SUREŚVARA'S VĀRTIKA
on
YĀJÑAVALKYA-MAITREYĪ DIALOGUE

Sureśvara's Vārtika on Yājñavalkya-Maitreyī Dialogue

Bṛhadāraṇyakopaniṣad
2.4 and 4.5

SHOUN HINO

MOTILAL BANARSIDASS PUBLISHERS
PRIVATE LIMITED • DELHI

First Edition: Delhi, 1982
Second Edition: Delhi, 1991

ISBN: 81-208-0729-4

Also available at:
MOTILAL BANARSIDASS
41 U.A., Bungalow Road, Jawahar Nagar, Delhi 110 007
120 Royapettah High Road, Mylapore, Madras 600 004
16 St. Mark's Road, Bangalore 560 001
Ashok Rajpath, Patna 800 004
Chowk, Varanasi 221 001

PRINTED IN INDIA
BY JAINENDRA PRAKASH JAIN AT SHRI JAINENDRA PRESS, A-45 NARAINA INDUSTRIAL AREA, PHASE I, NEW DELHI 110 028 AND PUBLISHED BY NARENDRA PRAKASH JAIN FOR MOTILAL BANARSIDASS PUBLISHERS PVT. LTD., BUNGALOW ROAD, JAWAHAR NAGAR, DELHI 110 007.

TABLE OF CONTENTS

FOREWORD

In the history of Advaita Vedānta Sureśvara occupies an important place inasmuch as he has presented the philosophy of Śaṅkara in his own way, i.e. as theory about the appearance of Reality. He presented this theory in his independent work called the *Naiṣkarmyasiddhi* and his commentarial works, the *Taittirīyopaniṣadbhāṣyavārtika* and the *Bṛhadāraṇyakopaniṣadbhāṣya-vārtika*. These two commentarial works, as their names indicate, have often revealed Sureśvara's deviation from his teacher and, further, they have referred to some important views of pre-Śaṅkara Vedāntins like Bhartṛprapañca, Dramiḍācārya and others. As such, they provide considerable rich material for filling up certain gaps in the history of Indian philosophy. It is, however, unfortunate that no full translation of the *Bṛhadāraṇya-kopaniṣadbhāṣyavārtika* has ever appeared in any language.

It is therefore gratifying that Dr. Shoun Hino brings forth a critical translation of the Vārtika on the famous dialogue between Yājñavalkya and Maitreyī from the *Bṛhadāraṇyako-paniṣad* which presents the pivotal doctrine of Yājñavalkya's philosophy. The careful annotation to the translation and the Introduction which presents an analytical study of the portion under translation mark Dr. Hino's first step towards the fulfilment of his stupendous undertaking, viz. translation of other portions of this work of Sureśvara. I believe that it is only such topic-wise (or section-wise) studies that would enable him (and his collaborators) to secure his (their) aim.

Dr. Hino deserves all compliments for taking this first step and, I feel confident, his work will be delightfully received by the scholarly world.

K. P. Jog
Professor of Sanskrit,
Deccan College Research
Institute, Pune 411006

Deccan College, Poona-6
November, 1981

ACKNOWLEDGEMENTS

At the outset, I should express my gratitude to Prof. S. D. Joshi, Director, C.A.S.S. University of Poona, and later Prof. Dr. H. Kitagawa. It is under the exchange programme between the University of Poona and the University of Nagoya, established by the efforts of both of these that I got an opportunity to study Sanskrit at C.A.S.S., University of Poona, in September 1975. Later (in July 1976), Prof. Joshi permitted me to work on my research project for Ph.D. at C.A.S.S. And, all throughout my studies, he has been very kind to me—this enabled me to complete my studies unhampered.

My thanks are due to Dr. M. Tachikawa, Associate Professor, University of Nagoya, Japan, who has been encouraging me all the while, giving me a lot of useful suggestions.

I am greatly indebted to my supervisor, Prof. K. P. Jog, Professor of Sanskrit, Deccan College Research Institute, Poona. Without his guidance, my dissertation would not have seen this early completion.

I am extremely grateful to Pt. Sivaramakrishna Sastri of Deccan College and Prof. Anant Lal Thakur of the University of Burdwan for their valuable suggestions while I put my Ph.D. dissertation into the shape of a book. Also I cannot forget the kind help which Prof. S. D. Joshi of the University of Poona gave me while I pursued my work as a Ph.D. student and also later when I revised my Ph.D. dissertation for publication. I am thankful also to the authorities of the University of Poona for their permission to publish my dissertation.

SHOUN HINO

PREFACE

Histories of Indian philosophy have enumerated quite a number of philosophers and many modern scholars on Indian philosophy have produced treatises on quite a few of them. Nevertheless, then still remain a large number of individual philosophers, whose study, though indispensable, has escaped the attention of scholars. In the Advaita Vedānta, Sureśvara occupies high importance in that he is a direct disciple of Śaṅkara. Again, in the tradition of the Advaita Vedānta, he is identified with Mīmāṁsaka Maṇḍanamiśra. It is a matter of regret that only some of his works are properly studied. Thus, the *Naiṣkarmyasiddhi* (Nais) has been translated by a few modern scholars and considered as the basic text for delineating his philosophy. His other work, the *Taittirīyopaniṣadbhāṣyavārtika* (TUBV) has been just translated, its critical study is so far awaiting scholars' attention. His voluminous work *Bṛhadāraṇyakopaniṣadbhāṣyavārtika* (BUBV) has been all along neglected, though he gives in it a fuller explanation of his philosophy on the basis of the great Upaniṣad, the *Bṛhadāraṇyakopaniṣad*. It is with a modest desire to fill this gap in History of Indian philosophy that I have undertaken here the study of this work of Sureśvara. I have chosen for this purpose only a part of the voluminous work, viz. BUBV 2. 4 and 4. 5 inasmuch as it forms one complete unit in itself and gives fairly good idea of Sureśvara's contribution to the Advaita Vedānta. Since it is not the study of the whole of BUBV, it would be wrong to expect that all aspects of Sureśvara's philosophy have been covered in this work. But I hope to have offered some salient features of the same.

The procedure followed in this work is as follows :

(i) First, I have offered my translation of BUBV 2. 4 and 4. 5 together with the necessary Annotation. In the Annotation, I derived immense help from the *Śāstraprakāśikā* (Ānandagiri's commentary on BUBV) and at times the *Bṛhadāraṇyakavārtikasāra* of Vidyāraṇya and the *Nyāyakalpalatikā*. Occasionally, I had to refer to Nais, TUBV and the *Pañcikaraṇavārtika* also.

(ii) On the basis of the Translation and Annotation, I have tried to build up some picture of Sureśvara's philosophy—this I have given in the Introduction.

(iii) Then, I have appended Select Glossary which it was necessary to add because, being written in verse, this work would require certain modification in words and terms whose meanings are at times somewhat different from those of the other Advaitins.

Before closing a word is necessary on the mode of reference to the texts of BUB. As is well-known the Kāṇva recension of the *Śatapathabrāhmaṇa* consists of 17 *kāṇḍas*, the last of these being called the *Bṛhadāraṇyaka*. Again, the last six chapters (*adhyāyas*) of the *Bṛhadāraṇyaka*, i.e. chapters 3-8, are called the *Bṛhadāraṇyakopaniṣad*. BUB and BUBV refer to the chapter number in the *Bṛhadāraṇyaka* : E.g. *caturtha-adhyāya* for BU ch. 2 as found in BUBV 4. 5. 7. And BU chh. 1-2, i.e. the *Bṛhadāraṇyaka* chh. 3-4, constitute the Madhukāṇḍa; BU chh. 3-4, the Munikāṇḍa; and BU chh. 5-6, the Khila-kāṇḍa.

S.H.

PREFACE TO THE SECOND EDITION

It is great pleasure to have my first book on Sureśvara's Vārtikas reprinted, while I am busy with my work on further portions of the Vārtikas that are undergoing print. Indeed, my feeling that there is need of translating Sureśvara's work gets stronger and my attempts towards it, in collaboration with my Guru, could not have materialized without the readiness of the publisher for undertaking the serial publication of such translation of Sureśvara's Vārtika in its entirety and also his encouraging words, 'any volume of the serial publication should be ever available'. Though this book formed materially the whole of my Ph.D. dissertation and naturally involved some failings here and there, this is now being treated as an initial volume of the whole of Sureśvara's Vārtika of the *Bṛhadāraṇyakopaniṣad* in translation form and therefore I have made suitable changes therein.

I hope that this newly revised print will also be accepted by readers favourably.

SHOUN HINO

ABBREVIATIONS

ĀnSS	Ānandāśrama Sanskrit Series
ATUBV	Ānandagiri's commentary on TUBV
BG	*Bhagavadgītā*
BGB	*Bhagavadgītāśāṅkarabhāṣya*
BORI	Bhandarkar Oriental Research Institute
BSB	*Brahmasūtraśāṅkarabhāṣya*
BU	*Bṛhadāraṇyakopaniṣad*
BUB	*Bṛhadāraṇyakopaniṣacchāṅkarabhāṣya*
BUBV	*Bṛhadāraṇyakopaniṣadbhāṣyavārtika*
Cand	*Candrikā*
CSS	Chowkhamba Sanskrit Studies
CU	*Chāndogyopaniṣad*
CUB	*Chāndogyopaniṣacchāṅkarabhāṣya*
GKB	*Gauḍapādakārikāśāṅkarabhāṣya*
GK	*Gauḍapādakārikā*
GOS	Gaekwad Oriental Series
KaivU	*Kaivalyopaniṣad*
KathU	*Kaṭhopaniṣad*
KausU	*Kauṣītakyupaniṣad*
KeU	*Kenopaniṣad*
KSS	Kashi Sanskrit Series
MaiU	*Maitryupaniṣad*
MaU	*Māṇḍūkyopaniṣad*
MuU	*Muṇḍakopaniṣad*
Nais	*Naiṣkarmyasiddhi*
MBh	*Mahābhārata*
PK	*Pañcīkaraṇa*
PKV	*Pañcīkaraṇavārtika*

PU	*Praśnopaniṣad*
SP	*Śāstraprakāśikā*
SV	*Sambandhavārtika*
SK	*Sāṁkhyakārikā*
TUB	*Taittirīyopaniṣacchāṅkarabhāṣya*
TUBV	*Taittirīyopaniṣadbhāṣyavārtika*
U	*Upaniṣad*
Upad	*Upadeśasāhasrī*
VS	*Vedāntasāra*

PART I

INTRODUCTION

PRELIMINARY REMARKS

1.1 In Advaita Vedānta tradition, Sureśvara (720-770) is regarded as a direct disciple of Śaṅkara.[1] He is regarded to have been an eminent Mīmāṁsaka but, after being defeated by Śaṅkara in a debate, converted into an Advaitin and a disciple of Śaṅkara.[2] Tradition also records that Sureśvara was disallowed to write a commentary on BSB because originally he was not an Advaitin.[3]

1.2.1.1 The following works are ascribed to Sureśvara : The *Naiṣkarmyasiddhi*, the *Mānasollāsa*, the *Pañcīkaraṇavārtika*, the *Taittirīyopaniṣadbhāṣyavārtika*, the *Bṛhadāraṇyakopaniṣadbhāṣyavārtika* and the *Sambandhavārtika*.[4]

1.2.1.2 Nais is Sureśvara's independent work; it consists of four chapters and contains an exposition of the knowledge of the Brahman and the matters connected therewith, such as the ritualistic activity (*karman*) as a subsidiary means to liberation, the relation between the Brahman and the individual consciousness, ignorance about the nature of the Ātman[5] and the *mahāvākya* : *tat tvam asi* etc. This work may properly be called an epitome of Vedānta philosophy (*vedāntasārasaṁgraha-prakaraṇa*).[6]

1.2.1.3 The *Mānasollāsa* is the metrical commentary on the *Dakṣiṇāmūrtistotra* (ascribed to Śaṅkara). It aims at establishing the Advaita doctrine of ignorance, causality etc. by refuting other philosophical systems such as Vaiśeṣika, Sāṁkhya, Paurāṇika and Śaivāgama. The *Pañcīkaraṇavārtika* is a commentary on the *Pañcīkaraṇa* (ascribed to Śaṅkara). Sureśvara wrote commentaries on two Upaniṣad-Bhāṣyas of Śaṅkara, viz. the Bhāṣyas on the *Taittirīyopaniṣad* and the *Bṛhadāraṇyakopaniṣad*. The *Sambandhavārtika* is the introductory part of BUBV, i.e. BUBV 1.1, and yet has an independent status since it pertains to the relation between the ritualistic and philosophical portions of the Veda—a topic not purely Upaniṣadic. The reason why

Sureśvara has chosen just these two of the eleven Upaniṣadic commentaries of Śaṅkara for writing Vārtikas thereon is stated thus:[7] In deference to his master, who belonged to the *Taittirīya*-recension (*śākhā*) of the Yajur Veda, Sureśvara took up TUB and since he himself belonged to the *Kāṇva*-*śākhā* of Yajur Veda, he took up BUB. It is interesting to note that BUB follows the *Kāṇva*-recension of BU.[8]

1.2.2 BUBV comprising 11151 verses, approximating half the extent of the *Rāmāyaṇa*, is an extensive work on BU which is the greatest of the Upaniṣads in that it ably provides the bridge between *karmakāṇḍa* and *jñānakāṇḍa* of the Veda and consequently SV on BUB 1.1 evokes Sureśvara's exhaustive discussion on the relation of knowledge (*jñāna*) to action (*karman*). In this he elaborates the Advaita Vedāntins' refutation of the Mīmāṁsaka thought. BUBV contains every possible thought in the Advaita Vedānta and, therefore, serves as a veritable source book of the Advaita Vedānta.

1.3 BU consists of six chapters,[9] and the famous dialogue between Yājñavalkya and Maitreyī occurs in 2.4 and 4.5 and offers, it may be claimed, the very quint-essence of the Upaniṣads. It would not be wrong to say that one who has well understood this dialogue has understood the Upaniṣadic philosophy only too well. In the following work then are presented Sureśvara's comments on BUB 2.4 and 4.5 inasmuch as these discuss quite a number of essential problems of Advaita philosophy which are not (perhaps could not be) discussed in BUB 2.4 and 4.5, but are all the same necessary for understanding the philosophical data contained in the famous dialogue. It is this aspect of BUBV 2.4 and 4.5 that would make one believe it to contain Sureśvara's philosophy in a nutshell.

1.4 In the subsequent part of the Introduction are discussed some salient features of Sureśvara's philosophy, of course, basing the argument mainly on first ever critical translation (together with annotation) of Sureśvara's Vārtika.

1.5.1 For convenience, let us first note down, in brief, the gist of BU 2.4 (=4.5), BUB 2.4; 4.5 and BUBV 2.4 and 4.5 in order.

1.5.2 The contents of BU 2.4 may be summarized as follows:

Having decided to renounce the house-holder's life, the sage Yājñavalkya intends to obtain the consent of his wife, Maitreyī and announces to her that he would divide his property between her and her co-wife. Maitreyī refuses to accept any of the property and wants to receive from him the teaching regarding the way to immortality (*amṛtatva*). Then, pleased at her resolve, Yājñavalkya explains to her the lore of immortality, viz. the nature of the Ātman. Further, he declares to her that the uniqueness of the Ātman is realized, i.e. liberation is effected, through *śravaṇa*, *manana* and *nididhyāsana*.

In Yājñavalkya's teaching, we come across the famous and important passages, viz. *na vā are patyuḥ kāmāya patiḥ priyo bhavaty ātmanas tu kāmāya patiḥ priyo bhavati* (BU 2.4.4), *ātmā vā are draṣṭavyaḥ śrotavyo mantavyo nididhyāsitavyaḥ* (BU 2.4.5), *idam sarvaṁ yad ayam ātmā* (BU 2.4.6), *yatra hi dvaitam iva bhavati tad itara itaram jighrati....tat kena ka kaṁ jighret....* (BU 2.4.14).

This dialogue of Yājñavalkya and Maitreyī is repeated in BU 4.5 with a little deviation, e.g. BU 4.5.1 and BU 4.5.15 do not occur in BU 2.4; these deviations are, really speaking, of little significance.

1.5.3 Now we may note in brief Śaṅkara's observations on this passage from BU.

In the beginning, Śaṅkara points out the relation of BU 2.4 to the preceding portion, by way of offering a very brief summary of the contents. Then he turns to the discussion of the same.

The central teaching of Madhukāṇḍa (BU 1.2) is to describe the knowledge of the Brahman. In connection with the dialogue of Yājñavalkya and Maitreyī, on the occasion when Yājñavalkya proceeds to renounce, Śaṅkara stresses the point that this chapter intends to show that renunciation is a means to acquire the knowledge of the Brahman.

As regards the repetition of the dialogue of Yājñavalkya and Maitreyī (in BU 2.4) at BU 4.5, Śaṅkara says, "In Madhukāṇḍa, the truth of the Brahman is ascertained on the authority of the Śruti. Now in BU 3-4, the same is discussed by way of a debate, i.e. through reasoning, and then BU 4.5 forms a logical finale of the same."

The rest of BUB can best be described, more or less, as a word-to-word paraphrase of BU

Since BU 4.5 almost wholly agrees with BU 2.4, Śaṅkara only adds his elaborate discussion on how to interpret the Śruti passages which have an apparently mutual contradiction.

1.5.4 BUBV 2.4 starts with the discussion of renunciation. Sureśvara states that renunciation is an indispensable step towards liberation. Then he clarifies the aspects of renunciation from the point of view of daily life, e.g. it is necessary to get the consent of the wife before one repaired to the forest.

The central teaching of Vedānta is contained in the *mahāvākyas* such as *tat tvam asi*. This necessitates one's getting to know what is the Ātman. It is exactly for this purpose that Yājña-valkya announces to Maitreyī—*ātmā vā are draṣṭavyaḥ...* This Vedic passage might appear to some as an injunction. As such Sureśvara discusses the proper meaning of the same, proving in the end that it is not an injunction. In connection with the same sentence may come the necessary processes towards effecting liberation, through *śravaṇa*, *manana* and *nididhyāsana*. Sureśvara elaborates, therefore, that this is not some continued progressive action but this is the analysis of 'knowing' in terms of a process. BU, while clarifying its teaching, has employed certain illustrations—these are explained by Śaṅkara to some extent, but Sureśvara takes up the illustration of *dundubhi*, *śaṅkha* and *vīṇā* in BU 2.4.7-9 for quite a detailed discussion and brings out their purpose fully. Again, in connection with the passage *evaṁ vā are' sya mahato bhūtasya niḥśvasitam*, Sureśvara brings in another passage, viz. BU 2.4.10, with a view to ascertaining the authoritativeness of the Śruti which is not the outcome of some human effort. Discussing the Brahman as the one meeting point of all that is considered as knowledge on the basis of BU 2.4.11, Sureśvara elaborates the origin and merger of the world in keeping with the Sāṁkhya doctrine. Finally, while establishing the uniqueness of the Brahman in the light of BU 2.4. 14: *yatra hi dvaitam iva bhavati...*, he develops the topic of duality and non-duality under the lead of Gauḍapāda.

He does not discuss Śaṅkara's views in respect of interpretation of apparently contradictory Śruti passages.

NOTES

1. Traditional stories in the Advaita Vedānta are known from some texts: *Śaṅkaradigvijaya of Vidyāraṇya*, Poona: ĀnSS 22, 1932; *Śrī Śaṅkaravijaya of Anantānandagiri*, (ed.) N. VEEZHINATHAN, Madras: University of Madras, 1972; etc.; cf. R. BALASUBRAMANIAN, *The Taittirīyopaniṣad Bhāṣya-Vārtika of Sureśvara*, Madras : University of Madras, 1974, Introduction pp.1-10.

2. There is another detail of this traditional story : Maṇḍanamiśra was regarded as another name of Sureśvara before renunciation. In this matter, KUPPUSWAMI SASTRI refutes such a tradition of Maṇḍana-Sureśvara equation by pointing out eleven proofs. (*Brahmasiddhi* ed.), Introduction pp.xxv-lvii); his view may be taken as correct—any discussion on this point is not quite relevant here.

3. Cf. BALASUBRAMANIAN, *op. cit.*, p. 8.

4. There are two controversial matters in this connection, viz. (i) The authorship of the *Mānasollāsa* and the *Pañcīkaraṇavārtika*, (ii) the chronological order of Sureśvara's works. The *Praṇavavārtika* is sometimes ascribed to Sureśvara. On this, cf. A. MAHADEVA SASTRI, *Dakshinamurti Stotra of Śrī Śaṅkarāchārya*, Madras : Samata Books, 1978.

5. The Ātman sometimes signifies both the Brahman and the Jivātman as here.

6. Cf. Nais 1.1

7. The *Śaṅkaradigvijaya* 11.65-66: *satyaṁ yad āttha vinayin mama yājuṣīyā | śākhā tadantagatabhāṣyanibandha iṣṭaḥ | tadvārtikaṁ mama kṛte bhavatā praṇeyaṁ | sacceṣṭitam parahitaikaphalaṁ prasiddham || tadvat tvadīyā khalu kāṇvaśākhā | mamāpi tatrāsti tadantabhāṣyam | tadvārtikaṁ cāpi vidheyam iṣṭam | paropakārāya satāṁ pravṛttiḥ ||*

8. Cf. SV 2 and MAHADEVAN's note thereon, (T.M.P. MAHADEVAN, *The Saṁbandha-Vārtika of Sureśvarācārya*, Madras : University of Madras, 1972, pp. 2-3).

9. See remarks in the Preface.

SUREŚVARA'S WORK AS A VĀRTIKA

2.1.1 BUBV is the elaborate Vārtika on BUB written by Sureśvara. He also wrote Vārtikas on two most important of Śaṅkara's Bhāṣyas on Upaniṣads and other works and is therefore called Vārtikakāra. A *vārtika* means a work wherein there is the consideration of what is *ukta* (said), *anukta* (what is not said) and *durukta* (what is improperly said) by an author whose work is under the comment of the author of the Vārtika. In view of this, we expect to find in Sureśvara's works discussion of these aspects of Śaṅkara's Bhāṣyas. We often come across his elaboration of the *ukta* portions of Śaṅkara's works beside the *anukta* portions of his philosophical thought which occur in works not under comment. As for *durukta* portions, there are only very few of them.[1]

2.1.2 BALASUBRAMANIAN discusses this *ukta* etc. about TUBV and points out that there are many instances to this effect.[2] Here, in this section, I take up BUBV 2.4 as a specimen of Vārtika on Śaṅkara's works and discuss Sureśvara's treatment of the *anukta* ideas in relevant portions of BUB.

2.1.3 In BUB, Śaṅkara holds that renunciation is prescribed as a part of the instruction about the nature of the Brahman[3] and that this renunciation, which is characterized by abandoning of all the means, is subsidiary to the knowing of the Brahman.[4] On this point Sureśvara begins his discussion by pointing out how renunciation[5] is one of the stages towards liberation and then enumerates those stages which are noted below.

2.1.4.1 Since in Nais 1.52[6] also Sureśvara has expressed a similar idea about these stages, it would be worth while first to note the correspondence of the stages described in both these places and then to proceed to discuss Sureśvara's view of Śaṅkara's position. The following table shows these stages in the two works of Sureśvara :

BUBV 2.4.2-5		Sambandhokti of Nais 1.52
(1)	*nityakarmādy-anuṣṭhāna*	: *nityakarmānuṣṭhāna*
(2)		: *dharmotpatti*
(3)		: *pāpa-hāni*
(4)	*citta-śuddhi*	: *citta-śuddhi*
(5)	*niḥśeṣa-karma-hetūttha-phala-sāvadya-dhī*	: *saṁsāra-yāthātmyāvabodha*
(6)	*āgrajāt virakti*[7]	: *vairāgya*
(7)	*saṁsāra-jihāsā*	: *mumukṣutva* (or *mumukṣā*)
(8)	*tad-dhāne sādhana-spṛhā*[8]	: *tad-upāya-paryeṣaṇa*[9]
(9)	*aśeṣaiṣaṇā-tyāga*[10]	: *sarva-karma-tat-sādhana-saṁnyāsa*
(10)		: *yogābhyāsa*
(11)	*pratyag-yāthātmya-niścaya*	: *cittasya pratyak-pravaṇatā*
(12)	*vastu-vṛttātma-bodha*	: *tat-tvam-asy-ādi-vākyārtha-parijñāna*
(13)	*dhvasta-saṁsāra-kāraṇatva*[11]	: *avidyoccheda*
(14)	*vyāviddhāśeṣa-saṁsāratva*[12]	: *svātmany evāvasthānam*

2.1.4.2 Firstly, one is required to perform the daily and the occasional rites (*nitya-naimittika-karmans*), according to one's caste and the stage of one's life, in order to attain *cittaśuddhi* 'the purification of the intellect'. The word *ādi* of *nityakarmādy-anuṣṭhāna* in verse 2 refers only to the *naimittikakarman*, though there are four *karmans* counted, because firstly Sureśvara himself seems to support this idea in *evaṁ nitya-naimittika-karmānuṣṭhānena śudhyamānaṁ tu tac cittam* (Nais 1.45) and *nityaṁ naimittikaṁ karma sadaivātma-śuddhaye* (Nais 1.50) and secondly one reaches the status of a god by performing *kāmyakarman* and falls down to the hell by performing *niṣiddhakarman*;[13] these two *karmans* make one be reborn, suffer transmigratory existence and not attain liberation. Now BUBV 2.4 mentions *citta-śuddhi* as the second stage, but Nais speaks of two more intervening stages between *nityakarmānuṣṭhāna* and *citta-śuddhi* : One is *dharmotpatti* 'the generation of *apūrva*'[14] and the second is removal of (lit. loss of) the sins that are incurred in transmigratory existence.[15]

2.1.4.3 The fifth stage is one's becoming *niḥśeṣa-karma-hetūttha-phala-sāvadya-dhī* which is explained in the commentary as *saṁsārāsāratā-dṛṣṭi*.[16] Nais puts it as : *saṁsāra-yāthātmyāvabodha*, 'the knowledge of the true nature of the transmigratory existence' which is explained as *anitya-doṣa-darśana*[17] 'realizing the defects such as non-eternity etc.' This stage in Sureśvara's writing can be regarded as equivalent to *nityānitya-vastu-viveka* which is mentioned by Śaṅkara in BSB 1.1.1[18] as the first of the four prerequisites (*sādhana-catuṣṭaya*) for the knowledge of the Brahman. Although Śaṅkara admits the utility of *nityakarman* etc. for *citta-śuddhi*[19] he thinks it is possible for someone to attain *citta-śuddhi* and *nityānitya-vastu-viveka* even without performing these *karmans*.[20] In this one may see a deviation of Sureśvara from Śaṅkara; but since Sureśvara himself admits at SV 89-91 as an exception[21] the case of one who has attained *citta-śuddhi* without performing *nityakarman* etc., it is not a deviation but a difference of emphasis. The Mīmāṁsaka would emphasize the *karmaparatā* of the Upaniṣads on the basis of the aphorism of the *Jaimini-Sūtra* 1.2.1 : *āmnāyasya kriyārthatvāt*. ...But on the other hand, Śaṅkara would not admit of it and emphasize the *jñānaparatā* of the same. He has clarified his position in his elaborate commentary on the *Brahmasūtra* 1.1.4: *tat tu samanvayāt*. Hence it was only natural that Śaṅkara would not elaborate matters of the *karmakāṇḍa* such as *nityakarman* etc. This is why one could say that Sureśvara's clear statements of *nityakarman* etc. may be taken as elaboration of the *ukta* portion of Śaṅkara's comment elsewhere—of course, not much emphasized there. Sureśvara adopts the performance of *karman* as one of the essential stages for liberation and his theory of liberation does not appear to avert the view of the Mīmāṁsaka on *karman* . It cannot be overlooked that, on this point, he expressed his view in Nais ch. 1 etc.[22] where, immediately after the postulation of the Mīmāṁsaka's view in Nais 1.9-21 represented as *mukteḥ kriyābhiḥ siddhatvāt*, 'because liberation is attained through actions', he remarks, "*karman* serves for the removal of ignorance but it does not directly remove the same since, like knowledge, it is not opposed to it."[23] Thus, unlike the Mīmāṁsaka, Sureśvara rejects *karman* as a direct means to liberation, but adopts it in a preliminary stage to liberation; in other words, he accepts it as a necessary means of purifying the intellect and does not attach to it any more importance. For this reason, it might be said that Sureśvara is an adherent of *jñāna-karma-samuccaya.*

2.1.4.5 In Sureśvara's scheme, the sixth stage is *vairāgya* which is equivalent to *ihāmutrārtha-phalabhoga-virāga* in the *sādhana-catuṣṭaya* of Śaṅkara. But, unlike Śaṅkara who appears to put *śama-damādisādhanasaṁpat* between the two, Sureśvara places *mumukṣutva* immediately after *vairāgya* as the seventh stage. MARKANDEYA SASTRI guesses the reason thereof: "To become eligible for the Vividiṣā-Saṁnyāsa one should not only renounce the world but possess a positive desire for getting liberation. Otherwise mere renunciation of the world which is a negative act will result only in complete annihilation of the individual."[24] Let us not suppose that Sureśvara has neglected *śama* etc.; that he has *śama* etc.[25] in mind can be seen from BUBV 1.3.98-99 where he mentions that *śama* etc. is derived from *buddhi-śuddhi* (=*citta-śuddhi*) and leads to *jñānotpatti.*[26] Now, taking into account the eighth and the following stages, let us examine what he exactly understands by *śama* etc. According to Sureśvara, the eighth stage is *tad-dhāne sādhana-spṛhā* (=*tad-upāya-paryeṣaṇa*) 'search (longing) for the means to that, viz. abandoning of transmigratory existence' and the ninth stage *aśeṣaiṣaṇā-tyāga* (=*eṣaṇā-traya-tyāga, sarva-karma-tat-sādhana-saṁnyāsa*) 'renunciation of all desires (originating in *karmans* and their means)'. The ninth stage is the renunciation of three desires, viz. *putraiṣaṇā, vittaiṣaṇā* and *lokaiṣaṇā,* which a *vividiṣā-saṁnyāsin*[27] is expected to abandon as the *vividiṣā* text (=BU 4.4.22) points out.[28] Thus, the eighth and the ninth stages have nothing to do with *śama* etc. We should now consider the relation of the tenth and the eleventh stages to *śama* etc. As BUBV 1.3 98-99 shows *śama* etc. lead to the rise of knowledge; Nais 3.4 also says: "One who is possessed of *śama* etc. should see the Ātman in oneself without any effort."[29] This shows that *śama* etc. lead to the eleventh stage, *pratyag-yāthātmyāvabodha.*[30] One could therefore suspect if Sureśvara means that *śama* etc. are equivalent to *yogābhyāsa.* Cand says that *yogābhyāsa* consists in the performance of *śravaṇa, manana* and *nididhyāsana.*[31] However, for the person who has detached himself from the transmigratory existence and has given up the desires (i.e. has become a *vividiṣā-saṁnyāsin*), disciplines such as *yama* are necessary for knowing the teaching of the Upaniṣads.[32] As for *dhyāna* etc., it causes the rise of knowledge.[33] Therefore, *yama*, *dhyāna* etc. have to be the precedents of *śravaṇa* etc.[34] It is to be noted that the words *yama*, *dhyāna* etc. which are used here refer to disciplines prescribed in the *Yogasūtra* 2.30,[35] but it appears that Sureśvara has in mind *śama* etc. while he uses them.[36] So then, we can set aside Cand's remark and say that by *yogābhyāsa* Sureśvara means *śama* etc. and *śravaṇa* etc. as well.

2.1.4.6 Regarding the twelfth stage, *tat-tvam-asyādi-vākyārtha-parijñāna*, we should notice that, as is shown in Nais 2.8,[37] Sureśvara has employed the method of *anvayavyatireka*[38]—the method of analytical process of determining the word and the word-sense, thereby clarifying the sentence-sense (*vākyārtha*) (as shown in BUBV 2.4.111-112). But since the knowledge of the Brahman is *avākyārtha* '(that which is) beyond the sentence-sense',[39] the sentence-sense only indirectly leads to the knowledge of the Brahman— this is meant by the twelfth stage. One, who has acquired the sentence-sense (*vākyārtha*) by utilizing the method of *anvayavyatireka*, proceeds to remove the ignorance of the *mumukṣu* who has got the sentence-sense in order to attain the knowledge of the *avākyārtha*. And one succeeds in securing this *avākyārtha* with the help of the so-called *sambandha-traya-jñāna*, viz. the knowledge of *sāmānādhikaraṇya*, *lakṣaṇa-lakṣya* relation and *viśeṣana-viśeṣya* relation[40]— this is meant by the thirteenth stage. We should notice that *avidyoccheda*, 'the destruction of ignorance', and *brahma-jñānāvagati* 'the acquisition of the knowledge of the Brahman', are but two sides of one and the same coin and have no sequential order insofar as the thirteenth stage is concerned.[41]

2.1.4.7 Both the thirteenth and the fourteenth stages show the states of *jivanmukti* and *videhamukti* respectively. These two can be further expounded from the view-point of *karman*. There are three kinds of *karmans*, viz. *sañcitakarman*, *āgāmikarman* and *prārabdhakarman*. The *sañcitakarman* is that which has accumulated in the previous lives but has not begun bearing the result yet; the *āgāmikarman* is that which is done in the present life (perhaps even after acquiring the knowledge of the Brahman); and the *prārabdhakarman* is a part of the *sañcitakarman* which has started bearing the result through constituting the cause of generation of the present body. The knowledge of the Brahman nullifies the *sañcitakarman* and makes the *āgāmikarman* ineffective,[42] but the *prārabdhakarman* persists and keeps on producing experience[43]—this is called *jīvanmukti*. When the *prārabdhakarman* is exhausted by the decay of the body, one attains the final liberation, viz. the state of *videhamukti*. This view of the final liberation is supported by the Śruti: *tasya tāvad eva ciraṁ yāvan na vimokṣye' tha sampatsye* (CU 6.14.2).[44] If one had attained the final liberation immediately after acquiring the knowledge of the Brahman, the Śruti would not have spoken of one's awaiting the decay of the body. Thus, the state of *jīvanmukti* results from the knowledge of the Brahman which is the thirteenth stage, *avidyoccheda*. In this regard, the Śruti, *brahmaiva san brahmāpyeti* (BU 4.4.6) is cited in Nais 1.52[45] showing the fourteenth stage in the context. And the same Śruti is utilized together with the aforesaid Śruti (viz. CU 6.14.2) in Śaṅkara's description of *videhamukti* at BSB 4.1.19.[46]

2.1.4.8 It may be noted that Sureśvara has adopted the notion of these two types of liberation from BSB;[47] Sureśvara refers to them in PKV 56-60[48] and Nais 4.60 ff. also, basically following Śaṅkara's view. He metaphorically describes the state of *jīvanmukti* in Nais 4.60 thus:

nivṛtta-sarpaḥ sarpotthaṁ yathā kampaṁ na muñcati/
vidhvastākhila-moho'pi moha-kāryaṁ tathātmavit//

2.1.5.1 It is now possible to state precisely the correspondence of the ideas of Śaṅkara and Sureśvara.

(a) The first to the fourth stages, *nityakarmādyanuṣṭhāna* to *citta-śuddhi*, mentioned by Sureśvara are not included in Śaṅkara's *sādhana-catuṣṭaya*.

(b) The fifth stage of Sureśvara corresponds to *nityānitya-vastu-viveka* of Śaṅkara.

(c) The sixth stage *vairāgya*, corresponds to *ihāmutrārtha-phala-bhoga-virāga* of Śaṅkara.

(d) The seventh stage, *saṁsāra-jihāsā*, corresponds to *mumukṣutva* of Śaṅkara.

(e) Both the eighth and the ninth stages are not mentioned by Śaṅkara.

(f) The tenth stage, *yogābhyāsa*, stands for the remaining *sādhana-catuṣṭaya viz.*, *śamadamādisādhanasampat*, of Śaṅkara.

(g) In BSB, *sādhana-catuṣṭaya* is prescribed as the prerequisite of *brahma-jijñāsā* 'desire to know the Brahman' and this procedure from *brahma-jijñāsā* to *jīvanmukti* is not referred to by Śaṅkara in specific words.

(h) Both Śaṅkara and Sureśvara regard that the thirteenth and the fourteenth stages are states respectively of *jīvanmukti* and *videhamukti*.

2.1.5.2 The first to third stages of Sureśvara are not included in the *sādhana-catuṣṭaya*; in fact, Śaṅkara does not discuss these in his comment on BU 2.4 but, taking into account his statement of *sādhana-catuṣṭaya* in BSB 1.1.1 and of *nityakarman* in BUB 3.3.1, one can say that Sureśvara puts together these ideas of Śaṅkara and makes a systematic and thorough amplification of them under BU 2.4. So, we can say that the discussion by Sureśvara of the various stages to the knowledge of the Brahman agrees with one of the features of a Vārtika, i.e. it clarifies, and occasionally amplifies, the portion of the work under comment, at times drawing from other works of Śaṅkara and at others adding his own views.

2.1.5.3 According to Sureśvara, *vairāgya* is followed by *mumukṣutva* but, according to Śaṅkara, *śamadamādisādhanasampat* (= *prāpti*) should occur between the two. This can, therefore, be understood as a deviation of Sureśvara from Śaṅkara and may be called the rectification of the *durukta* in Śaṅkara's writing. It must be remembered, however, that here *durukta* cannot be taken as 'a wrong statement'; rather it should be considered as the disorderly mention of an item in the writing.

2.2.1.1 As mentioned above, Śaṅkara states in the introductory part of BUB 2.4 that renunciation is characterized by abandoning of all the means and is subsidiary to the knowing of the Brahman. Regarding this renunciation, Sureśvara follows Śaṅkara's standpoint and discusses the same in detail in BUBV 2.4.21 ff.

2.2.1.2 (a) In verses 22-23, Sureśvara stresses that renunciation is the best and indispensable means to liberation. Here, taking up the case of Yājñavalkya, who is a *vidvas* 'one who has known (the Brahman)', Sureśvara says that even a person like Yājñavalkya is requested to renounce so that he could attain liberation. Śaṅkara also discusses the necessity of renunciation for liberation in BSB 3.4.20-27. There are two types of renunciation, i.e. *vividiṣā-saṁnyāsa* 'renunciation as a preparation for the knowledge of the Brahman' and *vidvat-saṁnyāsa* 'renunciation of the knower of the Brahman'. Here the description in the case of Yājñāvalkya is that of *vidvatsaṁnyāsa.*

2.2.1.3 (b) In verses 27-29, Sureśvara states that renunciation is prescribed for one after one has paid debts at the stage of a student, of a householder, or of an anchorite. And, as SV 89[49] clearly shows, Sureśvara admits renunciation even at the stage of a student. In the case of one who has attained *citta-śuddhi*, there is no need of performing *nityakarman* etc. at the stage of a householder. This view is supported by JābālaU 4.[50] The case is the same with Śaṅkara in BSB 3.4.20. That is to say, Śaṅkara admits renunciation from the stage of a student, on the strength of JābālaU 4.

2.2.1.4 (c) Sureśvara's statements regarding renunciation such as renunciation after dividing the property in verse 45 etc., or renunciation after getting the consent of a wife in verse 39 show his awareness of the contemporary society. This idea is put in the mouth of Yājñavalkya. Both the statements are not referred to by Śaṅkara but are based on the Smṛti texts. This fact seems to be connected with Sureśvara's references to the normally accepted behaviour such as one's like, dislike or hate in worldly relationship shown in verses 66 etc. The matter of renunciation is important in the philosophical discussion of liberation, but he introduces and explains the same from the point of view of social behaviour.

2.2.1.5 Sureśvara's discussions (a) and (b) above are not found in the relevant portions of BUB, but they are available in Śaṅkara's other works, so they may be called the exposition of the *anukta* of Śaṅkara. The discussion (c) is not found anywhere in Śaṅkara's work, so this is also said to be entirely *anukta* by Śaṅkara.

2.3 On the word *brahman* in BU 2.4.6, Śaṅkara comments *brahma-brāhmaṇa-jātiḥ* without any reason. Sureśvara justifies this Śaṅkara's interpretation by putting forward the reason in verse 250 thus:

> "(In the word) *brahman*, there is the mention of the (Brahmin) caste owing to its use in the vicinity of (the word) *kṣatra*."

This can be considered as the *anukta* of Śaṅkara in BUB, that is to say: Sureśvara supplies certain detail to Śaṅkara's statement and justifies it.

2.4 As for the three illustrations of *dundubhi*, *śaṅkha* and *viṇā*, which are noticed in BU 2.4.7-9, Śaṅkara gives the reason for their occurrence: 'The use of many illustrations here is intended for declaring the manifold generalities, for there are different kinds of generalities and particularities in the form of the sentient and the insentient. It is to show how they are included in some supreme generality, viz. a mass of consciousness in some way or other that they are given'.[51] In connection with this statement of Śaṅkara, Sureśvara tries to clarify the 'manifold generalities' and 'how they are included in some supreme generality'. In verse 287, he points out that one great merger (*mahāsāmānya*) of all distinguishing attributes together is impossible and suggests that there are different stages of merger. And, in the succeeding verses, he clarifies the mode of merger in comparison with the illustration of a drum. In keeping with the three illustrations there are three, viz. particular (*viśeṣa*), species (*sāmānya*, *sāmānyetara*, *avāntarasāmānya*) and genus (*mahāsāmānya*). When there is a particular note of a drum (i.e. *viśeṣa*) it finally culminates into the sound of a drum (*dundubhiśabdatva*, i.e. *sāmānya*) which consists in 'sound' and persists in every particular note that arises from the beating of a drum. And this 'sound' (*śabdatva*) is the final merging place (i.e. *mahāsāmānya*). This is nothing but the Brahman. Thus, Sureśvara clarifies what Śaṅkara stated, viz. they are included in the supreme generality. This is Sureśvara's amplification of what is said by Śaṅkara.

2.5 Commenting on the word *niḥśvasita*, Śaṅkara writes thus: "...from the highest Ātman, which is the matter in hand, this has issued forth as if one breathed without (even) slight effort."[52]

Sureśvara develops the idea of the Veda as this *niḥśvasita*, together with its authoritativeness also (verses 304-312). Since Veda has arisen from the 'breath' of the Brahman, i.e. without any human effort, it is by its own nature eternal like the sky. Though whatever is produced is perishable, Veda is not what is produced and is therefore ever-existent.[53] Though Veda describes the nature of the thing (Ātman) as it has been in existence, it is not to be regarded as the product of any previous thought on the same. It is not like any human being's speech. Hence nothing disturbs its eternity.[54] Breathing out of the Ātman does not mean that Veda is artificial (*kṛtaka*) but that it appears as the very nature of the Ātman just in the same way as the rays of the Sun resemble the Sun.[55]

2 6 As long as one is infatuated by ignorance and does not become aware of the oneness of the Brahman, Veda is a means of knowing; Veda is *upāya* and liberation *upeya*. The excellence of the Veda lies in removing ignorance; that is why it is accepted as the authoritative means of knowing reality. When the Veda removes ignorance and one becomes aware of the oneness of the Brahman and the Ātman, the Veda cannot be any more a means. The thought that all is the Ātman occurs at this stage and continues to persist.

2.7 Such consideration with Sureśvara is not noticed in the relevant portion of BUB. However, one notices Śaṅkara discussing the authoritativeness of the Veda in BSB 1.1.3 etc. and, as such, we can say that Sureśvara's argument is the amplification of BUB in that, though not adduced by Śaṅkara in BUB, it is noticed in his other works. This is how the portion can be called *anukta* in BUB.

2.8 These details noticed above would certainly bring out the purpose served by the Vārtika on Śaṅkara's Bhāṣya. The Bhāṣya sought to render the contents of BU easy to understand, supplying some missing connections between the Upaniṣadic passages; whereas the Vārtika undertook to explain each and every detail that concerned the philosophical implications of both the Upaniṣad and the Bhāṣya, even when these were not clearly stated in them. This would show how important a place Sureśvara's work occupies in Vedānta literature.

NOTES

1. In the portion which forms the subject of this work, there is only one instance of *durukta* portion from Śaṅkara's work, viz. the words *itihāsa* etc., in BU 2.4.10 occurring in BUBV 2.4.313-317.

2. BALASUBRAMANIAN, *op. cit.*, pp. 10 ff.

3. Cf. BUB 2.4 (p.319): *asyā brahma-vidyāyā aṅgatvena, saṁnyaso vidhitsitaḥ.*

4. *Ibid.* (p. 320): *parivrājyaṁ sarva-sādhana-saṁnyāsa-lakṣaṇam .aṅgatvena vidhitsyate* /

5. Cf. C. MARKANDEYA SASTRI, *Sureśvara's Contribution to Advaita*, Venur: Sundari Samskrita Vidyalaya, 1974, pp 128 ff; V. PRASAD UPADHYAYA, *Lights on Vedānta*, CSS 6, 1959, pp 188 ff; P. HACKER, *Untersuhungen über Texte des frühen Advaitavāda*, 1 *Die Shüle Śaṅkaras*, Wiesbaden: 1950, pp. 88 ff.

6. *nityakarmānuṣṭhānād dharmotpatteḥ pāpahānis tataś citta-śuddhis tataḥ saṁsāra-yāthātmyāvabodhas tato vairāgyaṁ tato mumukṣutvaṁ tatas tad-upāya-paryeṣaṇaṁ tataḥ sarva-karma-tat-sādhana-saṁnyāsas tato yogābhyāsas tataś cittasya pratyak-pravaṇatā tatas tat-tvam-asyādi-vākyārtha-parijñānaṁ tato vidyocchedas tataś ca svātmany evāvasthānaṁ "brahmaiva san brahmāpyeti", "vimuktaś ca vimucyate" iti* /

7. Though the original words are *virakta āgrajāt*, I find it convenient to use this term in order to indicate a stage. Similar are cases under notes 8, 10, 11 and 12.

8. The original words are *tad-dhāne sādhana-spṛhaḥ.*

9. As to the meaning of the word *tat*, see 2.1.4.5.

10. The original word is *tyaktāśeṣaiṣaṇaḥ.*

11. The original word is *dhvasta-saṁsāra-kāraṇaḥ.*

12. The original words are *vyāviddhāśeṣa-saṁsāro vimukto nā vimucyate.*

13. Nais 1.41: *śubhaiḥ prāpnoti devatvaṁ niṣiddhair nārakīṁ gatim*/; and 1.46: *narakād bhīr yathāsyābhūt tathā kāmya-phalād api* /

14. Cand 1.52.

15. Cand cites the Śruti (*Mahānārāyaṇa* U 22.1): *dharmeṇa pāpam apanudati* /

16. SP 2.4.2.

17. Cand 1.52.

18. BSB 1.1.1 (P.5): *kim api vaktavyaṃ—yad anantaraṁ brahma jijñāsopadiśyata iti ucyate nityānitya-vastu-vivekaḥ, ihāmutrārtha-bhoga-virāgaḥ, śamadamādisādhana-sampat, mumukṣutvaṁ ca* /

19. BUB 3.3.1 (pp. 412-3): *yeṣāṁ punar nityāni nirabhisaṁdhīnyātma-saṁskārārthāni / teṣām ārād upakārakatvān mokṣa-sādhanāny api karmāṇi bhavantīti na virudhyate* /

20. Cf. MARKANDEYA SASTRI, *op. cit.*, p. 127; and H. DUTT SHARMA, *Brahmasūtra-catuḥsūtrī*, Poona: Oriental Book Agency, 1967, p. 42.

21. *yas tu janmāntarābhyāsāt kṣapitāśeṣa-kāmanaḥ /*
ādāv evādhikārī sa punaḥ karma na vīkṣate // (SV 89)
viraktasya tu jijñāsor mānān nānya-vyapeṣaṇam /
karmāpekṣā hi sādhye 'rthe siddhe 'rthe tad anarthakam // (SV 90)

vāmadevasya maitreyyā gārgyāś caiva samañjasam /
darśanaṁ brahmacaryādes tathā prāvrājya-śāsanāt // (SV 91)

22. Nais 1.22 ff., SV 46-158; e.g.—*ajñāna-hāna-mātratvān mukteḥ karma na sādhanam / karmāpamārṣṭi nājñānaṁ tamasīvotthitaṁ tamaḥ //* (Nais 1.24)
ekena vā bhaven muktir yadi vā sarva-karmabhiḥ /
pratyekaṁ ced vṛthānyāni sarvebhyo 'pyeka-karmatā // (*Ibid.* 25)
durita-kṣapaṇārthatvān na nityaṁ syād vimuktaye /
svargādi-phala-sambandhāt kāmyaṁ karma tathaiva na // (*Ibid.* 26)
sādhya-sādhana-bhāvo'yaṁ vacanāt pāralaukikaḥ /
nāśrauṣaṁ mokṣa-daṁ karma śruter vaktrāt kathaṁcana // (*Ibid.* 27)

And also see MARKANDEYA SASTRI, *op. cit.*, pp. 89-100, where he summarizes Sureśvara's standpoint in 26 items.

23. Nais 1.52: *karmaivaṁ syād avidyānivṛttaye / jñānavan nāvirodhitvāt karmāvidyāṁ nirasyati //*

24. *Op. cit.*, p. 129.

25. The six disciplines beginning with *śama* are as follows : *śama* 'mental control', *dama* 'control of the external senses', *uparati* 'abandoning of action and its fruit', *titikṣā* 'endurance of heat, cold etc.', *samādhi* (=*samādhāna*) 'concentration of mind' and *śraddhā* 'faith (devotion)'. On this, cf. the *Bhāmatī*, 1.1.1 (*Brahmasūtra Śāṅkara Bhāṣya with the commentaries Bhāmatī, Kalpataru and Parimala*, Bombay : Nirnaya Sagar Press, 1917, p. 73), and VS, Sec. 4, (p. 5) : *tasmād evaṁvic chānto dānta uparatas titikṣuḥ samāhito bhūtvātmany evātmānaṁ paśyati sarvam ātmānaṁ paśyati /*

This Śruti, viz. BU 4.4.23, is cited in the *Bhāmatī* (*loc. cit.*) as well as VS (*loc. cit*), and JACOB (*ibid.*, p. 143) remarks on this : "Rāmatīrtha points out that from this come the *śama, dama, uparati, titikṣā* and *samādhāna* of our text. But whence comes the *śraddhā*? It is added from the *Mādhyandina* recension of the same Upaniṣad, which reads *śraddhāvittaḥ* instead of the *samāhitaḥ* of the *Kāṇva*; so our author has combined the two in accordance with the *guṇopasaṁhāra-nyāya*." BUB 4.4.23 (p. 670) comments on the above Śruti in the following way :

yasmād evam akarma-sambandhyeṣa brāhmaṇasya mahimā neti netyādilakṣaṇas tasmād evaṁvic chānto bāhyendriya-vyāpārata upaśāntas tathā dānto 'ntaḥkaraṇa-tṛṣṇāto nivṛtta uparataḥ sarveṣaṇā-vinirmuktaḥ saṁnyāsī titikṣur dvandva-sahiṣṇuḥ samāhita indriyāntaḥkaraṇa-calana-rūpād vyāvṛttyaikāgryarūpeṇa samāhito bhūtvā /

And in this connection Sureśvara enters on a detailed discussion at BUBV 4.4. 1203-1271. The starting verse, viz. 1203, is as follows :

dānto bhūtvā tataḥ śāntaḥ tataś coparato bhavet /
artha-kramo balīyān syād yataḥ pāṭha-kramād iha //

Sureśvara changes the order of the first two disciplines, viz. *dama* and *śama*, though Śaṅkara follows the order stated in BU, as mentioned above. And Sureśvara begins his explanation thereof with *dama* in verse 1205 and proceeds to that of *śama* in verse 1205. This change of his is not out of metrical consideration but out of a philosophical reason. That is, he seems to think that *dama* 'control of the external senses' is preceded by mental control (*śama*) as is already pointed out by UPADHYAYA (*op. cit.*, pp. 187-8) or MARKANDEYA SASTRI (*op. cit.*, pp. 225-6)

26. *avidyāyā na cocchittau jñānād anyad apekṣyate |*
jñānotpattau na caivānyac chamādibhyo hy apekṣyate ||
śamādy-utpattaye nānyad buddhi-śuddher apekṣyate ||
buddhi-śuddhau ca nityādi-karmabhyo nānyad iṣyate ||

27. Cf. SP 2.4.4: *vividiṣā-saṁnyāsānantaram asakṛdanuṣṭhita-śravaṇādi-phalam āha |*

28. ...*te ha sma putraiṣaṇāyāś ca vittaiṣaṇāyāś ca lokaiṣaṇāyāś ca vyutthāyātha...*

29. *śamādi-sādhanaḥ paśyed ātmany ātmānam añjasā |*

30. Cand 1.52 explains this as *pratyagātmany evāprayatnenāvasthānam.*

31. *yogābhyāsaḥ śravaṇa-manana-nididhyāsanādīnām anuṣṭhānam |* It seems that Cand takes the support of SP : *vividiṣāsaṁnyāsānantaram asakṛdanuṣṭhita-śravaṇādiphalam āha |*

32. Cf. Nais 4.71 : *nāviraktāya saṁsārān nānirastaiṣaṇāya ca | na cāyamavate ceyaṁ vedāntārthapraveśanam ||*

33. Cf. BUBV 2.4.234 : *vijñānotpatti-hetutvaṁ dhyānādeḥprāg avādiṣam |*

34. Cf. SP 2.4.234: ...*dhyāna-sahita-śravaṇādi-phala-bhūta-vākyārthajñānokter iti draṣṭavyam |*

35. *yama-niyamāsana-prāṇāyāma-pratyāhāra-dhāraṇā-dhyāna-samādhayo 'ṣṭāvaṅgāni|*

36. Cf. SP 4.4.1217.

37. *tathā pada-padārthau ca na sto vākyam ṛte kvacit |*
anvaya-vyatirekau ca tāv ṛte stāṁ kimāśrayau ||

38. On this method, see HACKER, (*op. cit.*, p. 93) and Nais 3.74 where the analogical explanation thereof is offered, thus :

sthāṇuḥ sthāṇur itīvoktir na nṛ-buddhiṁ nirasyati |
vyanuvādāt tathaivoktir bhrāntim puṁso na bādhate ||

—The method of *anvaya* conveys the true nature of a thing . "This is a post." But merely this statement does not remove the misconception "This is a man". The nature of the post is required to be stated again and again by the method of *vyatireka* : "This is not a man". Thus, by denying what is grasped (viz. a man) and by stating what it is (viz. a post), one understands that this is not a man but a post. Also see section 7 below where the method of *anvaya-vyatireka* is fully discussed.

39. Cf. Nais 3.39 : *anvaya-vyatireka-puraḥsaraṁ vākyam evāvākyārtha-rūpam ātmānaṁ pratipādayatīti....|*

40. Nais 3.3 : *evaṁ kṛtānvaya-vyatireko vākyād evāvākyārthaṁ pratipadyata ity-uktam atas tad-vyākhyānāya sūtropanyāsaḥ |*

sāmānādhikaraṇyaṁ ca viśeṣaṇa-viśeṣyatā |
lakṣya-lakṣaṇa-sambandhaḥ padārtha-pratyagātmanām ||

41. Cf. MuU 2.2.8: *bhidyate hṛdaya-granthiś chidyante sarva-saṁśayāḥ* and 3.2.9 : *brahma veda brahmaiva bhavati.* And also cf. BUBV 1.3.83: *bhidyate hṛdaya-granthir brahmāpyetīti ca śruteḥ | na cārthavādataitasyāṁ juhvām iva phala-śruteḥ ||*

42. BSB 4.1.15 (p.475) : *apravṛtta-phale eva pūrve janmāntara-saṁcite, asminn api ca janmani prāg jñānotpatteḥ saṁcite, sukṛta-duṣkṛte jñānādhigamāt kṣīyete* /

43. *Loc. cit.* : *na tv ārabdha-kārye sāmibhukta-phale, yābhyām etad brahma-jñānāyatanaṁ janma nirmitam* /

44. *Loc. cit.*: *kuta etat? tasya tāvad eva ciraṁ yāvan na vimokṣye 'tha sampatsye* (CU 6.14.2) *iti śarīra-pātāvadhikaraṇāt kṣemaprāpteḥ* / *itarathā hi jñānād aśeṣa-karma-kṣaye sati sthitihetvabhāvāj jñāna-prāpty-anantaram eva kṣemam aśnuvīta* / *tatra śarīrapāta-pratīkṣāṁ nācakṣīta* /

45. See note 6 above.

46. BSB 4.1.19 (p. 478) : *anārabdha-kāryayoḥ puṇyapāpayor vidyā-sāmarthyāt kṣaya uktaḥ, itare tv ārabdha-kārye puṇya-pāpe upabhogena kṣapayitvā brahma saṁpadyate, tasya tāvad eva ciraṁ yāvan na vimokṣye 'tha saṁpatsye* (CU 6.14.2) *iti brahmaiva san brahmāpyeti* (*BU* 4.4.6) *iti caivamādiśrutibhyaḥ* /

47. On *jīvanmukti* in BSB, see notes 35 and 36 above and on *videhamukti* see notes 37 and 39 above.

48. *kṛta-kṛtyo bhaved vidvāñ jīvanmukto bhavet sadā* /
ātmany evārūḍhabhāvo jagad etan na vīkṣate //
kadācid vyavahāre tu dvaitaṁ yady api paśyati /
bodhātma-vyatirekeṇa na paśyati cid-anvayāt //
kintu paśyati mithyaiva diṅ-mohendu-vibhāgavat /
pratibhāsaḥ śarīrasya tadā prārabdha-saṁkṣayāt //
tasya tāvad eva ciram ityādi-śrutir abravīt /
prārabdhasyānuvṛttis tu muktasyābhāsa-mātrataḥ //
sarvadā mukta eva syāj jñāta-tattvaḥ pumān asau /
prārabdha-bhoga-śeṣasya saṁkṣaye tad-anantaram //

49. *yas tu janmāntarābhyāsāt kṣapitāśeṣakāmanaḥ* /
ādāv evādhikārī sa punaḥ karma na vīkṣate //

50. *yadi vetarathā brahmacaryād eva pravrajet gṛhād vā vanād vā. . .* /

51. *aneka-dṛṣṭāntopādānam iha sāmānya-bahutva-khyāpanārtham* /
aneke hi vilakṣaṇāścetanācetana-rūpāḥ sāmānyaviśeṣāḥ /
teṣāṁ pāraṁparyagatyā yathaikasmin mahāsāmānye 'ntarbhāvaḥ prajñāna-ghanaḥ kathaṁ nāma pradarśayitavya iti / (p. 322)

52. *. . .asya paramātmanaḥ prakṛtasya . . .*/ *yathā 'prayatnenaiva puruṣaniḥśvāso bhavaty evaṁ vā are* / (pp. 329-330).

53. BUBV 2.4.305.

54. *Ibid.* 306.

55. *Ibid.* 307.

ĀNANDAGIRI IN RELATION TO ŚAṄKARA AND SUREŚVARA

3.1.1 After this notice as to how Sureśvara has commented on Śaṅkara's Bhāṣya on BU, it may not be out of place to make a few observations on the comment of Ānandagiri on the works of both Śaṅkara and Sureśvara, since he has commented on almost every work of Śaṅkara as also on TUBV and BUBV, offering a great help in understanding them.[1]

3.1.2 In most cases when Ānandagiri writes an exposition of BUB, he takes support from Sureśvara's Vārtika which means that he recognises a complete agreement between the master and his disciple.

3.1.3 In the course of his comments on the philosophical discussions by Śaṅkara and Sureśvara, Ānandagiri stresses some particular point and clarifies the purpose of the remark—this is usually expressed in the form of possible doubt(s). However, while commenting on BUB, he adds necessary points from Sureśvara's Vārtika and makes the text of BUB more understandable.

3.1.4 But there are in the portion under study cases where Ānandagiri's commentary on BUB differs from that on BUBV (=SP). The most glaring case is that which pertains to the exposition of *śravaṇa*, *manana* and *nididhyāsana*.

3.2.1 Śaṅkara explains *śravaṇa* as 'hearing from a teacher and (then) from the Śruti' (*śrotavyaḥ pūrvam ācāryata āgamataś ca*), *manana* as 'pondering over (the Truth) by means of reasoning' (*mantavyas tarkataḥ*). Ānandagiri comments that, following these three mentioned in the injunction,[2] one attains the knowledge of the Brahman. It may be noted that, according to him, one's taking to the three items, viz. *śravaṇa*, *manana* and *nididhyāsana*, is quite essential for the knowledge of the Brahman. *manana* conveys the sense of reasoning (*tarka*) which establishes the falsity of duality and determining the truth by employing *śruti, liṅga* etc. as the means which help the removal of the defects in one's understanding of the Śruti texts. Sureśvara explains *śravaṇa* as 'hearing from the Śruti and a teacher'[3] and further adds that this *śravaṇa* consists in the clarification and ascertaining of the meaning of the Vedāntas in respect of the oneness of the Brahman with the help of the rules, viz. *śruti, liṅga* etc. (*ṣaḍ-liṅga*), which determine the meanings of the words in a sentence and the meaning of the sentence itself. These *śravaṇa* and *manana* are carried on until the knowledge of the Brahman manifests itself.[4] And one's understanding is merely verbal so long as one does not meditate on what is heard. Thus, he considers these two as one continuous logical process. Ānandagiri says that *śravaṇa* and *manana* are to be performed with the practice of six disciplines[5] and meditation (*dhyāna*).[6] This means that according to Ānandagiri *śravaṇa* and *manana* are actions intended by the injunction, *śama* etc., one of the four prerequisites (*sādhana-catuṣṭaya*) as stated in BUB 1.1.1, and *dhyāna* etc. are disciplines prescribed in the *Yogasūtra*.[7] Sureśvara admits their necessity for the knowledge of the Brahman.[8] But it is not clear if he associates *śama* etc. and *dhyāna* etc. with *śravaṇa* and *manana*. So far as Ānandagiri's statements in both the commentaries are concerned, there is no contradiction in respect of his explanations of the nature of *śravaṇa* and that of *manana*. That is to say : *śravaṇa* and *manana* are, according to him, of the nature of actions.

3.2.2 On Śaṅkara's explanation of *nididhyāsana* as 'meditation with determination' (*nididhyāsitavyo niścayena dhyātavyaḥ*), Ānandagiri comments that it is in keeping with an injunction. It should be seen, however, that Sureśvara differs a lot in respect of the nature of *nididhyāsana*. According to him, *nididhyāsana* is the culmination of the practice of *śravaṇa* and *manana* which is an indirect intuition of the Brahman[9] and *nididhyāsana* does not mean 'meditation' (*dhyāna*) but 'knowledge' (*vijñāna*).[10] In other words, Sureśvara considers that *nididhyāsana* consists in 'the understanding of the meaning of the Śruti on the basis of *vācya-vācaka* relation underlying the sentence, thanks to the removal of any hindrance to the knowledge of the Brahman consequent to *śravaṇa, manana* and the practice of *śama* etc.' Hence, there is no possibility of an injunction in respect of *nididhyāsana*. Ānandagiri follows this Sureśvara's view in SP and thus his statements in the commentary on BUB and those in SP are contradictory— this may be due to the fact that he set to himself the task of merely explaining the view of the author of each of the works under his comment; perhaps he did not want to make any observation of his own.

3.2.3 Again, on the relation of these three, viz. *śravaṇa*, *manana* and *nididhyāsana*, Śaṅkara insists on the combination of them but does not appear to hold the principal-subordinate relation among them; thus he writes : "When these (three) are combined, the true seeing of the oneness of the Brahman is accomplished; not in any other way, viz. by hearing alone."[11] Commenting on this, Ānandagiri clearly points out the principal-subordinate relation of the three thus: "*śravaṇa* is the principal because it is the consideration of a means of knowing and *manana* and *nididhyāsana* are subsidiary..."[12] On this relation, Vācaspati and the Vivaraṇa school hold different views and it will be useful for our discussion to note them here. Vācaspati holds that *śravaṇa*, *manana* and *nididhyāsana* are all a chain of causes, contributory to the knowledge of the oneness of the Brahman. Thus, *śravaṇa* is the cause of *manana* and *manana* of *nididhyāsana*. And the three of them are causes of the knowledge of the said oneness, without any principal-subordinate relation among them. This seems to clarify Śaṅkara's view stated above. The Vivaraṇa school holds that *śravaṇa*, is the principal cause, while *manana* and *nididhyāsana* are subsidiary inasmuch as they are helpful in accomplishing the fruit of *śravaṇa* viz. the knowledge of the Brahman, *śravaṇa* is important in the sense that it causes the cognition of the object of knowing. On the relation of the three and the reason therefor, the view of the Vivaraṇa school is similar to that of Ānandagiri in his comment on BUB.

3.3 Now, let us consider the views of Sureśvara and SP. Sureśvara holds the view that both *śravaṇa* and *manana* should be performed till the knowledge of the Brahman manifests itself[13] and *nididhyāsana* is the final limit of the performance of these two.[14] That is to say, the two culminate into *nididhyāsana* after the repetition of the two. Thus *śravaṇa* and *manana* are co-existent and *nididhyāsana* is their culmination and the precedent of the knowledge of the Brahman. This view of Sureśvara is derived from the natures of the three stated above. In SP on 2.4.128, Ānandagiri follows Sureśvara's view thus: "*nididhyāsana*, being the support for the culmination of *śravaṇa* etc. as associated with *śama* etc. is being clarified."[15] Here we notice the difference between Ānandagiri's commentary on BUB and SP. In the former, Ānandagiri puts *śravaṇa* as the principal and the other two as subsidiary to it (viz. *śravaṇa*) and, in the latter, he holds *śravaṇa* and *manana* together as co-extensive with *nididhyāsana*, it being the culmination of the previous two.

3.4 In the end we may be allowed to observe that it would prove fruitful if such cases of differences between Ānandagiri's comment on BUB and SP are taken up as a separate topic of study—and perhaps differences between Ānandagiri's comment on TUB and ATUBV also.

NOTES

1. These commentaries are : (i) On Śaṅkara's Upaniṣadbhāṣyas, viz. CUB, BUB, TUB, *Īśopaniṣadbhāṣya*, *Kaṭhopaniṣadbhāṣya*, *Kenopaniṣad-bhāṣya*, *Muṇḍakopaniṣadbhāṣya*, *Praśnopaniṣadbhāṣya* and *Aitareyopaniṣadbhāṣya* ; on BSB, BGB, GKB, Upad and PK and (ii) on TUBV and BUBV.
2. *vidhyanusāritvam evaṁ-śabdārthaḥ* (BUB, p. 325) in connection with Śaṅkara's words: *evaṁ hy asau dṛṣṭo bhavati*. Thus *evam* means *śrutyanusārataḥ*.
3. Śruti and a teacher are mentioned in the reverse order of that in Śaṅkara's statement thereon, i.e. *śrotavyaḥ pūrvam ācāryata āgamataś ca* /
4. BUBV 2.4.218.
5. SP 2.4.217 and 218.
6. *Ibid.*, 234.
7. This is already quoted under note 35 on section 2.
8. BUBV 1.3.98-99, 2.3.234; Nais 3.4, 4.71; Cand 1.52.
9. BUBV 2.4.217.
10. *Ibid.* 232-3.
11. *yadaikatvam etāny upagatāni tadā samyagdarśanam brahmaikatvaviṣayam prasīdati nānyathā śravaṇamātreṇa* / (BUB, p. 326)
12. *śravaṇasya pramāṇa-vicāratvena pradhānatvād aṅgitvaṁ manana-nididhyāsanayos tu*. . .(BUB, p. 326)
13. BUBV 2.4. 218.
14. *Ibid.* 217.
15. SP 2.4.218: *tasya śamādi-sahita-śravaṇādy-avasāna-bhūmitvam eva sphorayati* /

ON *ĀBHĀSA* IN SUREŚVARA'S WORK UNDER REFERENCE

4.1 Having thus discussed BUBV (relevant portion) as a Vārtika and also the difference between Śaṅkara and Sureśvara, with the help of Ānandagiri, we may now inquire if in BUBV (under reference) Sureśvara develops his cardinal theory of *ābhāsa* which occupies an important place among various theories in Advaita tradition that are propounded with a view to elucidation of the relationship between the Brahman and the world.[1]

4.2 Sureśvara has expressed in his works at various places, his view on the relationship between the Brahman and the world, known as *ābhāsavāda*. Naturally, therefore, while he gives in the course of his discussion of the dialogue of Yājñavalkya and Maitreyī (viz. BUBV 2.4.424 ff.) his philosophy in a nut-shell (this is already observed), he does not let go the occasion for discussing his theory of *ābhāsa*.

4.3.1 As such, it is necessary to note Sureśvara's exposition of the theory of *ābhāsa* on the basis of BUBV 2.4. Before entering into the discussion of the theory of *ābhāsa*, however, let us note his use of the word *ābhāsa* together with its meaning.

4.3.2.1 That Sureśvara uses the word *ābhāsa* in the sense of 'apparent' or 'appearing as real' is clear from such passages as BUBV 2.4.124: *pramāṇam apramāṇaṁ ca pramābhāsaṁ ca yad bhavet*; Nais 3.85: *pratyakṣābhāsaḥ pratyakṣe hy āgamābhāsa āgame* and the *Praṇavārtika* 59 : *prārabdhasyānuvṛttis tu muktasyābhāsamātrataḥ* (if this is really his wǒrk). In TUBV 2.650 also, he uses the word *pramābhāsa* 'knowledge which has the appearance of right cognition'. It follows from these statements that, in reality, the Brahman is one and the same with the Jīvātman but when it is limited by limiting adjuncts (due to ignorance), it is called the Jīvātman or *pratyagātman* 'individual consciousness'.[2] Sureśvara postulates the notion of *ābhāsa* while distinguishing between the Jīvātman and the highest Ātman (Brahman) as well as for the explanation of the function/mode of the Jīvātman. When the Brahman is said to possess properties, it is taken as the Jīvātman; the Jīvātman is the Brahman on which are superimposed (*adhyāsa*)[3] properties etc. which really do not belong to it. The Brahman assumes the appearance of the Jīvātman. Here we should note that *ābhāsa* is the result of *adhyāsa* which is rooted in ignorance. When a white flower appears red to one who is wearing red glasses, it is the glasses that make the white flower look red. Hence the word *ābhāsa* is used in such a way that the subject is kept in view and the word *adhyāsa*, which may here be compared with glasses is used, with the object in view. The notion of the Jīvātman arises from the superimposition on the Brahman of various properties, such as those of external entities (*bāhyadharma*) of the body (*dehadharma*), of sense-organs (*indriyadharma*) and of inner organs (***antaḥkaraṇadharma***).[4]

4.3.2.2. Verses BUBV 2.4.427-429 show the case of inner-organs, of the body and of the external entities thus:

> "What is described as the activity of the highest Ātman, viz. the knower etc., has the appearance of the individual consciousness residing in the intellect which is the effect of ignorance."
>
> "Likewise, he (the highest Ātman) would be having the form of one who listens, one who touches etc., thanks to the (different) organs and their functions. Also, he who is above (i.e. aloof from) the activity of the body, (appears as) miserable, fair and twice-born."
>
> "(The highest Ātman) is wealthy, or possessed of cows, or poor owing to his association with objects such as wealth etc., even though he does not have that; (he has) become known as described due to ignorance."

4.3.2.3 In BUBV 2.4.350-351, the word *ābhāsa* is used in relation to the function of the intellect:

> "This (commonly known) relation of the enjoyer and the enjoyable (for) the Ātman is caused by that (intellect). This (commonly known) function of Ego which belongs to the intellect, being the encompasser of misery, encompasses the

knower and the object of knowing also (encompasses) its own semblance. There does not arise the function of Ego in a body without there being any external change."

On the common language level, the function of the intellect is: As appearance of sentiency, it pervades and takes the shape of an object. Only then the object appears to be seen.

4.3.2.4 On the basis of BUBV 2.4.346 and 390, we can speak of *ābhāsa* on the cosmological level:

"...(And) the *prāṇa* which has the appearance of sentiency, exists (in the body), pervading the (common) function (of the intellect)" (i.e. the function shared by the intellect with Ego and *manas*).

"(Take for instance:) This (vital force) is said to be a mass of knowledge not because of the knowledge through the intellect; it is called Prājña because of its connection with the apparent rise of the knowledge on the part of the individual consciousness."

As is commonly known, according to GK 1.11,[5] Prājña is the individual consciousness bound by *kāraṇa* and the enjoyer of joy and necessarily connected with the intellect. And this is not really different from the individual consciousness abiding in the state of deep sleep also. And BUBV 2.4.303 uses the word *pratyagiśvara* which means *pratyagātman* 'individual consciousness'. We may note here that Īśvara (cf. GK 1.28) is the Brahman in the state of deep sleep and corresponds to Prājña.

4.3.3 According to Sureśvara, existent things in any worldly dealing that originates from ignorance are of two types, viz. (i) the Ātman (=Jīvātman) of the nature of *cidābhāsa* and (ii) the non-Ātman (all things) of the nature of *acidābhāsa*.[6] Sureśvara notes it thus : The Brahman is *cit*, the Jīvātman is *cidābhāsa*, and the non-Ātman is *acidābhāsa*. Even though the Brahman is in reality neither a cause nor an effect, it stands in the form of a cause or an effect[7], assuming the nature of *cidābhāsa*. The Brahman is taken to have attained the nature of causes and effects and also manifoldness by its limiting adjuncts such as the intellect, *manas* etc. which are but its own appearances, due to ignorance.[8] The manifoldness, meaning all the worldly phenomena here, is formed on the basis of mutual expectancy in the form of a cause and an effect. It should be noted from this that the notion of *ābhāsa* is fully utilized in the discussion of the causation of the world. The Brahman which is wrapped by ignorance is called *cidābhāsa* and this *cidābhāsa* is assumed to create the world in keeping with the cause-effect relation. Since causality is a matter of worldly dealing, we may here drop *cit.*, i.e. the Brahman. The *cidābhāsa* is the cause of the world. As Śaṅkara states in his refutation of causality, the cause of the world is expected to be a sentient being[9] with the Sāṁkhya. So far as worldly dealing is concerned, *cidābhāsa* can be regarded as the sentient being. This *cidābhāsa* is called the Jīvātman (*pratyagātman*), Prāṇa and Prājña from microcosmic standpoint as stated above. From macrocosmic standpoint, as already pointed out in conformity with GK 1.28, it is called Īśvara.[10] To this effect, BUBV 1.4.371 states the following:

asya dvaitendra-jālasya yad-upādāna-kāraṇam |
ajñānaṁ tad-upāśritya brahma kāraṇam ucyate ||

"The Brahman is said to be the source of this illusory duality, on one's resorting to ignorance which is the material cause (of all of it)."

Thus, the Brahman, jointly with ignorance, is the material cause of this world. We notice in Nais 3.1 and 29 a support for this proposition, viz. that ignorance is connected with the causal Brahman, thus: Ignorance is the essence of the non-Ātman; the non-Ātman is born of ignorance (*anātmanaś cājñāna-prasūtatvāt*, Nais 3.1).[11]

Now TUBV 2.145[12] describes ignorance as the cause of creation and in TUBV 2.57 we find that the Brahman itself is the cause[13]—ATUBV thereon points out that the cause is material cause;[14] further, BUBV 1.4.375 also mentions the Brahman as the cause.[15] From these diverse statements there arises some problem : These statements and that in Nais as well do not use the term *upādāna* 'material' (cause). What then is Sureśvara's view ? In answer, we may say the following : Though the matter of the material cause (*upādānakāraṇa*) and the efficient cause (*nimittakāraṇa*) of the world is a controversial point in Advaita, we have to infer that Sureśvara does not draw a distinction between the *upādāna* and the *nimitta*. In this regard, HACKER says : "We come to know that Sureśvara does not draw a distinction between the material cause and the efficient cause."[16] In this connection we may observe that, according to Sureśvara, everything else than the Ātman is but to be negated and so he does not feel the need for using the term *upādāna*, since that might indicate the reality of the world.

As stated above, so far as worldly dealing is concerned, Sureśvara's word *cidābhāsa* as the cause of the world can be said to follow Śaṅkara's standpoint that the cause of the world should be the sentient being.

4.4 The foregoing review of Sureśvara's theory of *ābhāsa* should, in connection with the dialogue between Yājñavalkya and Maitreyī, raise two important questions : (i) Since the dialogue reaches its climax in the sentence *ātmā vā are draṣṭavyaḥ* what kind of activity has one to undertake in relation to what is *cidābhāsa* and/or *acidādhāsa* ? and (ii) if *draṣṭavyaḥ* is to be understood as *jñeyaḥ*, what kind of *jñāna* is that ? Is this knowledge similar to our common knowledge, though it is related to *cidābhāsa* and *acidābhāsa* ? It is to these questions that we shall have now to turn.

NOTES

1. They may be enumerated as *ajātivāda* (of Gauḍapāda), *vivartavāda* (of Śaṅkara), *pratibimbavāda* (of Padmapāda and his followers, the Vivaraṇa school), *ābhāsavāda* (of Sureśvara) and *avacchedavāda* (of Vācaspatimiśra and his followers, the Bhāmatī school).

2. So far as Sureśvara's use of the word *ātman* is concerned, *ātman* means at times the Brahman and some times the Jīvātman. Cf. note 5 on section 1.

3. Śaṅkara's theory of *adhyāsa* is very clearly accepted by Sureśvara.

4. BSB 1.1.1 (p.3) : *adhyāso nāma atasmiṁs tad-buddhir ity avocāma / tad yathā — putra-bhāryādiṣu vikaleṣu sakaleṣu vā aham eva vikalaḥ sakalo veti bāhyadharmān ātmany adhyasyati tathā deha-dharmān—sthūlo'haṁ kṛśo'haṁ gauro'haṁ tiṣṭhāmi gacchāmi laṅghayāmi ceti / tathendriya-dharmān—mūkaḥ kāṇaḥ klībaḥ badhiraḥ andho'ham iti / tathā'ntaḥ-karaṇa-dharmān—kāma-saṁkalpa-vicikit-sādhyavasāyādīn /*

5. SP on BUBV 2.4.390 refers to GK 1.11: *prājñaḥ kāraṇabaddhaḥ*, and 1.3 : *ānandabhuk tathā prājñaḥ*.

6. BUBV 2.4.424.

7. *Ibid.* 422

8. *Ibid.* 423-425.
9. See section 10.2 ff.
10. See section 9.3.1 ff.
11. Cf. HACKER, *op. cit.*, pp. 61 and 65.
12. TUBV 2.145 : *bhaviṣyaty asty abhūc ceti yato vandhyaṁ viśeṣaṇam/ uṣṭrādivad aṇos tasmād avidyaivātra kāraṇam //*
13. TUBV 2.57 : *yāvān kaścid vikāro 'tra brahma tasmān nivartitam / bhajate kāraṇatvaṁ tat tathā-caitanya-dharmakam //*
14. ATUBV 2.57 : "As an undesired consequence, it would follow that (Brahman) is senseless like clay etc."
15. *idaṁ tat sarva-vedeṣu yathābhūtārthc-vittaye / sad evetyādibhir vākyaiḥ kāraṇaṁ brahma gīyate //*
16. HACKER, *op. cit.*, p. 66.

SUREŚVARA ON SO-CALLED INJUNCTION IN VEDĀNTA

5.1.1 The first question we have just now raised is far more important than it appears: It raises a problem of the fundamental difference between the two types of sentences of the Veda, viz. those from the Brāhmaṇa texts and those from the Upaniṣads. Similar in form as they are, one would see in them the same import as regards activity one has to undertake. And such is indeed not the view of the Advaita Vedāntins. Sureśvara has therefore to clarify his position at the very outset.

5.1.2 It may be noticed in this context that, in the introductory portion of BSB, Śaṅkara describes his work as *śārīrakamimāṁsā* 'a methodical exposition of the (Vedānta) texts pertaining to the individual consciousness'. But one may say that this description of BSB can pertain to his other writings as well. And therefore the natural consequence would be the delight of the Mīmāṁsaka whose method of sentence-interpretation is evidently borrowed by Śaṅkara, (in his view) in all respects thereof. Śaṅkara and, following him, Sureśvara are aware of this and the latter has already taken care to show his basic differences with the Mīmāṁsakas as regards the interpretation of Vedic sentences.[1] But he does not speak of them while he comments on BU 2.4 and 4.5 where occurs the well-known *mahāvākya, ātmā vā are draṣṭavyaḥ*. . .which could easily be taken by the Mīmāṁsakas as an injunction. Sureśvara has, therefore, felt it necessary to take up this issue for discussion. His purpose is to show that, that sentence is not an injunction proper. Let us see how.

5.2. The Mīmāṁsaka holds the view that liberation is attained by action and a statement of the Śruti has action for its purpose (*āmnāyasya kriyārthatvāt.* Cf. the *Jaimini-Sūtra* 1.2.1) and is (generally) expressive of action. Hence, for the Mīmāṁsaka, the statement of an injunction is of paramount importance.

Contrary to this, the Advaita Vedāntin holds the view that liberation is attained only through understanding the purport of a *mahāvākya* which presupposes ineffectiveness of action. Śaṅkara says in this connection, "Knowledge, however, arises from the Śruti and that whose object is reality (i.e. the Brahman) cannot be produced by a hundred commands."[2] The Śruti statement, *ātmā vā are draṣṭavyaḥ* (BU 2.4.6) looks like an injunction and is therefore likely to involve a discrepancy. In this connection Śaṅkara has elsewhere said, "Such commands like *ātmā vā are draṣṭavyaḥ*, as in ordinary speech, are meant to invite one's attention to reality, there is no injunction that one should actually attain any knowledge."[3] And Sureśvara, taking his cue from his teacher, carries on an elaborate discussion on this point in BUBV 2.4.95-212.

5.3.1 It will, however, be useful to note the general idea of an injunction before we enter into Sureśvara's discussion on this matter.

An injunction is expressed generally by *liṅ* 'potential mood' which is therefore called *vidhiliṅ*. This *vidhiliṅ* gives rise to *bhāvanā* 'imperative force'. *bhāvanā* also is two-fold; *ārthibhāvanā* 'imperative force dependent on sense' and *śābdibhāvanā* 'imperative force dependent on sound'. On the basis of these two *bhāvanās*, one can speak of two kinds of an injunction; *ajñātajñāpakavidhi* and *apravṛttapravartakavidhi*. The first variety of injunction (i.e. *ajñātajñāpakavidhi*) informs a man of three different earlier unknown things in this way: The action has (i) *sādhya*, (ii) *sādhana* and (iii) *itikartavyatā*—this is called *ajñātajñāpakatva* of the Śruti statement. When knowledge about an unknown action/thing has been thus imparted, the other variety of injunction (i.e. *apravṛttapravartaka*) enjoins a person to perform an action which he has not as yet performed. It may then be noted that certain injunctions in the Śruti may be of the first or the second variety, but it is also possible that there can be an injunction that combines the characters of both these varieties. Our problem is to see if at all a *vidhi*-like sentence from the Upaniṣad belongs to any of the two varieties or combines their character into one.

5.3.2.1 Keeping in view these notions about an injunction, we may examine Sureśvara's discussion on the sentence, *ātmā vā are draṣṭavyaḥ* . . . His discussion can be divided into six arguments thus:

(I) Knowledge of the oneness of the Ātman and the Brahman cannot be the object of an injunction.

(II) No action is possible in the Ātman, so an injunction is impossible in respect of it.

(III) An injunction is possible only in the sense of *ajñātajñāpana*. [These three are more important than the following three which are incidental.]

(IV) Neither *niyamavidhi* nor *parisaṁkhyāvidhi* is possible as regards knowing the Ātman.

(V) An injunction is compared with a simple affirmation (*abhidhāśruti*).

(VI) An injunction is not required for constant meditation.

5.3.2.2 Argument (I):

An objector, who holds that the sentence *ātmā vā are draṣṭavyaḥ* is an injunction, would say that the sentence prescribes not the knowing of the Ātman which has been already known, but the securing of the knowledge of the oneness of the Jīvātman and the Brahman.[4] To this Sureśvara replies thus: Such an injunction is possible when either (i) the oneness is not known, or (ii) the oneness is known. Now, the act of knowing presupposes the distinction between the knower and the object of knowing. In the case (i), the object of knowing is not known. And alternatively an injunction presupposes the distinction between the one who is enjoined to act and the object towards which one's action is directed (*niyojya-viṣaya*) which cannot be made in the case (ii)[5]. As such, the sentence *ātmā vā are draṣṭavyaḥ* cannot be the object of the injunction in respect of knowledge of the oneness of the Brahman and the Jīvātman. An injunction about the knowing of the Brahman is therefore impossible.[6]

Sureśvara refutes in three ways the view that the Ātman is the object of an injunction:

(a) The experience which is the result of the various means of knowing is the nature of the Brahman. This cannot be enjoined like other fruits of action such as attainment of heaven. Therefore, the Ātman cannot be the object of any injunction.[7] (b) All means of knowing etc. appear to be imagined in sentiency. The Brahman is partless, is of the nature of sentiency and becomes the support of many attributes. And the Ātman is of the nature of sentiency, homogeneous and invariable. Hence, such a sentient being cannot be the object of any injunction.[8] (c) The Ātman cannot be the object of any injunction[9] in view of the following Śruti passages: "By what, my dear, should one know the knower?" (BU 2.4.14), "You cannot see the seer of seeing." (BU 3.4.2). The same is affirmed by the nature of the Brahman, i.e. it is ever in the form of understanding (*sadāvagatirūpa*), it is shining as a circle of light (*jyotiścakrāvabhāsin*) and is by nature a light that shines by itself (*svayaṁjyotiḥsvabhāva*).

5.3.2.3 Argument (II):

Wherever there is cause-effect relation there is usefulness of action, for action makes a cause manifest itself into the form of an effect. Only in such a case, i.e. when action is possible, can an injunction be assumed.[10]

Sureśvara discusses the possibility of action regarding the Ātman in two ways:

(i) There are three possibilities as regards existence:

(a) That whose existence depends on origin etc., e.g. a pot, (b) that whose existence is independent of origin etc., and (c) non-existence, e.g. that of a sky-flower. The case (a) needs action, while the cases (b) and (c) do not.[11] As to (a), action may lead to one of the four results, viz. origin, attainment, change or purification.[12] The Ātman cannot be said to originate from anything else, because it is not what is made and has a beginning. It is not what is attained, because it is of the nature of what is eternally attained. It cannot be modified, because it is not finite but invariable. It is not what is purified, because it is devoid of qualities and therefore, no speciality can attach itself to it. Hence, the Ātman is not the case (a). As the Ātman is self-established, there can be no injunction with reference to it [case (b)]. Even if the Ātman be regarded as non-established like the sky-flower, it must be admitted that an injunction with reference to it would be futile [case (c)]. In either case, there is no place for human operation.[13] The Ātman is self-established and does not come into existence owing to any other thing (*svataḥsiddha*). But an injunction applies only to something that can be produced, as, for example, cattle which a particular sacrifice can produce.[14]

(ii) The knowledge of the Ātman arises owing to the strength of a thing which is to be known (*vastutantra*), i.e. the Ātman itself. In other words, it is not accompanied by a desire or some exertion on the part of a person, acting on an injunction (*puruṣatantra*). Hence, there is no injunction possible in respect of the knowledge of the Ātman.[15]

5.3.2.4 Argument (III):

Sureśvara admits the necessity of an injunction for the understanding of the meaning of at least two words which are required to form a proposition. This understanding takes place by the method of *anvayavyatireka*.[16] Thus he says:

> "Therefore there is the Vedic injunction as regards discrimination between the Ātman and the non-Ātman by the method of *anvayavyatireka*." (BUBV 2.4.107)
>
> "The awareness that the Ātman is eternally liberated can result straight from the Śruti statement. And the awareness of the sentence-sense is preceded by the remembrance of that which is signified by the word(s). One firmly recollects that which is signified by the word (s) by the method of *anvayavyatireka*. Thus one knows the Ātman as free from misery and inactive." (BUBV 2.4.111-112)

Again, one should note that there are two implications in respect of an injunction: (a) *ajñātajñāpana* '(an injunction) which makes known what is not known', (b) *apravṛttapravṛtti* '(an injunction) which inclines one towards some act (that one normally has not already taken to)'. As such, in the context of knowing the Ātman (as stated above), an injunction is understandable in the sense that it makes known what is not known before, but it does not incline one to get to know it. This is stated in the following:

> "And, therefore, the Vedānta sentence is to be considered as

an injunction informing one of what is known (before). But it does not stand to say that the injunction makes one inclined towards an action (which was never undertaken before) . . . " (BUBV 2.4.115)

"Therefore, it stands to reason that here (in this Śruti statement) there is an injunction which informs one of what is not known; but it cannot be held reasonable (to say that here there is) an injunction regarding doing what is not (previously) done." (BUBV 2.4.198)

5.3.2.5 Argument (IV):

It is already mentioned that the knowledge of the Ātman is for an individual ever-attained, and, therefore, no *apūrvavidhi* is necessary for knowing it. But even a *niyamavidhi* 'injunction for restriction' or a *parisaṁkhyāvidhi* 'injunction for exclusion' is not possible in connection with the same, since restriction and exclusion are possible only in the case of what has been already established either in part or as an alternative.[17]

5.3.2.6 Argument (V):

One may say: As in the *karmakāṇḍa*, an injunction is independently authoritative and non-injunctive statements are useful as its subsidiaries, so it is in the *jñānakāṇḍa* also.[18] In answer to this possible doubt Sureśvara compares an injunction with a simple affirmation (*abhidhāśruti*). A simple affirmation is that which informs one about the nature of the Ātman but does not enjoin one to act, e.g. the affirmations: *tat tvam asi*, *aham brahmāsmi* and *sarvaṁ khalu idam brahma*. The Ātman is well-known (*siddha*) and still it does not resemble the earth etc., because the Ātman is devoid of a form etc. On this, it may be said that a simple affirmation conveying the nature of the Ātman leads to such a cognition as is beyond sense-perception (*atīndriyabodha*)[19] and an injunction also leads to *atīndriyabodha*. But then there is a difference between the two: the difference lies in the object of knowing (*prameya*). The object of knowing by a simple affirmation is what is already established (*siddhavastu*) and that by an injunction is what is to be accomplished (*sādhya*).[20] The knowledge of the oneness of the Ātman is self-established; it is, no doubt, covered with ignorance, but it does not expect any action for uncovering itself. Since the imperative force rests on action, there is no imperative force possible in respect of the self-established thing. And so long as there is no imperative force operating, an injunction cannot be considered as the means of knowing (the Ātman).[21] Therefore no injunction can be held as necessary for knowing what is established.

Two verses, viz. BUBV 2.4.160-161, may be noted here since they significantly bear on the point. In verse 160, Sureśvara first refers to a possible stand that the presence of a verb—that always expresses action—is an invariable necessity in a sentence. Then he answers it in verse 161 thus: In Vedānta, verbs are expressive of mere existence; thus for instance, *asti*, *asmi* are sufficient for understanding the uniqueness of the Brahman and consequent liberation. As such, one can conclude that the verbal expressions like *draṣṭavyaḥ* etc. need not be treated in the same manner as other verbs in the Mīmāṁsā.[22]

An objector would say that the statement, 'There are fruits on the bank of a river' is the same as a simple affirmation such as *tat tvam asi.* To this Sureśvara replies: The statement *sarittīre phalāni santi* expects another means of knowing for connecting the things, viz. the fruits and the bank. This connection is known by a speaker who states, 'There are fruits on the bank of a river', only after he goes to the bank of the river and observes the fruits. So the statement is merely a repetition of what he has actually seen. Thus, the statement *sarittīre phalāni santi* has no independent authoritativeness, since it depends on another means of knowing (i.e. direct perception). It is contrary to this that the oneness of the Ātman is conveyed to one by a simple affirmation and has not to be supported by direct perception—already, it is beyond sense-perception (*atīndriyabodha*).[23]

Further, an injunction depends on one's capacity to perform the act enjoined. In other words, it depends on the imperative force which evokes action. Thus, an injunction cannot be independently authoritative. As against this, a simple affirmation which informs one of the oneness of the Ātman expects no other injunctive force.[24]

In the course of his comparison of an injunction and a simple affirmation, Sureśvara meant to imply that an injunction is not possible in respect of knowing the oneness of the Jīvātman and the Brahman—a simple affirmation about it is sufficient for the purpose of removing the cover of ignorance on it.

5.3.2.7 Argument (VI):

In this case, Sureśvara adduces a number of reasons:
(i) As to knowledge with its object and form, meditation is possible, because it is possible to assume the meditator-meditated relation in respect of the same. But such is not the case in respect of the knowledge of the Ātman. The Ātman knows itself; in this knowing there does not exist any subject-object relation. Hence any constant meditation is also not necessary in respect of it. That is, no injunction is required in that behalf.[25]
(ii) Just because the knowledge of the Ātman is not acquired by sense-organs, and also it is not grasped by *manas* which is nourished by constant meditation—thus, constant meditation is impossible in respect of the same.[26]
(iii) An injunction for constant meditation could be possible: (a) when the Ātman is already known, or (b) when the Ātman is not known. If (a), there is no need of constant meditation; there already exists the fruit of the injunction. If (b), there is no support for meditation—it is already clarified that the relation of the meditator and the meditated is not possible.[27]
(iv) An objector says: 'An injunction for constant meditation may be necessary, since knowledge which is once acquired does not remove ignorance.' To this Sureśvara replies: 'It is shown that knowledge and ignorance are so opposed that they cannot co-exist, even as darkness cannot co-exist with light. Hence this objection cannot be sustained.[28]

5.3.2.8 It may be clear from this study that the sentence *ātmā vā are draṣṭavyaḥ* may very well resemble an injunction only in form; however, it does not answer the requirements of a proper injunction.

NOTES

1. Cf. BSB 1.1.4 (p. 19): *kimarthāni tarhi 'ātmā vā are draṣṭavyaḥ śrotavyaḥ' ityādīni vidhicchāyāni vacanāni* |

2. BSB 3.2.21 (p. 363) : *jñānaṁ tu pramāṇa-janyaṁ yathābhūta-viṣayaṁ ca na tan niyoga-śatenāpi kārayituṁ śakyate* |

3. *Ibid.* (p. 362) : *draṣṭavyādi-śabdā api paravidyādhikāra-paṭhitās tattvābhimukhī-karaṇa-pradhānā na tattvāvabodha-vidhi-pradhānā bhavanti* /

4. BUBV 2.4.96.

5. *Ibid.* 97-99.

6. TUBV 2.633-4: *na cāpīhātma-vijñānaṁ codanābhir vidhīyate / svādhyāyo'dhyetavya iti hy etasmāt tasya siddhitaḥ // karmāvabodho na yathā niyogāntaram īkṣate / tathaivātmāvabodho'pi na niyogāntarād bhavet //*

7. BUBV 2.4.123.

8. *Ibid.* 124-5.

9. TUBV 2.681-2: *vijñātāram are kena vijānīyād iti śrutiḥ / na dṛṣṭer iti dṛśyatvaṁ niyogair eva vāryate // sadāvagatirūpasya jyotiś-cakrāvabhāsinaḥ / svayaṁjyotiḥ-svabhāvasya nyāyyaṁ tasmān na darśanam //* Cf. BUBV 2.4.134-6

10. BUBV 2.4.118-9.

11. *Ibid.* 117.

12. *Ibid.* 189 and SV 236 : *utpattir āptiḥ saṁskāro vikāraś ca vidheḥ phalam / muktir vilakṣaṇaitebhyas tenehānarthako vidhiḥ //*

13. SV 656 : *siddhe'siddhe'tha vaikātmye vidhir naivopapadyate / nākāśe nāpi tat-puṣpe puṁ-vyāpārānapekṣatā //*

14. TUBV 2.632: *naivaṁ yataḥ kriyaiveha codanābhir vidhīyate / svavyāpāre yatas tābhir niyoktuṁ śakyate pumān / dravya-svarūpe'sādhyatvāt kathaṁ tābhiḥ pravartyate //*

15. BUBV 2.4.120, 121, 151 and SV 30 : *kim atra vidhinā kāryam anṛtantratva-hetutaḥ / śruto'py anarthako'tra syād vidhy-arthāsambhavatvataḥ //*

16. TUBV 2.714-5 and 718: *prāktu vākyārtha-vijñānāt tan-niviṣṭa-padārthayoḥ / anvayavyatirekākhya-vivekāya vidhir bhavet // vākyārtha-pratipattau hi padārthājñānam eva ca / pratibandho yatas tasmād anvayādy-avalokanam // svasiddheḥ kāraṇaṁ nānyaj-jñānam ajñāna-hānaye / yasmād apekṣate tasmān na nididhyāsanāya tat //*

17. BUBV 2.4.144-6 and SV 412b-413a : *vidhayas tu kathaṁ rāgaṁ nirundhantīti bhaṇyatām / na hi te parisaṁkhyārthā nāpi caite niyāmakāḥ //*

18. BUBV 2.4.147.

19. *Ibid.* 153-4.

20. *Ibid.* 165-6.

21. *Ibid.* 157-8.

22. Normally a Mīmāṁsaka would understand the force of Potential forms in verbal forms of other moods also. Take for instance, (i) *dadhnā juhoti* where *juhoti*, and (ii) *samānayate juhvām upabhṛtas tejo vā* where *samānayate*—the Present Indicative—has the meaning of the Potential forms *juhuyāt* and *samānayet.* That is to say, his tendency is to connect all verbal derivatives with some action. Sureśvara wants to controvert this. He would make a

clear-cut difference between 'what one ought to do' and 'what is (in its own right)'.

23. *Ibid.* 159, 162-3.
24. *Ibid.* 179-81.
25. *Ibid.* 202-3.
26. *Ibid.* 204.
27. *Ibid.* 207.
28. *Ibid.* 208-9.

JÑĀNA AND VIJÑĀNA

6.1 It was earlier (in 4.4) pointed out that Sureśvara's theory of *ābhāsa* raises a question about the nature of the knowledge of reality, i.e. whether it is similar to our common knowledge, inasmuch as it is related to *cidābhāsa* and *acidābhāsa*. The question demands our attention just after we have considered the significance of the Upaniṣadic affirmation *ātmā vā are draṣṭavyaḥ* inviting our attention to the true nature of the Brahman, viz. it is knowledge itself.

6.2 We have already seen how Sureśvara holds that the dialogue between Yājñavalkya and Maitreyī does not seek to prescribe any injunction for one who desires liberation but instead stresses the need of *jñāna* towards that purpose. Now he feels the necessity of explaining the nature of that *jñāna* which would effect one's liberation. Nevertheless, like many writers of the past, Sureśvara also uses the words *jñāna* and *vijñāna* without always making a discrimination between the two. It may be noted that, in Vedānta tradition, the word *vijñāna* conveys the notion of knowledge based on differences such as *grāhya* and *grāhaka* which are caused by ignorance about reality. In other words, the sphere wherein the notion of *vijñāna* applies is *pramāṇaprameyavyavahāra*, there one notices a means of knowing such as direct perception, inference etc.; this may be described as *savikalpakajñāna*. Contrary to this, the word *jñāna* is 'realization of the Ātman etc. which is preached by the Śruti and the preceptor'[1], or 'knowledge of things taught in the Śruti'[2], i.e. knowledge of the oneness of the Brahman and the Jīvātman.[3]

6.3.1 In the course of my work on translation of the portion from BUBV, I am forced to translate both the words *jñāna* and *vijñāna* at times as knowledge (as in common life), as equivalent to *savikalpakajñāna*, and at some others as knowledge (of the oneness, i.e. uniqueness of the Brahman/Ātman), that is the same as *nirvikalpakajñāna*. As such, a justification has to be offered here for doing so.

6.3.2 First, let us examine Sureśvara's use of the word *jñāna* as *savikalpaka* as well as *nirvikalpaka* in verses 256-258. He writes :

> "The knowledge [*jñāna* (1)] wards away (ever-) variable cognition associated with ignorance arising from ignorance regarding the (nature of the) individual consciousness, owing to the strength of object of knowing within oneself (viz. the Ātman, *antarmeyabala*), (and) because it is (ever-) invariable." (verse 256)
>
> "(Now,) in time etc. there is absence of it on account of the origin of their nature (as such and such) only in ignorance about the individual consciousness; therefore, time etc. is not the remover of knowledge [*jñāna* (2)]." (verse 257)
>
> "They do not consider that cognition [*jñāna* (3)] as the remover of ignorance which is itself dependent on (some other cognition) produced from an object (whose reality is) disproved. Right knowledge [*samyagjñāna* (4)] is (accepted as) remover of ignorance, as the two are mutually opposed." (verse 258)

Thus, Sureśvara has used the word *jñāna* four times, viz. *jñāna* (1), *jñāna* (2) etc. The words *jñāna* (1), *jñāna* (2) and (*saṁyag-*) *jñāna* (4) are used in the sense of *nirvikalpakajñāna* and *jñāna* (3), as *savikalpakajñāna*. The former is *antarmeyabala* and invariable and the latter is variable and arises from ignorance (that is to say: *bahirmeyabala*). Knowledge which is *antarmeyabala* removes knowledge which is produced from ignorance and so there is *bādhaka-bādhya* 'stultifier-stultified' relation between the two In the passages above *jñāna* (1) (2) (4) is *bādhaka* 'stultifier' and *jñāna* (3) is *bādhya* '(to be) stultified'. It must, therefore, be noted in passing that both cannot co-exist.

6.3.3 Now it may be noted that Sureśvara uses the word *jñāna* in either of the senses also. Thus in *ghaṭādi-jñānavaj jñānaṁ bhinna-hetv-anapekṣataḥ* (verse 191), *prameya-bheda-bhinnatvaṁ jñānānām iva bhedakam* (verse 200), *sparśādi-jñāna-bhedānām* . . . (verse 329), *kaṭhinaṁ jñānaṁ* 'gross knowledge' (verse 344), *tvagādi-jñāna-śaktīnām buddhiḥ* 'The intellect (is said to be the generality) of the powers of knowing, viz. the skin etc.' (verse 367), *jñāna-*

kriyā-śakti (verse 371), *jñāna-śakti* (verses 368, 383 and 387) and *boddhṛ-taj-jñāna-viṣayair* ... (verse 483) of BUBV 2.4, *jñāna* obviously means *savikalpakajñāna* which is based on duality, i.e. subject-object relation. And in *nirastātiśaya-jñāna* (verse 22), *jñānam eva* ... *ātmānam* 'the Ātman which itself is knowledge' (verse 25), *jñānāt kaivalyam aśnute* '(only he, who has given up action) attains liberation through knowledge' (verse 26), *mohamātrāntarāyatvāj jñānamātram apekṣate* '(we think that) there is an obstacle only of ignorance (and therefore) only knowledge (of the oneness of the Ātman) is expected (by us)' (verse 31), *jñānaṁ saṁnyāsalakṣaṇam* (verse 32), *avidyāmātra-vidhvaṁsāj-jñānād evāmṛtam* ... 'immortality (results) only from knowledge which is destruction (i.e. removal) of ignorance alone' (verse 54), *amṛtatva-samprāptir jñānamātraika-hetunā* (verse 55), *muktyeka-sādhanaṁ jñānaṁ* 'knowledge, which is the sole means to liberation' (verse 64), *sarvānartha-nivṛttiś ca sarvāhlādāptir eva ca*. . . *jñānamātrāt* 'removal of all undesirable things and the acquisition of all pleasure merely on account of knowledge' (verse 89), *kaivalya-jñāna-vartmani* (verse 93), *ātma-jñāna* (verses 121, 238 and 482), *utpannam api saj jñānaṁ*. . . 'knowledge that has already arisen and is in existence' (verse 127), *yathāsthitātmavastūttha-jñāna* (verse 151), *avidyā-samucchittir jñāna-* (verse 195), *vāstavaṁ vṛttaṁ jñānam ajñāna-nāśa-kṛt* (verse 197), *ātmāsāmānyarūpotthaṁ jñānaṁ* 'knowledge which arises from the unique nature of the Ātman (verse 208), *saṁyagjñāna* (verses 209, 397 and 472), and *vāstavaṁ jñānam* (verse 450). Sureśvara uses the same word in the sense of *nirvikalpakajñāna* which consists in the knowledge of the oneness of the Brahman—this is expressed in various ways as seen from the translations given here.

6.4.1 Let us now turn to Sureśvara's use of the word *vijñāna* as *savikalpaka* and *nirvikalpakajñāna* as well. He refers to both *nirvikalpaka* and *savikalpakajñāna* in *vākyārthasya vijñānaṃ* 'the awareness of the sentence-sense' in verse 111. This *vākyārtha* is derived from the method of *anvayavyatireka* as we will discuss in the following section and is not the knowledge of the oneness of the Brahman. He also mentions in verse 203 *aviṣaya-vijñāna* 'that which is not an object of (common) knowledge' to signify the Ātman. Though here the compound itself signifies the knowledge of the Ātman, the word *vijñāna* refers to the common knowledge through some means of knowing. Again, in verse 221: *ananyāyatta-vijñāne śravaṇāder upāyataḥ / jāte* . . . 'when there arises knowledge which does not depend on anything else owing to the means 'hearing' etc.', he states that *śravaṇa* and *manana* cause the indirect knowledge of the Ātman, based on *tarka*; this *vijñāna* does not signify *nirvikalpakajñāna*. We may note also the instances where *vijñāna* signifies the knowledge of external objects through direct perception, based on duality, for example in *bhinnamātrādi-vijñāna* 'knowledge of various (things, viz.) knower etc.' (verse 223), *udbhūta-sparśa-vijñāna* (verse 342), *sparśādi-bheda-vijñāna* (verse 343), *sūkṣmaṁ(vijñāna* verse 345) and *viṣaya-vijñāna* (verse 377).

6.4.2 Sureśvara uses the word *vijñāna* (like the word *jñāna*) in either of the senses just noted. Thus in *brahma-yāthātmya-vijñāna* (verse 7), *ṛte'pi brahma-vijñānāt* (verse 17), *pratyagyāthātmya-vijñāna* (verses 331 and 470), *pratyagyāthātmya-vijñāna-janmane* (verse 38) and *aikātmya-vijñāna-phala* (verse 235), he uses the word *vijñāna* clearly to mean the knowledge of the oneness of the Brahman. So also in *nitya-muktatva-vijñāna* 'the awareness (that the Ātman is) eternally liberated' (verse 111) and *utpannam eva vijñānaṁ tadā prāg*. . . 'knowledge was already in existence even before' (verse 128), the word *vijñāna* refers to the knowledge which is ever-attained (*nityaprāpta*), but it is covered with ignorance before realization. It may be clearly noticed that this knowledge is nothing else than *nirvikalpakajñāna*. This is further elaborated by Sureśvara in *vijñānam bhāsvaram*, blazing knowledge' (verse 218), pointing to the self-luminous nature of knowledge (*svaprakāśatva*) of the *nirvikalpakajñāna*.

6.4.3 In verses 232 and 234, Sureśvara paraphrases *nididhyāsana* as *vijñāna-vijñānotpatti-hetutvaṁ dhyānādeḥ prāg avādiṣam / svārtham eva tu vijñānaṁ muktimātra-phalaṁ smṛtam //* "I have already mentioned that meditation etc. is the origin of knowledge but it is held that knowledge is for its own sake, it results only in liberation as its fruit." (verse 234). Since *nididhyāsana* is not the knowledge of the oneness of the Brahman but is the indirect knowledge of the same, this use of the word *vijñāna* is in the sense of *savikalpakajñana*.

6.5 Thus we have examined Sureśvara's use of the word *jñāna* and *vijñāna*. We can say that Sureśvara does not deliberately seek to make a clear-cut distinction between these two words; his use of the two words at times seems to depend on metrical consideration. It may be incidentally pointed out here that the case of Sureśvara's use of the word Ātman is similar; at times, he uses it in the sense of the Jīvātman 'individual consciousness' and, at others, in the sense of the unique consciousness, viz. the Brahman.

6.6 Lastly, let us note his terminological inaccuracy about other words such as *dhī*, *buddhi* etc. In this connection, HACKER correctly observes, "Sureśvara usually calls the inner-organs *buddhi* or *dhī*, sometimes *citta*, more seldom *antaḥkaraṇa* and quite seldom *manas*. Like his teacher, he does not convey the differentiation of the inner-organs (*antaḥkaraṇa* in *ahaṁkāra*, *buddhi*, *manas* and *citta*) which was customary in later Advaitins. But like his teacher, he occasionally distinguishes *buddhi* from *manas* without indeed fixing the functions of both of powers."[4] In the end I may add: This is further supported by the fact that Sureśvara uses these words in the sense of *nirvikalpakajñāna* such as *ātma-caitanya-rūpa-dhī* (TUBV 2.308), *aikātmya-buddhi* (SV 332), *aikātmya-dhī* (SV 340).

NOTES

1. BGB 3.41 : *jñānaṁ śāstrata ācāryataś cātmādīnām avabodhaḥ* . . .
2. BGB 6.8 : *jñānaṁ śāstrokta-padārthānāṁ parijñānam* . . .
3. SV 326 : *jñānād aikātmya-gocarāt* . . ./
4. *Op. cit.*, p. 44.

THE METHOD OF ANVAYAVYATIREKA AS A MEANS OF KNOWING

7.1 So far, we have noted some of the salient features of Sureśvara's philosophy, in the light of BUBV under reference. It is now necessary that we take into consideration an important aspect of his writing, viz. the method he has employed while clarifying the philosophical ideas in the relevant portions of both BU and BUB. A query like this would, it is hoped, throw light on how and what Sureśvara has contributed to the Vedāntic mode of philosophical argument.

7.2 Now, it is a matter of common knowledge that Śaṅkara follows the Vedānta tradition of adopting *tarka* as a means of ascertaining the truth conveyed by Vedānta texts. Naturally, therefore, Sureśvara also would follow him and support his observations on the writings of his master by suitable methods of *tarka*. One of these (one may not be wrong to say, the most important of these) is that of argument based on *anvayavyatireka* relation.

7.3 Sureśvara has explained the method of *anvayavyatireka* in Nais 3.74[1] through the analogy of a man and a post thus: There is a post, but one misunderstands it as a man; the method of *anvaya* conveys the true nature of the thing: 'This is a post.' But merely this statement does not remove the misconception; 'This is a man.' The nature of the post requires to be stated again—this by the method of *vyatireka*: 'This is not a man.' Thus, by stating what it is (viz. a post), and by denying what is (wrongly) grasped (viz. a man) one understands that this is not a man, but a post.

7.4 It would be useful to note how HACKER has explained the word *anvayavyatireka*. He writes[2] : "This explanation and discussion is the duty of logical thought which operates with the positive and negative argument. The former (i.e. *anvaya*) states what logically must belong to a thing and the latter (i.e. *vyatireka*) shows that the opposite cannot belong to it." Taking support from Nais 3.33, 34 and Cand 3.33,[3] he further says that *anvayavyatireka* is a fixed term for 'logical thought or logical method' and is the synonym of the word *anumāna* or *yukti*.

7.5.1 Further, Sureśvara uses the word *anvayavyatireka* in two contexts, i.e. in the philosophical context and in the linguistic context. In the former case, the method gives rise to 'discrimination of the Ātman and the non-Ātman' and in the latter, 'clarification of *pada* and *padārtha*'.

7.5.2.1 Let us, first consider his use of the method of *anvayavyatireka* in the philosophical context. Sureśvara does not elaborately explain the method of *anvayavyatireka* in a way done by the later writers of Vedānta, though he has introduced its basic idea in his writings, at various places. As such, before we consider Sureśvara's adoption of this method in BUBV under reference, let us note, for securing a better acquaintance with this method, what Madhusūdana, who has taken inspiration from Sureśvara in his philosophy, has to say about this method of *anvayavyatireka*. According to him, this method is of five kinds:[4]

(i) *dṛg-dṛśyānvayavyatireka*,
(ii) *sākṣis-sākṣyānvayavyatireka*,
(iii) *āgamāpāyi-tad-avadhy-anvayavyatireka*,
(vi) *duḥkhi-paramapremāspadānvayavyatireka*, and
(v) *anuvṛtta-vyāvṛttānvayavyatireka*.

These five kinds of *anvayavyatireka* are based on the mutually distinguishing pairs such as 'perceiver and perceived', 'witness and witnessed' and 'unchanged and changed.' And this method finally leads us to the discriminative knowledge about the two members of each pair. Since the purpose of the Upaniṣads is to clarify the true nature of transmigratory existence and that of reality, the Brahman, they (and Advaita Vedāntins also) clarify that this world of transmigratory existence consists in the dealings of knower(s) and the object(s) of their knowing (*pramāṇa-prameyavyavahāra*). These dealings arise from the false identification of the Ātman with the non-Ātman, viz. body, senses, *manas* and the intellect, due to ignorance.[5] To remove this false identification due to ignorance is the aim of the Vedāntin and, for achieving his aim, he finds the method of *anvayavyatireka* useful. It is through this method of *anvayavyatireka* that there arises the discriminative knowledge of the Ātman and the non-Ātman,[6] and yet ignorance continues to remain just as it does in the state of deep sleep where there is no duality.[7] Hence the expression of BUBV 2.4.114 above stated is vague, from the philosophical point of view. That is to say, the removal of one's ignorance may still not be effected even after one has acquired discriminative knowledge and therefore one might not attain liberation.[8] Nais 3.4 declares in this connection the necessity of mastering the six disciplines, viz. *śama*, *dama* etc.[9]

7.5.2.2 It is *viveka* that is produced from the adoption of the method of *anvayavyatireka* and is characterized by the discrimination between the Ātman and the non-Ātman.[10] Now, taking into consideration the Sāṁkhya who is called *vivekavādin*,[11] we shall make the point yet more clear. According to the Sāṁkhya, the transmigratory existence is rooted in the false identification of the intellect with *puruṣa* who is ever-free, non-attached, immutable; this is due to ignorance. But this ignorance can be removed through logical inference which shows that *puruṣa* is distinct and apart from other entities beginning with intellect. This removal of ignorance is *viveka* and is sufficient for one to be liberated.[12] Contrary to this, in the opinion of Sureśvara, ignorance remains on the part of one even after attaining *viveka*—in other words, *viveka* is also the effect of ignorance.[13] Hence, the means to liberation is not this *viveka*; it is the knowledge which arises from the Vedic sentence.[14]

7.5.2.3 Again, let us think over this method of *anvayavyatireka* from the point of view of *anvayavyatireka-anumāna* (or, *yukti*, *liṅga*)[15] equation. There exists distinction between the Ātman and the non-Ātman within the sphere of empirical means of knowing, such as direct perception, inference etc.[16] In other words, the method of *anvayavyatireka* ceases to operate when the distinction disappears. BOETZELAER says,[17] "Reasoning (*yukti*) takes an intermediate place between the Śruti (which is direct revelation) and perception." This method of *anvayavyatireka* bears the same fruits as *yukti* etc. This method gives rise to the discriminative knowledge and conveys that the Ātman alone exists, negating everything else than the Ātman,[18] but it does not lead to the final goal.[19] It does not allow the direct union with the Ātman. Just as we infer from the sight of smoke that fire exists and yet we do not know the nature of the fire, i.e. whether it is lit by burning logs of mango tree or oak-tree, so is the case with the method of *anvayavyatireka*. It is the indirect acquaintance with the Ātman that we can get through the method of *anvayavyatireka*. It is only through the Vedic sentence that we come to know the Ātman which is beyond existence and non-existence.[20] Thus, we have so far noticed the following points:

(i) The method of *anvayavyatireka* gives rise to the discriminative knowledge between the Ātman and the non-Ātman by nullifying the nature of duality, but

(ii) it leaves ignorance existent, and

(iii) *śama* etc. are necessary for the removal of ignorance;

(iv) this method leads us to the indirect acquaintance with the Ātman, and, therefore,

(v) the Vedic sentence is an indispensable means to get the direct union with the Ātman, i.e. liberation.

7.5.2.4 Now, let us take support from (iii) and (v) just stated and cast a glance at the remaining process to liberation to be achieved through adopting the method of *anvayavyatireka*. Not only in Nais 3.4 but in BUBV 1.3.98-99 [21] also Sureśvara declares the need of *śama* etc. Hence, one would suspect if *śama* etc. is equivalent to *yogābhyāsa*, one of the stages to liberation mentioned in Nais 1.52—this we have noted in section 2 above. But Cand 1.52 interprets the *yogābhyāsa* as the performance of *śravaṇa*, *manana* and *nididhyāsana*.[22] However, according to SP, Sureśvara holds that *śravaṇa* and *manana* and *śama* etc. are inseparably connected[23] and *nididhyāsana* is mentioned as the culmination of *śravaṇa* etc. together with *śama* etc.[24] and that one acquires complete understanding of the Vedic sentence through *nididhyāsana*.[25]

7.5.3 The other use of the method of *anvayavyatireka* by Sureśvara is found in the context of the clarification of *pada* and *padārtha* (*padapadārthaśodhana*). In fact, Sureśvara shows in Nais

2.9[26] that the understanding of the *vākyārtha* 'sentence-sense' necessarily presupposes the method of *anvayavyatireka.* In BUBV 2.4.111-112 also, he says the same thing thus:

> "The awareness (that the Ātman is) eternally liberated can result straight from the Śruti statement. And the awareness of the sentence-sense is preceded by the remembrance of that which is signified by the word(s). One firmly recollects (or, recognizes) by the method of *anvayavyatireka* that which is signified by the word(s). Thus does one know the Ātman as free from misery and inactive."

Sureśvara declares in Nais 3.39 that the method of *anvayavyatireka* helps one to understand the nature of the Ātman which does not form the *vākyārtha*;[27] so, one can acquire only indirect knowledge thereof.[28] The *mumukṣu,* who has acquired the sentence-sense by adopting the method of *anvayavyatireka,* then proceeds to remove his own ignorance in order that he should attain the knowledge of *avākyārtha.* And one succeeds in securing this *avākyārtha* after cognising the so-called *sambandha-traya,* viz. the knowledge of *sāmānādhikaraṇya, lakṣaṇa-lakṣya* relation and *viśeṣaṇa-viśeṣya* relation[29] between some two words such as *tat* and *tvam* in the *mahāvākya: tat tvam asi.*

7.5.4 We may note here the following points:

(i) In Nyāya and later Advaita Vedānta,[30] *anvayavyatireka* is used for establishing the *vyāpti* between *hetu* and *sādhya*; in Grammar, this is used in order to establish the relation between *pada* and *padārtha.*[31] Sureśvara's use of *anvayavyatireka* shows its nearness to that of Grammar, viz. in that the use is connected with *pada* and *padārtha.*

(ii) The method of *anvayavyatireka* gives rise to the *vākyārtha,* but needs cognizing of the *sambandhatraya* as a further step towards attaining the *avākyārtha.*

(iii) Śaṅkara employs the method of *anvayavyatireka* while explaining the Vedic sentence *tat tvam asi* in Upad.[32] But the later Advaitins, especially Sarvajñātman[33] (for the first time), employs three kinds of *lakṣaṇās* for the same, giving up Śaṅkara's method of *anvayavyatireka.* As for Sureśvara, he follows Śaṅkara in that he adopts, in his discussion, the method of *anvayavyatireka,* but goes a step further and takes the help of *sambandhatraya* in order to support the results of the use of the method of *anvayavyatireka*.

NOTES

1. *sthāṇuḥ sthāṇur itīvoktir na nṛ-buddhiṁ nirasyati | vyanuvādāt tathaivoktir bhrāntim puṁso na bādhate ||*
2. HACKER, *op. cit.*, p. 93.
3. *loc. cit.*
4. HIRIYANNA's note to Nais 3.1 (p. 253), K. S. MURTY, *Revelation and Reason in Advaita Vedānta*, Delhi : Motilal Banarsidass, 1974, pp. 152 ff., UPADHYAYA, *op. cit.*, pp. 234 ff., *Siddhāntābindu*, Baroda: GOS 64, p. 70. Cand insists on four kinds of *anvayavyatireka* in 3.1 and 4.7 thus: *caturvidhānvaya-vyatirekābhyām*; *dṛśyatvādi-caturvidhānvayavyatireka-lakṣaṇo nyāyaḥ* . . .
5. Nais 3.46, 2.97; TUBV 2.224-229.
6. BUBV 2.4.107; Nais 2.111; SP 2.4.272-4.
7. Nais 3.4: *anvayavyatirekābhyāṁ tyaktvā yuṣmad aśeṣataḥ ||*
8. Nais 3.33 and 57.
9. Nais 3.4: *śamādi-sādhanaḥ paśyed ātmany ātmānam añjasā |* On *śama* etc. see note 25 under section 2.
10. Nais 4.16: *yo'yam anvayavyatireka-jo viveka ātmānātma-vibhāga-lakṣaṇo. . .|*
11. The *Pañcadaśī* 9.98 and 131.
12. A. J. AISTON, (tr.), *The Realization of the Absolute*, London : Shanti Sadan, 1971, p. 148.
13. Nais 2.103: *sarva evāyam ātmānātma-vibhāgaḥ pratyakṣādi-pramāṇa-vartmany anupatito 'vidyotsaṅga-varty eva . . . |*
14. Nais 3.33 : *buddhyādīnām anātmatvaṁ liṅgād api ca sidhyati | nivṛttis tāvatā netīty ato vākyaṁ samāśrayet ||*

    Cand 4.16: *tena vākya-jam advaita-jñānam eva mukti-hetur na viveka-jñānam.*
15. J. M. van BOETZELAER, (tr.), *Sureśvara's Taittirīyopaniṣadbhāṣya-vārtikam*, Leiden : E. J. Brill, 1971, p. 44: The word *liṅga* is treated as the synonym of *anvayavyatireka.*
16. Nais 2.103.
17. BOETZELAER, *op. cit.*, p. 57.
18. Nais 3.53 etc.
19. Nais 3.34.
20. Nais 57 : *sad-asad-vyutthitātmāyam ato vākyāt pratīyate ||*
21. See note 26 under section 2.
22. *yogābhyāsaḥ śravaṇa-manana-nididhyāsanādīnām anuṣṭhānam.*
23. SP 2.4.217: *śravaṇa-manana-śamādi-yukte kṛtvā* . . .
24. SP 2.4.218 : *tasya śamādi-sahita-śravaṇādy-avasāna-bhūmitvam eva sphorayati.*
25. BUBV 2.4.217-218.
26. *anvayavyatirekābhyāṁ vinā vākyārthabodhanaṁ na syāt . . .||*

27. Nais 3.39 : *anvayavyatireka-puraḥsaraṁ vākyam evāvākyārtharūpam ātmānam pratipādayatīti . . .* /

28. On Nais 3.28: *iyaṁ cāvākyārtha-pratipattir anvayavyatirekābhijñsyaiva,* HIRIYANNA puts an alternative reading in the footnote (p. 124) thus : *iyaṁ ca vākyārtha-pratipattiḥ.* Nais 3.28 stresses that the acquiring of the knowledge of the Ātman is possible for one who has understood the *vākyārtha* of *tat tvam asi* by the method of *anvayavyatireka,* though the Ātman is not the *vākyārtha* 'sentence sense'. What Sureśvara means is : the *vākyārthapratipatti* is based on subject-object relation, but *ātmapratipatti* is 'not *vākyārthapratipatti*'—since the understanding is not based on subject-object relation.

29. Nais 3.3 : *sāmānādhikaraṇyaṁ ca viśeṣaṇa-viśeṣyatā / lakṣya-lakṣaṇa-sambandhaḥ padārtha-pratyag-ātmanām* // Nais 3.33 : *anvayavyatireka-puraḥsaraṁ vākyam eva sāmānādhikaraṇyādināvidyā-paṭala-pradhvaṁsa-dvāreṇa mumukṣuṁ svārājye 'bhiṣecayati na tvanvayavyatirekamātra-sādhyo 'yam artha ity āha* /

30. The *Vedāntaparibhāṣā,* ch. 2.

31. G. CARDONA, "Anvaya and Vyatireka in Indian Grammar," *The Adyar Library Bulletin,* vols. 31-32, (1967-8), pp. 313-352.

32. Śaṅkara employs the method of *anvayavyatireka* in explaining *tat tvam asi* thus : The method of *anvaya* helps one to understand the sense which both the words *tat* and *tvam* convey in common parlance. Among the various senses of the word *ātman,* the sense *pratyagātman* is conveyed by the word *tat.* The characteristic description of the *pratyagātman* as *nirduḥkhin* is also implied by the word *tat*; and the method *vyatireka* negates the sense which is indicated by the word *tvam* and also the characteristic description of the *pratyagātman* as *duḥkhin* 'miserable'. (This is nothing else than *saṁsārin* 'transmigratory') : But this sense of the word *tvam* is not implied by the word *tat* which is *nirduḥkhin pratyagātman.* Hence, the sense *duḥkhin* is discarded from amongst the senses of the word *tvam.*

33. The *Saṁkṣepaśārīraka* 1.154-157.

THE USE OF ILLUSTRATION (DṚṢṬĀNTA) IN PHILOSOPHICAL WRITING

8.1 Having discussed Sureśvara's method of *anvayavyatireka* in presenting the philosophical contents of the dialogue between Yājñavalkya and Maitreyī, we may now proceed to discuss another important aspect of his writing (and incidentally one of all philosophical writing), viz. the role of *dṛṣṭānta* in philosophical writing. This has become necessary in view of the fact that people would often accept reality to be such and such, only on the basis of *dṛṣṭāntas* 'illustrations' employed in the writing thereon and then there would result more misunderstanding about the same instead. And, certainly Sureśvara also has, following the lead of BU (relevant portion) itself, employed some *dṛṣṭāntas* in his own writing !

8.2 In philosophical discussion, the authors introduce a number of illustrations and try therewith to prove the point under consideration. This practice of theirs is well expressed in a brief sentence, *dṛṣṭāc ca adṛṣṭasiddhiḥ* 'the unseen is established with (the aid of) the seen'. Indeed, this is a useful method of arguing, there is nevertheless a certain difficulty that crops up; thanks to the authors' tendency to overstress the similarity between the *dṛṣṭa* and the *adṛṣṭa*. As examples of this tendency, we may refer to certain passages in BUBV and point out how Sureśvara brings out fuller import of the illustrations used by the Upaniṣadic seer and by his own teacher Śaṅkara as well.

8.3 Thus, while in the course of his exposition of the dialogue of Yājñavalkya and Maitreyī, Sureśvara explains the ideas in Śaṅkara's comment thereon, he finds occasions to discuss Śaṅkara's explanations of a number of illustrations and from his discussions it appears that there are certain differences between the master and his disciple. It would indeed prove profitable, therefore, to follow the arguments of the two and examine the role played by illustration in philosophical writing and then, in the light of that examination, study the differences between Śaṅkara and his disciple.

8.4 It may be pointed out in this connection that Śaṅkara clarifies the role of illustration while referring to the illustration of the *sūryaka* 'reflection of the Sun' in BSB 3.2.20[1]: "The parallel illustration (of the Sun's reflection in the water) is unobjectionable, since a common feature—with reference to which alone the comparison is instituted—does exist. Whenever two things are compared, they are so compared only with reference to some particular point they have in common. Entire equality of the two can never be demonstrated; indeed, if it could be demonstrated, there would be an end of that particular relation which gives rise to the comparison. Nor does the Sūtrakāra institute the comparison objected to on his own account; he merely sets forth the purpose of a comparison actually met with in scripture. Now, the special feature on which the comparison rests is 'the participation in increase and decrease'. The reflected image of the Sun dilates when the surface of the water expands; it contracts when the water shrinks; it trembles when the water is agitated; it divides itself when the water is divided. It thus participates in all the attributes and conditions of the water; while the real Sun remains all the same that time. Similarly, the Brahman, although in reality uniform and never changing, participates as it were in the attributes and states of the body and the other limiting adjuncts within which it abides; it grows with them as it were, decreases with them as it were, and so on. As the two things compared thus possess certain common features, no objection can be raised against the comparison." Likewise, in BSB 2.3.40[2] also, he emphasizes that only a particular characteristic is (or some particular characteristics are) intended for consideration when one compares any two objects. It is ridiculous to expect that the two objects compared should be on all fours in every respect; if that were so, there would be identity between them. And comparison is not identity. Hence while we examine an illustration we should clearly understand the implication and limitations thereof.

8.5.1 Keeping in view this remark of Śaṅkara, we shall now discuss (I) how Śaṅkara discusses the illustration in BU 2.4 (=4.5) and (II) how Sureśvara explains the same in BUBV.

8.5.2.1 The illustrations of the sound of a drum etc. found in BU 2.4.7-9 and in *yatra hi dvaitam iva bhavati* at BU 2.4.14 are to be taken up first. Since both Śaṅkara and Sureśvara explain these (in BUB and BUBV respectively), we shall note their attitudes to these illustrations in the course of the comparison of their views.

8.5.2.2 The illustrations of the sound of a *dundubhi*, *śaṅkha* and *viṇā* in BU 2.4.7-9:[3]

(i) In the introductory part of his commentary on this section of BU, Śaṅkara says, "Because consciousness is noticeable everywhere, it is understood that (everything) is of the nature of consciousness. In this respect is the illustration stated."[4] And hence it is possible to understand that all this is the Ātman. Sureśvara also says the same thing in BUBV 2.4.263-6, but again enters upon a detailed elucidation thereof.

(ii) Hereafter, we shall follow Sureśvara's elucidation and, from time to time, turn to Śaṅkara, if need arises. The words *dundubher hanyamānasya* 'when a drum is being beaten'[5] indicate *śabdatva* 'the common (*sāmānya*) nature of sound'. From this invariable common sound arises a variable particular and external sound.[6] Just as even a skilful man cannot hold a sword taken out from the sheath, i.e. he holds the sword together with the sheath, or just as one cannot distinguish a rope from a serpent imagined therein, so does one imagine a particular sound as only a common sound. Sureśvara employs here the notion of *adhyāsa* in respect of a particular (*viśeṣa*) and a common (*sāmānya*) sound. A particular sound is superimposed on a common sound and is erroneously identified therewith. And further, Sureśvara applies this to the case of the Ātman and the non-Ātman. The non-Ātman is superimposed on the Ātman and identified therewith—this is Sureśvara's addition to Śaṅkara's explanation.[7]

(iii) A question arises: "Does there exist between the Ātman and the non-Ātman *sāmānya-viśeṣa* relation which is the purport of the illustration."[8] Therefore, in connection with this question, Sureśvara first postulates two possibilities, viz. (a) both are identical or (b) both are different. If (a), there is no relationship possible between the Ātman (the *sāmānya*), which is the substratum, and the particular superimposed thereon (the *viśeṣa*). If (b), as in the case of an elephant and a rat, it is impossible to assume any *viśeṣa* which is somehow related to the *sāmānya* just as in the case of a serpent that is assumed in the place of a rope, since both of these have the same form (long and slender form). Thus, *sāmānya-viśeṣa* relation is not possible in respect of the Ātman and the non-Ātman, it is only imaginary. Thus is developed Sureśvara's argument on *sāmānya-viśeṣa* by way of introducing the notions of *adhyāsa* etc., though there is not seen a similar argument in BUB. So, while Śaṅkara offers a brief explanation of the illustration, Sureśvara picks up every possible aspect thereof and elaborates it intensively.

(iv) Also, in BUBV 2.4.286-9, Sureśvara argues the reason why there are three illustrations employed by Yājñavalkya. We shall first note Śaṅkara's remark in this regard: "The use of many illustrations here is intended for declaring manifold generalities, for they are different kinds of generalities and particulars in the form of the sentient and the insentient. It is to show how they are included in the supreme generality, viz. the mass of consciousness, in some way or other."[9] Thus, Śaṅkara is content with only giving the reason as to why many illustrations are given. Now let us turn to BUBV. Sureśvara is aware that, in this regard, one may observe, "The purport of the illustration is one, i.e. the Ātman alone does exist everywhere. Since one illustration is sufficient to prove this purport, it is useless to state any other illustration(s)" and, therefore, argues: In order to state the merger of the non-Ātman into the Ātman in the order of the many distinguishing attributes into species (*sāmānya* and *avāntarasāmānya*) and species into genus (*mahāsāmānya*), there are three illustrations. Thus Sureśvara supplies what Śaṅkara did not state.

8.5.2.3 Now about the illustration *yatra hi dvaitam iva bhavati* in BU 2.4.14.

(i) Sureśvara writes two verses, viz. BUBV 2.4.453-4, for explaining the word *yatra*. As a matter of course, we shall first see Śaṅkara's remark thereon. He states: "The word *yatra* means 'in the case where there exists some Ātman of a specific nature, viz. the individual consciousness, produced from the limiting adjuncts of the aggregates of the body and organs, conjured up by ignorance."[10] And Sureśvara amplifies the view of Śaṅkara and stresses that the word *yatra* refers to the state of ignorance wherein duality prevails. BUBV 2.4.453-4 are helpful for the clarification of the matter under consideration. In these Sureśvara states:

> "Whoever is one that has not known the Truth of the Ātman and has the intellect overpowered (lit. wrapped) by ignorance; is overwhelmed by wrong knowledge and has the notions of distinction such as the seer, the object of seeing etc."
>
> "The person, who has not known the real nature of the Ātman, has eyes covered by darkness (i.e. ignorance) about that; he, understands the Ātman as being possessed of properties such as the intellect etc. which have arisen from ignorance."

(ii) Then, in BUBV 2.4.455, Sureśvara says that the word *hi* expresses the reason supporting Śaṅkara's view.[11] And he adds in BUBV 2.4.457: "The word *hi* is employed to clarify the thing which has been already stated, it being an adverb", thus stressing what is said in verse 455.

(iii) Ignorance produces (=manifests) what is non-existent and knowledge, on the other hand, produces (=manifests) that which is existent, viz. the Brahman. This is stated in BUBV 2.4.456. In relation to the falsity of the world, Sureśvara intends to clarify the nature of knowledge and ignorance which are the main theme of Advaita, though Śaṅkara does not refer to the same in his Bhāṣya on BU 2.4. It may be pointed out that Sureśvara does all the while have a mind to elucidate his philosophical view.

(iv) In connection with the word *iva*, Sureśvara develops the notion of *upamāna* in BUBV 2.4.459-464. If duality is real, there would be contradiction to the concept of the oneness of the Brahman. If duality is not real, how could one think of and state *upamāna-upameya* relation? Such an objection, Śaṅkara answers through a Śruti quotation,[12] whereas Sureśvara develops the notion of *upamāna* in the process of proving that duality is not real and yet the action of *upamāna* is possible. His view is this: From the metaphorical standpoint, duality is not real and the Śruti alone is the reliable means of knowing reality. But, from the empirical standpoint, the use of *upamāna* is valid; in other words, the use of *upamāna* is possible and helpful in the state of ignorance. In the case of sleep or of a show by a magician, the seer of sleep or the knower of the magic show can make duality. In a similar way, it is possible to say that the Ātman appears to be dual even if there is no duality in the Ātman. Thus, the *upamāna-upameya* relation can be affirmed (i.e. stated) in respect of just one thing, the Brahman.

8.6 It may now be observed that Sureśvara carries on a more detailed discussion of the *dṛṣṭāntas* in BUBV 2.4 than what is noticeable in his master's writings. It would not be quite right, however, to hold that he has over-spun them, because he has adduced convincing reasons for giving additional arguments. One may consider these (additional) arguments of Sureśvara as an expression of what is really *anukta* 'unexpressed' in Śaṅkara's writing. As such, one should not fail to observe that Sureśvara fully deserves compliments for being a Vārtikakāra of high order.

NOTES

1. *yukta eva tv ayaṁ dṛṣṭānto vivakṣitāṁśa-sambhavāt / na hi dṛṣṭānta-dārṣṭāntikayoḥ kvacit kaṁcid vivakṣitāṁśaṁ muktvā sarva-sārūpyaṁ kenacid darśayituṁ śakyate / sarva-sārūpye hi dṛṣṭānta-dārṣṭāntika-bhāvoccheda eva syāt / na cedaṁ svamanīṣayā jala-sūryakādi-dṛṣṭānta-praṇayanam / śāstra-praṇītasya tv asya prayojana-mātram upanyasyate / kim punar atra vivakṣitaṁ sārūpyam iti / tad ucyate ṛddhi-hrāsabhāktvam iti / jalagataṁ hi sūrya-pratibimbaṁ jala-vṛddhau vardhate jala-hrāse hrasati jala-calane calati jala-bhede bhidyata ity evaṁ jala-dharmānuyāyi bhavati na tu paramārthataḥ sūryasya tathātvam asti / evaṁ paramārthato 'vikṛtam eka-rūpam api sad brahma dehādy-upādhy-antar-bhāvād bhajata ivopādhi-dharmān vṛddhi-hrāsādīn / evam ubhayor dṛṣṭānta-dārṣṭāntikayoḥ sāmañjasyād avirodhaḥ /* (p. 359). Translation is almost the reproduction of THIBAUT's. *The Vedānta-Sūtras*, pt. 2, SBE 38, pp. 158-159.

2. Cf. *takṣa-dṛṣṭāntaś cetāvatāṁśena draṣṭavyaḥ / takṣā hi viśiṣṭeṣu takṣaṇādi-vyāpāreṣv apekṣyaiva pratiniyatāni karaṇāni vāsyādīni kartā bhavati / svaśarīreṇa tv akartaiva / evam ayam ātmā sarvavyāpāreṣv apekṣyaiva mana ādīni karaṇāni kartā bhavati svātmanā tv akartaiveti /* (P. 293).

"The case of the carpenter must be considered as being parallel to the following extent. The carpenter is, in certain kinds of work, such as cutting wood and so on, an agent with regard to certain definite tools, such as the axe and so on, but a non-agent with his mere body; so this Self also is an agent in all its functions with regard to its instruments, such as the mind and so on, but is a non-agent by its own Self." (Translation THIBAUT's).

3. *sa yathā dundubher hanyamānasya na bāhyāñ śabdāñ śaknuyād grahaṇāya dundubhes tu grahaṇena dundubhy-āghātasya vā śabdo gṛhītaḥ // sa yathā śaṅkhasya dhmāyamānasya na bāhyāñ śabdāñ śaknuyād grahaṇāya śaṅkhasya tu grahaṇena śaṅkhadhmasya vā śabdo gṛhītaḥ // sa yathā vīṇāyai vādyamānāyai na bāhyāñ śabdāñ śaknuyād grahaṇāya vīṇāyai tu grahaṇena vīṇāvādasya vā śabdo gṛhītaḥ //*

4. *cinmātrānugamāt sarvatra cit-svarūpataiveti gamyate / tatra dṛṣṭānta ucyate /* (p. 327).

5. BUBV 2.4.267-8.

6. *Ibid.* 275-7.

7. Cf. BUB 2.4.7 (p. 328) : *dundubhes tu grahaṇena dundubhi-śabda-sāmānya-viśeṣatvena dundubhi-śabdā eva iti śabda-viśeṣā gṛhītā bhavanti / dundubhi-śabda-sāmānya-vyatirekeṇābhāvāt teṣām /*

8. BUBV 2.4.269-270.

9. *aneka-dṛṣṭāntopādānam iha sāmānya-bahutva-khyāpanārtham / aneke hi vilakṣaṇāś cetanācetanarūpāḥ sāmānya-viśeṣāḥ / teṣām pāramparya-gatyā yathaikasmin mahāsāmānye 'ntarbhāvaḥ prajñānaghane katham nāma pradarśayitavya iti /* (p. 329).

10. *yatra yasminn avidyākalpite kārya-karaṇa-saṁghātopādhi-janite viśeṣātmani khilya-bhāve hi yasmād dvaitam iva paramārthato 'dvaite brahmaṇi dvaitam iva bhinnam iva vastvantaram ātmana upalakṣyate /* (p. 340).

11. *hi yasmād dvaitam iva* . . . (p. 340) '(The word) *hi* means *yasmāt* 'for' '.

12. *vācārambhaṇaṁ vikāro nāmadheyam iti śrutyantarād* . . . (p. 340).

SUREŚVARA'S INDEBTEDNESS TO HIS PREDECESSORS

(Gauḍapāda in Particular)

9.1. We learn from tradition about many an earlier thinker who influenced the philosophical thought of Śaṅkara and the post-Śaṅkara Advaita Vedānta, viz. Ṭaṅka, Bhartṛprapañca, Bhartṛhari, Bhartṛmitra, Brahmadatta, Gauḍapāda etc. Among these thinkers, only Bhartṛprapañca and Gauḍapāda require notice for the purpose of this work. Again, even if there are references to the views of these in Sureśvara's other works or the other portions of BUBV, any particular attention is not paid to them, since this section is built up on the references from only BUBV 2.4.

9.2. Bhartṛprapañca, Brahmadatta and, together with these, Maṇḍanamiśra hold the theory of *jñānakarmasamuccaya* and Sureśvara discusses and refutes this theory in Nais 1.20, SV 356[b]-357[a] etc.[1] Bhartṛprapañca is an older writer whose view Sureśvara has to discuss because of the fact that Śaṅkara has taken note of it in BUB 5.1.1.[2] In BUBV 2.4.328-330, Sureśvara writes: "As the ocean having but one (and the same) name and form is the merger (i.e. the meeting-point) of rivers which have different names and forms—(and) merger means oneness—so is the skin etc. the one meeting-point of different knowledge such as touch etc. And the skin etc. also (get merged) into their own end (viz. *manas*) and so also is (the merger of) *manas* into the intellect. In the same way, the intellect (also) remains in the form of cause, when action gets destroyed. This is the (nature of) merger (everywhere) common and it is not preceded by any deliberate thinking." This is clearly a gist of Śaṅkara's view which is quoted here for facility of discussion: "The infinite effect manifests from the infinite cause. The manifested effect is also real at the present time, even in its dualistic form. Again, at the time of merger, taking the infinitude of the infinite effect into itself, the infinite causal form alone remains. Thus in all the three stages of origin, sustenance and merger the cause and the effect are infinite. It is just one infinite entity spoken of as divided into cause and effect. For instance, an ocean consists of water, waves, foam, bubbles etc. As the water is real, so are its effects: (waves, foam, bubbles etc. which appear and disappear as part and parcel of the ocean itself) real in the true sense of the word."[3] And Sureśvara refutes it in verses BUBV 2.4.354-355, as SP points out,[4] thus: "An effect is manifested only in the cause after something is superimposed on the cause due to misconception; it is impossible to assert that the effect is real as the cause is real." Thus is the *bhedābhedavāda* postulated by Bhartṛprapañca refuted by the Advaitin Sureśvara.

9.3.1 In relation to Gauḍapāda DASGUPTA quotes the end of GKB[5] and says, "It seems particularly significant that Śaṅkara should credit Gauḍapāda and not Bādarāyaṇa, with recovering the Upaniṣad creed."[6] Though it is doubted that Gauḍapāda is the author of the entire GK (consisting of four chapters), it is beyond doubt that GK contributed quite a lot to Advaita Vedānta expounded by Śaṅkara, from the point of view of the philosophical thought. This should be said about Sureśvara and Gauḍapāda also, since between Sureśvara and GK there is noticeable a close relationship so far as philosophical terms (as well as notions) are concerned. For instance, Nais4. 41 and 42 are quotations from GK 1.11 and 15 respectively. And the following pairs of verses convey similar notions, viz. GK 4.36 and Nais 2.19; GK 2.34 and Nais 2.112; GK 4.1 and Nais 3.17.[7]

9.3.2 KARMARKAR points out as an outstanding contribution of Gauḍapāda thus: "Gauḍapāda was the first to make the fullest use of the doctrine of the three states, waking, dreaming and deep sleep, described in the Bṛhadāraṇyaka and the Chāndogya for the purpose of establishing Advaita."[8] This doctrine has been handed down in Advaita tradition beginning with Śaṅkara. Śaṅkara declares this in his PK whose subject-matter is the same as that of MāU, i.e. the theoretical aspect of reality and the practical way of realizing one's identity.[9]

And Sureśvara's PKV totally follows Śaṅkara's PK in respect of the doctrine of three states. Here, noting down this doctrine in a tabular form, we shall discuss the matter relevant to BUBV 2.4 such as the words *prājña* etc.

Macrocosmic	*virāj vaiśvānara*	*sūtra* (*sūtrātman*) *hiraṇyagarbha*	*iśvara avyākṛta akṣara*
Microcosmic (*Upādhi*)	*viśva*	*taijasa*	*prājña*
	sthūlaśarīra	*sūkṣmaśarīra*	*kāraṇaśarīra*
States of Consciousness	*jāgrat* (=*jāgarita*) 'waking'	*svapna* 'dream'	*suṣupti* 'deep sleep'

(Note: The macrocosmic terms in PK and PKV do not appear in GK at all. These are introduced in some other Upaniṣads also.)

9.3.3 In waking state, the world consists of the aggregate of all the gross bodies which have undergone quintuplication (*pañcīkaraṇa*[10]). In this state, the sense-organs give rise to the knowledge of external objects.[11] In other words, the distinction between subject and object exists and consequently the knowledge derived therefrom is called *draṣṭṛ-dṛśyādi-bheda-dhī* (BUBV 2.4.453)[12] or *bheda-grahaṇa* (*ibid*). Thus here prevails *pramātṛ-prameyavyavahāra* as stated in *adhyāsabhāṣya* in BSB.

9.3.4 This is applicable to the dream state (*svapna*, BUBV 2.4.462, 465; Nais 2.117, 4.36, 37, 40, 42, 43, 48) too, because, though the sense-organs are inoperative there, the awareness which arises from the impressions (*saṁskāra*) of the waking state is formed in the relation of a knower and the object of his knowing.

9.3.5 In the state of deep sleep, just as the banyan tree is merged (i.e. concealed) into the seed, all thoughts vanish and the intellect merges into the causal condition. Here the macrocosmic consciousness is called Īśvara (BUBV 2.4.303). The individual consciousness of this state is called Prājña. According to GK, this is a mass of consciousness (*ghanaprajña*) and experiences (only) joy(*ānandabhuk*).[13] It is bound by only *kāraṇa* though the *viśva* and the *taijasa* are bound by *kāraṇa* as well as *kārya*[14] and there is no perception of duality in deep sleep.[15] Here there are two points to be discussed: (1) *prājña* and (2) *ajñāna*.

(1) As we have seen in the table (above), the word *prājña* (in verse 390) is used for the individual consciousness in deep sleep state. But we may note that Prājña called *prājñātman* by Śaṅkara, is always the highest Ātman.[16]

(2) Regarding that there is no duality, i.e. no other entity than the individual consciousness, in deep sleep, unlike in other two states, there are descriptions in Sureśvara's works such as TUBV 2.568; Nais 4.39, 40, 47; BUBV 4.3.5. In this connection Nais quotes two verses from GK 1.11 and 15:

kārya-kāraṇa-baddhau tāv iṣyete viśva-taijasau |
prājñaḥ kāraṇa-baddhas tu dvau tau turye na sidhyataḥ ||
(Nais 4.41 = GK 1.11)

anyathā gṛhṇataḥ svapno nidrā tattvam ajānataḥ |
viparyāse tayoḥ kṣīṇe turīyam padam aśnute ||
(Nais 4.42 = GK 1.15)

The terms *kārya* and *kāraṇa* of the former verse are interpreted respectively as *anyathāgrahaṇa* and *tattvāgrahaṇa* by Cand[17] as well as GKB.[18] Both these terms *anyathāgrahaṇa* and *tattvāgrahaṇa* approximately correspond to *mithyājñāna* and *ajñāna* respectively.[19] Thus, *kāraṇa* is *tattvāgrahaṇa* or *ajñāna* and *kārya* is *anyathāgrahaṇa* or *mithyājñāna*. So, we can say that *tattvāgrahaṇa* is more primordial than (i.e. the cause of) *anyathāgrahaṇa*. This *mithyājñāna* is the erroneous knowledge in that it identifies the non-Ātman as the Ātman and causes (awareness of) duality. In waking and dream states prevail this *mithyājñāna* (= *anyathāgrahaṇa*) and subsequent duality. After the removal of this *mithyājñāna* (*kārya*), in deep sleep, there exists no duality, but *ajñāna* (*kāraṇa*) remains. The justification of the existence of *ajñāna* in deep sleep is offered in Nais 3.58 in three ways thus:

(a) If *ajñāna* were not present, one would get liberated from transmigratory existence even without hearing Vedic sentences such as *tat tvam asi.*

(b) Deep sleep state is a state from which one returns to the waking and/or the dream state again. If *ajñāna* were not present, deep sleep would be liberation and this liberation would be temporary, for there would be return to the waking state.

(c) Though we are not aware of ignorance, the state of deep sleep is caused by the absence of a revealer, viz. *antaḥkaraṇa.* Thus, in deep sleep also, *ajñāna* does exist. In deep sleep *ajñāna* remains in its bare form characterized by the merger of all its products;[20] it prevails there and has no connection with the Ātman. Such deep sleep is of importance in Advaita Vedānta inasmuch as it reveals both (the ever-existing) Ātman and *ajñāna.*

9.4. In relation to GK, there are found in BUBV 2.4 some matters which can now be pointed out:

(1) BUBV 2.4.106 uses two words : *avyultita-manas* and *vyutthitātman.* The former means *manas* which is not operative. In this state, no subject-object relation (i.e. duality) is seen. This state of *manas* is possible in deep sleep and is like *amanībhāva* in GK 3.31.[21] The word *vyutthitātman* refers to the states of waking and dream. Yet, in the final analysis, it sees nothing else than the individual consciousness.

(2) BUBV 2.4.285 uses the word *saṁhata* 'that which is of the nature of a collection', a synonym of the word *saṁghāta* which is the notion used in the Sāṁkhya. Sureśvara rejects this notion on the support of GK 3.10: *saṁghātāḥ svapnavat sarve ātmamāyāvisarjitāḥ.*

(3) BUBV 2.4.324, "As a seed is noticed by direct perception, both in the beginning and in the end, therefore, in the middle stage of the effects also let the seed be (understood as) the cause", clearly originates from GK 2.6 (=4.31):

ādav ante ca yan nāsti vartamāne 'pi tat tathā |
vitathaiḥ sadṛśāḥ santo' vitathā iva lakṣitāḥ ||

The same idea can be found in Nais 2.12, 95; 3.55.[22]

NOTES

1. Cf. HACKER, *op. cit.*, pp. 88 ff.; HIRIYANNA, *op. cit.*, Introduction pp. xxii ff., etc.

2. *atraike varṇayanti—pūrṇāt kāraṇāt pūrṇaṁ kāryam udricyate / udriktaṁ kāryaṁ vartamāna-kāle'pi pūrṇam eva paramārtha-vastu-bhūtaṁ dvaita-rūpeṇa / punaḥ pralaya-kāle pūrṇasya kāryasya pūrṇatām ādāyātmani dhitvā pūrṇam evāvaśiṣyate kāraṇarūpam / evam utpatti-sthiti-pralayeṣu triṣv api kāleṣu kārya-kāraṇayoḥ pūrṇataiva / sācaikaiva pūrṇatā kārya-kāraṇayor bhedena vyapadiśyate / evaṁ ca....*/ *yathā kila samudro jala-taraṅga-phena-budbudādyātmaka eva / yathā jalaṁ satyaṁ tad-udbhavāś ca taraṅga-phena-budbudādayaḥ samudrātmabhūtā evāvirbhāva-tirobhāva-dharmiṇaḥ paramārtha-satyā eva /* (BUB 5.1.1, pp. 699-700)—Translation MĀDHAVĀNANDA's; *The Bṛhadāraṇyaka Upaniṣad,* (tr.), Calcutta : Advaita Ashrama, 1975.

3. BUB 5.1.1, see note 2 above.

4. Ānandagiri points out that this is the view of Bhartṛprapañca.

5. Cf. DASGUPTA's translation of the second verse in Śaṅkara's conclusion of the commentary: "he adores by falling at the feet of that great guru (teacher) the adored of his adored, who on finding all the people sinking in the ocean made dreadful by the crocodiles of rebirth, out of kindness for all people, by churning the great ocean of the Veda by his great churning rod of wisdom recovered what lay deep in the heart of the Veda, and is hardly attainable even by the immortal gods." (S. DASGUPTA, *A History of Indian Philosophy,* vol. 1, p. 422).

6. DASGUPTA, op. cit., p. 423.

7. GK 4.36 :

svapne cāvastukaḥ kāyaḥ pṛthag anyasya darśanāt /
yathā kāyas tathā sarvaṁ citta-dṛśyam avastukam //

Nais 2.19 :

ghaṭādivacca dṛśyatvāt tair eva karaṇair dṛśeḥ /
svapne cānanvayāj jñeyo deho 'nātmeti sūribhiḥ //

GK 2.34 :

nātma-bhāvena nānedaṁ na svenāpi kathaṁcana /
na pṛthaṅ nāpṛthak kiṁcid iti tattva-vido viduḥ //

Nais 2.112:

na svayaṁ svasya nānātvaṁ nāvagatyātmanā yataḥ /
nobhābhyām apy ataḥ siddham advaitaṁ dvaita-bādhayā //

GK 4.1 :

jñānenākāśakalpena dharmān yo gaganopamān /
jñeyābhinnena saṁbuddhas taṁ vande dvipadāṁ varam //

Nais 3.17 :

sāmānyāc ca viśeṣāc ca svamahimnaiva yo bhavet /
vyutthāpy avikārī syāt kumbhākāśādivat tu saḥ //

8. R. D. KARMARKAR, *Gauḍapādakārikā,* Poona : BORI, 1973, Introduction p. li.

9. This is clearly mentioned in the *Pañcadaśī* thus :

māṇḍūkyādau ca sarvatra nirguṇopāstir īritā // (9.63)

10. PK: *pañcīkṛta-pañca-mahābhūtāni tatkāryaṁ ca sarvaṁ virāḍ ity ucyate* /
PKV: *tataḥ sthūlāni bhūtāni pañca tebhyo virāḍ abhūt* /
pañcīkṛtāni bhūtāni sthūlānīty ucyate budhaiḥ //7
and
pañcīkṛtāni bhūtāni tatkāryaṁ ca virāḍ bhavet /
sthūlaṁ śarīram etat syād aśarīrasya cātmanaḥ // 11
11. PK: *indriyair arthopalabdhir jāgaritam* /
PKV: *indriyair artha-vijñānaṁ devatānugrahānvitaiḥ* /
śabdādi-viṣayaṁ jñānaṁ taj jāgaritam ucyate //13
PKV: *bāhyāntaḥkaraṇair evaṁ devatānugrahānvitaiḥ* /
svaṁ svaṁ ca viṣaya-jñānaṁ taj jāgaritam ucyate // 29
12. *tatra mithyāgrahagrasto draṣṭṛ-dṛśyādibhedadhīḥ* //
13. GK 1.1, 3; MāU 5
14. GK 1.11.
15. GK 1.13.
16. P. DEUSSEN, *The System of the Vedānta*, (Eng. tr. C. JOHNSON), Delhi: Motilal Banarsidass, 1972, p. 180, n. 82.
17. Cand 4.41.
18. GKB, p. 47.
19. HACKER, *op. cit.*, p. 60.
20. Cf. UPADHYAYA, *op. cit.*, p. 131, MARKANDEYA SASTRI, *op. cit.*, p. 140, and HACKER, *op. cit.*, p. 60, SINHA, *A History of Indian Philosophy*, vol. 2, p. 434.
21. *mano-dṛśyam idaṁ dvaitaṁ yat kiṁcit sacarācaram* /
manaso hy amanībhāve dvaitaṁ naivopalabhyate //
GK 3.32 uses the word *amanastā* instead of *amanībhāva*.
22. Nais 2.12 :
prāg anātmaiva jagdhaṁ sad ātmatām satyavidyayā /
srag-ālepanavad dehaṁ tasmāt paśyed viviktadhīḥ //
Nais 2.95 :
avagatyātmano yasmād āgamāpāyi kumbhavad /
sāhaṁkāram idaṁ viśvaṁ tasmāt tat syāt kacādivat //
Nais 3.55 :
prāg asad yāti paścāt sat sac ca yāyād asat tathā /
anātmābhijanaṁ tat syād viparītaḥ svayaṁ dṛśiḥ //

SUREŚVARA AND THE SĀṀKHYA

10.1 In the course of my translation of BUBV 2.4, I have often to take into account the Sāṁkhya notions and terms. As is known, the Sāṁkhya is the principal antagonist for the Advaita Vedānta. And the most clear-cut distinction between the Sāṁkhya and the Advaita Vedānta lies in the fact that while the former holds dualism the latter holds non-dualism. Hence Sureśvara has sometimes to introduce the Sāṁkhya doctrine signifying dualism as the defect to be avoided.[1] It is again worthwhile to note how Sureśvara's work (under reference) reveals differences and similarities with the Sāṁkhya in respect of (i) notion of causality, (ii) worldly phenomena, (iii) notion of *ajñāna* and (iv) terminology. And if we do not turn to note this, our observations on BUBV 2.4 and 4.5 would indeed remain incomplete.

10.2 (i) According to the Sāṁkhya, both *puruṣa* and *prakṛti* are eternally existent. Both of them are explained thus:

(a) The insentient *prakṛti* and the sentient *puruṣa* are existent independently of each other and have no beginning. *prakṛti* consists of three *guṇas* (*sattva*, *rajas* and *tamas*) in a state of equilibrium, before there is creation and *puruṣa* is indifferent (*udāsīna*) and inactive.

(b) When the equilibrium of the three *guṇas* is disturbed, creation begins. *prakṛti* is the material cause of the world and it is active by nature and *puruṣa* is not the efficient cause.[2]

(c) Although *puruṣa* is not the *prayojaka-kartā* 'prompter' of *prakṛti*, it is due to the *sannidhāna* 'nearness' of *puruṣa* that *prakṛti* becomes fit for creation. Śaṅkara criticizes such a dualistic causality in BSB 2.2.1-10.[3] His criticism is focussed on the point that the insentient *prakṛti* cannot be active on the occasion of creation. Refuting the idea that real *prakṛti* is the primary cause of the world, he points to the difficulty in holding dualism. For Śaṅkara, it is the Brahman that is the sole existential entity and is the material as well as the efficient cause of the world.[4] In order to justify his non-dualism he postulates two-fold Brahman, viz. *kāraṇātma brahman* ('causal Brahman') and *kāryātmabrahman* ('effect Brahman.')[5] The causal Brahman is the highest Brahman, which is of the nature of *sat* 'existence', *cit* 'sentiency' and *ānanda* 'bliss'. And the effect Brahman is the same Brahman being limited (covered) by ignorance. This effect Brahman is called in other words as *īśvara*,[6] *aparabrahman*[7] or *māyopādhikabrahman*.[8]

10.3 Sureśvara, being Śaṅkara's direct disciple, basically follows the Śaṅkara's view of non-dualism. He says: Because of ignorance, there are in worldly dealings existing things of two kinds; the Ātman of the nature of *cidābhāsa* and the non-Ātman of the nature of *acidābhāsa*.[9] Even though the Ātman is in reality neither a cause nor an effect, the Ātman of the nature of *cidābhāsa* stands in the form of a cause and an effect.[10] And this Ātman, having attained, due to ignorance, the nature of causes and effects, attains manifoldness.[11] Thus, this *cidābhāsa* is nothing but the causal Brahman postulated by Śaṅkara, which is the cause of the world. This *cidābhāsa* attains manifoldness, i.e. it creates the phenomenal world, as the causal Brahman or Īśvara of Śaṅkara. But *cidābhāsa* as well as its products are in reality, i.e. from real point of view (*paramārthasattā*), not existent because they are caused by ignorance. They are existent only from the empirical point of view (*vyāvahārikasattā*).

10.4 Thus, the difference between the Sāṁkhya and the Advaita Vedānta consists in their concepts about the cause of the world. The Sāṁkhya holds that an existent causal entity transforms into what is called an effect—this is *pariṇāmavāda*. As against this in the opinion of the Advaitin the existent Brahman is considered to be a causal entity which has undergone some transformation—this is called *vivartavāda*. It is useful to note here how the *Vedāntaparibhāṣā* defines both the terms, viz. *pariṇāma* and *vivarta*; it states: "What is called transformation (*pariṇāma*) is the result into an effect having equal reality with the material cause. What is called transfiguration (*vivarta*) is the result into an effect whose reality is not equal to that of the material cause."[12]

And the Sāṁkhya view of cosmology, *pariṇāmavāda*, is called *satkāryavāda*. The diverse world has projected from *prakṛti* which is real and it also is therefore real. Hence, not only are the many *puruṣas*, but all the evolutes from *prakṛti* also are real. And in the case when a particular *puruṣa* is liberated *prakṛti* only ceases to affect that *puruṣa*, it lasts forever and continues its creation for other non-liberated *puruṣas*. And contrary to this, the Advaita view of cosmology, *vivartavāda*, is called *satkāryavāda* since, though there does not really exist any causal entity, the entire world is considered to be projected from one. It is the Brahman alone that is existent. We should notice that the difference between the two systems stems from their view regarding the prime cause as real or non-real. But even for Advaita, the evolutes, viz. the diverse worldly phenomena which are only apparent and not real from the real point of view, are real from the empirical point of view. So long as we consider from the empirical point of view, the worldly phenomena are as much real as for the Sāṁkhya. And the process of evolution as well as the worldly system are really similar.

10.5 As for the worldly phenomena postulated by both the schools, SK 22-38 describe the eighteen evolutes of *prakṛti*, viz. the intellect, Ego, *manas*, five organs of action and five organs of knowing and five *tanmātras* (together with their natures and functions). As to the three inner-organs, the function of the intellect is *adhyavasāya* (SK 23), that of Ego is *abhimāna* (SK 24) and that of *manas* is *saṁkalpa* (SK 27). But as for the inner-organs, Sureśvara is slightly ambivalent. Thus he seems to agree with SK in BUBV 2.4.350, 369 and elsewhere, but in BUBV 2.4.353 he refers to *manas* and the intellect as two inner-organs; this is further clarified by SP (on the same verse) *antaḥkaraṇam eva dvidhocyate*. However in PKV 33-34[13] he refers to the inner-organ of four kinds; perhaps Sureśvara is thus a precursor of later Advaita Vedāntins. Five organs of action and five organs of knowing mentioned in SK 26 are accepted as such by Sureśvara in BUBV 2.4.362-372.[14] Five *tanmātras* and five *mahābhūtas* projected therefrom are mentioned in SK 28. The process of *tanmātras* becoming *mahābhūtas* is explained by the notion of accumulation. Five *bhūtas* are projected by *tanmātras* who have come to possess properties in the following way[15]:

ākāśa	: *śabda*
vāyu	: *śabda, sparśa*
agni	: *śabda, sparśa, rūpa*
ap	: *śabda, sparśa, rūpa, rasa*
pṛthivī	: *śabda, sparśa, rūpa, rasa, gandha*
mahābhūta	: *tanmātra* (*guṇa*)

The same is mentioned in TUBV 2.152 in the context of projection[16] and in BUBV 2.4.343 in the context of merger (*laya*); as to the order of projection and merger, merger is in the reverse order of projection.[17] Thus it may be seen that both hold a totally identical process and system of the worldly phenomena. Of course, for the Vedāntin, the process is *really* false.

10.6 In Nais 3.5, we see the discussion on *ajñāna* 'ignorance'. For the Sāṁkhya, *ajñāna* is *mithyājñāna* 'erroneous knowledge' in the form of regarding the non-Ātman as the Ātman. But this *mithyājñāna* can be removed by the logical thought.[18] For Sureśvara, however, knowledge obtained by removing *mithyājñāna* is nothing but the effect of *ajñāna*. And such a knowledge is that of distinction between the Ātman and the non-Ātman existing in the sphere of the direct perception etc.[19] *ajñāna*, the cause of such a knowledge, is removed not by logical thought but by hearing the Vedic statement, such as *tat tvam asi*, and grasping its meaning.

10.7 (a) The three kinds of hindrance to knowledge, viz. *ādhyātmika*, *ādhibhautika*, and *ādhidaivika*, mentioned in TUB[20] and ATUBV on TUBV 1.49[21] are the Sāṁkhya expressions which have been already used as the three kinds of pain in the *Tattvakaumudī* on SK 1.

(b) BOETZELAER finds the influence of the Sāṁkhya in TUBV 2.431,[22] "*ekārtha* 'just one aim': Cf. the Śāṁkhyaexpression *puruṣārtha*. Matter cannot form a body and its functions without the help/association of intelligence or sentient (being) or, as the Sāṁkhya puts it, without *puruṣa*. Matter exists for the sake of the *puruṣa* (i.e. *puruṣārtha*), this is its only aim."

(c) *ābrahma-stamba-paryanta* meaning 'beginning with the Brahman, i.e. Hiraṇyagarbha, up to the blade of grass' is used in the both: SK 54; BUBV 2.4.71, 93, TUBV 1. 133; 2.433; Nais 1.1, 41: 2.93, 97; 3.1.22.

(d) The word *kaivalya* means 'the absolute', 'state of liberation' in SK 17, 19 and 21; BUBV 2.4.26, 93 and 252; SV 26; TUBV 2.22; Nais 2.116; 3.9.58 also use it in the same sense.

(e) The word *saṁghāta* meaning 'collection' is used on various occasions (SK 17; BUBV 2.4.285); *sparśādivat-parārthatvāt* in BUBV 2.4.343 conveys the same idea as *saṁghāta-parārthatvāt* (SK 17), (because the *sparśādivat* is identical with *saṁghāta*). In the case of Nais 2.20 *dehādikāryakaraṇasaṁghāta*, *dehādikāryakaraṇa* and *saṁghāta* are linked as *karmadhāraya samāsa*. Here also *saṁghāta* means 'collection of the non-Ātman.'

(f) The word *mahadādiviśeṣabhūtaparyanta* meaning 'all the evolutes' is found in SK 56. Nais uses *buddhyādidehānta*, *dehādibuddhyanta* to mean 'the non-Ātman' in 2.14,15, 44; 3.33; 4.4.

(g) The word *parārtha* meaning 'for the sake of another' is used in SK 17; BUBV 2.4.343; Nais 2.74.

(h) The word *tamas* meaning 'ignorance' occurs in both : Advaita usually uses the word *tamas* in the sense of 'ignorance'. SK 13 says *guru varaṇakam eva tamaḥ*, '*tamas* is sluggish and enveloping'.

(i) The words *sthūla*, *sūkṣma* meaning 'gross, subtle' are used in Nais 2.21, 17; cf. BUBV 2.4.344 where *kaṭhina*, *svaccha* are used in place of *sthūla* and *sūkṣma* respectively.

(j) After stating the three-fold inner-organs and the is three discrete functions, SK states in the 29th verse that the common function of them all is the five winds. And the *Gauḍapādabhāṣya* and the *Tattvakaumudī* as well (on the verse) explain the five-fold winds. Similarly BUBV 2.4.345-6 states the five winds as the common function of the inner-organs. And verse 388 states the five-fold winds, viz. *prāṇa*, *apāna*, *vyāna*, *udāna* and *samāna*.

(k) In the discussion of *satkāryavāda*, SK 9 says : "Because the efficient can do only that for which it is efficient" (*śaktasya śakyakaraṇāt*) and BUBV 2.4.398 utilizes the notion of *śakti* 'efficiency' in the discussion of merger: "The merger consists in that the effects reside in their own cause in the form of efficiency. . ."

(l) The word *āvirbhāva-tirobhāva* 'appearance and disappearance' is seen in the *Tattvakaumudī* on SK 9 and TUBV 1.30, 2.93, 411: Cf. BUBV 2.4.371 and Nais 2.68 where *bhūtvā* and *vilīyate* suggest 'appear' and 'disappear' respectively.[23]

10.8 The above discussion will clearly show how Sureśvara makes a very able use of the Sāṁkhya doctrine while he sets up his own in the light of the dialogue between Yājñavalkya and Maitreyī, incidentally this may explain also the queer situation that almost all the available expositions of SK come from Vedāntins.

NOTES

1. BUBV 2.4.20; Nais 2.69; TUBV 2.268.

2. "SK does not give any definition of *nimitta*. The single causal substance in the form of *prakṛti* is both material cause and efficient cause. No ever-free divine personality is postulated here as the efficient cause of the world." A. SENGUPTA, *Sāṁkhya and Advaita Vedānta—a Comparative Study*, Lucknow : 1973, p. 67.

3. BSB, pp. 220-228: (i) The sentient should supervise in order that the insentient is active, just as the sentient potter should help the clay to become a pot. Thus, the insentient *prakṛti* cannot create the diverse world by itself (BSB 2.2.1-2). Milk and water do not flow of their own accord, i.e. without being directed by some (divine) personality. In the Sāṁkhya who does not postulate such a personality, *prakṛti* can never become active and undergo modification in any way (BSB 2.2.3-5). (ii) According to the Sāṁkhya, the sentient *puruṣa* is indifferent and inactive, though *prakṛti* needs someone sentient to set it in motion. Hence, there is no scope in the Sāṁkhya as far as creation is concerned. The Sāṁkhya holds that *puruṣa* is inactive and yet can direct *prakṛti* owing to its nearness just as the lame can give direction to the blind, but, if *puruṣa* is always near *prakṛti*, there would be permanence of creation. Hence, the indifferent *puruṣa* cannot contact *prakṛti* (BSB 2.2.7).

(iii) According to the Sāṁkhya, *prakṛti* consists of three *guṇas* and those *guṇas* are independent of one another and in a state of equilibrium before there is creation. Since among these three *guṇas*, the principal-subordinate relation is impossible, creation should be impossible unless and until they lose their independence by any external force (BSB 2.2.8) .

4. BSB 1.4.23: *upādāna-kāraṇaṁ ca brahmābhyupagantavyaṁ nimittakāraṇaṁ ca*/

5. BUB 5.1.1: *tad idaṁ viśeṣāpannaṁ kāryātmakaṁ brahma pūrṇāt kāraṇātmana ucyate....* / *....* / *pūrṇasya kāryātmano brahmaṇo....* /

6. BSB 1.1.5, 11, 22: 1.2.1, 10, 21, 22; 2.1.1, 22; e.g. *kāṇādāstv etebhya eva vākyebhya īśvaraṁ nimittakāraṇam anumimate...* / (BSB 1.1.5, p. 24).

7. Cf. PU 5.2 : *etad vai satyakāma paraṁ cāparaṁ ca brahma yad oṁkāraḥ* / Śaṅkara's Bhāṣya thereon: *paraṁ satyam akṣaraṁ puruṣākhyam aparaṁ ca prāṇākhyaṁ prathamajaṁ yat tad oṁkāraḥ....*/ and BSB 1.3.13.

8. BSB 1.4.3; 2.1.14; CUB 3.14.2.

9. BUBV 2.4.424.

10. *Ibid.* 422.

11. *Ibid.* 423-425.

12. *pariṇāmo nāma upādāna-samasattāka-kāryāpattiḥ* /
vivarto nāma upādāna-viṣamasattāka-kāryāpattiḥ / (p. 37).

13. PKV 33-34 describes the same more clearly :
mano-buddhir ahaṁkāraś cittaṁ ceti catuṣṭayam /
saṁkalpākhyaṁ manorūpaṁ buddhir niścaya-rūpiṇī //
abhimānātmakas tadvad ahaṁkāraḥ prakīrtitaḥ /
anusaṁdhānarūpaṁ ca cittam ity abhidhīyate //
Cf. Nais 3.56, 57 where the intellect is meant by the word *niścayavṛttimat.*

14. Also PKV 31-32 describes the same more clearly (like in the case of *antaḥkaraṇa* noted above) :
jñānendriyāṇi pañcaiva pañca karmendriyāṇi ca //
śrotra-tvaṅ-nayana-ghrāṇa-jihvā dhīndriya-pañcakam /
vāk-pāṇi-pāda-pāyūpasthāḥ karmendriya-pañcakam //

15. SK 38 and the *Gauḍapādabhāṣya* and the *Tattvakaumudī* thereon.

16. Cf. BOETZELAER, *op. cit.*, p. 79 and PKV 3-6.

17. Cf. 2.3.15 (p. 275) : *viparyayeṇa tu pralaya-kramo 'ta utpattikramād bhavitum arhati* /

18. *śarīrendriya-mano-buddhiṣv anātmasv ātmeti nissaṁdhi-bandhanaṁ mithyājñānaṁ....tasya cānvaya-vyatirekābhyām eva nirastatvān nirviṣayaṁ tat-tvam-asyādi-vākyam prāptam* /, cf. ALSTON, *op. cit.*, pp. 147 f.

19. Cf. Nais 3.6 : *bheda-saṁvid idaṁ jñānaṁ bhedābhāvaś ca sākṣiṇi* /
kāryam etad avidyāyā jñātmanā tyājayed vacaḥ //
Also Nais 2.103: *sarva evāyam ātmānātma-vibhāgaḥ pratyakṣādi-pramāṇa-vartmany anupatito'vidyotsaṅgavarty eva na paramātmavyapāśrayaḥ* /

20. TUB, p. 9.

21. Cf. BOETZELAER, *op. cit.*, p. 20; PKV 12, 14-28.

22. *bāhyendriyāṇām adhyātmaṁ saṁhatir yena lakṣyate* /
ekārtha-vṛtti-rūpeṇa sā dṛṣṭāsaṁhate sati //

23. Cf. DASGUPTA, *op. cit.*, p. 257.

PART II

TRANSLATION AND ANNOTATION

TRANSLATION AND ANNOTATION

BUBV 2.4

आत्मेत्येवेति सूत्रस्य व्याख्येयं प्रस्तुता स्फुटा ।
ब्रह्म तेऽहं ब्रवाणीति प्रारभ्याऽऽपूर्णवाक्यतः ॥ १ ॥*

1. Now begins a clear exposition of the aphoristic remark, "Let him meditate (on that Brahman) as the Ātman" (BU 1.4.7) etc., which began with, "I shall tell you the Brahman" (BU 2.1.1) and continued up to the end of last sentence of the previous section (viz. BU 2.3).

NOTES

The aphoristic remark, "Let him meditate (on that Brahman) as the Ātman," etc. which is the so-called *vidyāsūtra*, is enunciated in BU 1.4.7 which is the third chapter of the Madhukāṇḍa. The second chapter of BU (=the fourth chapter of the Madhukāṇḍa) which begins with *brahma te aham bravāṇi* is devoted to an elucidation of the purpose of the *vidyāsūtra*. In this connection BUB (pp. 318-319) remarks: "But in the second chapter, after introducing the individual consciousness which is the object of the knowledge of the Brahman in the passages 'I shall tell you the Brahman,' 'I shall let you know the Brahman,' the Śruti has taught the Brahman, the one reality where there is no duality, without all characteristics, all material qualities, directly indicated by the word *satya* ('truth'), having action, its functionaries and its results as its essential nature, by the negation 'not this, not this.'"

नित्यकर्माद्यनुष्ठानसंशुद्धधिषणः पुमान् ।
निःशेषकर्महेतूत्थफलसावद्यधीस्ततः ॥ २ ॥

*The Devanāgari text is taken from the Ānanda Āshrama edition (ĀnSS 16, 3 vols).

2. A man has his intellect purified by (i.e. through) the performance of the daily action etc.; later he comes to have (i.e. develop) the notion that the result arising from the cause in the form of the entire action is to be blamed.

NOTES

Sureśvara seems to accept the notion of *kramamukti*. I have discussed this point in the Introduction; cf. section 2.

विरक्त आग्रजात्सोऽयं तत्सावद्यसमीक्षणात् ।
संसारदुःखसंस्कारस्मृतिभिः प्रेर्यमाणधीः ॥ ३ ॥

उद्भूततज्जिहासः संस्तद्धाने साधनस्पृहः ।
त्यक्ताशेषैषणः सोऽथ प्रत्यग्याथात्म्यनिश्चयः ॥ ४ ॥

3-4. Having well (*saṁ*) seen that it (viz. the fruit of action) is full of blame, a person turns averse to the result of previously performed actions.[1] His intellect being stirred by impressions and memories of the misery of the transmigratory existence, he has a desire to abandon it (viz. the transmigratory existence) and (also) the wish for acquiring the means for abandoning the same; he gives up all the desires, and has then determined the true nature of the individual consciousness.

NOTES

(1) *āgraja* < *agraja*, i.e. produced by the earlier (performed action)—maybe, it is mostly prosperity like riches in cattle etc. acquired by rituals. Cf. TUBV 2.6 where BOETZELAER translates *āgraja* as "previously gained (possession)". At some other places, Sureśvara uses this word in the sense, 'belonging to (or, characteristic of Hiraṇyagarbha, the first born'. (cf. TUBV 2.537). But this meaning is not suitable in the context here.

वस्तुवृत्तात्मसंबोधध्वस्तसंसारकारणः ।
व्याविद्धाशेषसंसारो विमुक्तो ना विमुच्यते ॥ ५ ॥

5. The man, who has destroyed the cause of the transmigratory existence by means of his knowledge of the nature of

reality (viz. the Brahman) and his own self (viz. the individual consciousness), and (thereby) destroyed the entire transmigratory existence, becomes liberated.

यावत्किञ्चिदविद्यायाः कार्यं वैराग्यकारणम् ।
तत्संन्यासो विरक्तत्वात्स्वत एव न शास्त्रतः ॥ ६ ॥

ब्रह्मयाथात्म्यविज्ञानसाधनत्वं विनाऽऽगमात् ।
संन्यासस्य न विज्ञातं तच्छास्त्रेणेह बोध्यते ॥ ७ ॥

6-7. Whatever is the product of ignorance (becomes) the cause of aversion (to the transmigratory existence). The abandoning of the product of ignorance effects of itself, owing to one's being averse to it; (it is) not (effected) by Vedic injunction. That renunciation is the means to ascertaining the true nature of the Brahman is not known (except from the Śruti[1]). And this (lit. that) is preached here (i.e. in the Śruti).

NOTES

Śaṅkara remarks: *asyā brahma-vidyāyā aṅgatvena saṁnyāso vidhitsitaḥ*, "The Śruti wishes to enjoin renunciation as subsidiary (i.e. helpful) to (the acquisition of) the knowledge of the Brahman." (BUB, p. 319). But Sureśvara does not admit of any injunction either for urging renunciation or for prescribing renunciation as a means to the knowledge of the Brahman. The scriptural text is therefore merely informative of renunciation.

(1) The word *āgama* here refers to any Śruti which is traditionally handed down.

ब्रह्मविद्यासमुत्थानात्कार्यकारणलक्षणात् ।
व्युत्थाप्य नेति नेतीति परं ब्रह्म प्रदर्शितम् ॥ ८ ॥

8. The Brahman, the highest, has been explained in the words, "(The Brahman is) not this, not this...." (BU 2.3.6), after showing it (to be) apart from what is characterized as the cause and the effect, viz. that which has arisen from ignorance of the Brahman.

NOTES

Commenting on BUB (pp. 318-319): *caturthe tu brahma-vidyā-viṣayaṁ pratyagātmānaṁ brahma te bravāṇīti brahma jñāpayiṣyām ca prastutya tad-brahmaikam advayaṁ sarva-viśeṣa-śūnyaṁ kriyākāraka-phala-svabhāva - satya-śabda - vācyāśeṣa - bhūta-dharma - pratiṣedha-dvāreṇa neti netīti jñāpitam |*

[Up to the eighth verse, the intention of BU 2.3 is summarized in accordance with BUB (stated in the note on verse 8). Now, while proceeding to 2.4, an objection is raised which runs up to the 17th verse.]

तत्रैतच्छङ्क्यते चोद्यं ब्रह्मत्वासिद्धिदोषकृत् ।
निषिद्धं नेति नेतीति मूर्तामूर्तादि वस्तु यत् ॥ ६ ॥

9. In this regard, an objection is raised, pointing to the fault (which consists in) non-establishing of (viz. not proving) the nature of the Brahman. Whatever thing, concrete or abstract and so on,[1] is denied (to be the Brahman) in the sentence, "(The Brahman is) not this, not this. . .".[2]

NOTES

1. The word *mūrtāmūrtādivastu* means concrete or abstract things, *satya* or *asatya nāmarūpa* etc. which are discussed in the end of BUB 2.3. In short it refers to all that is the non-Ātman.

2. Cf. BU 2.3.6 : *athāta ādeśo neti neti,* also BU 3.9.26, 4.2.4, 4.4.22, 4.5.15: *sa eṣa neti netyātmā.*

किं तद्ब्रह्मानुगं सर्वं किं वा तस्माद्विविच्यते ।
यदि ब्रह्मानुगं ब्रह्म स्यादनर्थात्मकं तदा ॥ १० ॥

10. Is all that identical with the Brahman, or distinct from it ? (And) if it is identical with the Brahman, then the Brahman would be of the nature of evil.

NOTES

Regarding the relation between things and the Brahman three alternatives are possible :

(a) All that may be existent and identical with the Brahman,

(b) all that may be non-existent and identical with the Brahman, and

(c) all that may be different from the Brahman.

The discussion of this relation continues up to verse 14. In this verse, the alternative (a) is refuted *anartha* 'evil' consists in the body that originates from ignorance. Hence if (a), the Brahman would be produced from ignorance. On *anartha*, see TUBV 2.125: *avidyāhetavaḥ kāmāḥ kāmamūlāḥ pravṛttayaḥ | dharmādharmau ca tanmūlau deho 'narthāśrayas tataḥ ||*

अभावनिष्ठं तच्चेत्स्यान्मुख्यं ब्रह्म न सिध्यति ।
अभावस्य ततोऽन्यत्वादन्वयव्यतिरेकतः ॥ ११ ॥

11. If that (thing) is non-existent, then the highest[1] Brahman does not become established, for non-existence is different from that (Brahman) as (is clear) from the method of *anvayavyatireka*.[2]

NOTES

The alternative (b), as pointed out above, is refuted here. While refuting the case (b), the method of *anvayavyatireka* becomes useful. Thus one cannot specifically state what the *abhāva* 'is' and what it 'is not'. Again in the case (b), one would be required to say : 'Since all that (*mūrtāmūrtādi* of verse 8 above) does not exist, the Brahman does not exist.' This would disturb the Advaita doctrine which holds that it is the Brahman alone that exists. And all the efforts of Vedas in search of the Brahman would be useless.

1. The word *mukhya* is literally 'the principal'.
2. The word *anvayavyatireka* means 'the method of *anvayavyatireka*'; on this see the Introduction section 7.

नेतीत्यपि निषेधोक्तिस्तथा सति विरुध्यते ।
वैदिकश्च प्रयासोऽयं सर्वः स्यात्तुषकण्डनम् ॥ १२ ॥

12. In that case (viz. in case it is held that all that is distinct from the Brahman), the statement of rejection in the

Vedic passage: "(The Brahman is) not this, not this . . . ", would also be opposed, and all the (lit. this) effort of the Vedas would be useless like the (effort of) pounding the husk.

NOTES

The alternative (c) is refuted. In case argument (c) is accepted, the negative assertion of the Śruti *neti neti*. . .would be contradicted.

विविच्यते ब्रह्मणश्चेन्मैवं दोषस्तथाऽपि हि ।
ब्रह्मत्वं ब्रह्मणो न स्याद् द्वितीये सति वस्तुनि ॥ १३ ॥

13. If again (you would say that) that thing is definitely taken as different from the Brahman, do not (say so, for) in that case also there would be wrong reasoning: (That is to say), the Brahman would not remain the Brahman (any more), if there existed a second thing (i.e. a thing apart from the Brahman).

अव्यावृत्ताननुगतं वस्तु ब्रह्मत्वमश्नुते ।
एतच्च दुर्लभं तस्य द्वितीये सति लक्षणम् ॥ १४ ॥

14. (Also), the entity which is not differentiated from (all that) and not followed (by all that) is called the Brahman (lit. obtains the nature of the Brahman); and this definition (of the Brahman) would be difficult to assert, if there existed a second entity.

NOTES

The alternative (c) is refuted further: The Śruti defines the Brahman as *ekam evādvitiyam* 'The Brahman is one where there is no second entity.' This definition would prove false, if one accepted the existence of thing(s) other than the Brahman.

अथाब्रह्मात्मकं वस्तु जग्ध्वा चेद्ब्रह्म तद्भवेत् ।
प्रतीचो ब्रह्मणाऽत्तत्वान्न मोक्षो नापि संसृतिः ॥ १५ ॥

15. If (one were to say that) all the non-Brahman would become the Brahman after the Brahman contained (lit. ate) it

within itself,[1] there would be neither liberation nor the transmigratory existence for the individual consciousness because it would be contained in (lit. eaten up by) the Brahman.

NOTES

The first line proposes further possibility, viz. the Brahman would include the second entity and then the following alternatives would be assumed: (A) The individual consciousness is included in the Brahman, (B) the individual consciousness is not included in the Brahman. The second line refutes (A).

1. The words *jagdhvā* (< √*jakṣ* 'to swallow') and *atta* (< √*ad* 'to eat up') are used in figurative sense, they show the merger of the entity into the primordial entity. Cf. TU 3.1: *yato vā imāni bhūtāni jāyante* | . . . | *tad brahmeti* |

संसारिणो न चेदत्ति संसार्येव प्रसज्यते ।
नाऽऽप्नोति ब्रह्मतां साक्षात्सत्सु संसारिवस्तुषु ॥ १६ ॥

16. If (the Brahman does) not eat up (i.e. withdraw within itself) numerous individual consciousnesses, then it would result that the Brahman itself is transmigratory. (If it is held that) there actually exist transmigratory entities, it would not attain the status of the Brahman.

NOTES

(B) is refuted: If (B), again two other alternatives could be assumed, viz. (i) the Brahman is identical (in nature) with the numerous individual consciousnesses, (ii) the Brahman is different (in nature) from them (i.e. numerous individual consciousnesses). If (i), the question of withdrawing the others within itself (by the Brahman) does not arise. If (ii), there is nothing which has the status of the Brahman, as required by the definition.

संसारे चापि जग्धेऽस्मिन्ब्रह्मणा निखिले सति ।
ऋतेऽपि ब्रह्मविज्ञानात्सर्वे स्युर्मुक्तबन्धनाः ॥ १७ ॥

17. And further if the whole of the transmigratory existence was withdrawn (lit. eaten up) by the Brahman, all beings would be released even without having obtained the knowledge of the Brahman.

NOTES

A doubt could be this: 'Even if the transmigratory things and the Brahman are identical in nature, the Brahman cannot be said to be transmigratory, because the Brahman is said to withdraw the transmigratory things within itself and it does not get withdrawn in any other thing.' The answer is stated in the following verses.

अन्वयादिनिषेधाय सर्वमात्मेति वाक्यतः ।
मैत्रेयीत्यादिको ग्रन्थस्तस्मादारभ्यते परः ॥ १८ ॥

18. Therefore, in order to reject (the argument regarding) the method of *anvayavyatireka* by means of (i.e. through the help of) the sentence, "All (this) is the Ātman,"[1] (now) begins the subsequent work starting with the words, "O Maitreyī".

NOTES

Now begins the answer to the objection stated in verses 10-17. That the world is nothing but the individual consciousness is proved by the Śruti "All (this) is the Ātman" which negates the method of *anvayavyatireka*. In connection with this begins the present section.

1. Perhaps the statement, "All (this) is the Ātman" is a brief paraphrase of (*idaṁ*) *sarvaṁ* (*yad ayam*) *ātmā* in BU 2.4.6.

सर्वाब्रह्मनिषेधेन तदर्थो वेह निश्चितः ।
तस्य संसिद्धिविषयमैकात्म्यमधुनोच्यते ॥ १९ ॥

19. Or,[1] (since) the entity which is expressed by the word *tat* (viz. the Brahman) is ascertained by rejecting all the non-Brahman entities (in the preceding sections to this, i.e. in BU 2.3.6) now is being declared (lit. stated) the oneness of that

(Brahman with the non-Brahman)[2] pertaining to the realization[3] in its real form.

NOTES

In verse 18 reference is made to the introduction of the section "O Maitreyī . . ." as an answer to the question in verses 10-17, but now is stated another answer. By rejecting the non-Ātman such as a concrete thing etc., the entity expressed by the word *tat*, viz. the Brahman, has been ascertained. Now is to be ascertained the oneness of the Brahman with the entity expressed by the word *tvam*, viz. the individual consciousness.

1. The word *vā* marks first alternative way of introducing comment on "O Maitreyī. . .". Note the word *vā* in the following verse.

2. Cf. SP: *tasya* (= *tadarthasya*) *tvamarthenaikyam.*

3. The word *saṁsiddhi* literally means 'establishing (in real form)', but here it is the synonym of *mukti* = *avagati.*

नेतीति ब्रह्मणोऽन्यत्र मूर्तामूर्तव्यवस्थितौ ।
प्रसक्ते सांख्यसिद्धान्ते सर्वमात्मेति वोच्यते ॥ २० ॥

20. Or if on the basis of the statement, "(The Brahman is) not this. . .," (one accepted) the existence of concrete and abstract things (apart from the Brahman), (and) would (thus) be led to the acceptance of the Sāṁkhya doctrine,[1] then, (in order to obviate that difficulty) is stated "All this is the Ātman."

NOTES

1. According to the Sāṁkhya, both *prakṛti* and *puruṣa* are existent. Hence, the Sāṁkhya is called a realist and dualist. He holds that all the worldly phenomena are real, since they originate from real *prakṛti*. As suggested by 'if...(one accepted) ...' in the verse, the Vedāntin would not remain in any way different from the Sāṁkhya. That is, the Advaita Vedāntin would be forced to hold the duality, giving up *kevalādvaita*, 'absolute-monism'.

सत्यपि ब्रह्मवेदित्वे नासंत्यक्तैषणो यतिः ।

मुक्तिभागिति चेहोक्तः संन्यासेन समुच्चयः ॥ २१ ॥

21. An ascetic, who has not given up the desire, may not attain liberation even if he is a knower of the Brahman.[1] Therefore, the combination (of the knowledge of the Brahman) with renunciation is mentioned here (as a means to attaining liberation).

NOTES

In verses 19-20, the purpose of this section (viz. BUBV 2.4) was introduced, i.e. the oneness of the Brahman and the Ātman, all this is the Ātman. Here another purpose is described: Though it was stated before that renunciation is subsidiary to the knowledge of the Brahman, now is declared the combination of renunciation with the knowledge of liberation.

1. Here we find the suggestion of *vidvat-saṁnyāsa*. Thus the necessity of renunciation for liberation is introduced as one of the purposes of this section.

निरस्तातिशयज्ञानो याज्ञवल्क्यो यतो गृही ।

कैवल्याश्रममास्थाय प्राप तद्वैष्णवं पदम् ॥ २२ ॥

22. Because Yājñavalkya, a householder, who possessed the knowledge of that which surpassed all excellence, obtained the highest place of Viṣṇu,[1] after attaining the state of renunciation[2] (hence the combination of knowledge with renunciation is essential for liberation).

NOTES

By taking up the example of Yājñavalkya, the Vārtika confirms what was stated in the preceding verse, i.e. even if one has the knowledge of the Brahman, one cannot attain liberation without renunciation; the combination of knowledge with renunciation is essential for liberation.

1. Sureśvara uses the words *vaiṣṇavaṁ padam* in PKV 62 also in order to convey the sense of the Brahman. And a similar expression *viṣṇoḥ paramaṁ padam* found in SV 219 is first used in KathU 3.9 conveying the same idea. One

could notice the influence of Vaiṣṇavism on Sureśvara's expression for the Brahman. In TUBV also the word *viṣṇu* appears twice, i.e. at 2.374 and 380, conveying the sense of the Brahman. Also cf. Nais 1.1 which uses the word *hari* in a similar context.

2. The word *kaivalya* means *pārivrājya* 'separation from wives etc.' This stresses *saṁtyaktaiṣaṇo yatiḥ* in the preceding verse.

त्याग एव हि सर्वेषां मोक्षसाधनमुत्तमम् ।
त्यजतैव हि तज्ज्ञेयं त्यक्तुः प्रत्यक्परं पदम् ॥ २३ ॥

23. Indeed, renunciation is, for all, the best means to liberation,[1] for it is only by one who has renounced (lit. is renouncing) that the highest state of the individual consciousness can be attained.[2]

NOTES

This verse is the same as SV 215.

It is proved by inference as well as by the Smṛti that the knowledge combined with renunciation is the cause of liberation.

1. This is based on passages which mention that renunciation is the best means. These are: *tyāgenaike amṛtatvam ānaśuḥ* (KaivU 2, *MahānārāyaṇaU* 10.5); *naiṣkarmya-siddhiṁ paramāṁ saṁnyāsenādhigacchati* (BG 18.49).

2. This is the reply to the possible objection: 'Renunciation is the cause of liberation and not knowledge combined with renunciation (SP).'

मुक्तेश्च बिभ्यतो देवा मोहेनापि दधुर्नरान् ।
ततस्ते कर्मसूद्युक्ताः प्रावर्तन्ताविपश्चितः ॥ २४ ॥

24. The gods, being afraid of (men who would get) liberation, covered them with infatuation[1] (i.e. ignorance). Then they (i.e. men), the ignorant ones, began conducting themselves in action.

NOTES

This verse is almost the same as SV 218. SV 218 uses the word *avicakṣaṇāḥ* instead of *avipaścitaḥ*. The idea of the fear of the gods is derived from BU 1.4.10. On this see MAHADEVAN's note on SV 218 (*op. cit.*, pp. 111-112).

1. The word *moha* is the synonym of *avidyā* or *ajñāna* 'ignorance'.

मोहमात्रैकहेतूनि तस्मात्कर्माण्यशेषतः ।
संन्यस्यैकात्म्यसंबोधाद्भित्त्वा मोहं विशुद्धधीः ।
ज्ञानमेवाऽऽत्मनाऽऽत्मानमुपासीनोऽमृतो भवेत् ॥ २५ ॥

25. Therefore, having completely abandoned actions which proceed only from infatuation (i.e. ignorance), the one of clear intellect[1] overcomes (lit. breaks or destroys) ignorance by knowing the oneness (of the individual consciousness with the Brahman); he of himself meditates on his own self (i.e. consciousness) as the Ātman which itself is knowledge (itself) and becomes immortal (i.e. liberated).

NOTES

1. Regarding *kramasaṁnyāsa* and *viśuddhadhīḥ*, see verse 2 and note on the same.

इति प्रमाणमत्रार्थे वचनं भाल्लविश्रुतौ ।
सर्वः संन्यस्तकर्मैव ज्ञानात्कैवल्यमश्नुते ॥ २६ ॥

26. In this respect, there is an authoritative statement in the Bhāllavi-Śruti, viz. Śruti attributed to Bhāllavin[1]: "Only he who has given up action attains liberation[2] through knowledge."

NOTES

1. Bhāllavi-Śruti is the scriptural passage belonging to the school of the Bhāllavins, but a text thereof is not available; cf. SV 220 where Bhāllavin is referred to: *iti bhāllavi-śākhāyām adhīyate| sarva-karma-nirāsena tasmād ātma-dhiyo janiḥ||*

2. The word *kaivalya* means 'liberation'. Cf. verse 22 note (2) where the word *kaivalya* is used in the sense of *pārivrājya*.

ब्रह्मचर्याद्गृहाच्चैव वनाच्चापि विधीयते ।
निःशेषकर्मसंन्यासो यतोऽतो नर्णबद्धता ॥ २७ ॥

श्रुत्या जाबालशाखायां तथा चानधिकारिणाम् ।
संन्यासस्य विधानाच्च कार्योऽतोऽसौ मुमुक्षुभिः ॥ २८ ॥

27-28. Since renunciation of the entire action is prescribed even at (lit. from) the stage of a student, or of a house (holder) and of an anchorite, there remains (for one) no bondage of debt.[1] In the same way, there in the Śruti of Jābāla school renunciation is prescribed for those who are not entitled to perform the prescribed action (i.e. they are not eligible for the same), therefore, renunciation has to be accepted (undertaken) by those who are desirous of liberation.[2]

NOTES

This is the reply to the possible objection: 'There is impropriety of renunciation owing to the contradiction with the Śruti and the Smṛti which prescribe paying off the three debts.' SP points out to Sureśvara's intention thus: 'It is established in SV that the authoritativeness of the *arthavāda* in the Śruti and the Smṛti is not accepted if it is contradictory to an injunction.' (Cf. SV 540b-541a, 564b-567a) This is why the verse refers to *saṁnyāsavidhāna*.

1. There is a mention in the Śruti and the Smṛti that a man has to pay back: (i) the debt to the sages, as a student; (ii) the debt to manes, as a householder; and (iii) the debt to gods, as a sacrificer; see the *Manusmṛti* 6.35: *ṛṇāni triṇy apākṛtya mano mokṣe niveśayet | anapākṛtya mokṣaṁ tu sevamāno vrajaty adhaḥ ||*; the *Taittiriyasaṁhitā* 6.3.10.5: *jāyamāno vai brāhmaṇaḥ tribhir ṛṇāvā jāyate| brahmacaryeṇa ṛṣibhyo yajñena devebhyaḥ prajayā pitṛbhyaḥ| eṣa vā anṛno yaḥ putrī yajvā brahmacārivāsi |* Cf. SV 436b-437a and SP thereon.

2. JābālaU 4: *yadi vetarathā brahmacaryād eva pravrajet gṛhād vā vanād vā | atha punar avrati vā vrati vā snātako vā asnātako votsannāgniko vā yad ahar eva virajet tad ahar eva pravrajet|* Cf. note (1) on verse 23 regarding the Śruti mentioning renunciation.

नरलोकादिकामानां सुतोत्पत्त्यादि साधनम् ।
तेभ्यो व्युत्थितचित्तानां संन्यासस्त्वात्मकामिनाम् ॥ २९ ॥

29. For those who have a desire for the world of men etc.,[1] begetting a son etc. is a means (to fulfilling the same,) but, in the case of those who are desirous of (the knowledge of) the Ātman (and) whose mind has risen above them (i.e. the objects of desire), renunciation is the means.

NOTES

This verse is the reply to the possible objection: 'Even if renunciation does not go against the authoritative Śruti in respect of *ṛṇa*, renunciation cannot be accepted as subsidiary to knowledge leading to liberation. It may be possible that by getting a son (etc.) or by acquiring the knowledge of the Brahman together with that (viz. getting a son etc.), one may get liberation. That is to say, renunciation is not all necessary.' Sureśvara replies that renunciation has to be accepted as subsidiary.

1. See BU 1.5.16 which mentions that *manuṣyaloka, pitṛloka* and *devaloka* are attained through a son, rites such as *agnihotra* and knowledge respectively: *atha trayo vāva lokā manuṣyalokaḥ pitṛloko devaloka iti so'yaṁ manuṣyalokah putreṇaiva jayyo nānyena karmaṇā pitṛloko vidyayā devaloko . . .* /

इममर्थं श्रुतिर्वक्ति सर्वकर्मानपेक्षिणी ।
प्रजादिना करिष्यामः किं तत्फलवितृष्णतः ॥ ३० ॥

30. The Śruti, indifferent to all action, states this[1] very thought: What should we do with a son etc., or with hankering for the fruit of having that, viz. a son etc.[2]

NOTES

1. BU 1.5.16: *atha trayo vāva lokā manuṣyalokaḥ pitṛloko devaloka iti so'yaṁ manuṣyalokaḥ putreṇaiva jayyo nānyena karmaṇā karmaṇā pitṛloko vidyayā devaloko devaloko vai lokānāṁ śreṣṭhaḥ tasmād vidyāṁ praśaṁsanti* /

2. The reading of the printed edition is *phalavitṛṣṇataḥ*, but the other reading in the footnote *phalavitṛṣṇavaḥ* (*phala-vi-tṛṣṇu*) 'not longing for fruit' is more suitable to the context. The manuscript of SP also shows this reading. But Sureśvara's

fondness for using ablative cannot be altogether overlooked. Cf. verses 170, 275 etc.

उत्पत्त्यादिविरुद्धोऽयं लोको येषामकर्मजः ।
मोहमात्रान्तरायत्वाज्ज्ञानमात्रमपेक्षते ॥ ३१ ॥

31. (We hold that in the case of those) for whom this world is not subject to (lit. opposed to) origination etc. and not produced by any action, (it exists) on account of the obstacle only of infatuation (i.e. ignorance) (and therefore their liberation) expects[1] only of knowledge (of the oneness of the Ātman).

NOTES

31a states the reason why there is no hankering for a son etc. This explains *phalavitṛṣṇavaḥ*.

1. The word *apekṣate* requires words *teṣām mokṣaḥ* as its agent. Also *apekṣate* is equal to the word *avalambate* 'depends (on. ..)'. Cf. SP: *mokṣaḥ sutādy-anapekṣaś cet kim apekṣya bhavati tatrā ha* |

प्रवृत्तिलक्षणो योगो ज्ञानं संन्यासलक्षणम् ।
तस्माज्ज्ञानं पुरस्कृत्य संन्यसेदिह बुद्धिमान् ॥ ३२ ॥

32. Yoga is characterized by activity and knowledge by renunciation. Therefore, having preferred knowledge (to Yoga) the intelligent one should renounce this world.

NOTES

This verse is a quotation from MBh 14.43.24b-25a and is the same as SV 217 as well as BUBV 3.5.4. It is shown on the basis of some Smṛtis that renunciation leads to knowledge.

भावितैः करणैश्चायं बहुसंसारयोनिषु ।
आसादयति शुद्धात्मा मोक्षं वै प्रथमाश्रमे ॥ ३३ ॥

33. Indeed this pure Ātman[1] attains liberation in the (very) first stage (of life) by means of the sense-organs properly brought under control in many transmigratory existences.[2]

NOTES

This verse is a quotation from MBh 12.313.26.

In verse 32 there is the prescription of renunciation. One would doubt if renunciation comes in following the order of the stages of life (*āśramas*). Sureśvara answers that one could renounce in any stage of life. In verse 34, he states that renunciation which is preceded by knowledge could not be overcome by any desire whatsoever.

1. This refers to one whose mind is purified. On this cf. the Introduction section 2. The word *ātman* refers to the Jīvātman. The case is the same with the Ātman in verses 37 and 38.

2. Cf. BG 4.5, 7.19 which speak of many births: *bahūni me vyatitāni janmāni tava cārjuna / tāny ahaṁ veda sarvāṇi na tvaṁ vettha paraṁtapa //* (4.5), *bahūnāṁ janmanām ante jñānavān māṁ prapadyate / vāsudevaḥ sarvam iti sa mahātmā sudurlabhaḥ //* (7.19). In tradition, chapter 18 of BG is called *mokṣasaṁnyāsayoga*; also cf. 18.2, 5-6, 12, 51-53; 2.47-48 and Ch. 5 which is called *saṁnyāsayoga*—this latter emphasizes *karmayoga*, 'action with detachment.'

तमासाद्य तु मुक्तस्य दृष्टार्थस्य विपश्चितः ।
त्रिष्वाश्रमेषु कोऽन्वर्थो भवेत्परमभीप्सतः ।। ३४ ।।

34. And in the case of one who has obtained that (liberation) (in the first stage[1]), i.e. in the case of the intelligent one who has seen (i.e. experienced) the desirable,[2] what purpose would be there in the (subsequent) three stages of life ?—he is one who is wishing for the highest.

NOTES

This verse is a quotation from MBh 12.313.27.

This is a discussion about one who would feel the necessity of the stage of a householder etc. when he has renounced at the stage of a student (SP). Sureśvara asserts, 'one who has renounced after feeling aversion to momentary fruits would get liberated and later would not feel the necessity of any stage of life.'

1. The statement that three stages of life are redundant implies *tam* (=*saṁnyāsam*) (*brahmacarye eva*) *āsādya*. SP also supports this view.

2. *artha*=*parārtha*=*mokṣa* 'liberation' as *param abhīpsataḥ* shows. There is a play on the word *artha* 'purpose'. In *dṛṣṭārtha* 'one who has acquired (lit. seen) the purpose' the author refers to *mokṣa* as the (highest) desirable object. Naturally, for such a *dṛṣṭārtha*, there is no *artha* in *gārhasthya* etc.

श्रुतयः स्मृतयश्चैवमस्मिन्नर्थे सहस्रशः ।
प्रत्यक्षा एव विद्यन्ते संन्यासप्रतिपादिकाः ॥ ३५ ॥

35. (Already) there exist thousands of Śrutis and Smṛtis[1] pointing to this thing, i.e. they preach renunciation.

NOTES

1. JābālaU 6: *saṁnyāsena dehatyāgaṁ karoti*; BU 3.5.1: *etaṁ vai tam ātmānaṁ viditvā brāhmaṇāḥ putraiṣaṇāyāś ca vittaiṣaṇāyāś ca lokaiṣaṇāyāśca vyutthāyātha bhikṣācaryaṁ caranti*; MuU 1.2.12; *parīkṣya lokān karmacitān brāhmaṇo nirvedamāyān nāsty akṛtaḥ kṛtena| tadvijñānārthaṁ sa gurum evābhigacchet samitpāṇiḥ śrotriyaṁ brahmaniṣṭham ||* and the *Manusmṛti* 6.31: *aparājitaṁ vāsthāya vrajet diśam ajihmagaḥ | ā nipātāc charīrasya yukto vāryanilāśanaḥ ||* Cf. note (1) on verse 23.

मुख्यार्थता वा प्रागुक्ता ब्रह्मेत्यस्य सदादृशि ।
प्रतीच्यथाऽऽत्मशब्दस्य मुख्यार्थो ब्रह्मणीर्यते ॥ ३६ ॥

36. Or rather it has been first stated that (the word) *brahman* has indeed as its primary meaning 'ever-seeing individual consciousness' and then is the primary meaning of the word *ātman* stated to be the Brahman.

NOTES

The first line of the verse states in brief the purport of the previous section, i.e. BUBV 2.3. And the second line states in brief the purport of the new section that has begun.

ततस्तदेतदिति च ब्रह्मात्मपदवाच्ययोः ।
मधुकाण्डार्थसर्वस्वं वाक्येन प्रतिपाद्यते ॥ ३७ ॥

37. And, therefore, by the statement, "This is that. . .," (which is to follow[1]) is expressed the essential meaning of the Madhukāṇḍa,[2] (viz. the oneness of meanings expressed) in the two words *brahman* and *ātman*.

NOTES

The aim of BU 1-2 is reconfirmed as showing the oneness of the Ātman and the Brahman.

1. *tad etad brahmāpūrvam anaparam anantaram abāhyam* |
2. The Madhukāṇḍa refers to BU 1-2.

प्रत्यग्याथात्म्यविज्ञानजन्मनेऽतः श्रुतिः स्वयम् ।
विधित्सन्तीह संन्यासं मैत्रेयीति प्रवर्तते ॥ ३८ ॥

38. Therefore, seeking to prescribe renunciation (as a means to liberation), for the emergence of the knowledge[1] of the true nature of the Ātman, the Śruti itself begins with the word, "O Maitreyī".

NOTES

Renunciation is prescribed as subsidiary to the knowledge of the oneness, viz. liberation. This is the reassertion of BUB (p. 320): *pārivrājyaṁ sarvasādhanasaṁnyāsalakṣaṇam aṅgatvena vidhitsyate* |

1. The term *vijñāna* means *brahmajñāna*.

भार्याद्यनुज्ञापूर्वो हि संन्यासो विहितः श्रुतौ ॥
अतोऽनुज्ञार्थमेवाऽऽह मैत्रेयीमृषिरात्मनः ॥ ३९ ॥

39. Indeed, in the Śruti[1], renunciation is prescribed only when it is allowed by a wife etc., therefore, the sage addressed (his wife) Maitreyī for (securing) her consent.

NOTES

1. This refers to the normal *kramasaṁnyāsa* 'renunciation at the fourth stage of life.' In the case of Yājñavalkya, the Śruti refers to *kramasaṁnyāsa*. This remark of Sureśvara is an answer to the possible question as to why Yājñavalkya who wanted to renounce sought the consent of his wife. Sureśvara does

not insist on *kramasaṁnyāsa* nor does he censure it. SP clarifies the idea of the verse thus: *mātaraṁ pitaraṁ bhāryāṁ putrān suhṛdo bandhūn etān anumodayitvā ye ca anyartvijas tān sarvān pūrvavad vṛṇītvā vaiśvānarim iṣṭiṁ kṛtvā sarvasvaṁ dadyād* /—this brings out the purpose of *ādi* in *bhāryādin*.

उद्यास्यन्वा अरे स्थानादस्माद्गार्हस्थ्यलक्षणात् ।
चिकीर्षवे मे संन्यासमनुज्ञां दातुमर्हसि ॥ ४० ॥

40. "I am about to renounce this stage of life which is characterized as of a householder. You should give consent to me who am desirous of renouncing," (says the sage Yājñavalkya).

NOTES

Commenting on BU 2.4.1, *udyāsyan vā are sthānād asmād* . . ., 'I am about to give up this stage of life. . . .'

The difference of word-order between BU and BUBV (i.e. *asmāt sthānād* and *sthānād asmād*) is owing to exigencies of metre.

युक्तमाह भवानस्माननुरूपं चिकीर्षति ।
यदेवं सति कर्तव्यं तत्क्षिप्रमनुशाधि माम् ॥ ४१ ॥

41. (The wife said,) "You have told me (lit. us) the proper thing. (Indeed,) you desire to do what is (only) proper; therefore, please tell me quickly what is to be done (by me), when this is the case (i.e. you propose to renounce)."

NOTES

From this verse up to the 45th verse, Sureśvara comments on BU 2.4.1: *hanta te 'nayā kātyāyanyāntaṁ karavāṇiti*, 'Let me now divide property between you and Kātyāyanī'.

[Verses 42-44 are Yājñavalkya's talk.]

अनुज्ञातोऽथ तामाह हन्तेत्यादि परं वचः ।
कात्यायन्या सपत्न्या ते विभागं करवाण्यहम् ॥ ४२ ॥

42. Thus allowed by her, he said to her, "Let me now divide my property between you and Kātyāyanī who is your co-wife.

NOTES

The word order of the original passage of BU is different from that of the present verse: the word *sapatnyā* is added after the word *kātyāyanyā* and the word *vibhāga* is substituted for the word *antam* on the basis of BUB (p. 322, *line* 9) *antaṁ vicchedam*.

निःस्वा स्त्री स्ववता पुंसा नियुक्ता कर्मसंपदि ।
मयि प्रव्रजिते तस्माद्युवयोर्नार्थसंगतिः ।। ४३ ।।

43. "(Since) a woman, who does not have (a right to own) any property[1], is appointed to (perform) some duty by her man who possesses the property, therefore, after I have renounced, there will not be any of your association with the property.

NOTES

In MBh 1.77.22, 5.33.57, there is a statement in this connection: *traya evādhanā rājan bhāryā dāsas tathā sutaḥ / tat te samadhigacchanti yasya te tasya tad-dhanam //* The quotation in SP is *bhāryā putraś ca dāsaś ca trayas te nirdhanāḥ smṛtāḥ / yat te samadhigacchanti yasya te tasya tad dhanam //* "The wife, the slave and the son——all these are devoid of property, whatever they earn is the property of him to whom they themselves belong" (Trans. G. JHA, *Śābara Bhāṣya*. GOS 70, p. 980). JHA says that the source of the latter quotation is the *Manusmṛti* 8.416. But it is worth noting that the quotation in SP closely resembles one from MBh. This latter is quoted in the *Śābarabhāṣya* 6.1.12 which discusses that whatever a woman earns would be the property of her husband.

1. *niḥsvā* (f), 'having no property of her own'.

स्ववानेव पुरा न्यासाद्युवयोः स्वेन सांप्रतम् ।
विभागं करवाणीति भार्या तेनाभ्यचोदयत् ।। ४४ ।।

44. "In respect of my wealth, before I renounce it[1], I am the master (or owner). To you two, therefore, I say, "Let me now divide my property". Therefore the wife urged on him (further).

NOTES

The last line of the verse should read. . .*bhāryā tenābhyacodyata*, (thus was the wife told by him) because the next verse is also the continued speech of Yājñavalkya. If we accept the reading of the printed edition, the sentence (therefore the wife urged on him) hangs loose.

1. The word *nyāsa* is brief for *saṁnyāsa*.

वृत्तिभिः संविभज्य स्वान्संन्यसेदिति चोद्यते ।
यतः शास्त्रेण तेनायं विभागः क्रियते मया ॥ ४५ ॥

45. "Since it is laid down in the Śāstras (i.e. scriptures and law books) that one should renounce only after having divided one's own (relations) in respect of their livelihood; just for that reason, I am making this distribution."

NOTES

KANE says: "Kauṭilya (II. 1) prescribes that if a person embraces the order of ascetics without making proper provision for his wife and sons he shall be punished with the first amercement (footnote: *putradāram apratividhāya pravrajataḥ pūrvaḥ sāhasadaṇḍaḥ*. . . .|) (P.V. KANE, *History of Dharmaśāstra*, Poona: BORI, 1941, vol. II, pt. 2, p. 932.). Though Kauṭilya's work is not strictly a Smṛti one can argue that it had an earlier Smṛti basis.

[Verses 46-50 are Maitreyī's talk.]

युक्तमेतद्व्यवसितं यद्वित्तं न प्रदित्ससि ।
भवत्संन्यासवन्नूनमस्मद्धितकरं धनम् ॥ ४६ ॥

46. "You have (indeed) properly decided that you do not want to give us what you possess (as property), viz. knowledge,[1] (since,) indeed, like your renunciation, your wealth (viz. knowledge) is beneficial to us.

NOTES

This is an explanation of BU 2.4.2, *sā hovāca maitreyi*,. . ."That Maitreyī said."

1. The word *vitta* can mean both 'knowledge' and 'wealth' (which one is possessed of). It appears that Maitreyī is playing on the word; cf. the contrast of *dhana* and *jñāna*.

In verses 46-48, Sureśvara is adding some of the possible thoughts that would pass in Maitreyī's mind.

महानुभावसंपर्कः कस्य नोन्नतिकारणम् ।
अशुच्यपि पयः प्राप्य गङ्गां याति पवित्रताम् ॥ ४७ ॥

47. "(Tell me), for whom is not the association with persons of great eminence the cause of prosperity? See, (for instance,) even unholy water, when united with[1] Gaṅgā, becomes holy.

NOTES

SP quotes BG 9.32: . . .*ye 'pi syuḥ pāpayonayaḥ | striyo vaiśyās tathā śūdrās te pi yānti paraṁ gatim ||* and says that since women are sinful by nature (*pāpayoni*), they do not have any right to *hitasādhana dhana*=*hitakara dhana* (i.e. *vitta*).

1. The word *prāpya* should be paraphrased as *saṁgamya* 'having united (with. . .)'.

भगवत्संगतेर्नान्यः पुरुषार्थोऽमृतत्वतः ।
पृच्छाम्यतोऽमृतत्वस्य साधनं स्यात्कथं धनम् ॥ ४८ ॥

48. "There is no end of human life other (i.e. higher) than immortality which results from the association with you. Therefore do I ask you: How can wealth be the means to immortality (viz. liberation)?

NOTES

This is an explanation of *yan nu me iyaṁ bhagoḥ* . . ., "If now, sir,. . ."

सारेण यदि नामेयं पूर्णा स्याद्वसुना मही ।
तावताऽप्यमृताऽहं स्यां किंवा नेत्युच्यतां यथा ॥ ४९ ॥

49. "If, indeed, this whole earth (*mahī*) were filled with excellent wealth,[1] will it be that I could be immortal with all of that? Or shall I not be that? (Please) tell me.

NOTES

The question of Maitreyī was stated in the previous verse cryptically; it is now elaborated.

1. The words *vasu*, *vitta* (BU 2.4.2) and *dhana*, all mean 'wealth'.

सत्तामात्रोपकारीणि धनानि धनिनां न हि ।
क्रियाद्वारोपकारीणि यतोऽतः पृच्छ्यते क्रिया ॥ ५० ॥

50. "Indeed riches of the wealthy are not useful (beneficial to others) by their mere existence; (rather), they are beneficial (only) through the actions (which become possible therewith). Therefore, I ask you the purpose (served by your wealth)."

NOTES

This is an explanation of BUB (p. 322, *line* 4): *pṛthivī pūrṇa-vitta-sādhyena karmaṇā* (*'gnihotrādinā*), "through the actions which çan be performed with (the support of) wealth which is abounding in the earth", which paraphrases *tena* in BU 2.4.2. (p. 322, *line* 4).

On the question 'whether or not wealth can be a means to liberation,' Śaṅkara says, 'There is remote connection between the ritual which can be performed with the support of wealth and immortality implied in the question, 'Would I be immortal by means of that (wealth)?' Śaṅkara in KeU 1.2 also states: *amṛtā amaraṇa-dharmāṇo bhavanti* / "*na karmaṇā na prajayā dhanena tyāgenaike amṛtatvam ānaśuḥ*" (KaivU 1.2). . .*ityādi-śrutibhyaḥ* /

प्रत्याह पृष्टः स्वां जायां नामृतत्वं धनादिति ॥ ५१ ॥

वित्तं चेन्नामृतत्वाय कस्माद् दित्सति तद्ब्रवान् ।
इति पृष्टोऽब्रवीद्वित्तसाधनस्य प्रयोजनम् ॥ ५२ ॥

51-52. Thus asked, he answered his wife, "There is (indeed) no immortality through wealth". (As he was again) asked, "Why do you wish to give (us) wealth, if it does not lead to immortality?", he told her the purpose served by wealth as a means.

NOTES

Verse 51 is an explanation of *neti hovāca yājñavalkyaḥ*, "No, answered Yājñavalkya". Verse 52 is based on *yathaivopakaraṇa-vatāṃ jīvitaṁ tathaiva te jīvitaṁ syād*...., "Your life would be like that which is in the case of those who are with means. . . ."

[Verses 53-54 are Yājñavalkya's talk.]

क्षयिष्णुसाधनाधीनं जीवितं स्याद्यथा नृणाम् ।
तथैव तव वित्तेन जीवितं नामृतात्मता ॥ ५३ ॥

53. "Just as the life of men is dependent on perishable means, in the same way, indeed, is your life (also dependent) on wealth (as perishable means). (There is) no immortality (for you, through that).

अविद्यामात्रविध्वंसाज्ज्ञानादेवामृतं यतः ।
अमृतत्वस्य नाऽशाऽपि वित्तसाध्येन कर्मणा ॥ ५४ ॥

54. "Since immortality[1] (results) only from knowledge which is destruction (i.e. removal) of total ignorance alone, there is no hope whatsoever of immortality through action (which) can be performed with (the support of) wealth."

NOTES

This is an explanation of BU 2.4.2: *amṛtatvasya tu nāśāsti vitteneti*, "However, there is no hope of immortality through wealth." On this passage of BU, BUB says *amṛtatvasya tu nāśā manasāpy asti vittena vittasādhyena karmaṇeti* / In the second line of the verse, *vittasādhyena karmaṇā* is taken from BUB as it is and *api* means *manasāpi* in BUB. What is meant is this: Even if there is no hope of acquiring immortality through action which can be performed with the support of wealth, hope can be entertained in thought or dream etc. But by the words *manasāpi* (or, *api*) total negation of hope is intended.

1. The word *amṛta* is substituted by *amṛtatva* owing to the exigencies of metre.

कुतोऽमृतत्वसंप्राप्तिर्ज्ञानमात्रैकहेतुना ।
न कर्म कारणं मुक्तेर्नाग्निस्तापस्य भेषजम् ॥
कर्मभ्यो जन्म नियतं जन्म चेन्निर्वृतिः कुतः ॥५५॥

55. (One would ask:) Whence (can one say that) one would attain immortality solely by means of knowledge ? Why, again, is not the action the means to liberation ? (The answer is:) Indeed, fire[2] is not a remedy against heat. It[3] is certain that birth follows from (various) action, and if there is birth, how could there be liberation ?[4]

NOTES

1. The first two lines of the verse contain two questions with a view to elaborating the idea that immortality can be obtained through knowledge alone.

2. Fire stands metaphorically for *karman*; it is not a remedy (*bheṣaja*) against heat which stands for the transmigratory existence.

3. The third line of the verse shows that action is a hindrance to obtaining liberation.

4. The word *nirvṛtiḥ* shows the condition of the being (individual consciousness) whose covering is taken away. Cf. *saṁvṛti* which is the opposite of *nirvṛti* in GK : *saṁvṛtyā jāyate* (4.57); *saṁvṛtyā jāyate tu saḥ* (4.74)

स्वभावादेव साधूनां प्रवृत्तिरुपकारिणी ।
अपकारिण्यपि जने किमु भक्तजनं प्रति ॥५६॥

56. The activity of the good is, by its very nature, beneficial even to (i.e. in the case of) harmful people. What to say, then, (about its being so) in the case of the devoted people ?

NOTES

Sureśvara's next verse is Maitreyī's question to Yājñavalkya and it implies some unaccounted for unkindness on the part of Yājñavalkya. Therefore, he wants to avert that possible implication and so this general maxim is prescribed.
[Verses 57-63 are Maitreyī's talk.]

नूनं ममापराधोऽयं यद्भवन्तोऽपि मां प्रति ।
प्रतिलोमं चिकीर्षन्ति कोऽन्यः स्याद्धितकृन्मम ।।५७।।

57. "Indeed, this (must be) my fault that even you (my lord) wish to do to me (something) that is against (my interest). (But tell me) who else (than you) would be my benefactor? (asked Maitreyī).

NOTES

In the usual way, Maitreyī blames herself for the unkind treatment Yājñavalkya had given her. Also, as SP says, the latter half of the second line implies Yājñavalkya's refusal to offer her beneficial advice.

अनुरक्तां प्रियां साध्वीं बद्ध्वा वित्तेन मां कथम् ।
कामोच्छित्तिमकृत्वा च संन्यसन्ति भवद्विधाः ।।५८।।

58. "How do (i.e can) persons like you renounce, having bound to wealth me (who am) devoted, beloved and faithful, without destroying desires (of my heart)?

वित्ताच्चेदमृतत्वं स्यात्तत्तित्यक्षा न युज्यते ।
वित्ताच्चेन्नामृतत्वं स्याद्वद तेन ममापि किम् ।।५९।।

59. "If (again) immortality could be (attained) through (acquisition of) wealth, then (your) desire of renouncing that does not stand to reason. (And) if immortality could not be (attained) through wealth, then, tell me, of what use that can be to me.

NOTES

This is an explanation of BU 2.4.3: *yena ahaṁ nāmṛtā syāṁ kim ahaṁ tena kuryāṁ yad eva bhagavān veda tad eva me brūhiti*, "What should I do with that through which I shall not be immortal? Tell me that, indeed, what you know, sir."

[Armed with the remonstrance in verses 55-58 and reasoning in verse 59, Maitreyī puts her request which continues up to verse 63.]

यद्यस्त्यनुजिघृक्षैवं करुणा वा मयीष्यते ।
यदेव भगवान्वेद तेन संविभजस्व माम् ॥६०॥

60. "If you wish to favour me or you want to be compassionate on me, then share with me that which you know (or possess[1]), with (the gift of) that separate me (from my co-wife[2]).

NOTES

1. Sureśvara puns on the word *veda* which stems from *vid* 'to know' or 'to possess'. Cf. note on verse 46.

2. On the authority of SP. This accounts for grammatical forms.

यद्विज्ञानात्परित्यज्य निःशेषं वित्तसाधनम् ।
स्वाराज्यमीप्सति भवांस्तदेव वसु देहि मे ॥६१॥

61. "(Please) give me only that wealth, through the knowledge of which you, having renounced the entire wealth and (other) means, wish to obtain the domain of light.[1]

NOTES

Śaṅkara comments *yad eva bhagavān kevalam amṛtatva-sādhanaṁ veda tad eva amṛtatva-sādhanaṁ. . .* , "That alone is the means to immortality indeed which you know to be the only means to immortality". Sureśvara elaborately comments on *yad eva bhagavān veda tad eva* in verses 61-63.

1. *svārājya* < *svar*+*rājya* 'domain of light' : (Since *svar* is (heavenly) light in the *Ṛgveda* etc., the brightest light is *svārājya*.) The word *svārājya* is used in KausU 4.20; CU 2.24. 12, 3.7.4; TU 1.6.2; **MaiU 6.36,** especially Śaṅkara comments in TUB 1.6.2 for *āpnoti svārājyam* (TU 1.6.2): *āpnoti brahma-bhūtaḥ svārājyaṁ svarāḍbhāvaṁ svayam eva rājādhipatiḥ bhavati* / Sureśvara uses this word in TUBV 1.92; Nais 3.33, 115 meaning 'liberation'.

नाऽऽदिर्नान्तो न मध्यं वा यस्य वित्तस्य विद्यते ।
भोगे न च क्षयं याति तदेव वसु दीयताम् ॥६२॥

62. "(Please) give (me) that wealth which has neither a beginning nor an end nor a middle and which does not perish even when enjoyed.

अनन्तवित्तो हि भवानन्तवद्दीयते कुतः ।
असतः कीदृशं दानं सदेवातः प्रदीयताम् ।।६३।।

63. "Indeed, you possess endless wealth (viz. knowledge[1]), why then do you give me that (wealth) which has the end ? What kind of a gift is that which is unreal (i.e. perishable)? Give me, therefore, that which is real[2] (i.e. perennial)."

NOTES

Here concludes the Vārtika on BU 2.4.3.

1. As in verse 60, here also, do we find a pun on the word *vitta* 'knowledge' or 'wealth'.

2. There is an indirect mention of *sat* = *ananta* and *asat* = *antavat.* SP paraphrases *sat* as *jñāna* and *asat* as *ajñāna.*

संसारपुरुषार्थेभ्यो यतो नाव्युत्थितात्मने ।
मुक्त्येकसाधनं ज्ञानं दातुं शक्यमिदं मया ।।६४।।

अमुमुक्षुत्वमाशङ्क्य भवत्यै तत्प्रदित्सितम् ।
संसाराच्चेद्विरक्ताऽसि गृहाणानुत्तमामृतम् ।।६५।।

64-65. (He said to her,) "Since it is not possible to impart knowledge, which is the sole means to liberation, to one who has not risen above[1] (i.e. raised himself above) the ends of human life[2] in this transmigratory existence and since I doubted whether you have a desire for liberation, I wished to give you that, viz. wealth. Now, if you have turned averse to the transmigratory existence, accept then excellent immortality (viz. knowledge which leads to immortality).

NOTES

This is an explanation of *sa hovāca yājñavalkyaḥ...* (BU 2.4.4), "Then Yājñavalkya answered. . . ".

1. *saṁsārapuruṣārthebhyo. . .avyutthitātmane* constitutes *sāpekṣa-samāsa* 'a compound whose dissolution expects the help of another word by the side of itself'.

2. The word *puruṣārtha* in this context means *dharma*, *artha* and *kāma*. Here Sureśvara develops his idea of four prerequisites (*sādhanacatuṣṭaya*), i.e. *nityānitya-vastuviveka* is prescribed for *dharma*, *ihāmutraphala-bhogavirāga* for *artha* and *śamadamādisādhanasampat* for *kāma*. And he says that wealth is to be given to those who have not gone beyond these ends of human life, viz. who are *amumukṣu*. To a *mumukṣu*, is to be given the knowledge of the Brahman which is the last of the four prerequisites. Cf. the Introduction section 2 in connection with *sādhanacatuṣṭaya*.

स्त्रीणां यदुचितं वाक्यं प्रतिलोमं न भाषसे ।
पूर्ववत्त्वनुकूलं त्वमिदानीमपि भाषसे ॥६६॥

66. "You have always spoken to me that which is (quite) natural for ladies to speak and is not disagreeable (to me); and even now you are speaking (to me) only (that which is) agreeable (even) as before.

NOTES

This is an explanation of *priyā batāre naḥ satī priyaṁ bhāṣase*, "Already dear to me as you are, you speak to me that which is agreeable."

SP points out how the women should speak to their husbands by quoting the *Manusmṛti* 5.152, 154: *viśīlaḥ kāmavṛtto vā guṇair vā parivarjitaḥ | upacaryaḥ striyā sādhvyā satataṁ devavat patiḥ || pāṇigrāhasya sādhvī strī jīvato vā mṛtasya vā | patilokam abhīpsantī nācaret kvacid apriyam ||* (but SP quotes *kuśīlaḥ* instead of *viśīlaḥ* and *pūjanīyaḥ* instead of *upacaryaḥ*.)

मोक्षं यान्तं नरं सर्वे मुञ्चन्ति सहजा अपि ।
अतिभक्तितया मां त्वं मोक्षेऽपि न जिहाससि ॥६७॥

67. "All persons, by their own nature, give up (the company of) a person who is seeking for liberation. You, however, do not wish to abandon me even while I am seeking for liberation because of your intense devotion to me.

NOTES

SP states the purpose of this verse thus: Śruti (the *Taittiri-yasaṁhitā* 6.1.8.5) has a statement, 'A wife is only half of oneself' (*ardho vā eṣa ātmano yat patnī*). Therefore Maitreyī shows agreeable intention towards him in both worldly and non-worldly ways. Yājñavalkya is pleased at the fulfilment of his wish (*svābhiprāyasaṁpattau tuṣṭaḥ*, BUB, p. 323) and intends to share his knowledge of immortality with her.

विभागमसहन्तीव मदतिस्नेहकारणात् ।
मुक्तावनुयियासि त्वं मदैकात्म्यपरीप्सया ॥६८॥

68. "Not tolerating (i.e. unable to endure) separation from me, as it were, owing to your great love for me, you wish to follow[1] me even in liberation with the full desire of being one with me.

NOTES

1. The verb *anuyiyāsi* contains the omission of the letter *sa* from *anu-yi-yā-sa-si*, since the desiderative should have been *-yi-yā-sa-si*. On such an un-Pāṇinean irregular formation, see HIRIYANNA's introduction to Nais (pp. xxxi-xxxii).

अतिस्नेहाऽपकृष्टोमा देहार्धं शूलिनः श्रिता ।
त्वं तु सर्वात्मनाऽऽत्मानं कृत्स्नं मामाप्तुमिच्छसि ॥६९॥

69. "Carried away by great love, Umā occupied half of Śiva's body. But you, on your part, wish to secure the whole of me, the Ātman, by your whole self.

NOTES

We find in this reference to Śiva whose half body is Umā, the mythological bias of Sureśvara. Cf. the *Raghuvaṁśa* 1.1: *vāgarthāv iva saṁpṛktau vāgarthapratipattaye / jagataḥ pitarau vande pārvatiparameśvarau //*

यत एवमतस्तुभ्यं वक्ष्याम्यमृतसाधनम् ॥
निदिध्यासस्व चेतोऽतो व्याचक्षाणस्य तन्मम ॥७०॥

70. "Since this is so, I shall, therefore, explain to you the means to immortality. And,[1] therefore, pay (complete) attention, while I am revealing (i.e. explaining) it to you now.

NOTES

This is an explanation of *ehy āssva vyākhyāsyāmi te vyācakṣāṇasya tu me nididhyāsasveti* (BU 2.4.4).

1. There are two ways of reading *cetaḥ*:
(i) *cetas* 'mind' and (ii) *ca itas* 'and ... now'. SP accepts (i) and explains the second line thus: 'And, therefore, desire to profoundly meditate on the meaning of the words having concentrated the mind on my exposition of that (knowledge for liberation)'. But this is not satisfactory. The alternative (ii) seems to be better. The word order of the second line would then be *ataś ca nididhyāsasva itaḥ vyācakṣāṇasya* . . .

आ ब्रह्मणोऽस्मात्संसाराच्छुद्धधीर्न विरज्यते ।
यावत्तावन्न विद्याया अधिकारी भवेन्नरः ॥७१॥

71. "As long as a person of pure intellect[1] does not become averse to this transmigratory existence beginning with the Brahman (i.e. Hiraṇyagarbha, up to the blade of grass[2]), he is not eligible for the knowledge (of the Brahman).

NOTES

Already in verse 2 above, there is a reference to *vairāgya* which is one of the prerequisites for knowing the Brahman. Sureśvara takes up that point again with a view to explaining the passage in BU 2.4.5: *na vā are patyuḥ kāmāya patiḥ priyo bhavaty ātmanas tu kāmāya patiḥ priyo bhavati. . . ātmanas tu kāmāya sarvaṁ priyaṁ bhavati*, "Indeed, not for love of the husband is a husband dear, but for love of the Ātman is a husband dear. . .(Indeed, not for love of all is all dear,) but for love of the Ātman is all dear." This verse shows that he who has not become averse (to this transmigratory existence) is not eligible for acquiring the knowledge of immortality.

1. On the word *śuddhadhiḥ* see verses 2 and 25 above and the Introduction sections 2 and 10.

2. The phrase *ābrahmaṇaḥ* suggests *ābrahmastambaparyanta*. On this see the Introduction section 10.

[The discussion on aversion (*vairāgya*) continues up to verse 77 and see note on verse 2 above referring to *vairāgya*. The eligibility for knowledge of the Brahman of one who has been averse to this transmigratory existence will be again discussed at verse 93 onwards.]

वैराग्यहेतावप्यस्मिन्नक्तो धर्मादिहेतुतः ।
यतोऽतः कर्मशुद्धात्मा भवादस्माद्विरज्यते ॥७२॥

72. "Since on account of merit etc.[1], a person attaches (himself to this world) even though this (transmigratory existence) is the cause of aversion, therefore, one is purified by (the performance of) action and then turns averse to this world[2] (viz. transmigratory existence).

NOTES

This is in reply to the possible objection: viz. 'Since a bondage is of very momentary nature, there is the absence of any cause of attachment to that. Therefrom the aversion is established, of itself. Consequently, there is no need of the Śruti speaking about that bondage.' (SP)

1. The link of causation is shown in Nais 1.1, TUBV 2.125-126 and BSB 1.1.4. Cf. BOETZELAER, *op. cit.*, p. 7.

avidyā-hetavaḥ kāmāḥ kāma-mūlāḥ pravṛttayaḥ |
dharmādharmau ca tan-mūlau deho 'narthāśrayas tataḥ ||
ato vidyā-nirodhe syān nirodho viduṣaḥ sadā |
niḥśeṣa-karma-hetūnāṁ vikārāṇāṁ tadaiva tu ||
(TUBV 2.125-126).

2. *bhava=saṁsāra*, from √*bhū* 'to become'; it refers to *utpattyādi*.

वैराग्यहेतून्संसारे तस्माद्यत्नादियं श्रुतिः ।
न वा अर इति ह्युक्त्या वक्तुं समुपचक्रमे ॥७३॥

73. "Therefore, indeed, it is that this Śruti text (which commences) with the words *na vā are* began specifically to state the cause of aversion to this world.

NOTES

BU asserts here the causes of one's aversion to worldly belongings etc., such as their perishable nature and so on and then proceeds to state the words *na vā are* . . . for one whose mind is purified through the performance of action, since even in that state one may yet desire for some enjoyment. Cf. SP. on the same.

यस्मिन्नेव परा सक्तिस्तस्मिन्नेव निरादरम् ।
कर्म कृत्वा परं यत्नादन्यस्यार्थयते फलम् ॥७४॥

74. "On performing action without any regard whatever to that (viz. the transmigratory existence) towards which one (naturally) has the greatest attachment, one desires the enjoyment (lit. fruit) of another (i.e. knowledge[1]).

NOTES

This is in reply to the possible objection: 'If the worthlessness of the transmigratory existence is stated for bringing about one's aversion to the results of action, how does action performed generate purity?' A worldly person has an extreme attachment in respect of heaven etc. On account of performing *kāmyakarman* (or *pratiṣiddhakarman*) he loses the respect for purity. But by means of performing *nityakarman* (or *naimittika-karman*) with no personal interest, he can get his intellect purified, become averse to the results of action, and might expect some unexcelled fruit of knowledge.

Cf. BG 3.19: *tasmād asaktaḥ satataṁ kāryaṁ karma samācara | asakto hy ācaran karma param āpnoti pūruṣaḥ ||*

"Therefore, do always perform action to be done without attachment. For, one who performs action without attachment attains the highest, viz. liberation (through the purification of mind)." The bracket is supplied with the help of BGB.

1. Cf. NKL, p. 830 footnote.

किमिक्षो रसमाप्नोति यत्नान्निष्पीडयन्न ना ॥७५॥

75. "Why ! Does not a man get the juice of sugarcane when he presses it with effort ?

NOTES

This is in reply to the possible objection: 'There is no desire to know the Brahman through purification of mind even by performing *nityakarman* etc. since such a desire is not noticed in the case of persons like us. Just as one obtains the juice of a sugarcane by pressing it in a machine, so does one obtain the fruit of action, viz. the desire to know the Brahman by performing *nityakarman* etc. with the intention to offer its fruit to God, on the basis of the Śruti; (quoted in SP) *yena kenacana* (not traceable yet).

तीव्रदुःखोद्भवो बुद्धौ संस्कारो यावदेव तु ।
तद्विपक्षः सुखं तावदल्पं तत्संक्षये क्षयः ॥७६॥

76. So long as there is an impression in the mind of that great grief (which is entailed in the ritualistic performances which lead to pleasures), there arises slight pleasure which is its opposite. When (however), there is destruction of that (viz. little pleasure), there occurs the destruction (of all misery).

NOTES

This is in reply to the possible objection: 'There is no desire to know (the Brahman) through purification (of the intellect) by means of performing *nityakarman* etc. because there is the experience of pleasure and therefore there is no aversion (also)'. Aversion depends not on purification of the intellect but on the need for that. Acute misery consists in the effort of performing what leads to pleasure. And so long as hankering (or pleasure) which has arisen from that (misery) is there, there is to follow the pleasure of senses and sense-objects which are opposed to that pleasure. And that pleasure is very short-lived and it ceases to be there when misery also ceases because of its invariable association with it. And therefore that pleasure also is not important and therefore one should not have any attachment to pleasure.

शीतमल्पं सुखं ग्रीष्मे तापोऽल्पः शिशिरे सुखम् ।
तदेव दुःखकृद्भूरि तद्धेत्वोरनवस्थितेः ॥७७॥

77. "In summer, cold (though only) little, is pleasant, (and) in winter, is heat (though only) little, pleasant; but the same would cause great misery when its causes (viz. summer and winter) have remained no more.

NOTES

The verse states the reason for the recognition of pleasure and its cause, in the light of an example in our daily life. It implies that pleasure, be it small or great, is essentially misery. As such, when the causes of pleasure, viz. *dharma* and *adharma*, are overcome, there remains no misery whatever.

शब्दोऽस्ति न प्रियः कश्चिदप्रियो वा स्वतस्तथा ।
रक्तद्विष्टमनो हेतुः शब्दाद्यर्थे प्रियाप्रिये ॥७८॥

78 "Word is not agreeable or disagreeable (to one), by its own nature. In case of a thing such as a word etc. (which is considered as) agreeable or disagreeable, the cause is one's mind which is attracted (towards it) or abhorrent (of it).

स्वतोऽखिलोऽप्रियोऽनात्मा प्रत्यङ्मोहैकहेतुतः ।
प्रत्यगाह्लादकारित्वादप्रियोऽपि प्रियो मतः ॥७९॥

79. "All the non-Ātman[1] is disagreeable by (its own nature), since it has the ignorance of the individual conciousness[2] as its sole cause. But (the same), though by nature disagreeable, is taken as agreeable when it causes delight to the individual consciousness.[3]

NOTES

Verses 78-79 state the agreeableness and disagreeableness of the non-Ātman. The first line points out that agreeableness and disagreeableness of the non-Ātman is not by its own nature. That which makes a thing agreeable is *manas* tinged with *rāga* etc., and preceded by the superimposition of *śobhanāśobhana*. Verse 79 elaborates the second line of verse 78: The superimposition of *śobhanāśobhana* on *manas* as a cause of agreeable or disagreeable feeling is pointed out to be the effect of ignorance of the individual consciousness. A second cause is added in the second line of verse 79: The non-Ātman, disagreeable as it is by nature, is the object of the function of *dhī* (= *buddhi*) which reveals the joy (*ānanda*), the nature of the individual consciousness. (SP)

1. The word *anātman* refers to *śabdādi* 'a word etc.' explained in the previous verse.

2. Here we can find full support for the fact that the *pratyag* in BUBV always means *pratyagātman*.

3. The second line gives the essence of *ātmanas tu kāmāya sarvaṁ priyaṁ bhavati* where *ātman* is a reflexive pronoun, expressive of the individual consciousness. Cf. E. ROER, *The Twelve Principal Upanishads*, Madras: Theosophical Publishing House, 1931, vol. II, p. 238.

जायादिरप्रियः सर्वः स्वत आद्यन्तदुःखकृत् ।
तद्धेतोरात्मनः प्रीतेर्जायादिः प्रिय उच्यते ॥८०॥

80. "All objects such as a wife etc. are disagreeable by their own nature, because they are the causes of misery both in the beginning and in the end. On that account (only), it is said that a wife etc. are agreeable, when they bring delight to the individual consciousness.

NOTES

Though every object is disagreeable from the philosophical point of view, viz. because it is *ādy-antaṁ-duḥkhakṛt*, it is taken as agreeable on the worldly level because it is *pratyagāhlāda-kāri*, viz. it causes delight in the individual consciousness. Also cf. verses 82, 84 and 85 below.

न कस्यांचिदवस्थायामात्मा लोकेऽप्रियो मतः ।
प्रियोऽप्रियश्च जायादिर्यथाऽनात्मा मुहुर्मुहुः ॥८१॥

81. "In no condition is the Ātman considered to be disagreeable (to anyone) in this world. A wife etc. like any non-Ātman is time and again considered agreeable and disagreeable as well.

NOTES

This is in reply to the possible objection: 'One's own self is unsteady, since a desire to cut oneself, viz. to commit suicide, can be sometimes seen. Although there is the desire to cut the body, no discrepancy would be concluded as to the love for its own nature. The Ātman is of the nature of pleasure alone.' (SP)

स्वत एवाप्रियोऽनात्मा ह्यात्मप्रीत्यर्थसाधनात् ।
जायादिः स्यात्प्रियो भक्त्या बन्धक्याः कामुको यथा ॥८२॥

82. "Although the non-Ātman such as a wife etc. is not agreeable by its own nature,[1] it is said to be an object of pleasure for the individual consciousness,[2] (only) secondarily, just as[3] a paramour (is considered to be agreeable) to a libertine.

NOTES

This is in reply to the possible objection: 'If the non-Ātman is by nature disagreeable, it cannot be agreeable even though it is meant for the Ātman since it is impossible for one to have the nature of the other. Supposing for instance, a man is not fire by his own nature, he can still be called fire in a secondary sense (*bhaktyā, lakṣaṇayā, upacāreṇa*), because he is of the nature of fire (i.e. cause of fear) and therefore the characteristic of fire is transferred to him. Likewise, the non-Ātman is disagreeable by nature, still it is secondarily agreeable since the Ātman (the individual consciousness) seeks it for pleasure and the nature of pleasure is then transferred to the non-Ātman.

1. This is already stated in the first line of verse 80.
2. *ātma-prīty-artha-sādhanāt = pratyagātmānandārtha-kāraṇāt.*
3. According to SP, *bandhakī* stems from *bandhahetu* and is the synonym of ***puṁścalī***, *asatī*, *kulaṭā itvarī*. (Cf. the *Amarakośa* 2.6.10). A reading *vardhakī* in place of *bandhakī* is noted by SP, though it is not supported by any manuscript used by the editor. A paramour is not really agreeable to a libertine but he becomes agreeable (i.e. acceptable) only because he gives her the pleasure of money.

निर्हेतुकी स्वतः प्रीतिरात्मन्येव यतस्ततः ।
भाक्तं प्रियं परित्यज्य मुख्यं प्रियमुपाश्रयेत् ॥८३॥

83. "Since the delight of the individual consciousness does not proceed from any cause, therefore one should give up the thing which is agreeable (only) metaphorically and take to the thing which is agreeable (only) primarily.

NOTES

This verse concludes the discussion that the Ātman is by nature agreeable and the non-Ātman is by nature disagreeable.

क्षयान्ता निचयाः सर्वे पतनान्ताः समुच्छ्रयाः ।
संयोगा विप्रयोगान्ता मरणान्तं च जीवितम् ॥८४॥

84. "All collections end in destruction, all rises (or riches) end in decline, all unions end in separation, (so also) all (worldly) life ends in death.

NOTES

This verse is quoted from MBh 13. appendix 15.3967-8 and the *Rāmāyaṇa* 2.105.16. Sureśvara uses this quotation with the intention of seeking the support of Vyāsa, the author of MBh, for pointing out the transitoriness of worldly pleasure and its cause.

Cf. the maxim: *itihāsapurāṇābhyāṁ vedaṁ samupabṛṁhayet*; also one cannot overlook the traditional belief that Vyāsa was the compiler of the *Brahmasūtra*.

न तदस्ति सुखं लोके यन्न दुःखकरं भवेत् ।
तदसम्प्राप्तिविच्छेदक्षयेष्वसुखकृद्यतः ॥८५॥

85. "There is no pleasure in this world which does not cause misery, since that (pleasure) causes misery (if and when it is) unobtained, or separated, or (has) a destruction.

NOTES

Cf. verse 77 above.

एवं चेत्साधनोद्भूतं यावत्किञ्चित्सुखं मतम् ।
तन्निःशेषं परित्यज्य सुखमात्यन्तिकं श्रयेत् ॥८६॥

86. "If, for this reason one considers as pleasure whatever is produced by some means, then giving it up entirely, one should be after (lit. take to, i.e. seek) the pleasure which is absolute.

NOTES

It is shown that as long as pleasure is caused by anything it causes misery.

सांसारिकसुखस्यास्य दुःखत्वादुक्तहेतुतः ।
निष्कृष्यातस्ततः प्रीतिं प्रतीच्येव निवेशयेत् ॥८७॥

87. "Since for the reason (thus) stated[1] all this worldly pleasure is misery[2], therefore,[3] one should first turn away (lit. draw out) (the idea of) pleasure from it (i.e. any object in the world) and then find (lit. place) it (viz. pleasure) in the individual consciousness.

NOTES

This is in reply to a possible **objection: 'The** love for pleasure derived from the sense-objects is considered by people as imperishable—this has been so stated in the Smṛti (as SP states); "Pleasure of those who cannot discriminate one object from another is imperishable". (Quotation untraced) Therefore, one might say one should not give up the enjoyment of the object.'

1. See the verses 80-81 above.

2. Whatever is called pleasure (*sukha*) is nothing but misery (*duḥkha*). Cf. SK 2: *dṛṣṭavad ānuśravikaḥ sa hy aviśuddhikṣayātiśayayuktaḥ* which points to the fact that the pleasure promised by *śrutivihitakarman* is also with an end and therefore a cause of sorrow.

3. The word *atas* refers to the earlier ablative, i.e. *duḥkhatvāt*.

स्रजि दण्डादयो यद्वत्स्रगज्ञानैकहेतुकाः ।
पतिजायासुताद्येवं प्रत्यगज्ञानहेतुजम् ॥८८॥

88. "As a stick etc. are (perceived) in the place of a garland solely on account of the non-perception (lit. absence of

proper knowledge) of a garland, so (also the notion that) a husband, a wife, a son, etc. (are a source of pleasure) is caused by ignorance about the individual consciousness.

NOTES

The illustration is given in order to show that the worldly notion of pleasure from a wife or a son etc. results from non-knowing of one's self.

सर्वानर्थनिवृत्तिश्च सर्वाह्लादाप्तिरेव च ।
प्रतीचि ज्ञानमात्राच्चेत्तदन्यत्प्रार्थ्यते कथम् ॥८९॥

89. "If there is, for an individual (consciousness), the removal of all undesirable results and the acquisition of all pleasures merely on account of knowledge, how is it then that a thing other than that (pleasure in the Ātman) is solicited (by one)?

NOTES

SP explains this verse thus: One should give up the non-Ātman and love the Ātman because no pleasure is possible in the non-Ātman which has arisen from ignorance and because two-fold human aims, viz. *dharma* and *mokṣa* are attained merely by the knowledge of the Ātman.

Sureśvara has in mind the Śruti: *yathā hy evaiṣa etasminn adṛśye 'nātmye' 'nirukte 'nilayane 'bhayaṁ pratiṣṭhāṁ vindate/ atha so 'bhayaṁ gato bhavati* / "For truly, when one finds fearlessness as support in Him who is invisible, bodiless, undefined, without support, then has he reached fearlessness." (TU 2.7. 1. Trans. S. RADHAKRISHNAN, *The Principal Upaniṣads*, London: George Allen and Unwin Ltd., 1953, p. 549).

यस्य सम्बन्धमाश्रित्य ह्यप्रियोऽपि प्रियायते ।
प्रियोऽप्यप्रियतां याति यस्य सङ्गतिकारणात् ॥९०॥

दृष्ट्वाऽनुभवतस्तत्त्वमात्मानात्मपदार्थयोः ।
उपादित्सा जिहासा च तत्कृतैवानुपाल्यताम् ॥९१॥

90-91. "(Pleasure should be sought in that, viz. the Ātman) depending on contact (with which) even a disagreeable thing becomes agreeable, (and) on account of whose close association whatever is agreeable becomes disagreeable. Having known the reality of objects denoted by the word *ātman* and *anātman* through experience[1], one should entertain a desire to accept or to abandon what is related to them[2] (i.e. *ātman* and *anātman*).

NOTES

1. The word *ātmapadārtha* means *asmatpratyayagocara* and the word *anātmapadārtha*, *yuṣmatpratyayagocara* respectively as shown in BSB 1.1.1.

2. The desire to accept (*upāditsā*) that the Ātman is the highest reality, i.e. *pumartha* 'the end of human life' and the desire to abandon (*jihāsā*) that the non-Ātman is not the highest reality, i.e. it is 'not the end of human life'.

नानाप्रकार आसङ्गो विषक्तो योऽस्य बाह्यतः ।
यथोक्तकारणात्सर्वं प्रतीच्येव निवेशयेत् ॥९२॥

92. "Whatever attachment of various kinds has clung to it, (viz. the Ātman) from (any) exterior (object) is owing to the reason (already) stated.[1] (Therefore) one should **place** (viz. find) (attachment) in the individual consciousness.

NOTES

The end of human life can be found only in the Ātman and nowhere else because of the reason stated in verse 90.

1. See verses 90 and 91.

नरकादिव निर्विण्णो यावन्नाऽऽब्रह्मणो नरः ।
न तावदधिकारोऽस्ति कैवल्यज्ञानवर्त्मनि ॥९३॥

93. "So long as a man is not averse to this whole universe beginning with the Brahman[1] (i.e. Hiraṇyagarbha), as if (averse) to the hell[2], he has no eligibility (to tread) on the path of knowledge of liberation[3].

NOTES

Up to the previous verse the aversion to the non-Ātman has been stated. Here is stated that no eligibility for knowledge is possible in the case of one who is not so averse to the non-Ātman.

1. See note (2) on verse 71.

2. He seems to express the idea that there exists such unpleasant abode for beings as *naraka* etc. whose descriptions we come across in later Purāṇas but do not have any description of *naraka* etc. in Upaniṣads or Śaṅkara's Bhāṣyas.

3. This term is used in the Sāṁkhya to denote final emancipation resulting from discrimination of *puruṣa* from *prakṛti*. See note (2) on verse 26.

सर्वासङ्गविनिर्मुक्तो मोक्षमात्रप्रयोजनः ।
अतोऽधिक्रियते प्रत्यग्ज्ञानोत्पत्तौ न रागवान् ॥९४॥

94. "Therefore[1], a person is eligible in respect of rise of knowledge of the individual consciousness if he is fully free from all attachment and he has liberation alone as his purpose and not the one who has any attachment."

NOTES

1. The word *atas* means that aversion is conducive to the rise of knowledge and attachment is obstructive to it.

आत्मा प्रत्यक्प्रसिद्धेः स्यात्तत्रैवाऽऽत्मानुभूतितः ।
इति प्रमेयनिर्देशो द्रष्टव्य इति तत्प्रमा ॥९५॥

95. The Ātman[1] is (talked about) on account of (the commonly accepted) knowledge of the individual consciousness, because one experiences it (viz. the Ātman) in that (viz. one's own consciousness). Thus (in the sentence "The Ātman is to be seen,...." which will follow) there is the mention of the object of knowing (and the word) *draṣṭavyaḥ* refers to the right knowing of it (viz. the object of knowing).

NOTES

Whatever has preceded explained the portion of the BU beginning with *na vā are patyuḥ* . . . up to what immediately precedes the sentence *ātmā vā are draṣṭavyaḥ*. Now is to be explained the meaning of the word *ātman*, used in the sentence *ātmā vā are draṣṭavyaḥ*. (SP) In the first line Sureśvara proves the commonly accepted meaning of the word *pratyag*. In the sentence *ātmā vā are draṣṭavyaḥ* the Ātman is stated as the object of knowing. When the Ātman (viz. the individual consciousness) is the object of knowing, the Vedic sentence is the means of knowing it. The Vedic sentence can give the correct way of knowing the nature of the Ātman. In this sense, the seeing (or knowing, *darśana*) of the Ātman (the individual consciousness) is the object of knowing, there possibly arises the objection as in BSB 1.1.1 (p. 2): *kathaṁ punaḥ pratyagātmani aviṣaye 'dhyāso viṣaya-tad-dharmāṇām? sarvo hi puro 'vasthite viṣaye viṣayāntaram adhyasyati | yuṣmat-pratyayāpetasya ca pratyagātmano 'viṣayatvaṁ braviṣi* | For such an objection there is a reply of Śaṅkara: *aparokṣatvāc ca pratyagātma-prasiddheḥ* | '**And** because the individual consciousness is established on account of its immediate presentation.'

1. The word *ātman* means the Jīvātman as stated earlier. In the following verses, this meaning is kept in view.

आत्मबुद्धिरियं तावत्सर्वेषां जायते स्वतः ।
अप्राप्ता सर्वमात्मेति सैवातो धीर्विधीयते ॥९६॥

96. As for the awareness of one's own individual consciousness, it is patent to oneself (i.e. it is cognized through itself, i.e. by its mere being there in one). (But the knowledge) "All this is the Ātman" is not obtained (in the same way.) Therefore, the knowing of that[1] (knowledge) is prescribed (in the injunction, "The Ātman is to be seen, ...").

NOTES

This verse refers to the view of a *vidhivādin* who holds *ātmā vā are draṣṭavyaḥ* as an injunction: The suffix *tavya* is known to be prescriptive (of some action) and then it prescribes (a) the seeing (viz. knowing) of the Ātman which has been already known to all, or (b) the securing of the knowledge, i.e. the oneness of the Brahman and the Ātman. The *vidhivādin* refutes the alternative (a) in the first line and accepts the alternative (b) in the second line.

1. The words *buddhi* and *dhī* have usually the same meaning 'knowledge', but here the word *dhī* is used to express the sense, 'act of knowing'.

द्रष्टृद्रष्टव्ययोर्भेदे सत्येवं धीर्विधीयते ।
नियोज्यविषयाभेदे घटते न विधिर्यतः ॥९७॥

97. Such (act of) knowing is prescribed only when there is (grasped, i.e. accepted, by one) the distinction between the knower and the object of knowing; for, (indeed), in case there exists no distinction between the one who is enjoined and the object towards which his action is directed, (the prescription of) an injunction does not stand to reason.

NOTES

To such a *vidhivādin's* view about an injunction in verse 96, Sureśvara says: Such an injunction is possible when (i) the oneness of the Brahman and the Ātman is not known, or (ii) the oneness is known. Not (i); because the object of knowing is absent (the first line). Nor (ii); because of no distinction between one who is enjoined and the object (*niyojya-viṣaya*) which is indispensable to an injunction. Hence the injunction is impossible as to the sentence *ātmā vā are draṣṭavyaḥ* ....

उत्तरोत्तरभूयांसि नामादीनि यथाक्रमम् ।
उपन्यस्याऽऽत्मयाथात्म्यं तत्तत्वं प्राब्रवीच्छ्रुतिः ॥९८॥

98. Having introduced in (order one after another), name etc.[1], each latter of higher importance, the Śruti text declared the real nature of the Ātman (and) that to be the 'Truth'.[2]

NOTES

After proving that there exists no distinction between *niyojya* and *viṣaya* (for the oneness of the Brahman and the Ātman is known), Sureśvara keeps in mind an objection on the basis of *bhūmā tv eva* . . . (CU 7.23.1) which concludes a series of injunctions as regards various objects of knowing as the Brahman and then answers it: Prescribing the 'Truths' beginning with ***nāma*** and ending with *prāṇa* in order, and showing that each latter 'Truth' is greater, he only goes to prove that the real nature of them all is *bhūman* 'infinite', viz. the Ātman, alone through taking support from the Śruti, *bhūmā tv eva vijijñāsitavyaḥ* . . . 'But the infinite is to be known. . .' (CU 7.23.1).

1. CU 7.1.4-7.15.4 declares *nāma*, *vāc*, *manas*, *saṁkalpa*, *citta*, *dhyāna*, *vijñāna*, *bala*, *anna*, *ap*, *tejas*, *ākāśa*, *smara*, *āśā* and *prāṇa* in ascending order (of the 'Truths'.) These 'Truths' are enumerated in CU 7.26.1 also. The word 'Truth' (*tattva*) does not really refer to the Brahman, but name etc. which are tentatively taken to be the Brahman in the course of discussion for the sake of understanding.

2. The reading should be *tat tattvaṁ* instead of *tat tatvaṁ*.

भूम्नश्च लक्षणं चक्रे यत्र नान्यदिति स्वयम् ।
अथ यत्रेति चाल्पस्य प्राणान्तस्य च लक्षणम् ॥९९॥

99. Further[1] (the Śruti text[2]) itself defined the 'infinite' *bhūman*, (i.e. the Brahman) in the words, "Where there is nothing else (that is called *bhūman*)," and defined also 'the finite' (*alpa*, i.e. small one) (whose enumeration begins with that of *nāma* and) ends with (the mention of) *prāṇa* in the words, *atha yatra*. . . .

NOTES

This verse points out how *bhūman* alone is the Brahman and therefore to be known. It points to the definition of *bhūman* in CU 7.24.1: *yatra nānyat paśyati nānyac chṛṇoti nānyad vijānāti sa bhūmā / atha yatrānyat paśyaty anyac chṛṇoti anyad vijānāti tad alpam /* Also cf. Nais 2.57 and Cand on the same.

1. There are three *cakāras* in this verse. The first *cakāra* in the first quarter expresses that verse 98 and 99 retain the same idea. The second *cakāra* in the third quarter combines with the first line. The third *cakāra* in the fourth quarter makes an additional argument that *nāma* to *prāṇa* are not the Brahman.

2. This Śruti, viz. CU 7.24.1, comes immediately after CU 7.23.1 which has been dealt with in the note of the previous verse.

अथात इति वाक्येन ह्यहमेवेति निश्चितेः ।
निषिध्यानात्मरूपं यत्ततो ऽहंकारनिह्नुतिः ॥१००॥

आत्मैवेत्यादिवाक्येन पूर्णब्रह्मावबोधिना ।
नाविध्वस्तं तमोऽतोऽस्ति न च ज्ञानमनुत्थितम् ॥१०१॥

नानिवृत्तस्तथाऽनर्थो नानवाप्तं सुखं तथा ।
कार्यज्ञेयसमाप्तिः स्यात्प्रत्यग्याथात्म्यबोधतः ॥१०२॥

100-102. (There is absence of an injunction also) because after (the rise of) the definite knowledge, viz. *aham eva* 'I myself (am Brahman[1])' by (the understanding of) the sentence which begins with *atha-ataḥ* 'Now therefore'[2]), one would have denied all that is of the nature of the non-Ātman and thence (would follow) the concealment of (i.e. overcoming) the notion of Ego.[3] By (understanding the purport of) the sentence which begins with *ātmaiva* '(There is) only the Ātman. . .'[4] which makes one know the whole Brahman, it is not that ignorance is not removed and that knowledge (of the Brahman) has not arisen. Moreover, it is not that the undesirable (viz. 'I') has not disappeared and also that pleasure is not unsecured. (Indeed) there would be the end of (all) that is to be done (and) that is to be known[5] on account of (the rise of) the knowledge of the real nature of the individual consciousness.

NOTES

It has been already stated that the world beginning with *nāma* and ending with *prāṇa* is only *bhūman* which is without a second. So there is the absence of the distinction such as *niyojya* and *viṣaya* (see verses 97 and 98) in knowing it; therefore, injunction is impossible. Here another reason for the absence of an injunction is being given.

According to SP, verse 100 and the first line of verse 101 refer to the destruction of the notion of 'I' and the second line of verse 101 and verse 102 refer to the attainment of the ultimate human end (*mukti*) by means of the knowledge of oneness. And attainment of all ends are *tamodhvaṁsa* 'destruction of ignorance', *jñānodaya* 'rise of knowledge', *anarthanivṛtti* 'cessation of evil', and (*parama*)*sukhāvāpti* 'attainment of the highest pleasure' and all these four are *kāryajñeyasamāpti*.

1. *aham evādhastād aham upariṣṭād ahaṁ paścād ahaṁ purastād ahaṁ dakṣiṇato 'ham uttarato' ham evedaṁ sarvam* / 'I alone am below, I above, I behind, I ahead, I to the right, I to the left; I alone am all this.' (CU 7.25.1). This shows, I am Brahman which is all-pervading.

2. *atha ato 'haṁkārādeśa eva*, 'Next follows the teaching through the notion of Ego (CU 7.25.1).

3. There is the denial of the notion of Ego by means of the understanding of the non-dual Ātman.

4. *ātmaivādhastād ātmopariṣṭād ātmā paścād ātmā purastād ātmā dakṣiṇata ātmottarata ātmaivedaṁ sarvam* / (CU 7.25.2)

5. The notions of *jñeya* and *kārya* are associated with *avidyā*, i.e. they are the products of ignorance. Once the true nature of the Ātman (individual consciousness) is known, there remains nothing for one to be accomplished or to be known.

सर्वासूपनिषत्स्वेवं प्रमात्रादेरनात्मनः ।
प्रत्यङ्मात्रैकयाथात्म्यं श्रूयते सोपपत्तिकम् ॥१०३॥

103. Thus (i.e. as in CU), in all the Upaniṣads[1] is heard, together with reason (about the same), that (all the) non-Ātman like a knower etc. is essentially, i.e. in reality, of the nature of the individual consciousness alone.

NOTES

This verse asserts the agreement of all the Upaniṣads on what is stated in CU, viz. what is stated in the preceding three verses. Cf. BSB 1.1.4 (p.11): *sarveṣu hi vedānteṣu vākyāni tātparyeṇaitasyārthasya pratipādakatvena samanugatāni. . .*/

1. E.g. *brahmaivedam amṛtaṁ purastāt*/ (MuU 2.2.12); also cf. CU 7.25.1.

इहापि नेति वाक्येन प्रतीचोऽतत्स्वभावकम् ।
व्युत्थापितमनूद्याऽऽह सर्वमात्मेति नः श्रुतिः ॥१०४॥

104. Even in this Śruti, i.e. BU, by the statement, '(The Brahman is) not this. . .,'[1] (the Upaniṣad) first states that which has arisen from the individual consciousness (and) does not have

the nature of it (viz. the Ātman), (and then) declares to us that all this is the Ātman.

NOTES

Here is an assertion of the correspondence of BU with CU and other Upaniṣads.

1. *sa eṣa neti nety ātmā* (BU 3.9.26, 4.2.4, 4.4.22, 4.5.15); also cf. *adeśo neti neti* (BU 2.3.6).

भावाभावात्मना स्थानं न निषेध्यस्य वस्तुनः ।
यतोऽतः सर्वमात्मैव प्राब्रवीच्छ्रुतिरञ्जसा ॥१०५॥

105. Since a thing which is to be denied[1] cannot have existence as an entity or a non-entity, therefore the Śruti text declares in clear terms that all this is the Ātman.

NOTES

1. The word *niṣedhya-vastu* means any object of our awareness, which is denied by BU 3.9.26 to be the Brahman; cf. note on the preceding verse.

नाव्युत्थितमनाः कश्चित्प्रतीचोऽन्यत्प्रपश्यति ।
व्युत्थितात्माऽपि चाऽऽत्मानं पश्यन्नेवान्यदीक्षते ॥१०६॥

106. A person whose *manas* has not become operative[1] does not perceive anything other than the inner consciousness. Also a person whose Ātman has[2] become operative perceives things other than the inner consciousness, while it is perceiving the inner consciousness as well.

NOTES

Sureśvara has already pointed out why injunction is not required when the Brahman is both known and unknown. Now he points out another reason for it.

1. The word *avyutthitamanas* is explained thus: *avyutthitamanas* means *manas* which is not operative. In this state, no subject-object relation (viz. duality) is perceived. This state of *manas* is possible in deep sleep and is like *amanibhāva* in GK 3.31: *manodṛśyam idaṁ dvaitaṁ yat kiñcit sacarācaram/ manaso hy-*

amanībhāve dvaitam naivopalabhyate|, Mai U 6.34. (*amanastā* in GK 3.32).

2. For *vyutthitātman* cf. verse 104 above.

स्वातन्त्र्यं यत्र कर्तुः स्यात्तत्र कर्ता नियुज्यते ।
अन्वयव्यतिरेकाभ्यामात्मानात्मविवेचने ॥१०७॥

107. An agent is enjoined to do that (thing) in (respect of) which he has a freedom (to choose the course of action). (Therefore, there is the Vedic injunction[1]) as regards discrimination between the Ātman and the non-Ātman by the method of *anvayavyatireka*.[2]

NOTES

'If in respect of the knowledge of the Ātman, whether known or unknown, there cannot be any injunction, what then is enjoined by the word *draṣṭavyaḥ* ?' In reply to this objection a statement is made as to when an injunction is laid down.

1. This is supplied on the basis of SP: *viddhir iti śeṣaḥ*.
2. See the Introduction section 7.

वचोर्थंप्रतिबोधस्य पदार्थाज्ञानमेव तु ।
यतोऽन्तरायस्तद्धानौ तेन तत्र नियुज्यते ॥१०८॥

108. Since ignorance of that which is signified by the word(s) alone is a hindrance to becoming aware of the sentence-sense; therefore a person is enjoined to determine[1] that which is signified by different words, i.e. to remove ignorance of that which is signified by word(s).

NOTES

One might object: The *vākyārtha* can be understood merely from the sentence; what is then the need of an injunction that one should find out the *padārtha* by the method of *anvayavyatireka*. This verse is in reply to that.

1. The words *taddhānau* and *tatra* mean *padārthājñānadhvastau padārthaśodhane* respectively, according to SP.

एवं ज्ञातपदार्थः सन्यथा पूर्वमवादिषम् ।
ब्रह्म वा इदमित्यत्र न्यायेनैकात्म्ययायिना ॥१०९॥

निरन्तरायो वाक्यार्थं वाक्यादेवावगच्छति ।
अव्यावृत्ताननुगतप्रत्यक्तत्त्वसमीक्षणात् ॥११०॥

109-110. Thus having known that which is signified by the word(s) (in a sentence), as I have said in consonance with the rule that is related to the oneness (of the Brahman and the Ātman) a person gets to know the sentence-sense in the sentence, "The Brahman is indeed all this", from the sentence itself without any hindrance, on the proper pondering over the true nature of the individual consciousness which is not differentiated from and followed by anything else.

NOTES

Here Sureśvara refers to his comment on BU 1.4.10 and 11 which is to this purport: On hearing the Vedic sentence, one immediately understands (i.e. realizes) its meaning; the method of *anvayavyatireka* helps one to assert the meanings of the words in a sentence. This makes one aware of the real nature of the inner consciousness. This awareness is not produced (i.e. conveyed) by any means like a sentence in common parlance.

नित्यमुक्तत्वविज्ञानं वाक्यादेवाञ्जसा भवेत् ।
वाक्यार्थस्य च विज्ञानं पदार्थस्मृतिपूर्वकम् ॥१११॥

अन्वयव्यतिरेकाभ्यां पदार्थः स्मर्यते ध्रुवम् ।
एवं निर्दुःखमात्मानमक्रियं प्रतिपद्यते ॥११२॥

111-112 The awareness[1] (that the Ātman is) eternally liberated can result straight from the Śruti statement.[2] And the awareness of the sentence-sense is preceded by the remembrance of that which is signified by the word(s) One firmly recollects (or, recognizes) by the method of *anvayavyatireka*[3] that which is signified by the word(s). Thus does one know the Ātman as free from misery and inactive.[4]

NOTES

Verse 111 is almost same as SV 206 whose second quarter is *vākyād bhavati nānyataḥ* and verse 112 is the same as SV 207.

1. The word *vijñāna* is loosely used as equivalent to *jñāna*.

2. Sureśvara expresses his agreement with Śaṅkara in that the knowledge of the Brahman is acquired only from Vedānta sentence. Cf. BSB 1.1.4 (p.11) : *tad brahma sarvajñaṁ sarvaśakti jagadutpattisthitikāraṇaṁ vedāntaśāstrād eva avagamyate*|

3. Sureśvara replies to an objection: 'What is the purpose in explaining *padārtha* by the method of *anvayavyatireka* ?'

4. Through the knowledge of Vedic sentence such as *tat tvam asi* there remains (only) the immovable (i.e. consciousness).

प्रत्यङ्मोहोद्भवानात्मप्राधान्येन तमोन्वयात् ।
आत्माऽऽत्मानं पुराऽज्ञासीद्वाक्यार्थज्ञानजन्मतः ॥११३॥

अनात्मनोऽत आत्मानमन्वयव्यतिरेकतः ।
निष्कृष्याऽऽत्मन्यथाऽऽत्मानं सर्वमात्मेति पश्यति ॥११४॥

113-114. Before the rise of the knowledge of the sentence-sense the Ātman (i.e. the individual consciousness) is in association with ignorance and therefore it knows itself as principally being the non-Ātman (which has but) arisen from ignorance on the part of the individual consciousness. Therefore, one first distinguishes (lit. separates) the Ātman from the non-Ātman by the method of *anvayavyatireka*[1] and then[2] one knows (lit. sees) the Ātman (viz. the Brahman to be) in the Ātman (viz. individual consciousness) and also that all this is the Ātman.

NOTES

Once again Sureśvara asserts here that the limitation of knowing only the sentence-sense by the method of *anvayavyatireka* is in respect of the words in it.

1. See the Introduction section 7.

2. The word 'then' refers to 'removal of ignorance together with its effects.' Here 'effect' means 'grasping reality otherwise (*anyathāgrahaṇa*)', caused by ignorance, and also, joy etc. derived from *anyathāgrahaṇa*.

अज्ञातज्ञापनं चातो विधिरत्राभिधीयते ।
अप्रवृत्तप्रवृत्तिश्च न्यायाभावान्न युज्यते ॥११५॥

115. And, therefore, the Vedānta sentence is to be considered as an injunction informing one of what is not known (before). But[1] (lit. and) it does not stand to reason to say that the injunction makes one inclined towards an action (which was never undertaken before), for there is no reason[2] (of such a doing).

NOTES

It is shown that an injunction has been laid down in respect of explaining the **padārtha** which is understood by the method of *anvayavyatireka*. Now it will be shown that it would not be wrong to accept that there is an injunction which makes known what is not already known (*ajñātajñāpana*), viz. the knowledge of the sentence-sense.

There are two implications in respect of an injunction, (i) *ajñātajñāpana* regarding the matter of knowing and (ii) *apravṛttapravṛtti* 'instigation towards some act which one normally does not take to.' In the context of the knowledge of the Brahman, the injunction is intended to be *ajñātajñāpaka* but not *apravṛttapravṛtti* (*kāraka*). Sureśvara clarifies that no action is possible in respect of knowledge—see BSB 1.1.4: *nanu jñānaṁ nāma mānasī kriyā* . . . where Śaṅkara has elaborately discussed that knowledge is not action.

1. The reading in the **footnote** is *tu* instead of *ca*. The word *tu* seems better because the two lines of the verse state two implications in contrast.

2. Here the word *nyāya* means 'reason'. Verse 168 uses the word in the same sense; cf. GK 2.3: *abhāvaś ca rathādīnāṁ śrūyate nyāyapūrvakam* for *nyāya* in this very sense; Śaṅkara's comment on it is *yuktitaḥ*.

नित्यं न भवनं यस्य यस्य वा नित्यभूतता ।
न तस्य क्रियमाणत्वं खपुष्पाकाशयोरिव ॥११६॥

116. As in the case of sky-flower or sky, so in the case of that whose being produced is never (possible) or that which is ever being (i.e. whose existence is eternal), there cannot be (an injunction as to its) being produced.

NOTES

This verse (which is identical with TUBV 2.15 and BUBV 4.3. 1596) clarifies why the previous verse uses the word *nyāyābhāva*:

The example of sky-flower or sky points to the general rule as regards the impossibility of producing the knowledge (or awareness of the Ātman which is ever existent). A sky-flower, eternally non-existent, or sky, eternally existent, cannot be ever produced and therefore there cannot be any injunction as to the production of the same. This would point to the futility of any injunction in respect of *ātmajñāna*.

उत्पत्त्यादि स्वतो यस्य यस्य चात्यन्तमेव न ।
क्रियानपेक्षसिद्धत्वात्स्वतः सिद्धं तदुच्यते ॥११७॥

117. That is called self-established which exists in its own right, and whose origin etc. (from anything else) cannot (or, is not) asserted; for it is (already) existing independent of (anybody's) activity.

NOTES

There are three kinds of existents: (i) those whose existence depends on origin etc., e.g. a pot, (ii) those whose existence is independent of origin etc., e.g. sky, and (iii) non-existence, e.g. a sky-flower. Though the case (i) needs action for its existence, the cases (ii) and (iii) do not. The Ātman is the case (ii); it already exists and does not come into existence on account of any other thing. This is called *svataḥsiddha* 'self-established'.

उत्पत्त्यादौ तु यच्छक्तं हेतुमात्रमपेक्षते ।
साफल्यं कर्मणस्तत्र तदभिव्यक्तिकृद्धि तत् ॥११८॥

118. Whatever is capable of origin etc. expects only a cause. In such a case (somebody's) action becomes fruitful. For, that (i.e. action) causes the manifestation of it (i.e. effect).

NOTES

The first line of this verse is identical with TUBV 2.14 (first line) and BUBV 1.4.814 (first line).

Wherever there is *kārya-kāraṇa* relation there is usefulness of action. For, action makes *kāraṇa* manifest in the form of *kārya*. Only in such a case, i.e. when action is possible, an injunction can be assumed. To the contrary, there is no *kārya-kāraṇa* relation, i.e. no origin etc. is possible in case of the Ātman; therefore, neither action nor an injunction is possible. Here the idea of *kāryakāraṇa* relation is introduced. Cf. SK 9: *asad-akaraṇād upādāna-grahaṇāt sarva-sambhavābhāvād | śaktasya śakya-karaṇāt kāraṇa-bhāvāc ca satkāryam ||*

कार्यं कारणतन्त्रं स्यात्ततस्तस्याऽऽत्मलाभतः ।
अन्यकार्यमकार्यं च नान्यत्कारणमीक्ष्यते ॥११९॥

119. An effect depends on a cause, because it (the effect) comes into existence owing to that (the cause). We do not see there any cause of that which is not the effect of another or which is not (of the nature of) an effect.

NOTES

The impossibility of an injunction regarding the Ātman and its knowledge is being mentioned on the basis of the *kārya-kāraṇa* relation.

सर्वमात्मेति या बुद्धिः स प्रमेयबलाद्भवेत् ।
प्रमातृतन्त्रा सा चेत्स्यात्प्राप्ता लोकाग्निबुद्धिवत् ॥१२०॥

120. The knowledge that all (this) is the Ātman arises from the strength of a thing (which is) to be known (i.e. the Ātman itself). If that knowledge depended on a knower (viz. the individual who possesses a body, sense-organs etc., it could be) obtained like (the knowledge of) the worldly fire.

NOTES

A question may be asked: 'What do you want to prove by showing that there is no injunction possible in respect of the Ātman and its knowledge?' In reply Sureśvara says: Since the Ātman is not something to be achieved through action, there is no expectation of an injunction; its knowledge also, though possible on the strength of a means of knowing etc., is not *puruṣatantra*, i.e. it is not to be accompanied by desire or exertion on the part of a person dependent on an injunction in that respect. The second line is in reply to the objection: 'It is not established that the knowledge of the Ātman does not depend on a person's desire or effort'. On this cf. BSB 1.1.4. (P. 18): *nanu jñānaṁ nāma mānasī kriyā/na/vailakṣaṇyāt/ kriyā hi nāma sā yatra vastusvarūpanirapekṣaiva codyate puruṣacittavyāpārādhīnā ca / yathā "yasyai devatāyai havir gṛhītaṁ syāt tāṁ manasā dhyāyed vaṣaṭ kariṣyan" iti "saṁdhyām manasā dhyāyet" iti caivamādiṣu / dhyānaṁ cintanaṁ yady api mānasaṁ tathāpi pūruṣeṇa kartum akartum anyathā vā kartuṁ śakyaṁ puruṣatantratvāt / jñānaṁ tu pramāṇajanyam / pramāṇaṁ ca yathābhūta-vastuviṣayam / ato jñānaṁ kartum akartum anyathā vā kartuṁ na śakyaṁ kevalaṁ vastutantram eva tat na codanātantraṁ nāpi puruṣatantram / tasmān mānasatve 'pi jñānasya mahadvailakṣaṇyam/ yathā ca "puruṣo vāva gautamāgniḥ" "yoṣā vāva gautamāgniḥ" ity atra yoṣitpuruṣayor agnibuddhir mānasī bhavati / kevalacodanājanyatvāt tu kriyaiva sā puruṣatantrā ca / yā tu prasiddhe 'gnāv agnibuddhiḥ na sā codanātantrā nāpi puruṣatantrā / kiṁ tarhi pratyakṣaviṣayavastutantraiveti jñānam evaitat na kriyā / evaṁ sarvapramāṇaviṣayavastuṣu veditavyam /*

अतोऽपुरुषतन्त्रत्वान्नात्मज्ञाने विधिर्भवेत् ।
अन्वयादिक्रिया त्वस्य तत्तन्त्रत्वाद्विधीयते ॥१२१॥

121. Therefore there is no injunction possible in respect of the knowing of the Ātman,[1] since it (i.e. knowing the Ātman) does not depend on a person (i.e. his desire or effort). However, the process of *anvaya* etc. is prescribed here because it depends on that (viz. a person).

NOTES

The statements in the Śruti such as *dyauḥ agniḥ*, *lokaḥ agniḥ*, *yoṣid agniḥ* etc. lead to one's congnition of fire at least for some while. But the knowledge of the Ātman would not arise from the statement: *idaṁ sarvaṁ yad ayam ātmā*, for if the statement were taken as an injunction, it would point to the limitation on the Ātman like in the case of *loka* etc. With such an objection in view, the author writes the present verse.

1. *ātmajñāne vidhiḥ = ātmaviṣaye ātmajñānaviṣaye ca vidhiḥ*; cf. SP: *ātmani tajjñāne cety arthaḥ*

श्रवणं मननं तद्वत्तथा शमदमादि यत् ।
पुमाञ्शक्नोति तत्कर्तुं तस्मादेतद्विधीयते ॥१२२॥

122. In the same way (are prescribed) hearing about (and) pondering over (the nature of the Ātman). Also whatever (be it, whether) mental control, control of the external senses etc., a person can do it; therefore (all) this is enjoined.

NOTES

The first line explains the idea of *anvayādikriyā* 'the action of *anvayavyatireka*' done by a person and the second clarifies it further. [Verses 123-125 state two reasons why the Ātman is not the object of an injunction.]

विशिष्टेहानुभूतिश्च सर्वमानफलं यतः ।
फलं च न विधेयं स्यादतो नेदं विधीयते ॥१२३॥

123. And since here a peculiar kind of experience is the result of all means of knowing, and because the result is not the object of any injunction,[1] therefore this (viz. the knowing of the Ātman) is not enjoined.

NOTES

Another reason is given why there is impossibility of the Ātman being the object of an injunction. The experience which is the result of all means of knowing and is characterized by *satya*, *ānanda* etc. is the very nature of the Ātman; it cannot be enjoined, like other fruits of action such as attainment of heaven.

1. An injunction is always in respect of some activity which produces some result. The knowledge of the Ātman is not in any way produced by any human activity.

प्रमाणमप्रमाणं च प्रमाभासं च यद्भवेत् ।
चैतन्याकारमेवैतत्प्रथते सर्वमेव तत् ॥१२४॥

124. Whatever be it—a means of knowing, no means of knowing and appearance of right knowledge—all that is (i.e. these things are) nothing but a form of sentiency.

NOTES

Regarding that the knowing of the Ātman is not enjoined, yet another reason is given in this verse: The means of knowing etc., all appear to be imagined in sentiency. Therefore, since the sentient being is the substratum everywhere, it is not to be an object towards which one is enjoined to act.

नानाकारानुपादत्ते चैतन्याकारमेव सत् ।
प्रतीच्यव्यभिचार्येकं तदन्ये व्यभिचारिणः ॥१२५॥

125. The existent, which has the form of sentiency, itself assumes manifold forms; it is but one invariable present in the individual consciousness. All other things, viz. the non-Ātman, are variable.

NOTES

The Brahman is partless and of the nature of sentiency; it becomes the support of many particulars having attributes. Therefore, the Brahman, which has no attributes of its own, cannot be enjoined as an object of some action. The second line states a further reason: The nature of the Ātman, sentiency, is homogeneous (*ekarasa*), and it is invariable, while the non-Ātman is always variable.

मात्रादिव्यभिचारेऽपि संविदव्यभिचारिणी ।
मिथः कृत्स्नेऽपि जगति तदन्यद्व्यभिचारि तु ॥१२६॥

126. Although objects of sense or sense-organs etc.[1] are variable, the cognizing principle[2] is ever invariable. But in the entire world, all things other than that (viz. cognizing principle) are variable in relation to one another.

NOTES

This is a reply to a possible objection: 'Sentiency of the Ātman is also variable in deep sleep.'

1. The word *mātrā* may mean 'object of cognition' or 'means of cognition, sense-organs.' However, in his Bhāṣya on BG 2. 14: *mātrā-sparśās tu. . .*, Śaṅkara clearly states that the word *mātrā* means 'sense-organs such as the ear'. However,

one might be inclined to interpret *mātrādi* to stand for *mātṛ*, *māna* and *meya* which give rise to experience in the state of sleep. But the contrast between *saṁvid* and *mātrādi* does not allow one to do so. The word *mātṛ*, thus understood, is really not different from the word *saṁvid* which stands for 'knower' as well as 'knowing'.

2. The word *saṁvid* means cognizer, i.e. individual consciousness (cf. SP which says *saṁvid* means *cit*) or knowledge itself.

उत्पन्नमपि सज्ज्ञानं प्रमातृत्वाद्युपग्रहात् ।
तदनुत्पन्नवद्भाति तद्व्युत्पत्तेः पुरा नृणाम् ॥१२७॥

127. The knowledge (about the Ātman) does not appear to have come into existence even though it has already arisen and is in existence (as we say in our common dealings) because it has been grasped as a knower etc., before one has really understood[1] (the nature of the knowing which is not other than the objeet of knowing).

NOTES

In reply to the objection: 'if the Ātman is of the nature of sentiency, its knowledge is always established, therefore, an injunction such as hearing etc. about the Ātman would be useless.', Sureśvara states: Even though the knowledge is always present in the individual consciousness, it is overpowered by notions about it as a knower etc. and therefore appears as not obtained. For this reason, hearing etc. are prescribed, in the worldly way. Cf. BSB 1.1.1 (p.2): *tam etam avidyākhyam ātmānātmanor itaretarādhyāsaṁ puraskṛtya sarve pramāṇa-prameya-vyavahārā laukikā vaidikāś ca pravṛttāḥ. . . .*

1. This is possible with the help of what looks like an injunction, viz. *śrotavyaḥ* etc.

व्युत्पाद्यते यदा साक्षाद्यथोक्तन्यायवर्त्मना ।
उत्पन्नमेव विज्ञानं तदा प्रागपि मन्यते ॥१२८॥

128. When this awareness is directly brought to one, following the argument[1] (already) stated, the person considers that knowledge[2] was already in existence even before.

NOTES

The result of one's following the injunction discussed above, is given: Through hearing etc. one gives up the misconception about the Ātman as a knower etc. and knows the meaning (significance) of the word *tvam* as the Ātman without a second. We say: 'This knowledge is attained' though it was there, only covered with illusion.

1. The word *nyāya* means reasoning. Cf. note on verse 115.
2. The word *vijñāna* is nothing but *jñāna*. Cf. note on verse 112.

स्वसाक्षिकैव सर्वस्य न वेद्मीत्यपि या मतिः ।
किमु वेद्मीति बुद्धिः स्याच्चिद्वतोऽव्यभिचारिणी ॥१२९॥

129. Whatever be the thought of an individual, be it the thought 'I do not know', also be it the thought 'I do know', it has only the individual consciousness as the cognizer;[1] the cognizing principle (viz. sentiency) is not different (lit. variable) in every cognition.

NOTES

One might object that knowledge is variable because of non-observation of particular kind of knowledge before enlightenment and because one feels that one has obtained enlightenment. In reply Sureśvara states that the Ātman is invariable. *cit* 'sentiency' is *sākṣin* of *jñāna* and *ajñāna*, which has the form of cognition: 'I do know' and 'I do not know'. That is, both *jñāna* and *ajñāna* rest on sentiency.

1. The word *cit* means *saṁvid*. See note on verse 126.

आत्मेति मेयनिर्देशो वैशब्दस्तत्स्मृताविह ।
प्रमातृक्रियया व्याप्तिर्द्रष्टव्य इति भण्यते ॥१३०॥

शब्दानुरोधतस्तावदीदृगत्रोपजायते ।
श्रुतेरनुभवः साक्षाद्यथावस्तु न वेति वा ॥१३१॥

विचार्यमाणोऽनुभवो रूप्यशुक्त्यनुभूतिवत् ।
प्रमाणमप्रमाणं वा मेयसंगत्यसंगतेः ॥१३२॥

130-132. Here (i.e. in the Vedic sentence, *ātmā vā are draṣṭavyaḥ*) (the word) *ātman* refers to (or, denotes) the object of knowing and the word *vai* states the remembrance of it as the ascertained (decided) object.[1] By (the word) *draṣṭavyaḥ* is stated the acquisition (i.e. attaining proper understanding of the object of knowing) by the activity (viz. effort) of a knower. In this respect (i.e. in respect of the knowing the Ātman) such (knowledge) arises when one follows (the meaning of) the word. (As compared to the knowledge obtained) from the Śruti, experience may or may not be in conformity with the object (to be known).[2] The experience which is subject to reasoning[3] is like the experience of (a piece of) silver or conch-shell; it is valid or invalid knowledge because of its agreement or disagreement (with the nature) of the object of knowing.[4]

NOTES

In earlier portion, it has been refuted that the sentence, *ātmā vā are draṣṭavyaḥ* was intended to be an injunction. Now follows the refutation of the meanings obtained from the words severally.

1. The word *vai* means *niścitam* as noticed in Brāhmaṇa literature several times.

2. I.e. it is not as certain (right).

3. The words *vicāryamāṇo 'nubhavaḥ* are explained by SP as *brahmātmani mātrādibhedadhīḥ*. The words *mātṛ+ādi* used by SP can be understood in three ways: (i) *mātṛtādi* 'a knower etc.', (ii) *mātrā+ādi* where *mātrā* is 'cognitive mechanism such as senses' or alternative (iii) *mātrā+ādi* 'object of knowing'. Even though the use of (ii) is seen in verse 126, it does not hold good in this case. In the case of (i) *mātrādibhedadhīḥ* means 'cognition of distinction such as a knower in respect of the Ātman, but this leaves some vagueness. But, on second thought (when we take into consideration the next verse, *pramātṛmeyabhedo. . . .*,) this appears intended by Sureśvara. In the case of (iii): *mātrādibhedadhīḥ* means *vividhaviṣayabhedagrahaṇa*, 'cognition of various objects', for that is subjected to reasoning, compared as it is with *rūpyaśuktyanubhava* 'experience of (a piece of) silver or conch-shell'.

4. The word *rūpyaśukti* can be better taken as *vaikalpika dvandva*, i.e. *rūpyaṁ vā śuktir vā*. This seems to be justified by *meyasaṁgatyasaṁgateḥ*. The experiences of silver in silver and of conch-shell in conch-shell are cases of *meyasaṁgati*, but the experiences of silver in conch-shell and of conch-shell in silver are cases of *meyāsaṁgati*. Thus is explained the word *meyasaṁgatyasaṁgati*.

प्रमातृमेयभेदोऽत्र न तावद्गम्यते मितेः ।
प्रत्यग्धीमात्रगम्योऽर्थो यस्मादात्मेति निश्चितः ॥१३३॥

133. To begin with, there do not arise from (what is taken as) accurate knowledge in this respect (i.e. in respect of the Ātman), discrete notions such as (this is) a knower (and this is) an object of knowing etc. since the object to be understood only from the (correct) knowledge of the individual consciousness is determined to be (none other than) the Ātman itself.

NOTES

Here Sureśvara states the reason for explaining the ideas of the preceding verses. The general rule which has been given in the second line of the preceding verse does not hold in the case of the knowledge of the Brahman, because there are no discrete notions of a knower and an object of knowing and he supports this by stating the Vedāntic conclusion that the Ātman is self-luminous.

प्रत्यग्धीगोचरो नो चेदनात्माऽसौ घटादिवत् ।
ब्रह्मादिमध्यपातित्वं ततश्चास्य प्रसज्यते ॥१३४॥

134. If the Ātman were not grasped as identical with (lit. within the sphere of) the individual consciousness, it would be the non-Ātman like a pot etc. and thence would (necessarily) follow that the Ātman is included among the (range of) objects beginning with the Brahman[1] (i.e. Hiraṇyagarbha) (up to the blade of grass).

NOTES

This verse is for refuting the doubt: 'It is not established that the Ātman is self-luminous', which arises on hearing the argument of the preceding verse. The word *pratyagdhīgocara* is to be understood as *pratyagdhīmātragamya* in the previous verse. The argument is: As a pot which is the object of knowing for an individual is distinct from the consciousness within him (i.e. the pot is the non-Ātman), so, would the Ātman (mentioned in the preceding verse as the object of knowing) be the non-Ātman.

1. Cf. the phrase *ā brahmastambaparyanta*; see note (2) on verse 71.

विभिन्नद्रष्टृदृष्ट्याप्तिर्घटादेरिव नाऽऽत्मनः ।
न चाभेदेऽस्ति संव्याप्तिरैकात्म्यादेव कारणात् ॥१३५॥

135. In the case of the Ātman, the aquisition of a certain understanding by a knower (who is distinct from the object) is not possible as it is in the case of a pot etc. And (when a knower and an object of his knowing are) not distinct, there is no (possibility of) acquisition (of any kind) just for the reason of the oneness (i.e. uniqueness) of the Ātman.

NOTES

In verse 134 is stated that the Ātman cannot be an object. Now in the first line of this verse Sureśvara states that the Ātman does not enter on 'the activity of knowing'. The first half of the second line states that there is absence of *saṁvyāpti* (=*samāpti* as SP states) of the Ātman. The second half refers to *aikātmyajñāna* as the cause for its being so.

न च द्रष्टाऽऽत्मनोऽन्योऽस्ति द्रष्ट्रन्तरनिषेधनात् ।
न च द्रष्ट्रोर्द्वयोर्लोके द्रष्टृदृश्यत्वसंगतिः ॥१३६॥

136. There is no seer (of the Ātman) other than the Ātman itself, for there is a denial (in the Śruti) of another seer[1] and it is nowhere seen in the world that the character of a seer and an object of seeing can be spoken of two seers.

NOTES

The possible argument 'somebody else than the Ātman is its knower', is refuted: The first line takes support from the

Śruti: *nānyo'to 'sti draṣṭā nānyo 'to 'sti śrotā. . .*(BU 3.7.23). The refutation in the second line is clarified by SP thus: When we accept two seers, we should consider (a) two seers are equal, or (b) they are not equal. If (a), it is impossible to suppose a subject and an object like in the case of a lamp which needs no other lamp for its illumination. If (b), there is no means to prove inferior and superior nature between two sentient (beings). Thus, it is impossible to establish the knower of the Ātman. SP points out the outcome of this discussion: The Ātman is not understood by the discrete knowledge.

1. Cf. BU 2.4.14: *vijñātāram are kena vijānīyāt*; BU 3.8.11: *nānyad ato 'sti draṣṭṛ.*

क्रियाविरोधः प्राप्नोति द्रष्टुः स्वात्मसमीक्षणे ।
तद्दृष्टेर्नित्यसंप्राप्तेर्विध्यानर्थक्यसंगतिः ॥१३७॥

137. If (we accept the notion that) a seer can see himself, (there would follow) impossibility of that activity.[1] And since (in that case) he[2] (the seer) would always possess the knowledge (of himself), it would be only reasonable to understand the injunction as useless.

NOTES

The view of a possible opponent is given—it pertains to another defect in the view that the Ātman is the seer of itself.

1. SP explains *kriyāvirodha* thus: There is one act of seeing, i.e. knowing. And if it is held that the Ātman is both the seer (i.e. the agent) and the seen (i.e. the object), then it would mean that only one entity, the Ātman, has prime importance as the subject (i.e. agent) and secondly as the object—herein lies the difficulty: One and the same word is related to the verb twice.

2. Since the Ātman can see with its own will there is no need of an injunction. Or, the Ātman's action does not depend upon an impulse from a Śruti passage.

[The previous verse has dispensed with the need of an injunction for an individual whose act of seeing the Ātman (i.e.

the individual's own consciousness) depends on his own will. Yet an objector would persist in stressing the need of such an injunction. His objection is as regards the nature (qualification—*adhikāra*) of the Ātman who may be (i) transmigratory, or (ii) non-transmigratory; this objection is refuted in the following verses, i.e. 138-142.]

संसार्यात्मनि दृष्टेऽपि न च किंचित्प्रयोजनम् ।
अयमेव च नोऽनर्थो यत्संसार्यात्मदर्शनम् ॥१३८॥

138. It serves no purpose to get to know (lit. see) that the Ātman is subject to the transmigratory existence, for it is indeed undesirable for us to get to know that the Ātman is transmigratory.

तदन्यस्याप्रसिद्धेश्च कथं स्यात्तत्समीक्षणम् ।
अथ प्रसिद्धोऽसावात्मा तद्दृष्टिः किं विधीयते ॥१३९॥

139. If the other (i.e. the non-transmigratory, is supposed to become known), (we say) it is not established (i.e. known as such). 'How then will it be possible to see it ?' If, on the contrary, (it is held) that the Ātman is established,[1] (we ask) 'where is the need to enjoin that one should see the Ātman?'

NOTES

1. The argument on *prasiddhatva* or *aprasiddhatva* of the Brahman is found in BSB 1.1.1: *tat punar brahma prasiddham aprasiddhaṁ vā syāt. . .*, where Śaṅkara says that the Brahman is generally known, still not known in detail, for the detailed knowledge sake, *jijñāsā* is necessary.

द्रष्टृदर्शनदृश्यानां प्रात्यक्ष्यान्नाऽगमेक्षणम् ।
द्रष्टुरात्मा पृथक्चेत्स्यात्पृथगात्मेति दुर्वचः ॥१४०॥

140. (If it is thus held that) a seer, (his) act of seeing and the (object he has) seen are within the purview of direct perception, there is no need of the injunction of the Śruti[1] for seeing (the Ātman). Also, if the Ātman is (held to be) different from the seer, (we reply) it is wrong to say that the Ātman is different (from the seer).[2]

NOTES

Verse 140 states yet another reason for that the seeing of the transmigratory Ātman cannot be the purpose of any injunction.

1. Because a thing which is directly perceived in the world does not expect any Vedic injunction for seeing it. The very idea of a Vedic injunction involves the laying down of what is not known otherwise, i.e. from any means other than the Vedic injunction.

2. The reason for this has already been accounted for in verse 134 above.

न चाऽऽत्मन्यप्रसिद्धे स्यात्संसारस्य प्रसिद्धता ।
न ह्यप्रसिद्धसम्बन्धी सम्बन्धः क्वचिदिष्यते ॥१४१॥

141. And if the Ātman is not established, the transmigratory existence (of it also) could not be established, because nowhere is such a relation[1] observed (lit. desired, or accepted) as existent of which the constituents are not established.

NOTES

Verse 141 continues the discussion of the second line of verse 140: Suppose we accept that the Ātman exists apart from the seer, i.e. as the object of his action of seeing. Even then a Vedic injunction regarding the seeing of it by one is necessary, for the Ātman is not like other objects of experience; its properties such as being above hunger etc. are not known except from the Vedic text. Next the verse raises some important and pertinent questions: How can one assert that the Ātman, which is accepted as the object of seeing, is subject to the transmigratory existence, for such an assertion is based on grasping the relation of the Ātman and other objects of the transmigratory existence? To say that the Ātman is not known as other existential entities and also that it is related to other known things is only unwise.

1. SP paraphrases the word *sambandha* as *saṁsāra*.

न चेदात्माभिसम्बन्धः संसारोऽयं समीक्ष्यते ।
तन्मुमुक्षत्वमायातं कुतो हेतोरितीर्यताम् ॥१४२॥

142. If (it is held that) this transmigratory existence is not related to the Ātman, then it should be pointed out as to how the desire of liberation has arisen (on the part of the Ātman).

NOTES

One might take a stand on what the Sāṁkhya says, viz. that transmigratory existence is related to the *antaḥkaraṇa* but not the Ātman. To this Sureśvara answers: Since now the Ātman is not related to the transmigratory existence *mumukṣutva* cannot be asserted on it, because *mumukṣutva* is possible only on the transmigratory.

अनृतन्त्रे विधिर्नेष्टो वन्ध्यापुत्रोद्भवे यथा ।
मातृतन्त्रे तथैवायं न विधिः प्रत्यगीक्षणे ॥१४३॥

143. An injunction[1] is impossible if it (i.e. the activity involved in it) does not depend on (the activity or desire of) a person as the birth of a son of a barren woman (which does not depend on any person). So also an injunction regarding seeing (viz. thinking of the individual consciousness) is not (possible) since (that seeing) depends on the cognizing principle[2] itself (viz. the individual consciousness).

NOTES

1. It has been established that the seeing of the Ātman, whether transmigratory or non-transmigratory, cannot be the object of an injunction. This is proved through an illustration. It is stated that the Ātman cannot be the object of one's seeing because it does not depend for its existence on anyone else.

2. On the word *mātṛ*, see note (3) on verse 130. It means here only 'cognizer'.

नानाद्रव्यसमायोगे वियोगे च घटात्मनः ।
वियत्संपूर्णता नित्या वियत्सक्तेरवर्जनात् ॥१४४॥

शब्दादिबाह्यसम्बन्धे विभागे च तथा धियः ।
प्रत्यक्चैतन्यसम्बन्धो नित्यो नित्यात्मसाक्षिकः ॥१४५॥

यतोऽतः पाक्षिकी प्राप्तिर्नेहास्त्यैकात्म्यदर्शने ।
नियमः परिसंख्या वा न तेनेहोपपद्यते ॥१४६॥

144-146. A thing which is called (i.e. possesses the nature of) a pot is eternally possessed of ether, while it is and it is not in contact with other diverse objects, because its close association with ether is never given up (in any case). In the same way, knowledge is eternally in contact with the individual consciousness within while it stands in relation to the external things such as sound, etc. and it is in separation from the same because it (viz. that contact) has the eternal Ātman as the witness. Since (it is clear) from this that there is no optional acquisition of the knowledge of the oneness of the Ātman, therefore *niyamavidhi* or *parisaṁkhyāvidhi* is impossible in this respect.

NOTES

An injunction is normally *apūrvavidhi*, that is to say, it makes known what is not known (*ajñātajñāpaka*). It is already shown in this work that such an injunction is not possible (i.e. cannot be thought of) in the case of 'seeing of the Ātman' (*ātmadarśana*) etc. One might then point out: 'If that is so, why not think that there is *niyamavidhi* or *parisaṁkhyāvidhi*?' To this Sureśvara answers: The knowledge of the Ātman is for one ever-attained (*nityaprāpta*), therefore, neither *niyamavidhi* nor *parisaṁkhyāvidhi* is possible, *niyamavidhi* is an injunction which enjoins a thing which is established in alternatives (*pakṣe aprāpta*). But the knowledge of the Ātman is ever-attained (*nityaprāpta*), i.e. ever-known (*jñāta*), and not alternatively non-attained (*pakṣe aprāpta*), i.e. a sort of *ajñāta* 'non-known'. Therefore, no *niyamavidhi* is applicable in respect of the knowledge of the Ātman. *parisaṁkyāvidhi* is an injunction which excludes one of the two alternatives which become simultaneously available (*tatra cānyatra ca prāptā sā*), where choice or restriction is undertaken for what has been attained (*prāpta*). But no such restriction etc. is possible in respect of the Ātman.

कर्मकाण्डे यथा मानं तथैवोपनिषत्स्वपि ।
विधिरेवानपेक्षत्वात्सापेक्ष्यान्नाभिधाश्रुतिः ॥१४७॥

147. (Objection:) Just as in respect of the ritual-section, so in the Upaniṣads also, is the injunction the means of knowing, because it expects no other means of knowing. (Here the means of knowing) is not a simple affirmation,[1] because it expects (i.e. depends on) other means of knowing.

NOTES

One might object: In the ritual-section (*karma-kāṇḍa*) an injunction is independently authoritative and non-injunctive statements are useful as its subsidiaries. In the same way, in the knowledge-section (*jñāna-kāṇḍa*) also, an injunction must be an authoritative means of knowing. But a simple affirmation (*abhidhāśruti*), which informs about (the nature of) the Ātman but does not enjoin one to act, cannot be a means of knowing, because the Ātman which is conveyed by the simple affirmation is already known by (i.e. it depends on) another means of knowing.

1. The simple affirmation (*abhidhāśruti*) is the Śruti passage which contains a mere utterance in contradistinction to an injunction which enjoins one to act. The four *mahāvākyas*, i.e. *tat tvam asi* (CU 6.8.7), *aham brahmāsmi* (BU 1.4.10), *ayam ātmā brahma* (BU 2.5.19), *sarvaṁ khalu idaṁ brahma* (CU 3.14.1), are simple affirmations. Here, in the course of discussion of the Vedic sentence *ātmā vā are draṣṭavyaḥ*, Sureśvara asserts that this sentence is not an injunction but a simple affirmation.

मैवं मानान्तराप्राप्तसम्यगैकात्म्यबोधतः ।
अभिधाश्रुतेः प्रमाणत्वं सुप्तोत्थापकवाक्यवत् ॥१४८॥

148. (Reply:) It is not so. As an address which wakes up a sleeping man, so is the simple affirmation the means of knowing because of the perfect (lit. right) cognition of the oneness of the Ātman which does not arise from any means of knowing (other than the Śruti).

NOTES

A reply is given to the objection stated in verse 147: 'The sentence *ātmā vā are draṣṭavyaḥ* is an injunction and, therefore, an authoritative means of knowing.' The sentence *ātmā vā are draṣṭavyaḥ* is not an injunction but a simple affirmation. And this simple affirmation can be authoritative (and therefore useful) in respect of the knowledge of the oneness of the Ātman and the Brahman like an address which wakes up a sleeping man.

अकारकैकात्म्यमात्रं मेयं वस्त्विष्यते यतः ।
तदन्यस्य यतो मानाद्व्यतिरेको न लभ्यते ॥१४९॥

149. Since it is understood (lit. desired) that a thing to be known is only of the nature of the oneness and not productive, therefore,[1] one cannot obtain the distinction from it of anything other than itself.

NOTES

Again a doubt is raised about a simple affirmation being considered as the means of knowing: 'The oneness of the Ātman and the Brahman cannot be the object of knowing by a simple affirmation, because the object of knowing is known by a knower; the distinction of a knower and an object of knowing is presupposed. Then there would be the contradiction between oneness and distinction'. To this doubt Sureśvara replies: As long as the distinction between a knower and an object of knowing persists in the worldly dealing, the doubt would be right. But in the stage of the knowledge there is no distinction of a knower or an object of knowing.

1. The word *yataḥ* means *ataḥ* 'therefore', as SP points out.

मुक्त्वैकात्म्यस्य चाज्ञानं नान्तरायान्तरं यतः ।
विधितन्त्रस्य कार्यत्वान्नाज्ञाने प्रभविष्णुता ॥१५०॥

150. Since apart from ignorance about the oneness there is no other hindrance (to the knowledge of the Brahman), (no procedure is therefore laid down by an injunction,) (for) being of the nature of an action to be performed, it (i.e. injunction) is not authoritative in respect of (the removal of) ignorance.

NOTES

Yet another possibility is pursued about the usefulness of an injunction in Vedānta: 'Even if no injunction is possible regarding the means of knowing in Vedānta, the injunction is required since knowledge which is laid down in the Śruti (*vihitajñāna*) is expected for the purpose of removing the hindrance between the Brahman and the Ātman.' In reply to this Sureśvara assumes the alternative regarding what the hindrance is: The hindrance is (i) something other than ignorance, or (ii) ignorance. If (i), the injunction would be prescribed for the sake of removing it and not for acquiring knowledge (which removes ignorance). If (ii), knowledge dependent on an injunction would not be a right means of knowing, and, therefore, it would not have the capacity to remove ignorance.

यथास्थितात्मवस्तूत्थज्ञानं मुक्त्वा तमोह्नुतौ ।
नान्यो हेतुर्यतस्तस्मान्न त्रय्यन्ते विधिः प्रमा ॥१५१॥

151. Since for the removal of darkness (i.e. ignorance) there is no means other than knowledge that arises out of the existential entity (viz. the Ātman) as it is, one, therefore, cannot envisage that there is an injunction in the Vedānta texts,[1] conducive to the right knowledge.

NOTES

1. The word *trayyanta* 'end of three (Vedas)' means Vedānta; cf. verse 418, SV 12 and the word *vedāvasāna* in Nais 1.8 meaning the same.

नियोज्यस्य च नैश्वर्यं धीसम्यक्त्वं प्रतीष्यते ।
तस्य मेयैकहेतुत्वान्नैव स्यान्मातृतन्त्रता ॥१५२॥

152. It is not accepted that one on whom the injunction is enjoined has no freedom (liberty, capacity, power) insofar as rightness of knowledge is concerned. Since it (right knowledge) originates only from the (so-called) object of knowledge, therefore it does not depend on the knower (i.e. his activity, effort to acquire it).

NOTES

An objection is raised to the previous verse : 'It is not reasonable to hold that whatever depends on an injunction does not lead to the right knowledge, because it does not remove ignorance and because regarding knowledge, which is laid down in the Śruti, the authoritative means of knowing is effected by a person with intellect.' To this Sureśvara answers in the first line. And in the second line he confirms that the knowledge of the oneness of the Brahman and the Ātman is not *puruṣatantra* but *vastutantra*, so then an injunction which involves a *puruṣatantra* has no scope in acquiring knowledge of the oneness of the Brahman and the Ātman.

विधेरिवानपेक्षत्वं वेदान्तेष्वभिधाश्रुतेः ।
अनृतन्त्रत्वसामान्यात्तथाऽतीन्द्रियबोधतः ॥१५३॥

153. In the knowledge-section the simple affirmation does not depend on any other means of knowing (as the injunction in the ritual-section), on account of similarity in respect of not being dependent on (the activity or desire of) a person[1] and because it leads to cognition which is beyond sense-perception.[2]

NOTES

The first line is a reply to a possible objection: 'The simple affirmation refers to the thing already known, is dependent (i.e. expects another means of knowing) and, therefore, is not an authoritative means of knowing.'

1. Both a simple affirmation and an injunction are *anṛ-* (= *apuruṣa-*) *tantra*.

2. Both a simple affirmation and an injunction are *atīndriyabodha*, i.e. they lead to the knowledge of what is beyond the capacity of sense-organs.

अक्षाद्यविषयं प्रत्यक्स्वतः सिद्धेरसाधनम् ।
अभिधा बोधयन्तीयं नान्यत्किञ्चिदपेक्षते ॥१५४॥

154. A simple affirmation regarding the individual consciousness[1] which is not the object of direct perception etc.[2] and

does not need any means of knowing, since it is self-established does not need any other (support).

NOTES

The reply is given to an objection: 'Because like earth etc. the Ātman can be known by other means of knowing, how do you say that it is beyond sense-perception?' The Ātman is a well-known entity and still it is not like the earth etc. because the Ātman is devoid of a form etc. (*rūpādihīna*); it is self-luminous (*svaprakāśa*, like a lamp); it needs no means of knowing (*sādhanānapekṣa*); and it is not known by direct perception etc. (*pratyakṣādyayogya*). (Cf. direct perception is *indriyārthasaṁnikarṣajñāna*). Therefore, the simple affirmation referring to the Ātman does not need the help of an injunction. Cf. BSB 2.1.6. which declares that the Brahman is not established by direct perception or inference: *rūpādyabhāvād dhi nāyam arthaḥ pratyakṣa-gocaraḥ | liṅgābhāvāc ca nānumānādīnām |*

1. Meaning the Brahman as SP points out.
2. The word *akṣādi* means *pratyakṣa, anumāna* and *upamāna*.

तस्माद्विधेः प्रमाणत्वं साध्यसाधनबोधने ।
अतीन्द्रिये तदन्येन ज्ञातुं शक्यं न तद्यतः ॥१५५॥

155. Therefore, (it follows that) an injunction is an (authoritative) means of knowing the end and the means in respect of things beyond sense-perception, because it is impossible to know the same (lit. it) by any other (means than the injunction).

NOTES

In respect of the well-known entity one does not expect an injunction. An injunction is relevant in respect of a command (*niyoga*), therefore in respect of the Brahman it is naturally set aside. My translation above differs from SP which appears to divide this verse into two different sentences.

साध्यसाधनसम्बन्धो न शक्योऽभिधया यथा ।
प्रतिपत्तुं स्वतः सिद्धोऽशक्यो विधिगिरा तथा ॥१५६॥

156. Just as the relation between the means and the end is impossible to understand by simple affirmation (about it), so it

is impossible (to understand) by the words of an injunction that (relation) which is self-established.

NOTES

According to SP, the intention of the verse is: A simple affirmation leads to the inferential knowledge which is opposed to knowledge about the Brahman that is unstultified, unobtained and undoubted.

ऐकात्म्यस्य स्वतः सिद्धेर्न क्रियाऽपेक्ष्यते यतः ।
ततश्च भावनाभावो भावनायाः क्रियाश्रयात् ॥१५७॥

विरहे भावनायाश्च न विधेस्तत्र मानता ।
स्वतःसिद्धार्थबोधित्वादभिधायास्तु मानता ॥१५८॥

157-158. Because the oneness (of the Brahman and the Ātman) is self-established on account of the fact that it does not expect any act, therefore there is the absence of the injunctive force,[1] for the injunctive force (ever) rests on an act. And in case there is no injunctive force (operating), an injunction cannot be the means of knowing. But the simple affirmation is an authoritative means of knowing, since it only informs one of a certain thing which is self-established.

NOTES

This is another reason why an injunction is not a means of knowing in respect of the well-known entity, viz. the Ātman.

1. The word *bhāvanā* is a technical term of the Mīmāṁsakas; it means 'productive force, imperative power etc.' *bhāvanā* is of two kinds, (i) *ārthī bhāvanā* and (ii) *śābdī bhāvanā,* and is closely related to an injunction; it is both *ajñātajñāpaka* and *apravṛttapravartaka.* An *ajñātajñāpakavidhi* informs one of the unknown three-fold *ārthī bhāvanā* in this way—one's action has *sādhya, sādhana* and *itikartavyatā* while an *apravṛttapravartaka-vidhi* informs one of threefold performances which one has not performed. Thus, *bhāvanā* operates in order to enjoin one to some act, so then it constitutes the necessary function in an injunction.

सापेक्षत्वादमानं चेदभिधा लोकवर्त्मना ।
अभिधा तत्त्वमस्यादि सरित्तीरफलोक्तिवत् ॥१५९॥

159. Since a simple affirmation is not (accepted as) a means of knowing because it has an expectation (of some other proof); then following the worldly way, (one can say that) the simple affirmation 'Thou art that' etc. (would also not be authoritative) (just) like the statement, 'There are fruits on the bank of a river.'[1]

NOTES

An objection is raised on the strength of an illustration of *sarittīraphala* which is nothing but an affirmative statement.

1. This illustration is found in the *Śābarabhāṣya* 1.1.2 (p. 13): *nanv atathābhūtam apy arthaṁ brūyāc codanā yathā yat kiṁcana laukikaṁ vacanaṁ nadyās tīre phalāni santīti* / This is used as a worldly illustration of a simple affirmation. But it is not so. On this Sureśvara's discussion follows in verses 162 ff. Cf. BOETZELAER's note on TUBV 2.611 (p. 155), Nais 3.47 etc.

संहत्यनुपपत्तिश्च पदानामभिधाश्रुतौ ।
आख्यातपदहेतुत्वात्सर्वत्र पदसंहतेः ॥१६०॥

160. (Objection:) In a simple affirmation, the proper construe is wholly impossible, since everywhere a word gets properly construed (with other(s) in the statement) only because of a verbal form.

NOTES

An objection is raised: An injunction is required not only for the sake of authoritativeness in Vedāntas but also for the sake of effecting proper construe of words. This objection is noted in Sureśvara's concept of an injunction which is essentially ever-connected with some action as against a simple affirmation of the Vedānta which is not connected with any action. A question, therefore, arises: What is the purpose of the verb in the simple affirmation? Cf. in this context: *kṛtiḥ ākhyātārthaḥ yathā caitras taṇḍulaṁ pacatītyādau tiṅarthaḥ sarvatra ākhyātārtho bhāvaneti mīmāṁsakāḥ*/ (the *Nyāyakośa*, p. 103)

The word *ca* in the first line combines the objection in verse 159 with the objection in this verse. The objection stated in this verse is refuted in the next verse, and the objection in verse 159 later, in verses 162-164 below.

नाऽऽख्यातपदसद्भावात्स्यादेव पदसंहृतिः ।
अस्त्यस्म्याद्याख्यातपदमस्त्येवेहाभिधाश्रुतौ ॥१६१॥

161. (Reply:) No. Construing of the words would be possible on account of the existence of the verb; here in the simple affirmation (of the Vedāntas) are indeed used the verbs such as *asi*, *asmi* etc.[1]

NOTES

The objection in the preceding verse, viz. an injunction is required for establishing a proper construe of words, is refuted.

1. The word *ādi* refers to the verbs *veda, bhavati* etc. The verb *asmi* is in the sentence *ahaṁ brahma asmi*, the verb *asi* is in *tat tvam asi*. In *ayam ātmā brahma*, *sarvaṁ khalu idaṁ brahma*, the word *bhavati* is intended, also see the sentence *brahma veda brahmaiva bhavati*.

The second line is an answer to the other objection: 'It was stated that the verbal form exists in the simple affirmation. This would result in the necessity of an injunction because the verbal form is nothing but a word expressive of action.' If the Vedāntin also takes this position, he is in full agreement with the Mīmāṁsaka who holds: *āmnāyasya kriyārthatvāt*... Sureśvara wishes to set aside this possible argument.

सरित्तीरे फलानीति युक्ताऽपेक्षाऽभिधाश्रुतेः ।
प्रत्यक्षमानग्राह्यत्वात्फलतीरार्थसंगतेः ॥१६२॥

162. In the case of the simple affirmation, 'There are fruits on the bank of a river,' it is reasonable to say that there is some expectation of help from elsewhere because the connection between things, viz. fruits and the bank, is grasped by means of knowing, viz. direct perception (of them).

NOTES

As regards the illustration of *sarittiraphala* stated in the verse 159, there is a condition (*upādhi*) that it is the object of another means of knowing. Yet the simple affirmation like 'This is the Ātman' does not depend on any such outside help.

प्रत्यक्षग्राह्य एषोऽर्थो न तदन्यप्रमाणकः ।
यतोऽतो नाऽऽगमादेव तादृशेऽर्थे विनिश्चितिः ॥१६३॥

163. This thing is grasped by direct perception and not by any other means of knowing. Since (the oneness of the Brahman and the Ātman) is not grasped by this (viz. direct perception) therefore any definite idea about it (lit. a thing of that nature) is formed only from (i.e. with the help of) the Śruti statement.[1]

NOTES

Impossibility of direct perception of the oneness of the Brahman and the Ātman is denied clearly. A thing called the connection between fruits and the bank of a river is directly known by a speaker who states 'There are fruits on the bank of a river' only after he went to the bank of a river and saw fruits. So, the sentence is merely a repetition of what he has seen. Thus in respect of *sarittiraphala*, there is no authoritativeness in simple affirmation about it since it needs another means of knowing, viz. direct perception.

1. See note on verses 6-7.

अपूर्वादिवचोऽर्थे तु न प्रत्यक्षाद्यपेक्षते ।
प्रत्यक्षाद्यप्रमेयत्वादैकात्म्याख्यस्य वस्तुनः ॥१६४॥

164. In respect of the thing about which there is a statement '(It is) without preceding[1] . . .' there is no expectation (i.e. necessity) of direct perception etc., for the reason that the thing called the oneness of the Ātman is not the object of knowing by direct perception etc.

NOTES

SP begins with *sādhanavyāptiṁ pratyāha*: 'The author answers (the objection in respect of) the dependent character of the means (which is here simple affirmation).' This needs some clarification. The objector's view of *sādhanavyāpti* appears to be this: As regards the illustration of *sarittiraphala* for the simple affirmation, *sādhanavyāpti* is possible thus, *yatra yatra abhidhā tatra tatra sāpekṣatvaṁ yatra yatra sāpekṣatvaṁ tatra tatra amānatvam*. Though *sarittiraphala* has been introduced as the illustration for the simple affirmation, it is *sāpekṣa*, i.e. it can be apprehended by direct perception. As such, one might say, it is not the simple affirmation but direct perception that is authoritative in apprehending *sarittiraphala*. This leads to the conclusion that simple affirmation cannot be authoritative. Sureśvara's verse is against this view of *sādhanavyāpti* in respect of simple affirmation. He means: In the case of a sentence like 'That Brahman is without preceding. . .', there is no dependence on any other means (cf. *nāyaṁ pratyakṣagocaro 'rthaḥ*) though there is simple affirmation about the Brahman because the *sādhanavyāpti* in respect of simple affirmation about the Brahman cannot be established.

1. *tad etad brahmāpūrvam anaparam anantaram abāhyam* (BU 2.5.19), "That Brahman is without preceding or succeeding, without internal or external."

अपौरुषेयवाक्यत्वं समानमभिधाश्रुतेः ।
अतीन्द्रियार्थबोधित्वं समानं चोदनोक्तिभिः ॥१६५॥

165. Simple affirmation (in Vedānta texts) shares (with an injunction) a common (characteristic), viz. it does not have a human agency (or authorship). (And) with an imperative injunction it shares (another) common (characteristic), viz. it has the capacity to inform one of a thing which is beyond sense-perception.

NOTES

In this verse, Sureśvara shows the similarity of simple affirmation in Vedāntas with both *anuvāda* and *codanokti*. Simple affirmation is the same as *anuvāda* in the Śruti in one respect, viz. it is an *apauruṣeyavākya*, but it is different from it, since *anuvāda* is supported by direct perception while simple affirmation is not. For instance, *agniḥ himasya bheṣajam* (the *Vājasaneyisaṁhitā* 13.10) is a simple affirmation, supported by direct perception. Simple affirmation (in Vedānta) is the same as an injunction in two respects; (i) it is an *apaureṣe-*

yavākya, and (ii) *nirapekṣā*, but it is different from the latter since it does not lead us to undertake some activity.

सिद्धसाध्यप्रमेयत्वभेदो यदि परं तयोः ।
प्रामाण्ये त्वतिशीतिस्तु न काचिदपि दृश्यते ॥१६६॥

166. If at all there is a difference between simple affirmation and injunction[1] in having the object to be known[2], what is established and what is to be accomplished, no difference[3] is noticed insofar as an authoritativeness is concerned.

NOTES

The defect *sāpekṣatva* in inference consists in 'dependence on another means of knowing.' The object of knowing by simple affirmation is *siddha*, viz. the Brahman and that by injunction is *sādhya* 'that which is to be accomplished, like heaven etc.' Thus, both are different in respect of the object of knowing (*prameya*), but identical in that both are authoritative. Cf. BSB 1.1.1 (P. 4) on *prameyabheda*: . . . *phalajijñāsyabhedāc ca / abhyudayaphalaṁ dharmajñānaṁ tac cānuṣṭhānāpekṣaṁ / niḥśreyasa-phalaṁ tu brahmajñānaṁ na cānuṣṭhānāntarāpekṣam /*

1. The word *tayoḥ* means *abhidhāśruti* and *codanokti* stated in the previous verse. SP says that *tayoḥ* means *karmajñānakāṇḍayoḥ*. The intended meaning is the same, still SP has loose expression and is not exact.

2. The reading *prameyatva* should be *prameyatvāt* as the footnote points out.

3. The word *atiśiti* means *atiśaya* or *bheda*; this is an instance of Sureśvara's deriving help from Śaṅkara.

प्रमोपजायते तावदहं ब्रह्मेत्यलौकिकी ।
तत्त्वमस्यादिवाक्येभ्यः श्रवणात्समनन्तरम् ॥१६७॥

167. An uncommon (lit. non-worldly) right knowledge, viz. 'I am Brahman' arises immediately after hearing passages like 'Thou art that' etc.

NOTES

A possible objection may be: 'It has not been established that Śruti sentences give rise to the right knowledge. Then, how can you say that the Śruti is a means of knowing? To this objection is the reply: In the case of a proper (eligible) person the right knowledge resulting from (hearing/understanding) the Śruti cannot be repudiated (that is to say, we have to accept that the Śruti enlightens an eligible person). Cf. *brahma veda brahmaiva bhavati* or other passages whose hearing is immediately followed by the knowledge of the Brahman.

एवं चेदप्रमाणत्वं किमिवेहाभिधाश्रुतेः ।
विधेरपीह मानत्वं नोक्तन्यायातिरेकतः ॥१६८॥

168. If one were to declare the unauthoritativeness of this type, what indeed is achieved by simple affirmation? An[1] injunction is also not held authoritative in supercession of any reason.[2]

NOTES

1. On the contrary, an injunction is also to be taken as unauthoritative if an opposite is proved. This is given in the second line.

2. It must be possible to point out the opposite of an injunction as otherwise proved. Cf. note (2) on verse 115 above.

स्वशक्तिः सर्वमानानां यथा वस्त्ववबोधने ।
अभिधायाश्च साऽस्त्येव किमिति स्यादमानता ॥१६९॥

169. Just as all the means of knowing have each one of them a capacity in informing about something, simple affirmation also has that power. How then do you consider that simple affirmation is not a means of knowing?

NOTES

The Śrutis are also the means of knowing what is meant by them, just like the other means of knowing like direct perception etc.

नाप्यर्थेऽतीन्द्रिये सिद्धे मानं लिङ्गाद्यपेक्षते ।
योगिप्रत्यक्षमानं वा तयोरविषयत्वतः ॥१७०॥

170. Moreover, in respect of an entity which is (already) established as one beyond sense-perception one cannot expect

any characteristic mark etc. as the means of knowing it;[1] nor[2] also direct perception of the ascetics.[3] (This is so) because the two are devoid of any object[4].

NOTES

1. It may be objected: 'True. The Brahman is not known by direct perception, but it would be possible to know the same by means of inference etc. and, therefore, the Vedānta are not a means of knowing the Brahman.' The first line answers the objection thus: Inference holds good in respect of a thing with characteristics (*liṅgavat*) but not, in respect of a thing which is without any characteristics, i.e. the Brahman. One could yet further argue: 'Though the Brahman is not the object of our direct perception etc. it could be grasped by direct perception (at least) of the ascetics who are distinguished from us, ordinary folks.' To this, the second line gives an answer.

2. The word *vā* indicates the continued use of the word *na* together with the verb *apekṣate*.

3. There is the description of *yogipratyakṣa* in the *Tattvakaumudī* on SK 5: *viṣayāḥ pṛthivyādayaḥ sukhādayaś ca asmadādīnāṁ aviṣayāḥ tanmātralakṣaṇāḥ, yogināṁ ūrdhvasrotasāṁ ca viṣayāḥ/* Direct perception by the ascetic(s) can be authoritative in respect of the subtle object (*sūkṣma*) but not, an object beyond sense-perception.

4. Like Śaṅkara, Sureśvara also holds that the Brahman is *pratykṣādyagocarārtha*, i.e. it does not have any characteristics. Naturally, therefore, it cannot be the object in any inference from some characteristics. Direct perception, even *yogipratyakṣa*, is already ruled out automatically.

Sureśvara thus rules out the possibility of the Brahman being the object of *yogipratyakṣa* and *laukikānumāna*. This is elaborated in the following two verses.

नेतीत्यस्थूलमित्यादिवाक्याद्योऽर्थोऽवगम्यते ।
योगिप्रत्यक्षगम्योऽयं न तत्प्रत्यक्त्वहेतुतः ॥१७१॥

171. A thing which is understood from words like '(The Brahman) is not this[1]', '(The Brahman) is non-gross. . .[2]' etc. is not obtained by direct perception of the ascetics,[3] because it (viz. that thing) is already within themselves.[4]

NOTES

The reason is stated for the argument in the last quarter of the preceding verse.

1. BU 2.3.6 etc., see note on verse 104.
2. BU 3.8.8.
3. But this argument: 'Since the ascetics also cannot observe any characteristic, how can ordinary people notice any?' —to be inferred.
4. The characteristics of what is within one cannot be 'directly perceived' by one, even by Yogins.

प्रत्यक्षानवताराच्च नानुमानेन मीयते ।
धर्मधर्म्यभिसम्बन्धे नागृहीतेऽनुमा यतः ॥१७२॥

172. And[1] therefore the knowledge of the Ātman cannot be comprehended through inference, since direct perception also cannot acquire it, viz. its characteristic, because knowledge[2] by inference is not possible when the close[3] relationship between *dharma* and *dharmin* is not apprehended.

NOTES

1. Another reason why the Brahman cannot be known by inference is given in the first line.
2. A question arises: 'Even if the Brahman is not known by two kinds of direct perception (i.e. common and ascetic's), how is it not possible to assume that the Brahman is not known by inference?' To this question Sureśvara gives an answer in the second line.
3. The word *abhisambandha* is the loose expression for *vyāpti*. In the sentence *parvato vahnimān dhūmāt*, *dhūma* is *dharma* and *vahni* is *dharmin*, because the *vyāpti* '*yatra yatra dhūmaḥ tatra tatra vahniḥ*' is possible. Cf. BSB 2.1.6 as a support for this which has been referred to in verse 154.

[Verse 173 introduces the rule regarding the excellence of an object and verses 174-75 discuss the excellence of a means of knowing. Both these verses occur in Kumārila's *Ślokavārtika*: *codanāsūtra* 113-114.]

यज्जातीयैः प्रमाणैस्तु यज्जातीयार्थदर्शनम् ।
भवेदिदानीं लोकस्य तथा कालान्तरेऽप्यभूत् ॥१७३॥

173. (Indeed) whatever kind of objects are now known to people and by whatever means of knowing, they had become known to people of some other (i.e. earlier) time also by the same (means of knowing) and as of the same kind.

NOTES

An objection could be: 'Even if the Brahman is not known by direct perception in this time, it could have been in another time by some excellence in it (direct perception).' The answer is that direct perception of today also depends on the sense-organs as in earlier times. Means of knowing have not changed in the course of time. Cf. *adyatvavad eva kālāntare' pi pramāṇasvabhāvo nānyādṛśa iti* (the *Nyāyaratnākara* on the *Śloka-vārtika* 113, p. 60).

यत्राप्यतिशयो दृष्टः स स्वार्थानतिलङ्घनात् ।
दूरसूक्ष्मादिदृष्टौ स्यान्न रूपे श्रोत्रवृत्तिता ॥१७४॥

174. Where[1] again one sees a certain excellence, that results from seeing it from after and/or with closer attention, but (certainly) not going beyond the object of its own. Never indeed can any form be the object of the sense of hearing.

NOTES

One might say that since there is no excellence in our sense-organs now, the Brahman would not be their object. On this Sureśvara argues on the basis of the idea that whatever is devoid of excellence is not known by sense-organs. (SP) If sense-organs would at some time proceed towards objects beyond perception such as *dharma*, the Brahman etc., then it would be possible that ears would proceed also towards a form which is grasped only by the eyes.

1. There are two possibilities in the word *yatra*; (i) *yatra viṣaye* (ii) *yatra pramāṇe*. In this verse (i) is applicable and (ii) in the next verse—this verse refers to the excellence of the object and the next to the excellence of the means of knowing.

योगिप्रत्यक्षमानादेर्न चेदैकात्म्यमेयता ।
तत्प्राप्तमपि किं कुर्यात्स्वात्मायोग्यासु भूमिषु ॥१७५॥

175. If the oneness (of the Brahman and the Ātman) cannot become the object of the means of knowing, viz. direct perception of the ascetics etc.[1] of what use will they be, even if one possessed them, in matters which cannot properly be their own objects ?

NOTES

Where direct perception of the ascetics does not operate, inference might be useful, but it must be remembered that it could be so only in the case of objects other than the Brahman.

1. Cf. *māna* = *pramāṇa* in verse 170 above. Here 'etc.' refers to *anumāna* 'inference'. SP points out the purpose of the mention of *yogipratyakṣa* as it is more prominent than any other means, as seen from the preceding two verses.

अक्षादिमेयासारूप्यादैकात्म्यं स्यान्न तत्प्रमम् ।
यथा विधेयासारूप्यान्नैकात्म्यं स्याद्विधेस्तथा ।।१७६।।

176. The oneness is not correctly learnt from that (viz. any injunction) owing to the fact that it does not possess the form as an object to be enjoined; (this is) in the same way as that (oneness) is not known by direct perception etc.[1], for it does not possess the form as an object of knowing it (i.e. direct perception etc.).

NOTES

This verse is a reply to the possible objection: 'Even if the oneness of the Brahman and the Ātman is not made known by direct perception etc. because of the rule stated above, how can the Śruti be a means of knowing without depending on any other means of knowing when the oneness is understood by the injunction?'

1. Cf. note (2) on verse 154 above.

संभाव्यते चेदक्षादि ह्यैकात्म्यार्थे फलादिवत् ।
न तद्वारयितुं शक्यं लोके विधिशतैरपि ।।१७७।।

नासमीक्ष्य स्वसामर्थ्यं पुमान्विधिशतैरपि ।
प्रवर्ततेऽनपेक्षत्वं कुतो विधिवचः स्वतः ।।१७८।।

177-178. If direct perception etc. could prove effective, (i.e. it could grasp, or it could be the means of knowing the object) in the case of the object, viz. the oneness, as (it would be) in the case of a fruit etc.[1], then it would be impossible to ward it off (i.e. to deny it to be so) even by hundreds of injunctions,[2] (i.e. by any Śruti). Without having well-considered one's own capacity, one does not enter on any act even (though impelled) by hundreds of injunctions; how then is it possible to say that injunctive statements of the Śruti are themselves independent of (anything else) ?

NOTES

After stating that the Vedāntas are authoritative means of knowing the oneness, without expecting help from any other means of knowing, Sureśvara further goes to say that even an injunction stands expectant of some other means of accomplishing an act to be accomplished.

1. Cf. note on verse 159 above.

2. Verse 177 echoes Śaṅkara's idea regarding a hypothetical contradiction between direct perception and the Śruti; cf. BGB 18.67 (p. 535): *na hi śrutiśatam api śīto 'gnir aprakāśo veti bruvat prāmāṇyam upaiti* |

अपाक्येषु नियुक्तोऽपि कृष्णलाञ्श्रपयेदिति ।
न तच्छक्तिं विना कश्चित्पुमांस्तत्र चिकीर्षति ॥१७९॥

179. No one desires to do anything without having the capacity for (doing) it, even if he is enjoined (to cook) the uncookable (as in the statement), 'Let him cook black berries.'[1]

NOTES

Here is an illustration which supports that an injunction depends on one's capacity to perform the act enjoined; it consists in the eligibility or capacity of a person (*adhikārigatapravṛttiśaktisāpekṣa, puruṣaśaktyapekṣa*).

1. Sureśvara has stated this illustration in TUBV 2.626 also. "The maxim refers to a thief (who engaged himself) as a cook. His inability to perform the duties, however, lead to

his discovery and arrest. This is intended to teach the folly of undertaking to do some thing quite beyond one's power." (BOETZELAER's note, p. 159).

एवं चेदनपेक्षत्वं विधेः किमिति भण्यते ।
न भावनानपेक्षोऽसौ विधिर्यस्मात्प्रवर्तते ॥१८०॥

180. If this is so, why is it said that injunction (in the Śruti) depends on nothing else, (indeed) because an injunction does not operate when independent of any injunctive force?[1]

NOTES

This is a reply to the possible objection: 'Injunction expects only the capacity of one who is enjoined to act.' Sureśvara again stresses that injunction is not authoritative independently, because it certainly depends on the injunctive force of the words.

1. On the word *bhāvanā* see note (1) on verses 157-158 above.

न भावनान्तरमियं न च मानान्तरं तथा ।
अपेक्ष्याभिधयैकात्म्यमवबोधयति श्रुतिः ॥१८१॥

181. This Śruti text, by (mere) simple affirmation, informs one of the oneness of the Ātman, without expectancy of any other injunctive force,[1] or of any other means of knowing.

NOTES

An objection could be raised thus: 'In the case of a simple affirmation such as *tat tvam asi* also, there is similarly an expectancy as regards the said capacity on account of the acceptance that Veda gives rise to the right knowledge only if there is an eligible person.' To this, the answer is given in the first quarter.

SP is elaborate and useful: In both Vedānta and Veda, there is equal expectancy for the capacity of a person. As regards the capacity of one for activity and the *bhāvanā*, the discrepancy of expectancy arises only in the case of injunctions. Yet one might object: 'Since injunctions are authoritative independently, they do not therefore expect any other means of knowing for their support.' To such an objection Sureśvara replies: A command (*niyoga*) is insentient, so there is the necessity of another means of knowing, for otherwise the capacity in an injunction would not be grasped at all. But in the case of the Ātman the position is different; the Ātman is not the object of any means of knowing because it is self-luminous. The understanding of the meaning (*śaktigraha*) stands to reason. Therefore the Śruti, enlightening the oneness of the Ātman by mere affirmation which is devoid of an injunction does not expect any other means of knowing or the capacity for activity, except one's concentration (*niṣṭhā*) on the Brahman. The Śruti only by its own greatness enlightens the eligible person as regards the oneness of the Ātman.

1. This refers to simple affirmation in Vedānta texts.

अतोऽनपेक्षता युक्ता सर्वदैवाभिधाश्रुतेः ।
अभिधानाभिधेयार्थज्ञानमेव व्यपेक्षते ॥१८२॥

182. Therefore, it is reasonable to accept that simple affirmation in the Śruti is at all times expectant of nothing. It depends only on understanding the thing which is to be conveyed by means of direct expression.

NOTES

This verse concludes that simple affirmations in Vedāntas are different from injunctions.

One may now say: 'If one always holds non-expectancy of simple affirmations in the Vedāntas, there would follow the absence of expectancy as regards the understanding of the meaning of such affirmations also. And in that case even one who knows nothing would desire the cognition of the oneness only on hearing the sentences *tat tvam asi* etc.' The second line of the verse answers this.

The word *anapekṣatva* of simple affirmation in Vedāntas means the *anapekṣatva* of the direct expression (*abhidhāna*) whichever consists in the use of words that are rooted in the accepted convention (*saṁketa*) in respect of their meanings.

ज्ञानक्रिया प्रमातृस्था न यथावस्तुबोधकृत् ।
प्रमेयकर्तृकैवासौ यथावस्त्ववबोधिनी ॥१८३॥

183. The act of knowing, which enlightens one about a thing as it is, does not belong to the knower; that (viz. act of knowing), which enlightens one about a thing as it is, is caused by the object of knowing.[1]

NOTES

It has been established through logical reasoning that Vedāntas are independently authoritative even without that injunction. Now it is proved that knowledge enjoined serves no purpose. See verse 120 above. Also cf. BSB 1.1.4 (P. 18) which questions if knowledge is a *kriyā* : *nanu jñānaṁ nāma mānasī kriyā / na/vailakṣaṇyāt /* . . ., see note on verse 120.

1. Although SP says that the word *prameyakartṛkā* means *mānameyādhina* , no justification is possible.

न चान्यदीयव्यापारे ह्यन्योऽशक्तेर्नियुज्यते ।
न ह्यग्निसाध्ये शोषादौ नियोगो घटतेऽम्भसः ॥१८४॥

184. And[1] no one can be employed to do any activity that can be accomplished by anyone else on account of one's incapacity for it.[2] Indeed, it does not stand to reason that a pitcher of water is employed for the act of drying up (something) etc. which is accomplished by fire.[3]

NOTES

One may ask: 'Even if such a knowledge, viz. *vastutantra-jñāna* may result from mere hearing a sentence like *tat tvam asi*, why not enjoin a person to get to know it?' Here is a reply to the question.

1. The printed edition reads: *na cānyadiya* . . ., but the edition of NKL reads: *na hy anyadiya*. . . .

2. SP states: Although it is possible to enjoin the son in respect of an activity of his father, the injunction is of no use when the son has no independence. This is stressed by the word *hi* used here.

3. The illustration in the second line points out that because of the incapability of one, there is no command given to one.

[One may argue thus: 'In order that the knowledge related to an injunction has a fruit, an injunction is required for getting to know (*pratipattividhi*). This may imply four possibilities: (i) Its fruit is the destruction of difference, (ii) it is the cessation of ignorance, (iii) it is the attainment of the Brahman by the Jīvātman, (iv) something else. The answer is made in verses 185-189.]

ब्रह्मणोऽविद्यया योऽपि स्यादवच्छेद आत्मनः ।
तदवच्छेदविध्वस्तौ न साधनमपेक्षते ॥१८५॥

185. Whatever differentiation is (grasped) between the Brahman and the Ātman owing to ignorance, no injunction[1] is expected for the removal of that (differentiation).

NOTES

Regarding (i) there can be two alternatives: (a) The differentiation in question results from ignorance, or (b) it is natural. If (a), there is no need of an injunction, for knowledge of the oneness gives rise to the destruction of any differentiation.

1. *sādhana* = *vidhi*. (SP)

अनवच्छिन्नयाथात्म्यब्रह्मैकात्म्यादविद्यया ।
अवच्छिन्नवदाभाति क्षेत्रज्ञो रज्जुसर्पवत् ॥१८६॥

186. On account of the oneness of the Brahman whose real nature is not differentiated (from the individual consciousness), the consciousness within an individual[1] only appears to be differentiated by ignorance, like a serpent (appears) in a rope.

NOTES

The alternative (b) under (i) is refuted in this verse.

1. *kṣetrajña* 'one who knows the body', i.e. 'consciousness within an individual'.

न चाविद्यानिरास्यत्र प्रत्यग्याथात्म्यबोधतः ।
साधनं किञ्चिदापेक्ष्यं स्वर्गे यागादिवत्क्वचित् ॥१८७॥

187. (Apart from) knowing the real nature of the Ātman, nothing else is expected in this matter (as the means) for the removal of ignorance on the part of this (Ātman[1]) just as a sacrifice and the like (are sometimes[2] expected) for attaining the heaven.

NOTES

This is an answer to alternative (ii) which is like this: 'Even if one holds that the destruction of the body is produced by the removal of ignorance there is need of knowledge for purposes of removing ignorance. Therefore, in this respect at least an injunction is required.' For refuting this second alternative this reply is given.

1. Cf. *atra pratīci yāvat* in SP.

2. SP holds : *kvacid deśe kāle vā*; but *kāle* alone would convey better sense after understanding *atra* as *pratīci. .* , for *pratyak* implies some *deśa* invariably.

न चापि मुख्यया वृत्त्या साध्येऽसति जगत्यपि ।
किञ्चित्साधनमित्येवं भण्यते लोकवेदयोः ॥१८८॥

188. 'And indeed even in (this) world there is no means which (can accomplish) by its primary operation an object which does not exist (as the end of it)'.————so it is said among the people and in the Veda.

NOTES

Now an answer to the alternative (iii) : 'It is proved that the attainment of the Brahman by the Jīvātman can be achieved by the knowledge enjoined. So an injunction is required in order that one acquires knowledge.' For refuting this alternative is given this verse. Even if the Brahmanhood is attained by knowledge, it does not mean that it is attained by the primary sense of a word. The Brahman is ever-attained in a primary sense, so the Brahman is never attained by any means such as an injunction. It is generally accepted that when *sādhya* in a primary sense does not exist, *sādhana* too does not exist in any worldly dealing. And, therefore, no injunction is possible. (SP) SP clarifies how the general principle in this verse is applicable even in the knowledge of the Brahman.

साध्यं च लोकतः सिद्धमुत्पत्त्यादिचतुष्टयम् ।
प्रमाणस्य न तन्न्याय्यं सिद्धार्थव्यञ्जकत्वतः ॥१८९॥

189. And an object which is to be accomplished in any worldly dealing and is accepted to be four-fold,[1] i.e. it has origin etc., has been already established; but it is not proper to say that an object can be accomplished by a means of knowing since it (the latter) is merely capable of revealing an already existential entity.

NOTES

This is the refutation of alternative (iv) : Any fruit other than that stated in (i)-(iii) would be possible. Origin (*utpatti*), attainment (*āpti*), change (*vikṛti*) and purification (*saṁskṛti*) are attained by an injunction. And a means of knowing can prove a thing which has already come into existence. Therefore no injunction is possible.

1. The four fruits of act are origin, attainment, change and purification. Cf. BUBV 3.3.26, TUBV 2.13, Nais 1.53, BSB 1.1.4 etc.

नाऽऽत्मलाभातिरेकेण व्यञ्जकस्य मनागपि ।
सम्भाव्यतेऽपरं रूपमज्ञातत्वापनोदकृत् ॥१९०॥

190. It is again impossible to think of even a slightly different form of any means of knowledge that exists apart from its being merely a manifestor (or an already existent thing) so that it can be said to remove the condition of being not known.

NOTES

One might postulate: 'After the validity of an injunction in respect of the knowledge resulting from the Śruti (*śābdajñāna*) is refuted, one might urge that the injunction is required for the constant meditation on that knowledge since that would destroy ignorance.' The answer is: Such an injunction is not necessary, since when knowledge arises ignorance gets immediately destroyed.

आत्मासामान्यरूपोत्थं न चाभूत्वोपजायते ।
घटादिज्ञानवज्ज्ञानं भिन्नहेत्वनपेक्षतः ॥१९१॥

191. Without coming into existence, the knowledge which was (already) existing owing to (lit. born of) the peculiar nature of the Ātman, does not arise like the knowledge of a pot etc., because it does not expect any cause (for its coming into existence).

NOTES

It has been stated that an injunction is not required for the sake of knowing, or for constant meditation on it. Yet one may require it for the purpose of knowing the nature of the Brahman. One is then given the following reply.

Knowledge of the Brahman arises from the Ātman itself, it does not depend on anything else. That is to say, knowledge of the Brahman is not an effect; it is not the object of any injunction. Cf. verse 187.

स्थास्न्वनुभवमात्रत्वात्कार्यकारणवस्तुनः ।
अभूतभूतिर्नैवातो युज्यतेऽनुभवात्मनि ॥१९२॥

192. Since the thing which is both the cause and the effect[1] (viz. the Brahman) is merely of the nature of permanent experience, it is not proper to hold in the case of what is of the nature of the experience that there comes into existence one that did not exist.

NOTES

The knowledge is *sthāṇvanubhavātmaka*, the injunction is *abhūtabhūtyātmaka* (*sādhya*). It is stated that an injunction is useful for a thing to be attained but useless for an ever-attained thing (viz. *jñāna*). Knowledge does not expect any cause apart from itself.

1. Here the Brahman is described as *kāryakāraṇavastu* only in the empirical sense, not in absolute sense. Cf. verse 422 below where the Brahman, i.e. the Ātman, is described as *akāryakāraṇa*.

प्रत्यगज्ञानहेतूत्था भावनेयं न तु स्वतः ।
प्रत्यग्याथात्म्यजिज्ञासोः कथं सा विषयो भवेत् ॥१९३॥

193. The injunctive force[1] arises from the cause, viz. ignorance about the Ātman and not of its own. How then can it be an object (to be achieved) for a person who is desirous of knowing the real nature of the individual consciousness.

NOTES

An injunction may be meant either (i) for one who is desirous of knowing the Brahman, or (ii) for one who knows it. In the case of (i), the injunction is prescribed either (a) regarding the means of knowing the Ātman, or (b) for any other purpose. This verse refutes (b); (a) being acceptable.

1. See note (1) on verse 157 above.

क्रियाकारकभेदोऽयमज्ञातैकात्म्यवस्तुनः ।
तज्ज्ञानेऽसावसम्भाव्यस्तद्धेतूच्छित्तिकारणात् ॥१९४॥

194. This distinction between action and that which helps action[1] (arises) out of a thing which has only the oneness (i.e. the Ātman[2]) and has not been known (as such). When it (viz. the Ātman) is known that (viz. distinction) is not possible (to think of) because of the eradication of its cause.[3]

NOTES

The alternative (ii) stated in the note on the previous verse is refuted: Injunction is possible when ignorance persists and causes distinction and the enjoining force. But on the part of one who knows the Brahman, ignorance is already removed, therefore, no injunction is possible.

1. It means *kartṛ* 'agent (of an action)' or *karaṇa* 'a means (of achieving the action)'.

2. The Ātman here refers to the Jīvātman, i.e. the individual consciousness (*pratyagātman*) which is really not different from the Brahman.

3. See next verse referring to ignorance as the cause of distinction.

न चाविद्यासमुच्छित्तिर्ज्ञानोत्पत्त्यतिरेकतः ।
संसारनाशोऽविद्याया नाशान्न व्यतिरिच्यते ॥१९५॥

195. And eradication of ignorance is not possible by anything else than the rise of knowledge (of the oneness of the Brahman and the Ātman). The disappearance of the transmigratory existence is not different from that of ignorance.

NOTES

This is a reply to a possible objection: 'There is no eradication of ignorance, i.e. cause of differentiation. Because if ignorance has not been created, how can the remover thereof be possible in the absence thereof ? If ignorance has been created, it would be not opposed to the transmigratory existence. As the removal of darkness consists in the light of a lamp, there is no sequence between the rise of knowledge and eradication of ignorance.'

One could argue: 'Although destruction of ignorance invariably follows the rise of knowledge, the injunction is yet required for the constant meditation on the oneness of the Brahman and the Ātman for the sake of destruction of products of that ignorance.' This is answered in the second line.

न चाप्यविद्यानाशोऽत्र संसर्गः कारणात्मनि ।
तद्ध्वस्तेर्वस्तुवृत्तत्वान्मृदि लोष्टादिनाशवत् ॥१९६॥

196. Destruction of ignorance is not its merger into the (material) cause (viz. the Ātman), since that merger (of ignorance) consists in the *vastuvṛtta*. '(mere) existence of reality'; it is like merger (lit. destruction) of a lump of clay etc. into clay (which is its material cause).

NOTES

There are two kinds of merger, i.e. *sānvayanāśa* and *niranvayanāśa*. In the case of the former, a product merges into its material cause as a lump of clay merges into clay, its material cause. Hence, merger (destruction) of a lump of clay precedes the appearance of clay, i.e. the remainder. In the case of the latter (viz. *niranvayanāśa*), there remains nothing behind after merger (destruction). This is the case with the merger of ignorance. Because ignorance is not the effect (product) of the Brahman which could be stated as the material cause.

आदाय वास्तवं वृत्तं ज्ञानमज्ञाननाशकृत् ।
वस्तुयाथात्म्यवृत्तेन तमोऽपह्नूयते सदा ॥१९७॥

197. Only on understanding (lit. taking into consideration) the real nature of the thing (viz. the Ātman), (one may hold that) knowledge is the destroyer of ignorance, since then darkness (viz. ignorance) is for ever removed by the (very) nature of the thing as it is.

NOTES

Here is explained how the destruction of ignorance is nothing else than the rise of knowledge of the Ātman.

अज्ञातज्ञापनं तस्माद्विधिरत्रोपपद्यते ।
अकृतस्य क्रिया त्वत्र विधिर्नैवोपपद्यते ॥१९८॥

198. Therefore, it stands to reason that here (in this Śruti statement) there is an injunction that informs one of what is not known; but it cannot be held reasonable (to say that here there is) an injunction regarding doing what is not (previously) done.

NOTES

Cf. verse 115 above.

द्वैविध्यं चाप्यविद्याया न च युक्त्याऽवसीयते ।
ऐकात्म्यमात्रवस्तुत्वादविद्यैकैव युज्यते ॥१९९॥

199. Now as regards the two-fold nature of ignorance, it cannot be concluded (i.e. determined) even by reasoning. Ignorance can reasonably be accepted as unifold, since it pertains (only) to the oneness of the Brahman and the Ātman.

NOTES

'Ignorance can be understood as two-fold; (i) non-grasping of reality (*agraha*) and (ii) grasping the thing (i.e. reality) as otherwise (*anyathāgraha*). The *agraha-ajñāna* is destroyed by the very rise of knowledge and the *anyathāgraha-ajñāna* is destroyed by the knowledge laid down in the Śruti.' This view of some is refuted by the first line. One could determine the nature of ignorance if it really existed apart from the Brahman. If one could discern two distinct objects as a man and a tree then alone one could say that objects are two-fold. Hence it is impossible to speak of two-fold character of ignorance.

The second line refutes the objection: 'Unifold ignorance is impossible because of the absence of reasoning etc.' Because there is complete absence of any other substratum for ignorance, there cannot be any other kind of ignorance. This is supported by the following verse.

प्रमेयभेदभिन्नत्वं ज्ञानानामिव भेदकम् ।
नाविद्याया यतोऽस्तीह द्वैविध्यं तेन दुर्घटम् ॥२००॥

200. Since in the case of ignorance there is no variety of objects to be known as in the case of other knowledges (form and knowledge) which would here be the cause of differentiation, therefore it is difficult to accept the diverse nature of ignorance (in respect of the individual consciousness).

प्रत्यगज्ञानमेवेह तदन्यद्वस्तुकारणम् ।
तदन्यकारणासत्त्वाद्द्वैविध्यं तमसः कुतः ॥२०१॥

201. Here (i.e. in our worldly dealing) ignorance about (the nature of) the individual consciousness is the cause of (awareness of) a thing other than itself. Since there is no cause other than ignorance (about the nature of the individual consciousness), how could there be the two-fold nature of darkness (i.e. ignorance)?

NOTES

The first line repeats the idea of Śaṅkara, i.e. *tam imam adhyāsam avidyākhyaṁ puraskṛtya sarve pramāṇaprameyavyavahārā laukikā vaidikāś ca pravṛttāḥ* (BSB 1.1.1, p. 2). That is to say, we hold other things as existent only because we do not know the real nature of the Ātman.

With the help of the Śruti, *indro māyābhiḥ pururūpa iyate* (the *Ṛgveda* 6.47.18), 'Indra moves in various forms due to his miraculous powers', it is held that ignorance of the individual consciousness is the cause of the non-Ātman world. And the argument against bringing two things at one time by just one thing, i.e. ignorance (primarily), conceals the Ātman and secondly causes the world also; this is justified by the *kulyāpraṇayananyāya* according to which a thing made for some one purpose subserves another purpose also. Cf. *yathā śālyarthaṁ kulyāḥ praṇīyante tābhya eva pānīyaṁ ca pīyate tadvat*/ 'Canals are dug for purposes of bringing water to the paddy field (for the growth of paddy), but their waters are used for drinking purposes also.', quoted from G. A. Jacob, *A Third Handful of Popular Maxims*, Bombay: 1910, p.36).

न चाभ्यासाद्यपेक्षाऽपि स्वतोमुक्तत्वकारणात् ।
न घटादेर्घटत्वादि घटाद्यभ्याससंश्रयम् ॥२०२॥

202. There is again no expectation of constant meditation etc.[1] (on the part of an individual, i.e. individual consciousness) because of its (already) being liberated by itself. (Take, for instance,)[2] the potness of a pot etc. that does not depend on the constant meditation on a pot etc.

NOTES

One may yet argue: 'An injunction is required for constant meditation on knowledge because the liberated nature of the Ātman results from the constant meditation of knowledge.' This possible objection is answered in this verse.

1. The word *ādi* means *yoga* 'physical practices such as *prāṇāyāma*' 'controlling breath'.

2. This illustration is given in order to stress that an ever-liberated being does not expect constant meditation.

न चाविषयविज्ञानमनाकारं च भाव्यते ।
भावकप्रत्यगात्मत्वादाकृतेश्च निषेधतः ॥२०३॥

203. And that which is not an object of (common) knowledge[1] and does not have any form (indeed) cannot be known,

because one who meditates[2] is the individual consciousness itself and because[3] there is a (clear-cut) denial of its having a form.

NOTES

The knowledge with its object and a form such as an eagle is constantly meditated, but knowledge of the Ātman is otherwise; the Ātman knows itself, there is no subject-object relation in this respect. Therefore, no constant meditation for the knowledge of the Ātman is necessary. No injunction is, therefore, required regarding the same.

1. The word *vijñāna* here means *savikalpakajñāna* 'knowledge of object outside the subject' which is to be distinct from the knowledge of the oneness. On *vijñāna* and *jñāna*, see note on verse 112 and the Introduction section 6.

2. The word *bhāvaka* refers to one who repeatedly meditates on the nature of the Ātman.

3. The Śruti to that effect is *aśabdam asparśam arūpam*—(KaṭhU 3.15).

नेन्द्रियेण ग्रहोऽस्यास्ति शब्दाद्यर्थानुपातिना ।
दुःखादिवच्च नैवाऽऽत्मा चितेः स्वार्थैकरूपतः ॥२०४॥

204. The Ātman is not grasped by the (external) sense-organs, which follow (lit. run after) the objects, sound etc. The Ātman is not grasped, like misery etc. also since knowledge[1] is of the same nature as that of its object.

NOTES

Here is denied any possibility that the knowledge of the Ātman is grasped (i) by the external sense-organs, or (ii) by *manas*.

1. *citi* = *cit*. Knowledge consists in the one who knows; here there is no distinction between object and subject.

भावनोपचितं चेतो न च कैवल्यकारणम् ।
तस्यैहैव समुच्छेदात्तद्धेत्वज्ञानहानतः ॥२०५॥

205. And indeed *manas*[1] which is nourished by constant meditation[2] is not accepted as the cause of (bringing about) the

state of the absolute (Ātman), since there is complete negation of itself in the state[3] of the absolute (Ātman) (which proceeds) from abandoning ignorance which causes it (viz. *manas* etc.).

NOTES

But some say that *manas* with repeated meditation laid down in the Śruti is the cause of liberation and so they want an injunction as regards constant meditation on the nature of the Ātman. To them, Sureśvara replies in the first line.

That cause of liberation may be either (i) *upādānakāraṇa* or (ii) *nimittakāraṇa*. The alternative (i) is refuted in the second line of the verse.

1. The word *cetas* is used for *manas*.

2. The word *bhāvanā* has to be understood as *abhyāsa*, i.e. constant thinking about it; cf. the use of the causative of √*bhū* in verse 203 above; also in Śaṅkara's *Mohamudgaraḥ*: *artham anartham bhāvaya nityaṁ nāsti tataḥ sukhaleśaḥ satyam* |

3. The word *iha* is used for *jñānasattvāvasthā*.

स्वकार्यार्थानुगामित्वं भावनाज्ञानकर्मणाम् ।
अकार्यकारणात्मत्वात्कैवल्येऽनुगतिः कुतः ॥२०६॥

206. Constant meditation, knowledge (and) activity follow (i.e. are) in consonance with their own objects (to be known and) to be accomplished. (But) because (the Ātman) is not of the nature of a cause or an effect, how can there be such following on the part of its state of the absolute (Ātman)?

NOTES

Here is refuted the alternative (ii) mentioned in the note on the previous verse.

साक्षादात्मप्रसिद्धौ च नाभ्यासस्तत्फलस्थितेः ।
ज्ञानाभावादसिद्धौ च क्व न्वभ्यासव्यपेक्षणम् ॥२०७॥

207. Since the Ātman is already known directly, there is no need of constant meditation; there (already) exists its fruit; and while (the Ātman is) not known, where could there be any support for constant meditation.

NOTES

An injunction for constant meditation could be reasonable (i) when the Ātman is already directly known (*prasiddha*) or (ii) when the Ātman is not known (*aprasiddha*). Both these alternatives are refuted by the first and the second lines respectively.

आत्मासामान्यरूपोत्थं ज्ञानमज्ञानमात्मनि ।
सकृज्जातं न चेद्धन्ति ज्ञानमेव न तद्भवेत् ॥२०८॥

208. If knowledge which arises from the unique nature of the Ātman is once obtained and it does not remove ignorance on its own part, it would not at all be knowledge.

NOTES

'The knowledge which has been once obtained does not remove ignorance. Therefore an injunction is required for constant meditation.' To such a doubt is given this answer. Because the mutual contradiction between knowledge and ignorance has been established, both cannot co-exist.

सम्यग्ज्ञानं यदाश्रित्य तन्मोहोऽपि तदाश्रयः ।
अबाधितं तमोऽत्रास्त इत्युक्तिर्जडवक्तृका ॥२०९॥

209. Ignorance of that resorting to which there arises right knowledge also resorts to that. The statement that darkness (i.e. ignorance) remains unsublated here (i.e. in the Ātman) is made (only) by a stupid person.

NOTES

An objector may say : 'Ignorance may not necessarily be removed merely by the rise of knowledge but it would be definitely removed by the constant meditation on the knowledge.' To this Sureśvara replies with an illustration. It is never found that darkness (i.e. ignorance) also remains where there is illumination (knowledge).

इत्येवमादि यच्चोक्तं पूर्वमेवातिविस्तरात् ।
तत्कृत्स्नमनुसन्धेयं सर्वविकारहानिकृत् ॥ २१० ॥

210. Thus, whatever has been said before in great detail is all to be borne in mind as that which removes all objections (in respect of an injunction).

NOTES

SP refers *pūrvam uktam* to the earlier refutation of the idea that the Vedāntas have prescribed any injunction in respect of the knowledge of the Brahmaṁ at several places in SV.

सर्वमात्मेत्यतः पश्येदात्मानात्मविभागवित् ।
आत्मा द्रष्टव्य इत्युक्त्या ह्येषोऽर्थोऽत्राभिधीयते ॥२११॥

211. Therefore, knowing the distinction between the Ātman and the non-Ātman, one should see that all (this) is the Ātman; this is the only[1] thing conveyed by the statement, 'The Ātman is to be seen.'

NOTES

This asserts the final position that the sentence *ātmā vā are draṣṭavyaḥ* does not prescribe any action for one but expresses the proposition: 'All this is the Ātman'. The long discussion beginning with verse 95 is concluded here.

1. Cf. SP : *prāg uktam arthāntarāsambhavaṁ hetuṁ kartuṁ hi śabdaḥ.*

सर्वमानप्रसक्तौ च सर्वमानफलाश्रयात् ।
श्रोतव्य इत्यतः प्राह वेदान्तावरुरुत्सया ॥२१२॥

212. (Now) since it becomes necessary to hold the Ātman as the cause of all means of knowing on account of its being the very basis of the results of all means of knowing, (the seer of the Upaniṣad) declared, '(The Ātman has) to be heard about with a desire to declare the Vedānta texts (as the only means of knowing it).

NOTES

The suffix *tavya* in the sentence *ātmā vā are draṣṭavyaḥ* does not intend to 'enjoin' but to 'express' the Ātman as 'worthy of seeing'. Therefore, the meaning of the sentence is that the

NOTES

One could argue : 'It is not proved that the notion about the Ātman that it is a cause and also an effect has originated from ignorance.' To this argument, is this verse a reply. The means of knowing does not put forth an object which is contradictory to the means of knowing, because the nature of being the means of knowing (*pramāpakatva, jñāpakatva*) expects non-contradiction———this is stressed in the second line by the word *hi*.

1. Cf. BU 2.5.19 already cited under verse 229 above.

नैतस्माज्जायते किञ्चिन्नायं जातः कुतश्चन ।
आत्मेत्येवं श्रुतिर्वक्ति कारणादिनिषेधकृत् ॥२४४॥

244. Nothing (else) is born from this (Ātman), nor is this born from anything (else). Thus (lit. this) does the Śruti declare, (thereby) rejecting the cause etc.[1]

NOTES

The Śruti, 'The Ātman has nothing preceding . . .' (BU 2.5.19), does not establish the uniqueness of the Brahman, at the most it may point to its being unrelated to anything else. Therefore there is reference to *na jāyate mriyate vā kadācin nāyam bhūtvā bhavitā vā na bhūyaḥ* (Kath U 2.18), which is the authoritative Śruti (Also cf. BG 2.20).

1. Meaning *kāraṇa*, *kārya* and *kartṛ*.

ज्ञेयं यत्तत्प्रवक्ष्यामि यज्ज्ञात्वाऽमृतमश्नुते ।
अनादिमत्परं ब्रह्म न सत्तन्नासदुच्यते ॥२४५॥

यस्मात्क्षरमतीतोऽहमक्षरादपि चोत्तमः ।
अतोऽस्मि लोके वेदे च प्रथितः पुरुषोत्तमः ॥२४६॥

यो मामेवमसम्मूढो जानाति पुरुषोत्तमम् ।
स सर्वविद्भजति मां सर्वभावेन भारत ॥२४७॥

245-247. I am going to declare that which is the object of the knowledge (and) by knowing which one attains (lit. enjoys) immortality. It is said (i.e. declared in the Śruti) that the highest Brahman is beginningless, and neither existent nor non-existent. Because I am beyond the destructible and beyond also the indestructible, therefore I am widely (*pra*)[1] known as the best of men, both in the world and in the Śruti[2] as well. He who, unperplexed, knows me as the best of men, is a knower of everything and resorts to me in all objects (viz. with all sincerity), O son of Bharata !

NOTES

In this regard, SP points out that Sureśvara takes the support of the Smṛti. It is citations from BG 13. 12, 15. 18-19.

1. Or 'ever'.

2. CU 8. 12. 13 : *sa uttamaḥ . . . puruṣaḥ* and cf. BG 8. 1. 10. 15, 11. 3 referring to *puruṣottama*.

इति वेदात्मनः साक्षाद्वचनं श्रुतिसम्मतम् ।
सर्वान्तर्यामिणः शौरेर्नोपेक्ष्यं तद्भवादृशैः ॥२४८॥

248. Thus is the direct speech of Śauri[1] who himself is Veda and resides[2] within all, it is supported by the Śrutis; therefore, it should not be ignored by those[3] who are like you.

NOTES

The Smṛti passages cited are stated by the lord who is *sarvajña* and *yathārthavaktā* (viz. *āptavacana*); therefore, they are authoritative.

1. The descendent of Śūra clan; this is Śri Kṛṣṇa of MBh, the lord of the song, called BG.

2. Cf. BG 18.61: *iśvaraḥ sarvabhūtānāṁ hṛddeśe 'rjuna tiṣṭhati*; and also the *Māhānārāyaṇa U* 17.5.

3. The followers (i.e. knowers) of the Veda—, Maitreyī was conversant with Vedic lore.

तत्रैवं सति यो मूढः कार्यकारणदर्शनः ।
पराङ्मुखं निवध्यात्तमात्माकृत्स्नत्वदर्शिनम् ॥२४९॥

249. This being the case, the Ātman would turn him away

whosoever ignorant sees (the Ātman as consisting in) the cause and the effect, and (therefore) does not see the wholeness[1] (of the Ātman).

NOTES

After stating the general meaning (purport) of ***brahma taṁ parādādyo'nyatrātmano brahma veda kṣatraṁ taṁ sarvaṁ veda.*** (BU 2.4.6) the literal meaning is briefly stated. Though the Ātman is free from duality, a non-discriminative person sees it as the cause and himself as an effect. The notions of a brahmin, a kṣatriya etc. are falsely seen; they take the person who sees such differences away from the human goal.

1. It refers to 'partlessness'. That is to say: The Ātman cannot be divided into *kārya* and *kāraṇa*. Cf. the Śruti passages to the same effect: *virajaṁ brahma niṣkalam* (Mu U 2.2.9), *tad etat pūrṇam apravarti* (CU 3.12.9).

ब्रह्मेति जातिनिर्देशः क्षत्रसन्निधिकारणात् ।
ब्रह्मजातिः परादध्यादसम्यग्दर्शिनं नरम् ॥२५०॥

250. (In the word) *brahman*, there is the mention of the (brahmin) caste owing to its usage in the vicinity of (the word) *kṣatra*. The (notion of the) brahmin caste would put him away from reality, the one who does not see correctly !

NOTES

This verse reiterates the purport of the previous verse; here Sureśvara supplies the reason to Śaṅkara's commentary, *brahma brāhmaṇajātiḥ*.

यदस्ति तन्न जानाति यन्नेहास्ति तदीक्षते ।
इत्येवमपराधोत्थकोपाविष्टेव बालिशम् ॥२५१॥

कैवल्यात्तं पराकुर्याद्विप्रजातिः पराङ्मुखम् ।
अजातिब्रह्मतत्त्वं मां योऽयं जात्यात्मनेक्षते ॥२५२॥

251-252. The[1] (notion of the) brahmin caste would turn him away from reality[2], who is ignorant[3] that he does not know what[4] exists and sees what does not exist as if full of anger which has arisen out of this fault (of his), (with this thought:) this one is indeed looking upon me as of the nature of caste (etc., even if) I am the truth, viz. the Brahman, and one not having a caste.[5]

NOTES

The word *asamyagdṛṣṭi* 'seeing incorrectly' is further explained.

1. The word *viprajāti* means *brahmajāti*. Cf.
janmanā brāhmaṇo jñeyaḥ saṁskārair dvija ucyate|
vidyayā yāti vipratvaṁ tribhiḥ śrotriya-lakṣaṇam||
(the *Padmapurāṇa*, *sṛṣṭikhaṇḍa* 43. 134, Ānss 131, vol. 3, 1894).

2. The counter-entity of *parākaraṇa* 'taking away', viz. *kaivalya*, is stated.

3. The word *bāliśa* means 'childish person' or 'one who is not good at discrimination.' (SP) Cf. GK 4.83.

4. 'What exists' refers to *ātman* and 'what does not exist', *anātman*.

5. Context wants the idea of caste; though, by pun, one could understand 'not-born (at all)'.

किं तेन न कृतं पापं चोरेणाऽऽत्मापहारिणा ।
योऽन्यथा सन्तमात्मानमन्यथा प्रतिपद्यते ।।२५३।।

253. What sin is not committed by the thief, who is concealing (the real nature of) the Ātman and looks upon the Ātman as different from what it is?

NOTES

Verse 253 is a quotation from MBh 1.68.26, with the difference that the lines of the original verse have been reproduced here in the reverse order. The second line of the verse explains the concept of the 'theft' involved with respect to the Ātman.

यो न वेदाऽऽत्मयाथात्म्यं वेद जात्यादिमत्तया ।
स यद्यतोऽस्तो जातिस्तं परादध्याज्जडं नरम् ।।२५४।।

254. If he, who does not know the real nature of the Ātman (in the expression *brahman*), knows the Ātman as having the sense of a caste etc. (and takes it) apart from this *brahman*), then the (notion of) caste would keep him, the foolish, away (from reality).

सर्वदाऽव्यभिचार्येकं व्यभिचार्यर्थबुद्धिषु ।
यत्तत्वं गम्यते प्रत्यक्तदेवानात्मवस्तुनः ॥२५५॥

255. That is the individual consciousness which is understood[1] as essence (i.e. basic reality), the ever invariable, the one in all cognition of variable objects of consciousness, (apart) from the non-Ātman.

NOTES

An objection may be: 'If the brahmin caste etc. is understood as different from the Ātman, there would result non-acceptance of monism. If it is taken as identical with the Ātman, it would be what, in your opinion, is the non-Ātman.' Sureśvara gives a reply to this.

1. The word *gamyate* is the same as *pratiyate* or *anubhūyate*.

अन्तर्मेयबलाज्ज्ञानं प्रत्यङ्मोहजसंश्रयम् ।
बाधतेऽव्यभिचारित्वाद् व्यभिचारि तमोन्वयम् ॥२५६॥

प्रत्यक्तमोजयाथात्म्यमात्राभिजनहेतुतः ।
कालादौ तदभावोऽतो न ज्ञानस्यापवादकृत् ॥२५७॥

256-257. The knowledge wards away (i.e. sets away or destroys) (ever-) variable cognition associated with (i.e. marked by) darkness (i.e. ignorance) arising from (i.e. related to) infatuation (i.e. ignorance) regarding the (nature of the) individual consciousness, owing to the strength of the object of knowing within oneself (viz. the Ātman), (and) because it is (ever-) invariable. (Now,) in time etc.[1] there is absence of it[2] on account of the origin of their nature (as such and such) only in ignorance about the individual consciousness; therefore, (time etc.) is not the remover (i.e. destroyer) of knowledge[3]

NOTES

If the Ātman (*tat*) is the essence of all, how then is this every other thing (*itara*) set aside as false by knowledge (about the Ātman) arising from the Śruti ? Why is the essence (*tat*) itself not set aside by the well-known time etc., since there is no difference between *tat* and *itara*? To such a doubt a reply is given in 257 (after the doubt above.) The discussion from the previous verse is on *bādhaka-bādhya* relation between knowledge, and time etc. Knowledge, which is invariable, is *bādhaka* owing to *antarmeyabala*. On the other hand, time etc., which is variable, cannot be *bādhaka*. It is *bādhya*, although it is knowledge, since it has arisen from ignorance about the Ātman, the unique real.

1. According to some thinkers, time etc. is 'eternal'. These are notions different from the Ātman—they are false since they originate from ignorance about the Ātman. As to time etc., cf. GK 1.6-9 where nine thinkers regarding the origin of creation are enumerated; they regard the origin as *praṇava, puruṣa, vibhūti, svapnamāyā, icchā, kāla, bhoga, krīḍa* and *svabhāva*.

2. I.e. *antarmeyabala* mentioned in verse 256; thus it refers to the absence of the Ātman in these others postulated by other thinkers apart from it.

3. This is the same as the Ātman.

न बाह्यजव्यपेक्षं हि ज्ञानं बाधकमिष्यते ।
तयोर्मिथो विरोधित्वात्सम्यग्ज्ञानं तमोपनुत् ॥२५८॥

258. They do not consider that cognition as the remover of ignorance which is itself dependent on (some other cognition) produced from an object (whose reality is) disproved. Right knowledge is (accepted as) remover of darkness (i.e. ignorance), as the two[1] are mutually opposed.

NOTES

When knowledge (common knowledge) and time etc. are similar in that both have arisen from ignorance, this difference, viz. one is *bādhaka* and the other *bādhya*, is not proper. However, right knowledge is *bādhaka* because it has not arisen from ignorance and also because it is *antarmeyabala*. For instance, knowledge about silver as silver is *antarmeyabala*, therefore this is right knowledge. But knowledge about conch-shell as silver is not *antarmeyabala* but produced from ignorance, therefore this knowledge is removed (*bādhya*) by right knowledge, viz. *bādhaka*.

1. (a) Right knowledge, viz. that the Ātman is one and only real, and (b) knowledge produced from (i.e. based on) ignorance about the real nature of the Ātman.

[A doubt has arisen accidentally regarding the Ātman as the essence of all.]

आत्मानं यो यथा वेत्ति सम्यग्वा यदि वाऽन्यथा ।
यथादर्शनमेवासौ फलमाप्नोति मानवः ॥२५९॥

इति ब्रह्म तमित्यादेः संक्षेपार्थः समीरितः ।
संसरत्यन्यथाज्ञानात्सम्यग्ज्ञानाद्विमुच्यते ॥२६०॥

259-260. The man who knows the Ātman in a manner which is either right or wrong (lit. otherwise), obtains a fruit according to his perception (of the Ātman). Thus is declared in brief the meaning of the passage *brahma taṁ*. . . Due to false knowledge, men undergo the transmigratory existence; but due to the right knowledge is one freed.

NOTES

Here concludes Sureśvara's commentary on *brahma taṁ parādād yo*...

[In the following two verses, Sureśvara comments on the Śruti passage *idam brahmedaṁ kṣetram ime lokā*. . .*idaṁ sarvaṁ yad ayam ātmā*.]

अपोदितत्वाद्ब्रह्मादिदर्शनस्येति किं पुनः ।
द्रष्टव्यमित्यतो वक्ति त्विदं ब्रह्मेति नः श्रुतिः ॥२६१॥

261. (One may ask:) "Now that the vision of the brahmin caste etc.[1] is (already) blamed[2], what again is recommended to be perceived ?" Therefore (in order to answer the question) the Śruti text declares to us, '(All) this is the Brahman.'

NOTES

Beginning with a question in the first line, the verse affirms the purport of the Vedānta.

There are three *itis* in this verse (which are marked by (a), (b) and (c) in my translation.) The first *iti* indicates that 'if the vision . . . is thus blamed.' The second *iti* indicates that 'this is the purpose'. And the third *iti* indicates a quotation in my translation.

1. The word 'etc.' indicates *kṣatra, lokas, devas, bhūtas* which are described in BU 2.4.6.

2. Cf. verses 250-254 above.

प्रत्यक्त्वेन य आभाति प्रत्यग्बुद्धिप्रमाणकः ।
तावन्मात्रैकयाथात्म्यं ब्रह्मेत्युक्तं प्रतीयताम् ॥२६२॥

262. "The Brahman is the true nature of only that one who appears (in a body) as the individual consciousness and is the perceiver of the individual's awareness[1] 'I am this'."

NOTES

This is reiteration of the affirmation in the Śruti sentence, in a clearer form.

1. The word *buddhi* is translated here as awareness so as to indicate that there may not be reference to any object outside.

एवं श्रोतव्य आत्माऽयं समाप्तः श्रवणे विधिः ।
अथ मन्तव्य इत्यस्य प्रपञ्चः पर उच्यते ॥२६३॥

263. In this way is this Ātman to be heard. Thus is complete (our discussion of) the injunction in respect of hearing (about the Ātman.) Now hereafter is stated an elaborate explanation[1] of the injunction, viz. '(The Ātman) is to be meditated on'.

NOTES

Verses 263-266 are the introductory part of the discussion on BU 2.4.7. In earlier portion, there was merely a statement or report about the purport of the Śruti passage. Hereafter, there is reasoning about the same in a manner following the Śruti (*śrutyanusārī tarka*).

1. By elaborate explanation Sureśvara means a detailed examination of the illustration in the passages to follow.

नामरूपादिसम्भिन्नं जगदेतत्कथं पुनः ।
आत्मैव सर्वमित्येवं द्रष्टुं शक्यमिहाञ्जसा ॥२६४॥

264. (Objection :) How could it be logical[1] thus[2] to look upon (i.e. accept) this entire world, marked by (i.e. made up of) name, form etc., as the Ātman ?

NOTES

The objector means : "The Śruti 'All this is the Ātman' is contradictory to the direct perception etc."

1. Cf. verse 266 below for the word *añjasā* 'logically' or 'clearly'.

2. In the manner shown in the preceding portion which has brought out the purport of the Śruti; cf. *iheti nāmavyavahārabhūmir uktā.* (SP)

अव्यावृत्तविसंवादिप्रत्यग्धीव्याप्तिकारणात् ।
एतद्विरुद्धबुद्धीनामेवमेव हि शक्यते ॥२६५॥

265. (Reply :) (This is so possible) because the individual intelligence, (in reality, the individual consciousness itself) which is not variable and not contradictory pervades (all that is namable etc.) Only this[1] (awareness) is possible in the case of those whose intellect is opposed to (the cognition of) this (world mentioned in the previous verse).

NOTES

The first line is a reply to the objection raised in the previous verse. The second line justifies how the first line is a suitable reply. SP holds that this is the reply to the possible objection that the cognition, namely "all this world is only sentiency" does not arise in the case of persons like us. Thus, the verse brings out the contrast between those who are ignorant of reality and those who are the perceivers of it.

1. SP regards that the word *etat* refers to *nāmarūpasambhinnajagaddvaita* and constitutes compound with *viruddha*, meaning 'opposed to this world which is divided into name, form etc.' But it appears that *etat* indicates that which has preceded, viz. *avyāvṛttavisaṁvādipratyak*, and so here it refers to *vyāvṛttavisaṁvādipratyagdhiḥ*.

व्यभिचारिषु बोधेषु बोधोऽव्यभिचारवान् ।
तत्प्रमाणार्पितो मेयो ग्रहीतुं शक्यतेऽञ्जसा ॥२६६॥

266. It is possible to understand (lit. grasp) the object of knowing clearly (i.e. logically) when it is grasped on the authority of that cognition which (though) among many that are variable, does not vary.

NOTES

The verse aims to point out that it is possible for persons like us also to understand the uniqueness of the Ātman and sentiency of the world, not only for the wise.

[There is now a discussion on generality and particularity and it will continue up to verse 274.]

यथा दुन्दुभिशब्दत्वसामान्यादुत्थितान्पृथक् ।
नाऽऽदातुं शक्नुयात्कश्चिद्विशेषानसिकोशवत् ॥२६७॥

तद्वदात्मातिरेकेण नाऽऽत्मीयार्थो मनागपि ।
यतः समीक्षितुं शक्यस्तेनासौ रज्जुसर्पवत् ॥२६८॥

267-268. Just as nobody would be able to grasp (lit. take up) particular notes which have arisen (from a drum) separately (only) from sound in general, like a sword (which is covered) in a sheath; in the same way, (it is not possible)[1] for the Ātman to grasp even a single object (*manāk*)[2] apart from the Ātman itself; since (this is so) it is possible to see it (viz. the Ātman) just as (one sees), the rope-serpent.[3]

NOTES

The words 'when a drum is being beaten' indicate the nature of sound (*śabdatva*) and particular external sounds which have arisen from the drum are different from it (viz. sound).

1. This is the repetition of *nādātuṁ śakyaḥ*
2. The word *manāk* literally means 'even a little'.
3. The well-known example of *anirvacanīyakhyāti*; cf. verses 236 and 245 above.

विशेषैरन्वयो नापि सामान्यान्वयवत्क्वचित् ।
सामान्यस्याविशेषत्वान्नातः सामान्यधीग्रहः ॥२६९॥

विशेषैरन्वयो नो चेदिभाखुव्यक्तिवन्मिथः ।
खण्डवत्स्याद्विशेषादौ यत्सामान्यमितीरितम् ॥२७०॥

269-270. Nor also (is it possible for the Ātman) to be associated with a number of particularities, like generality, for generality has no particularities. Therefore, there is no understanding (the Ātman) as generality. If there is distinction between generality and particularity as between an elephant and a rat, then what is called generality will be like parts of different particularities.

NOTES

One could argue : 'The generality-particularity relation is found in the illustration, so the same relation should be found in the illustrated; because the illustration is based on equality of both.' In order to refute this, one may assume that (i) generality is identical with particularity, or (ii) generality is different from particularity. But here, (i) is not possible. Like the identity of particularities with generality, identity of particularity with generality cannot be found anywhere in respect of the Ātman, as the Ātman who is the basis of all imaginations is not associated with all particularities which are imagined.

द्विष्ठत्वादन्वयस्यापि व्याप्यव्यापकयोर्मिथः ।
व्यतिरेकमतो मुक्त्वा मिथो व्याप्तिर्न सिध्यति ॥२७१॥

271. Since (what we call) association is related to (two) different particulars, the relationship of concomitance between

two particulars cannot be obtained if we leave out the notion of mutual difference (between the pervaded and the pervasive).

NOTES

After refuting in verses 269-270, the assumption that generality and particularity are identical or different, Sureśvara anticipates another possible argument which pertains to *vyāpti* 'concomitance' between the two and proceeds to refute the same. The particular is *vyāpya* (*vyāpta*) 'less pervasive'. But unless there is difference between them, there can be no *vyāpti*. The relation in the form of *vyāpti* has the nature of staying on the two, and it expects the difference. Therefore, there is no *vyāpti* in the absence of any difference between the two, which has been already shown. Nor is there any other relation between the two, the generality-particularity relation is purely imaginary.

प्रत्यग्बोधानिरस्तोऽर्थः प्रत्यग्वन्न हि सिध्यति ।
न चाभावमुखोऽनात्मा नान्वयेनाप्यतो दृशि ॥२७२॥

272. A thing which is not denied by the knowledge of the individual consciousness cannot indeed (be proved to) exist like the individual consciousness. Therefore, there does not exist the non-Ātman whether of the nature of non-existence or as related to the Ātman by *anvaya*.

प्रत्यङ्मात्रैकरूपत्वादात्मा नानात्मतां स्वतः ।
सहते नापि चानात्मा स्वार्थादन्यत्र सिध्यति ॥२७३॥

273. Since the Ātman is merely of the nature of individual consciousness, it does not allow any notion of the non-Ātman of itself. And the non-Ātman also does not get established except in itself.

NOTES

One may raise a doubt that even if the method of *anvayavyatireka* cannot properly be conceived in respect of the Ātman and the non-Ātman, *anvayavyatireka* of the Ātman with the non-Ātman is possible because of the vicinity of the latter. Sureśvara answers this possible objection in this verse.

अनात्मवस्तुनः प्रत्यक्प्रत्यक्त्वान्नातिरिच्यते ।
पराङ्नान्वेति चाऽऽत्मानं व्यतिरेकात्मकत्वतः ॥२७४॥

274. The individual consciousness cannot exist outside the non-Ātman, because it is always its (i.e. of then non-Ātman) individuality. The non-Ātman (also) cannot co-exist with the Ātman owing to its nature consisting in its difference from the Ātman.

NOTES

This verse shows how the Ātman and the non-Ātman appear to be different and yet co-exist. In reality, one cannot make the Ātman from the non-Ātman. And yet the non-Ātman cannot be shown to be related to the Ātman by the method of *anvayavyatireka*.

दुन्दुभ्यन्वितशब्दस्य सर्वत्राव्यभिचारतः ।
पुंस्प्रयत्नादिलब्धात्मव्यभिचारिरिवात्मसु ॥२७५॥

275. Owing to the invariable occurrence of the sound connected with a drum, (one grasps the common character[1] of the sound) in the notes of varying nature that have come into being thanks to the effort of some man etc.

NOTES

Sureśvara introduces the reason for grasping the common nature of the sound (*śabdatva*); cf. verse 267 above.

1. Cf. *prakṛte vākye sāmānyopādānam iti śeṣaḥ* (SP)

उच्चनीचाविभेदेषु मिथः स व्यभिचारिषु ।
दुन्दुभिध्वनिरेवैकः सर्वत्राव्यभिचारवान् ॥२७६॥

276. The sound of a drum alone is unvarying among all the mutually varying differences such as high, low etc.

NOTES

Sureśvara aims to stress that generality resides among variable different particulars.

दुन्दुभिध्वनिसामान्यव्यतिरेकेण तेन ते ।
निरात्मका न शक्यन्ते तद्विशेषाः समीक्षितुम् ॥२७७॥

277. Therefore, particularities of the notes of a drum are not possible to think of (lit. see) as having their own character (which is) different from the common character, viz. (they are) the sound produced from the drum.

NOTES

Here concludes the comment on *sa yathā dundubher hanyamānasya na bāhyāñ śabdāñ śaknuyād grahaṇāya.*

दुन्दुभिध्वनिरित्येतत्कुतो लब्धं विशेषणम् ।
दुन्दुभेर्ग्रहणेनेति लब्धमेतद्विशेषणम् ॥२७८॥

278. (Objection:) Whence is the distinguishing attribute[1], viz. the sound of a drum, obtained ? (Reply:) This distinguishing attribute is obtained from the use of (the word) 'of the drum.'

NOTES

An objector might say : 'In the words, 'when a drum is being beaten . . . ', there is mention only of a drum, the distinguishing attribute of the drum, viz. the sound, is not mentioned. What leads you to use it then?' To this Sureśvara replies : It is possible to understand the distinguishing attribute from the remainder of the sentence (*vākyaśeṣa*). Indeed there is no understanding of any particular sound possible when only the stick is mentioned, i.e. the *dundubhi* is uttered; and a sound in general is indicated (*lakṣita*) by the word *dundubhi*, and the distinguishing attribute, i.e. the sound (in general) is to be obtained from the (other) word *hanyamānasya* 'being beaten.'

1. On language level, the word *viśeṣaṇa* means 'adjective' but here it means 'distinguishing attribute'.

दुन्दुभेस्तु रवा एत इत्येवं ग्रहणे सति ।
गृहीतास्तद्विशेषाः स्युस्तेषां तादात्म्यकारणात् ॥२७९॥

279. When there is the grasping (of the sense) that 'these are the notes of the drum', then their particularities are also understood on account of the fact (lit. reason) that they are of the same nature.

भेर्याघातग्रहाद्वाऽपि तद्विशेषग्रहो भवेत् ।
वीरादिरससंयुक्तो दुन्दुभ्याघात उच्यते ॥२८०॥

280. Or,[1] by grasping (or, stopping) the beating of a drum, one can grasp (or, stop) the particularities. The[2] beating of a drum is always said to be associated with *rasas*[3] beginning with *vira*, (viz. the heroic).

NOTES

This is the comment on the sentence, *dundubhyāghātasya vā śabdo gṛhītaḥ*.

1. Or, by grasping intermediate generality in the form of the common nature of the sound, there is grasping of its particularities. This is an alternative to what is stated in the preceding verse.

2. This is the explanation of 'the beating of a drum'. This sound of a war-drum etc. which is a symbol of one of nine *rasas* 'emotional contents' and is heard in the battle etc. is known as the beating of a drum. When the sound is heard, its particularity, viz. the *rasa*, is also understood because both are of the same nature.

3. The nine *rasas* are *śṛṅgāra*, *hāsya*, *karuṇa*, *raudra*, *vira*, *bhayānaka*, *bibhatsa*, *adbhuta* and *śānta*; cf. the *Nāṭyaśāstra* 6.15: *śṛṅgārahāsyakaruṇaraudravirabhayānakāḥ* / *bibhatsādbhutasaṁjñau cety aṣṭau nāṭye rasāḥ smṛtāḥ* //
And later the ninth *rasa*, i.e. *śānta*, is added in the *Kāvyālaṁkārasārasaṁgraha* 4.4 : *bibhatsādbhutaśāntāś ca nava nāṭye rasāḥ smṛtāḥ* //

उपलब्धोऽस्ति सन्कुम्भो लम्बोष्ठो देशकालवान् ।
पूर्वपूर्वातिरेकेण नोत्तरोऽर्थोऽनुभूयते ॥२८१॥

एवं चिदन्वयात्सर्वस्तदध्यस्तः समीक्ष्यते ।
सामान्यं वा विशेषो वा चिदसम्बोधहेतुतः ॥२८२॥

281-282. The existing jug (pitcher) with its portruding brim (lit. lip) is always grasped as related to time and place, but a thing of each later (moment and place) is not experienced as apart from it of each previous moment. In the same way, all that on which is superimposed sentiency, whether common character or particular, may be seen on account of its co-existence with sentiency and (also) due to the non-knowing of sentiency.

NOTES

After introducing the illustration, viz. *dundubhes tu grahaṇena dundubhyāghātasya vā śabdo gṛhītaḥ* (verses 279 and 280), Sureśvara clarifies the illustrated (*dārṣṭāntika*) as he has already done so in verses 267 and 268 above.

The objection may be : 'If that which has to be enlivened (*cetya*) does not exist, apart from sentiency (*cit*), how can one think of *vyatireka* relation between them?' To such an objection does Sureśvara reply in verse 282: In reality there is no difference between *cetya* and *cit*; however, generality etc. are superimposed on *cit* owing to ignorance; and there appears *cetya*.

प्रत्यग्रूपस्य संसिद्धौ प्रतीचोऽन्यत्र कारणम् ।
अनात्मवत्तदप्यात्मविशेषणतया भवेत् ॥२८३॥

283. There[1] is no reason other than the individual consciousness for proving the existence of the individual consciousness and, like[2] all the non-Ātman, that[3] (viz. the cause, the individual consciousness) also would be (established) as the distinguishing attribute of the Ātman.

NOTES

1. A doubt may arise : 'If the non-Ātman appears as the sentient Ātman, that Ātman also would appear as something else like a lamp. Then there would result infinite regress.' To this doubt is there an answer in the first line of this verse.

2. In proving the non-Ātman, there is a certain proof for its existence in the form of a knower.

3. A possible objection is : 'Since you accept something else (viz. a knower etc.) to prove the existence of the non-Ātman, it means that you give up the theory that the Ātman proves all, viz. a knower etc. exist apart from the Ātman.' The reply is that, what proves the non-Ātman, in the form of a knower, can be said to prove the Ātman only as subsidiary, for the Ātman alone has assumed the nature of it. Therefore, there is no abandoning of the theory.

कर्तृत्वकञ्चुको यद्वदात्माऽनात्मानमीक्षते ।
कूटस्थदृष्टिमात्रत्वान्न तथाऽऽत्मानमीक्षते ॥२८४॥

284. As the Ātman which has put on (viz. assumed) a robe[1] of the character of an agent sees any non-Ātman in the same way, it does not see itself, since the Ātman is of the nature of immutable seeing power alone.

NOTES

Sureśvara has the following passage in mind : *yatra hi dvaitam iva bhavati tad itara itaraṁ jighrati . . .* (BU 2. 4. 14)

1. On the word *kañcuka*, cf. TUBV 2.314; Nais 3.60; this is a technical term in the Kashmir Śaivism.

संहतो गम्यतेऽनात्मा प्रत्यक्षेण यथा सदा ।
गम्यतेऽसंहतस्तद्वदात्मा प्रत्यग्धियाऽऽत्मना ॥२८५॥

285. As one knows by direct perception that the non-Ātman is ever made up of parts[1], so does one know by the knowing principle within[2] that the Ātman is not made up of parts.

NOTES

An objection may arise: 'Since it is possible to assume that the Ātman is a knower etc., it may be said that the Ātman cannot be accepted as ever immutable seeing power.' To this is a reply given : As the non-Ātman, which is gross and accompanied by other objects, is known by direct perception, so is the Ātman, which is subtle and free from action, known by sentiency itself but not by anything outside itself, for that thing does not exist.

1. The word *saṁhata* means 'that which is of the nature of a collection' and is a synonym of the word *saṁghāta*. On this see SK 17: *saṁghātaparārthatvāt triguṇādiviparyayād adhiṣṭhānāt / puruṣo'sti bhoktṛbhāvāt kaivalyārtham pravṛtteś ca //* Here Sureśvara refers to the Sāṁkhya notions of *saṁghāta*, *sthūla* and *sūkṣma* which are the basis of the notion of *saṁghāta*. He rejects these notions perhaps on the support of GK 3.10: *saṁghātaḥ svapnavat sarva ātmamāyāvisarjitaḥ /*

2. *pratyagdhi* is the same as *pratyagātman.*

[Verses 286-289 correspond to BUB 2.4.9 : *anekadṛṣṭāntopādānam iha sāmānyabahutvakhyāpanārtham / aneke hi vilakṣaṇāś cetanācetanarūpāḥ sāmānyaviśeṣāḥ / teṣāṁ pāramparyagatyā yathaikasmin mahāsāmānye' ntarbhāvaḥ prajñānaghane kathaṁ nāma pradarśayitavya iti / dundubhiśaṅkhavīṇāśabdasāmānyaviśeṣāṇāṁ yathāśabdatve 'ntarbhāvaḥ / evaṁ sthitikāle tāvat sāmānyaviśeṣāvyatirekād brahmaikatvaṁ śakyam avagantum /* Śaṅkara restricts his statement to the reason why many illustrations are given. But Sureśvara goes further, viz. he mentions why it is necessary to state the reason.]

दार्ष्टान्तिकार्थासम्भित्तेरेकेनैव कृतार्थतः ।
दृष्टान्तेन बहूनां तु किमर्थोक्तिरितीर्यते ॥२८६॥

286. One might object : 'Since there is no variety in the illustrated, one illustration is sufficient to prove the point; why is it then that the point is stated by means of many illustrations ?' —therefore, it is (now) said (in reply) :

NOTES

An objection is raised : 'Though there are many illustrations mentioned such as *dundubhi*, *śaṅkha* and *vīṇā* (BU 2.4.7,8 and 9), the illustrated is one, viz. the Ātman alone exists everywhere. Therefore, merely by one illustration can be proved the illustrated; it is useless to state many illustrations !'

महासामान्य एकस्मिन्विशेषाणामशेषतः ।
विलयः स्यात्कथं नाम व्यावृत्तान्वयरूपिणाम् ॥२८७॥

287. How can there be a merger in one great generality of all the distinguishing attributes which are of the forms mutually distinguished and related ?

NOTES

The reply to the question in verse 286 continues up to verse 289. The seer of the Upaniṣads has employed three different illustrations in order to state the merger, in order, of many distinguishing attributes, generality and both of them into the unique Brahman, which occupies the place of the great generality.

महासामान्यदृष्टान्तो दौन्दुभो रव उच्यते ।
सामान्येतररूपस्य दुन्दुभ्याघात इष्यते ॥२८८॥

288. The sound of a drum is called the illustration for the great generality (and) the beating of a drum is called (lit. desired to be, the illustration) of the form other than generality.

NOTES

Now Sureśvara further clarifies the significance of the three illustrations. By the mention of the drum, the seer points to generality which consists in 'sound' and persists in every particular note that arises from the beating of a drum. It can therefore be the illustration for 'great generality', viz. the Brahman which persists in every particular thing of which it is also the origin. And when the seer refers to the beating of a drum, i.e. to some particular note produced from it, he has in mind some particular note that corresponds to any particular (so-called) product of the Brahman. The *kārya-kāraṇa* relation, 'the relation between the origin and its product(s)' is in both the illustration and the illustrated only the product of imagination, i.e. unreal.

बाह्यानिति तथाचोक्तिर्विशेषाणां तु केवलम् ।
इत्युक्तार्थप्रसिद्ध्यर्थमित्युदाहरणत्रयम् ॥२८९॥

289. And the expression, '(to) the external (notes) (in the objective case)' refers only to the particular notes. The three

illustrations (are related), therefore, only for establishing the matter (already) stated.

NOTES

In keeping with three illustrations there are three, i.e. particular (*viśeṣa*), species (*sāmānya*, *sāmānyetara*, *avāntarasāmānya*) and genus (*mahāsāmānya*). Particular is some particular note of a drum, species is the sound of a drum (*dundubhiśabdatva*) and genus is sound (*śabdatva*). Hence, as all particular notes of a drum are first understood as 'the sound of a drum' and then (later) as 'sound', so all things are related first to individual consciousness and then to the Brahman.

अन्वयव्यतिरेकाभ्यामभाववपुषाऽथवा ।
सद्धीगम्याद्बहिरुग्वस्तु न मानेनावसीयते ॥२९०॥

290. Neither by the method of *anvayavyatireka*, nor by (a means in) the form of non-existence is the existent within ascertained. Indeed, (it is understood) only by experience that it exists.

षष्ठ्यर्थासम्भवोऽतः स्याद्द्वितीयासम्भवात्सतः ।
यथा सति तथा विद्यात्प्रतीच्यनन्यमानके ॥२९१॥

291. In the case of the individual consciousness, for (understanding) which there is no means other (than itself), one should get to know in the same way as in the case of an existent thing. (One understands that) there is the impossibility of the meaning conveyed by the genitive[1] owing to the absence of the second existential entity.

NOTES

This is an answer to the following argument which is possible. If particularity and generality are identical, what follows ? When there do not exist many individuals, particularity and generality cannot be related. So, the nature of generality and particularity cannot be proved in the case of the Brahman.

1. It is impossible to think of any relation between the Brahman and any other thing, since in grammar the genitive case becomes helpful to express two things existent. In the case of the Brahman the use of genitive case or suffix is very naturally precluded.

सामान्यभेदरूपाणां विशेषाणामशेषतः ।
महासामान्य एकत्र भूयसां स्याद्यथा तथा ॥२९२॥

मिथोभिन्नपदार्थानां नामरूपक्रियात्मभिः ।
स्थूलाद्यनभिसम्बन्धे कार्यकारणरूपिणाम् ॥२९३॥

292-293. As each and every of many particularities which are of the nature of the various generality finally exists together in one great generality, so the different things which are distinct in the nature of name, form and function (and) which are also of the nature of the cause and the effect, (exist finally in the Brahman) which has no connection with the gross etc.

NOTES

The discussion on the illustration is concluded.

सूक्ष्मताव्यापिते ज्ञेये भूम्यादेरुत्तरोत्तरम् ।
प्रत्यगात्मावसानेषु पूर्वपूर्वप्रहाणतः ॥२९४॥

नामादीनि च तत्त्वानि प्राणान्तानि तथाऽऽत्मनि ।
पूर्वपूर्वप्रहाणेन यान्त्यस्तं केवलाद्वये ॥२९५॥

294-295. Of (the elements,) earth etc., each preceding one gives up its own nature and is merged into each succeeding one and finally ends in the individual consciousness (which is) the object of knowing and (which is) marked by subtlety. The Truths beginning with name and ending with *prāṇa* get merged into the absolute non-duality, each preceding one giving up (its own nature and merging into the more and more subtle).

NOTES

Sureśvara takes the support of Śaṅkara's view, viz. all modifications merge into the individual consciousness in order among *pṛthivī*, *ap*, *tejas*, *vāyu*, *ākāśa*, *ātman*—each succeeding one is more subtle than its preceding one. Sureśvara takes the support of CU. 7.25.1ff., cf. verse 98 above.

दृष्टान्तत्रितयं तावत्स्थितिकाल उदाहृतम् ।
महासामान्यवत्प्रत्यक्सर्वानात्माप्ययः स्वतः ॥२९६॥

[Now follows an explanation of the illustrations in BU 2.4. 10 : *sa yathārdraidhāgner abhyāhitāt pṛthag dhūmā viniścaranti*, it continues up to verse 303.]

296. As for the three aspects of illustration[1], they are mentioned with reference to the time of sustenance (of other existent objects), since the individual consciousness is itself, like the great generality, the (place of) merger of all the non-Ātman.[2]

NOTES

1. *dṛṣṭāntatritaya* should not be three illustrations but possibly the three aspects of the illustration (viz. *mahāsāmānya*, *sāmānya* (*itara=avāntara*) and *viśeṣa*). On this see note on verse 289.

2. This is a statement of the purport of the three aspects of the illustrations : As the existential particularities, viz. the non-Ātman, culminate into but one existence, the individual consciousness, nothing else remains after the merger into it.

स्थितिकाले यथैकात्म्यं शक्यते ज्ञातुमञ्जसा ।
यथोक्तन्यायतस्तद्वदुत्पत्तावपि शक्यते ॥२९७॥

297. As it is possible to know the real nature of the Ātman (only) clearly at the time of sustenance (of other existent objects), so is it possible to know it at the time of its origin, with the help of the manner (already) stated.

NOTES

Now, Sureśvara states in brief the purport of BU 2.4.10.

धूमार्चिर्विस्फुलिङ्गादि यथापूर्वं विभागतः ।
अग्निरेव न धूमादिभेदः कश्चन लक्ष्यते ॥२९८॥

प्राणलोकादिरप्येवमनात्मा प्राग्विभागतः ।
अपूर्वानपरानन्तप्रत्यगात्मैव केवलः ॥२९९॥

298-299. Smoke,[1] flame, sparks etc. are, before separation[2], nothing but fire (and) no distinction like smoke etc. can be observed, in the same way,[3] the non-Ātman, like *prāṇa*, world etc. is (before separation) nothing but the individual consciousness which is only one and does not have any preceding, any succeeding and an end.

NOTES

1. This is the literal meaning of the illustration stated in BU 2.4.10.
2. This refers to the origin (*janma*).
3. The illustrated is stated.

एकजातौ हि भिन्नानां शब्दानां शब्द एव तु ।
दृष्टमैक्यं न भिन्नानां भिन्नजातौ तथेति चेत् ॥३००॥

धूमादिभेदभिन्नानां यथैकत्वं विभावसौ ।
नामरूपादिभिन्नानामैकात्म्यं तद्वदात्मनि ॥३०१॥

300-301. If one were to object, 'one notices (i.e. grasps) the identity of different words with word when all of them belong to the same category; whereas, if they belong to the different categories, the case is not the same'; (we reply), 'as particulars like smoke etc. which are distinct from one another on account of distinction (among them) have (but) oneness in (i.e. with) fire, so is there identity of different things like name, form etc. with the Ātman.'

NOTES

In order to prove the other purport of BU 2.4.10 than that stated in verse 297 the objection is raised : 'The identity of its distinguishing attributes with the sound can be seen not like the case of things belonging to different categories such as a pot etc. in the fragrant herb etc. Therefore the identity of the world made up of different things such as name etc.

with the Ātman, for they belong to different categories.' The reply refers to both the illustration and the illustrated.

बोधाविशेषादथवा भेद एव न विद्यते ।
कार्यकारणयोस्तत्त्वमुभयोरविलक्षणम् ॥३०२॥

302. Or, perhaps, on account of the non-distinction in realization, the difference (between objects) does not exist. The nature of the two, i.e. the cause and the effect, is not varied in characteristics[1].

NOTES

The mention of 'different things' in the preceding verse implies acceptance of various reality. This is explained away here in the verse. Sureśvara asserts that the different things are nothing but sentiency and, as such, there is no mutual exclusion among them. Indeed, we mention them as causes and their effects; however, they are but one, viz. the individual consciousness.

1. Meaning 'does not have different characteristics'.

स्वार्थसाधनयत्नादीननपेक्ष्योत्सृजेद्यथा ।
धूमादीन्हुतभुक्तद्वत्प्राणादीन्प्रत्यगीश्वरः ॥३०३॥

303. As the fire would give out smoke etc. without any regard for the effort for the means of its own existence, so does the lord[1], the individual consciousness, would give rise to *prāṇa* etc.

NOTES

This verse is in answer to a possible objection which can be stated thus : 'If the individual consciousness is assumed to be a cause, there must be an effect, because one, who acts after having thought about the action, does not undertake any activity that does not bear any effect. Also one cannot do without any means, or the procedure, for attaining the effect. It should therefore follow that the individual consciousness abandons its nature of being one whose desire is fulfilled (*āptakāma*). Indeed, thinking about some effect to follow and *āptakāmatva* are mutually contradictory.' Cf. GK 1.9 : *devasyaiṣa svabhāvo 'yam āptakāmasya kā spṛhā.*

1. *pratyagiśvara*=*pratyagātman*, since the individual consciousness completely controls the creation around itself.

श्रोतव्यः श्रुतिवाक्येभ्य इत्यत्राऽऽशङ्क्यते यतः ।
प्रयत्नानन्तरः शब्दोऽनित्यः कुम्भादिवद्भवेत् ॥३०४॥

इत्यस्य परिहारार्थं निःश्वासोदाहृतिस्त्वियम् ।
अप्रयत्नोत्थितो वेदो नित्यः स्याद्व्योमवत्स्वतः ॥३०५॥

304-305. Since a doubt may be entertained as regards the Śruti sentences, '(The Ātman) is to be known (lit. heard) from the Śruti passages,', viz. that a word follows the effort (of a speaker) and therefore it would be non-eternal, like any pitcher etc.[1]; therefore, in order to answer it away, there is this statement in the Śruti of the *niḥśvāsa* ('breath' of the great being)[2]. Indeed, the Veda has arisen without any effort (of anyone) and is therefore by its own nature (*svataḥ*) eternal, like the sky.

NOTES

The argument proceeds from the notion that the Veda was made by the lord and must, therefore, be non-eternal like the statement of persons (like the Buddha—SP) as it would be dependent on some one's efforts.

1. The axiom is : Whatever is produced is perishable (non-eternal).

2. The refutation is clarified further : The Veda is not non-eternal because the Veda is manifested from the highest without any effort, just as the sky which only seems to be produced as the sky in a pot. In reality, it has ever been existent; there is nothing produced. The Veda is, by nature, eternal.

[The discussion on *niḥśvasita* continues up to verse 312.]

अबुद्धिपूर्वकत्वाच्च यथावस्त्वनुरोध्यपि ।
बुद्धिवन्नाप्रमाणत्वं वेदस्येहोपपद्यते ॥३०६॥

306. Since the Veda is not preceded by any deliberate thinking it cannot be considered as unauthoritative, like human intellect in our world (*iha*), even though it follows (the nature of) the thing as it is[1].

NOTES

This is an answer to the objection regarding *kṛtakatva* of the Veda that leads to its *anityatva*. The adjective of the Veda *yathāvastvanurodhī* would invite further difficulty. It is held that any worldly knowledge is true if and only if it conforms to its object as it is : The truth of this knowledge depends upon the proper grasping (*niścaya*) of the nature of the objects by the intellect (*buddhi*). As such, the information about the Brahman which the Veda gives, must be grasped only by intellect—this constitutes some efforts of someone before the Veda was created. That is to say : We must accept the Veda as non-eternal. Sureśvara firmly asserts that this objection cannot arise, simply because the Veda is the breathing out of the great being—it is not preceded by any thought. Nor is it like any human being's speech. As such, the Veda must be accepted as eternal.

1. I.e. the existent Brahman.

सर्वथा यदनेनोक्तं तच्छ्रद्धेयं बुभूषता ।
भानुप्रकाशवच्छब्दो नित्योऽयं न तु कृत्रिमः ॥३०७॥

307. Certainly whatever is stated by the Veda must be believed by one who wants to know[1]; like the light of the sun,[2] this word (viz. Veda) is eternal and not at all a product.

NOTES

1. SP clarifies *bubhūṣatā* as *bhavitum icchatā*, i.e. by one who seeks for liberation.

2. The second line answers an implied doubt, viz. 'that even though the Veda proceeds like breath, it is still not eternal because it is artificial (*kṛtaka*).' The Veda is just the very nature of the lord, like the rays of the sun. (SP mentions that the Veda is the *vivarta* of the lord.)

पर एवाऽऽत्मनाऽऽत्मानं प्रतिपाद्य नरं श्रुतिः ।
कार्यकारणवत्पीत्वा स्वात्मनैवावतिष्ठते ॥३०८॥

308. (Since) it has been established that the consciousness[1] in a human being is the Ātman[2], the Śruti is the highest (Ātman itself). (Then having) negated (lit. swallowed/drunk off) this (mundane existence) made up of *kāraṇa* 'cause(s)' and *kārya* 'effect(s)' it stands (firmly established as eternal) on its own (support).

NOTES

One could say : 'If the eternity of the Veda is derived from the manifestation as shown in the previous verse, other things are also eternal because they are the manifestations of the lord, too. A distinct note of the Veda is useless.' Therefore, it is stated as to why the Veda alone can be said to be eternal. Purifying the objective things misconceived by a man by stating that they are identical with the non-dual Brahman and thereby sublating the world by means of knowledge, the Śruti remains as the Brahman. The excellence of the Śruti lies in that it removes the ignorance.

1. Just 'consciousness' (sentiency in a human being).
2. The consciousness (=*paramātman*).

वेदामात्वप्रसक्तौ वा सर्वमात्मेतिवाक्यतः ।
वेदामात्वापनुत्त्यर्थं स यथेत्यागमः परः ॥३०९॥

309. Indeed if one were forced to consider the Veda as non-authoritative means to knowledge, then after making the statement, 'All (this) is the Ātman' with a view to removing the idea of the Veda as non-authoritative means to knowledge, the latter (part of the) Śruti[1] proceeds in words *sa yathā*.

NOTES

Three different explanations of the purport about the sentence *sa yathārdraidhāgner* .... have been given in verses 297-308. Now, yet another purport thereof follows.

One might argue that from the sentence, 'All this is the Ātman', it may be concluded that the Veda is not authoritative. Without accepting falsity of all this world, one does not understand it as the Ātman. And when all is false, the Veda also, being included in all, is false and therefore not a means of knowing, like the appearance of smoke certainly leading to knowing of fire. In order to refute this argument, Sureśvara points to the Śruti, *sa yathā* . . . .

1. On the word *āgama*, cf. note on the verses 6-7.

तदयुक्तं पुमर्थस्य तदुक्त्यैव समाप्ततः ।
सर्वोपायोऽनुपायः स्यादुपेयावसितौ यतः ॥३१०॥

स्वोपेयार्थप्रसिद्धौ च नोपायानामुपायता ।
न चोत्सर्गापवादोऽपि साक्षाद्वेदग्रहश्रवात् ॥३११॥

310-311. It is not proper (to say that the Veda is not the authoritative means to knowledge), because it has been declared by the Veda itself that the end of human life is obtained (only) by the (knowledge of the) Vedic statement. When the purpose of a means (viz. Veda) is served, it does not (any more) remain a means. And the means do not have the nature of the means when the thing to be obtained by them is well-known. And there is not an exception to the general rule, (in the case of the Veda also), on account of the direct hearing (i.e. understanding) of the Veda.

NOTES

A means (*upāya*) is possible when one still has something to accomplish (*upeya*). Then once *upeya* is accomplished, a means (*upāya*) cannot remain a means any more. On verbal level, Veda is a means (*upāya*) and liberation is *upeya*. Once one is aware of the oneness of the Brahman and the Ātman, Veda cannot remain a means any more. One might object : 'If all is the Ātman, Veda which is included in all is also the Ātman. How can the Veda be a means ?' A reply is : All is the Ātman is the thought which occurs later. As long as one does not become aware of the oneness, all is not the Ātman and Veda is a means.

बालोन्मत्तोक्तिवच्चाहं वक्तुं दूषणमादरात् ।
जिह्रेमि बहुशोऽत्रोक्तौ तस्मादेवोपरम्यते ॥३१२॥

312. On account of my great regard (for the Vedānta) I feel reluctant in stating the faults (that are) in many ways (or, at many times) attached to the word of the Veda (by others), in the manner of the speech of a child (ignorant one) or of a mad man. Therefore, I stop talking further.

NOTES

On account of my having made statement several times in this regard I stop talking.

[Sureśvara now proceeds to comment on BU 2.4.10 : *yad ṛgvedo yajurvedaḥ sāmavedo 'tharvāṅgirasa itihāsaḥ purāṇaṁ vidyā upaniṣadaḥ ślokaḥ sūtrāṇy anuvyākhyānāni vyākhyānāny asyaivaitāni niḥśvasitāni*. The comment runs up to verse 326.]

ऋग्वेदादिगिरोच्यन्ते ऋग्यजुःसामलक्षणाः ।
अथर्वाङ्गिरसस्तद्वन्मन्त्राः स्युर्ब्राह्मणोद्धृताः ॥३१३॥

313. By the words *ṛgveda* etc. should be understood *mantras* which are characterized (by names) Ṛg, Yajur, Sāma and Atharvāṅgiras[1] as well (and) which are quoted in the Brāhmaṇa texts.

NOTES

1. *atharvāṅgiras* denotes 'the two elements which make up the Atharvaveda'; see A. A. MACDONELL and A. B. KEITH, *Vedic Index*, Delhi : Motilal Banarsidass, 1958, vol. 1, p. 18, also BLOOMFIELD, *Hymns of the Atharvaveda*, pp. xviii ff.

इतिहासादिसम्भेदभिन्नं ब्राह्मणमेव तु ।
ग्राह्यमत्र प्रसिद्धस्तु नेतिहासादिरिष्यते ॥३१४॥

314. But, in this respect[1], by the words (i.e. prose compositions) marked as variety of Itihāsa (narratives) etc.[2] only Brāhmaṇa is to be understood. Indeed, it is not intended to refer to the well-known *itihāsas*[3].

NOTES

1. The word *atra* refers to the sentence under discussion, viz. BU 2.4.10

2. Itihāsa etc. refers to narratives in the Brāhmaṇa texts such as *ākhyāna*, *nārāśaṁsi* etc. that are related to the *mantras* of Ṛg etc. Refer to the eight-fold Brāhmaṇa as understood in BUB (pp. 330-331), i.e. *itihāsa*, *purāṇa*, *vidyā*, *upaniṣad*, *śloka*, *sūtra*, *anuvyākhyāna* and *vyākhyāna*.

3. MBh, which is called *itihāsottama*, and the *Rāmāyaṇa* are meant here.

अभिधेयार्थजन्मापि ह्यभिधासम्भवोक्तितः ।
द्रष्टव्यं नाभिधानं स्यादभिधेयमृते क्वचित् ॥३१५॥

315. One should understand (lit. see) that the thing to be signified originates indeed from a statement which originates from (the function called) expression. Never could there be any expression without (there being) what is to be expressed.

NOTES

The idea is perhaps to explain *yasya niḥśvasitam....* That is to say : If there did not exist the Great Being, there could be no (power of) expression, no expression and there could not be any such things as Ṛg etc. The Brahman is *sarvaśaktimat* and *cit*, so it is capable of utterance. Therefore, there is the rise of words and the signification, i.e. the signified.

मन्त्रब्राह्मणयोर्वेदनामधेयत्वकारणात् ।
ऋग्वेदादिगिरा तस्मान्मन्त्रब्राह्मणयोर्ग्रहः ॥३१६॥

यथासिद्धमितिहासपुराणाद्यपि गृह्यते ।
लोकप्रसिद्धिमुल्लङ्घ्य यतोऽन्याय्योऽन्यथाग्रहः ॥३१७॥

316-317. Since the *mantra* and the Brāhmaṇa have the name *veda*, therefore, one grasps (i.e. understands) by the word *ṛgveda* etc. the *mantras* and the Brāhmaṇa (texts). Also Itihāsa, Purāṇa etc., as they exist[1], are also understood here, even going beyond the popular usage (of the word); understanding them in some other way is improper[2].

NOTES

1. That is already declared by the Śruti as the breathing out of the Great Being, i.e. they are already existent.

2. *anyāyyo'nyathāgrahaḥ* is Sureśvara's objection to Śaṅkara's explanation of the words *itihāsa* etc., i.e. he considers it as *durukta*.

इतिहासपुराणाभ्यां वेदं समुपबृंहयेत् ।
इत्यादिमनुनाऽप्युक्तं कथं तत्त्यागमर्हति ॥३१८॥

318. Even[1] Manu says, "One should amplify (i.e. support/explain) the Veda by means of Itihāsa and Purāṇa."[2] How does it deserve to be given up ?

NOTES

1. The word *api* is used to indicate that Atri has said the same thing. (SP)

2. *itihāsapurāṇābhāym vedaṁ samupabṛṁhayet|*
bibhety alpaśrutād vedo māṁ ayaṁ prahariṣyati||

This verse cannot be found in the *Manusmṛti*, but one finds it in MBh, i.e. 1.1.204. However, Sureśvara ascribes it to Manu. This means tradition held this as an opinion of Manu, the time-honoured authority on Vedic learning. Cf. *yan manur avadat tad bheṣajaṁ bheṣajatāyāḥ*.

इतिहासपुराणादेर्वेदमूलत्वकारणात् ।
प्रामाण्यं नान्यथा तस्य प्रामाण्यमुपपद्यते ॥३१९॥

319. Since Itihāsa and Purāṇa etc. have their source (lit. roots) in the Veda they are authoritative; otherwise their authoritativeness would not stand to reason.

NOTES

If the meaning of the Veda is clarified by Itihāsa etc., it would bring about an undesirable result, viz. that the Veda is not independently authoritative. Such an argument cannot be entertained. The verse gives reason for the same. The Veda is the basis or cause of Itihāsa etc. That is to say; if one ascertains the meaning of the Veda from words of some expounder, it would not mean that the Veda gives up its independent authoritativeness.

From significance, meaning is ascertained. Itihāsa etc. are taken by the learned to be based on the Vedic tradition (*vedamūlatva*) and therefore, if one entertains a doubt about a Vedic passage it should not mean that the Vedic passage is unauthoritative. One should interpret Vedic passages in the light of interpretation supplied by Itihāsa etc. SP refers to *na hi vyākhyānato viśeṣapratipattiḥ*; on this see the *Paribhāṣenduśekhara of Nāgojibhaṭṭa*, Poona: BORI, 1962, p. 1.

प्रत्यक्षवेदवचनविरुद्धं तेषु यद्वचः ।
बुद्धवाक्यादिवत्तादृक्त्याज्यं श्रुतिविरोधतः ॥३२०॥

320. Whatever statement in them would be noticed as directly opposed to the Vedic statement, like the statements of (Gautama) Buddha, it is to be given up on account of its contradiction to the Śruti statement.

NOTES

Here is a reason given for accepting the Itihāsa etc. as authoritative even like the Veda; these are not opposed to the Śruti statements. Sureśvara affirms his opinion that anything opposed to the Veda cannot be authoritative and whatever follows the Śruti is, on the other hand, authoritative.

न चेश्वरातिरेकेण कश्चित्स्त्रष्टाऽभ्युपेयते ।
इतिहासपुराणादेस्तदन्यस्येह कार्यतः ॥३२१॥

321. Further, (in the case) of Itihāsa and Purāṇa no creator other than the Īśvara[1] is accepted in our view on the ground that they are some effect.

NOTES

1. Īśvara = the Lord.

कारणत्वं प्रमाणेन यस्य साक्षाद्विनिश्चितम् ।
अपि तत्कार्यकर्तृत्वे तदेवाभ्युपगम्यते ॥३२२॥

322. That whose nature as the cause is ascertained directly by some means of knowing is itself accepted as the creator of the effect (i.e. its own effect) also.

NOTES

The idea is that Vyāsa is the author of MBh, Purāṇa etc. but the Brahman is the creator of Vyāsa. Therefore finally, the Brahman is the creator of MBh.

As to SP's quotation from MBh (appendix 2.2 pr. appendix 3. 2 pr.), in the critical edition of MBh this verse is given in an appendix which records passages that are left out by the editor, on the ground that they are later additions. At least in Ānandagiri's age, these passages were there in MBh.

बीजमेवाङ्कुरादीनां यथा कारणमिष्यते ।
अङ्कुराद्यात्मना तद्वद्बीजमेव तु कारणम् ॥३२३॥

323. As a seed is held to be the cause of a sprout etc., so is that seed itself understood as the cause of the nature of the sprout etc.

NOTES

This is not a strictly logical argument; that which seed produces, viz. sprout (1), in its turn produces seed (2).

आद्यन्तयोर्यतो बीजं प्रत्यक्षेणावसीयते ।
तस्मात्तन्मध्यकार्येषु बीजमेवास्तु कारणम् ॥३२४॥

324. As a seed is noticed by direct perception, both in the beginning and in the end, therefore, in the middle stage of the effects also let the seed be (understood as) the cause.

NOTES

The illustration of the seed-sprout relation depending on the deciding factor is elaborated; cf. GK. 2.6 : *ādāv ante ca yan nāsti vartamāne 'pi tat tathā* /

न च वेदोक्तितो वेदः श्रद्धेयार्थ इहेष्यते ।
किंत्वमानत्वहेतूनां वेदवाक्येष्वसम्भवात् ॥३२५॥

325. It is not intended here to state that the Veda has to be believed in, (only) on (the basis of) the statement in the Veda, but (it is intended to state) that there is no possibility of (stating) any reasons to determine the unauthoritativeness of the sentences of the Veda.

NOTES

The purport of this verse is to point out that the Śruti is authoritative owing to the fact that it is not and cannot be opposed by any other means of knowing.

प्रामाण्यं वेदवाक्यानां न च मानान्तराश्रयात् ।
अक्षादेरपि मानत्वं यथोक्तादेव कारणात् ॥३२६॥

326. That the sentences of the Veda are authoritative does not follow from one's resorting to other means of knowing. Direct perception etc.[1] are also accepted as authoritative means of knowing just for the reason mentioned before.

NOTES

yathoktakāraṇa may refer to *amānatvahetūnām asaṁbhavāt*. Then, ordinarily, means of knowing are considered authoritative, since there is no opposition to them by any other means. Therefore, let one not suppose that the words of Veda are unauthoritative because they use the same word as in common parlance. In reality, the Veda signifies that which cannot be understood by any other means though the words of Veda may be the same as those of the daily speech.

1. For the word *akṣādi*, cf. note (2) on verse 154 above.

प्रज्ञानव्यतिरेकेण यथैव स्थितिसर्गयोः ।
वस्त्वन्तरं न संभाव्यं प्रलयेऽपि तथोच्यते ॥३२७॥

327. As it is impossible to conceive of (i.e. accept) any other thing over and above (i.e. beside) knowledge (i.e. Brahman), which is supposed to be existing at the time) of the creation and sustenance (of the world), so it is said to be there at the time of the merger also.

NOTES

This is a comment on *kiṁ cānyan na kevalaṁ sthityutpattikālayor eva prajñāna-vyatirekeṇābhāvāj jagato brahmatvaṁ pralayakāle ca* (BUB, p. 332), which explains the introductory part of BU 2.4.11 : *sa yathā sarvāsām apāṁ. . . .*

[Now follows a comment on *sa yathā sarvāsām apāṁ samudra ekāyanam evaṁ sarveṣāṁ gandhānāṁ nāsike ekāyanam evaṁ sarveṣāṁ rasānāṁ jihvaikāyanam evaṁ sarveṣāṁ rūpāṇāṁ cakṣur ekāyanam evaṁ sarveṣāṁ śabdānāṁ śrotram ekāyanam evaṁ sarveṣāṁ saṁkalpānāṁ mana ekāyanam evaṁ sarveṣāṁ vidyānāṁ hṛdayam ekāyanam* (BU 2.4.11) ; it continues up to verse 377 below.]

विभिन्ननामरूपाणां सरितां सागरो यथा ।
अभिन्ननामरूपैकः प्रलयोऽयनमेकता ॥३२८॥

स्पर्शादिज्ञानभेदानां त्वगाद्येकायनं यथा ।
स्वान्ते त्वगादयस्तद्वद्बुद्धौ च मनसस्तथा ॥३२९॥

कर्मक्षयात्तथा बुद्धिः कारणत्वेन तिष्ठति ।
एष साधारणस्तावत्प्रलयोऽबुद्धिपूर्वकः ॥३३०॥

328-330. As the ocean having but one (and the same) name and form is the merger[1] (i.e. the meeting-point) of rivers which have different names and forms——(and) merger means oneness——so is the skin etc. the one meeting point of different knowledge such as touch etc. And the skin etc. also (get merged) into their own end[2] (viz. *manas*) and so also is (the merger of) *manas* into the intellect. In the same way, intellect (also) remains in the form of cause,[3] when action gets destroyed. This is the common[4] (nature of) merger (everywhere) and it is not preceded by any deliberate thinking.

NOTES

1. The word *pralaya* has two senses, (i) 'the act of merger' and (ii) 'the point of merger' (the place where the merger takes place). In order to set aside the sense (i) the word *ayana* meaning (ii) is used. And the word *ekatā* 'oneness' is used in order to obviate the idea of void—oneness means becoming 'one'.

2. The word *svānte* means 'in their own . . .', viz. *manas.*

3. *kāraṇatvena=kāraṇātmanā* (SP), it takes the form of *prakṛti.*

4. Referring to two types of *pralaya* : *sādhāraṇa* and *asādhāraṇa.* This verse refers to the first variety of *pralaya.*

प्रत्यग्याथात्म्यविज्ञानाद्वस्तुवृत्तानुरोधतः ।
प्रलयोऽज्ञानविध्वंसाद्यस्त्वसौ बुद्धिपूर्वकः ॥३३१॥

331. But that merger, which (results from) the destruction of ignorance, the knowledge of the real nature of the individual consciousness and is owing to following (i.e. accepting) the real nature of the thing (viz. the Brahman), is preceded by some deliberate thinking.

NOTES

This verse refers to the second type of merger, viz. the uncommon merger (*asādhāraṇa* and *buddhipūrvaka*).

Cf. *evam eva khalu somyemāḥ sarvāḥ prajāḥ sati sampadya na viduḥ sati sampadyāmaha iti / ta iha vyāghro vā siṁho vā vṛko vā varāho vā kiṭo vā pataṅgo vā daṁśo vā maśako vā yad yad bhavanti tad ābhavanti /* (CU 6.9.2-3), which intends that all beings get merged into the highest and again come into existence at the time of creation. Also cf. CUB on the same and BSB 2.1.9.

अब्धिरेकायनं यद्वत्सर्वासां सरितां तथा ।
त्वग्गोचराणां स्पर्शानां त्वगेवैकायनं परम् ॥३३२॥

332. As the ocean is the one meeting-place of all the rivers, so is the skin the one meeting-place of all the touches which are the objects of the skin.

स्पर्शशब्देन विषयस्त्वग्ग्राह्योऽत्राभिधीयते ।
तथा गन्धादिशब्देन घ्राणादिविषयो मतः ॥३३३॥

333. The word *sparśa* (here) expresses (only) the object grasped by the skin. Similarly, by the words *gandha* etc. are to be understood the objects of the nostrils etc.

गन्धादिसंहतिः पृथ्वी रसान्तानां तथा जलम् ।
तेजस्त्रयाणां वायुस्तु द्वयोरेकात्मकं नभः ॥३३४॥

334. Earth is the collection of (five objects such as) the smell etc., water (is likewise the collection of four objects) ending with the taste. Fire is (the collection) of three. As for wind, it is of two and ether (is) of the nature of one.

NOTES

Here is introduced the merger of the elements.

Element (*bhūta*)	: Property (*guṇa*)
pṛthivi	: *śabda, sparśa, rūpa, rasa, gandha*
ap	: *śabda, sparśa, rūpa, rasa*
agni	: *śabda, sparśa, rūpa*
vāyu	: *śabda, sparśa*
ākāśa	: *śabda*

एवं लक्षणतः पञ्च भूतान्येतानि निर्दिशेत् ।
मूर्तामूर्ताविष्करणं गुणाविष्कृतिरिष्यते ॥३३५॥

335. From this explanation, one should understand (the nature of) these (five) elements. (And) their manifestation of concrete and abstract[1] are understood as the manifestation of their *guṇas* 'properties'.

NOTES

The five elements are collection of five *guṇas* 'properties' beginning with the smell and ending with the sound which increase and decrease as shown in the previous verse. The rise of the five elements from their own causes is nothing but the manifestation of the smell etc. from the primordial cause, in ascending order. And the merger of the element into a subtler element is not else than the merger of *guṇas*.

1. Among the five elements, ether is *amūrta* and the rest are *mūrta*.

संहतोक्तविशेषाणां भूतानां कारणात्मता ।
तत्र स्पर्शग्रहेणैव वायोरंशोऽत्र गृह्यते ॥३३६॥

तेजसस्तु तृतीयांशश्चतुर्थोऽपां तथा भुवः ।
पञ्चमस्तद्गुणैर्भेदस्तथा स्पर्शे समीक्ष्यताम् ॥३३७॥

गन्धादिषु तथा योज्यो भेदोऽयं गुणभेदतः ।
पृथिव्यंशस्य बाहुल्यात्कर्कशः स्पर्श उच्यते ॥३३८॥

शीतश्च पिच्छिलश्चापां बाहुल्यात्स्पर्श इष्यते ।
भूयस्त्वात्तेजसश्चोष्णः सुकुमारस्तथा मरुत् ॥३३९॥

बाहुल्यादिति विज्ञेयो यथोक्तगणसंश्रयात् ।
ध्वस्ताशेषविकारस्य ब्रह्मणोऽविद्ययाऽऽत्मनः ॥३४०॥

स एष परिणामः स्यात्तेजोवन्नाद्युपक्रमः ।
स्पर्शनाद्यात्मनाऽत्यन्तं परं काठिन्यमागतः ॥३४१॥

336-341. The[1] objects (lit. elements), which possess these (already) mentioned distinct properties collected together, have the nature[2] of the cause. Among these (elements) is understood the element of wind by the mere mention of touch. And the third is that of the fire; the fourth, of water and the fifth, of earth. Again distinction (of five elements) in touch may be noticed by means of (the distinction of) their *guṇas* : So also, this distinction (of the five elements) as regards the smell etc. has to be associated with the difference of *guṇas*, thus[3] : The touch is stated to be rough owing to the abundance of the earth (element in an object). (Again), touch is taken to be cool and slippery when there is abundance of the water (element in an object). The wind (also) is taken to be hot or pleasant when there is abundance of fire (element in an object). Thus this mention of the transformation having its beginning in (the mention of) fire, water, food etc. should be (treated as) of the Brahman[4], whose entire modification is denied (lit. destroyed), (as possibly existing), owing to its basis on the *guṇas* already stated (and) the ignorance (about the real nature) of the Ātman (Jīvātman) —(this modification) has attained to (lit. has come to) extreme grossness (etc.)[5], owing to its (havintg *guṇas*) touch etc.

NOTES

1. Here in SP the reference is to *guṇa* which occurs in the previous verse. It is that which would give rise to the doubt. The doubt expresses a possible interpretation of verse 335 (last line) according to the Vaiśeṣika theory. The first line of the verse 336 is the answer to it.

2. The theory of causation which Sureśvara accepts (for the sake of argument, not in reality) resembles that of the Sāṁkhya. Therefore all these *guṇas*, together in a substance assume the forms of the cause and the effect. Thus, Sureśvara rejects the *asatkāryavāda* of the Vaiśeṣika. In other words, the elements can exist in both the forms, the cause and the effect — this explains their *jani* and *laya*.

3. One could entertain a doubt: 'Since there is a mention in the Śruti (only) of *guṇas*, viz. touch etc., it intends to refer to the merger of the elements which have not been mentioned.' This doubt is answered in the next two sentences. The mention of *guṇa* is indicative of *guṇin*. This is done only after accepting the difference of *guṇa* and *guṇin* in normally spoken language of every day life. It is not real.

4. This sentence is an answer to the doubt: 'There is the transformation of the highest in the form of the earth etc. which is of the nature of the touch etc.' Sureśvara thinks that without ignorance about the nature of the Brahman and / or of the Ātman (= Jīvātman) which is inner and immutable, such a talk of transformation is impossible — the world is 'caused' by ignorance of the Brahman.

5. Cf. SP's mention of the two types of hardness (etc.) — One is *sthūla* (gross) and the other *sūkṣma* (subtle). (Etc.) is necessary in view of *sparśādi*, 'touch etc.' *kāṭhinya* is literally 'hardness'; however, it is translated as grossness in view of Sureśvara's use of the adjectives *kaṭhina* and *svaccha* as pair in verse 344 below.

उद्भूतस्पर्शविज्ञानस्त्वचा तस्य समागमात् ।
स्पर्शभेदपरिज्ञानं ततोऽभिव्यज्यते दृशेः ॥३४२॥

342. (This transformation wherein) that knowledge of the touch has arisen is owing to its (i.e. of the Ātman)[1] association with the skin, (for) the complete knowledge of distinct touches[2] is said to be of the seer (= the Ātman[3]) from (i.e. by means of) that (i.e. the skin).

NOTES

How is the transformation of the touch etc. proved ? When one has got a knowledge in the form 'This is a touch' etc., that cognition results from the association of the Ātman with the skin etc. SP's explanation of the compound *udbhūtasparśa-vijñānaḥ* is not satisfactory. One can take the compound as an adjective of the *pariṇāma* (mentioned in earlier verse) and *tasya* as *ātmanaḥ*.

1. The Ātman in verse 340—this association is rooted in ignorance. See for that verse 344 below.

2. Cf. *sparśādibhedavijñānam* in the next verse as further support.

3. Alternatively translated as; 'the complete knowledge of distinct touches is manifested to the seer.'

स्पर्शादिभेदविज्ञानं स्यादचेतनमेव तु ।
स्पर्शादिवत्परार्थत्वात्स्वार्थं तन्न तु साक्षिवत् ॥३४३॥

343. Indeed[1], the knowledge of distinct (objects), touch etc., is insentient[2], because it is for the sake of another[3], as (is) the touch etc. (for another), it is not for its own sake, accompanied (as it is) by the witness (Ātman)[4].

NOTES

This is the refutation of some opponent's view that even if this is not inferred, it is known by a witness, because it is self-luminous.

1. The word *tu* is used for emphasis.
2. Sureśvara follows the Sāṁkhya theory of cognition.
3. Cf. SK 17 which has been already quoted in the note on verse 285 above.
4. The construction is thus: *sākṣivat* (*sat*) *tat* (= *sparśādibhedavijñānam*) *na svārtham.*

अतीव कठिनं ज्ञानं त्वचातोऽस्य समागमात् ।
मनसा तस्य संयोगे ततः स्वच्छैव धीर्भवेत् ॥३४४॥

344. The very gross[1] (of the Ātman), (arises) on account of its association with the skin (etc.). (And) when it comes into contact with *manas*, there arises only subtle knowledge.

NOTES

The idea of *laya*, as mentioned in notes on 336-341, is explained here further. One takes *jani* and *laya* according as one's knowledge is gross or subtle.

1. the word *kaṭhina* means *sthūla* or 'gross' and the word *svaccha*, *sūkṣma* or 'subtle'; (as noted earlier in the note on verse 341 above.)

ततोऽपि सूक्ष्मं विज्ञानं बुद्धिसंयोगजं भवेत् ।
यावद्रुधिरसंव्याप्तिः शरीरे तावदेव तु ॥३४५॥

बुद्धेः सामान्यवृत्त्येह व्याप्तिरादेहसंक्षयात् ।
चैतन्याभासवत्प्राणस्तां वृत्तिं व्याप्य तिष्ठति ॥३४६॥

345-346. Yet[1] subtler knowledge would occur (to the Ātman) owing to its association (only) with the intellect. The intellect wholly pervades a body by its common function so long as there is pervasion by blood all through the body until the fall of it. (And) the *prāṇa*,[2] which has the appearance of sentiency, exists (in the body), pervading the (common) function (of the intellect).

NOTES

1. The same knowledge would be subtler because the intellect is subtler than *manas*.

2. *prāṇa* is one of the winds in the body. It resembles sentiency in the body because of their *avinābhāva*. One should remember here the common function of the three-fold inner-organs, *prāṇādidhāraṇa*. Cf. SK 29 referring to the common function of the three inner-organs: *sāmānyakaraṇavṛttiḥ prāṇādyā vāyavaḥ pañca*.

अकार्यकारणस्त्वात्मा तमपह्नुत्य तिष्ठति ।
कण्टकादिसमायोगे शरीरे विक्रिया यदा ॥३४७॥

तदाऽधर्मादितो दुःखं विक्रियातोऽभिजायते ।
देहैकदेशगं दुःखं विशिनष्टि स्वदेशगाम् ॥३४८॥

धियं तद्देशदुःखित्वाद्दुःखित्वं जायते धियः ।
तस्यावच्छित्तये वृत्तिर्दुःखभूत्यैव जायते ॥३४९॥

347-349. As for the Ātman, which is neither a cause nor an effect, it remains after covering that *prāṇa* which is mentioned just in the previous verse. If there is a change in a body when there is a contact of it with a thorn etc., then there is pain (on the part of the Ātman) due to the (so-called) demerit etc.[1] consequent to the change (in the body). The pain[2] in one part of the body qualifies the intellect belonging to that part, (for) the condition of the misery of the intellect arises from the pain of that part (of the body). (And) for the eradication of (the condition of) that (misery), the function (activity of the intellect) results only from the abundance (i.e. intensity) of the misery.

NOTES

1. A pun on the word *adharma*. It means (i) demerit (as commonly understood) and (ii) (in reality) not its property—this latter points to unreal pain.

2. This sentence is an answer to the possible doubt : 'When misery has arisen in one part of the body, how can one say that misery rests on the intellect?' The reply is: Since the intellect

pervades the entire body, therefore, misery in any part of the body stays on the intellect also.

भोक्तृभोग्याभिसंबन्धस्तन्निमित्तोऽयमात्मनः ।
बुद्धेः सेयमहंवृत्तिर्दुःखावच्छेदिनी सती ॥३५०॥

परिच्छिनत्ति बोद्धारं बोद्धाऽप्याभासमात्मनः ।
न बहिर्विक्रियां मुक्त्वा देहेऽहंवृत्तिसंभवः ॥३५१॥

350-351. This (commonly known) relation of the enjoyer and the enjoyable (for) the Ātman is caused by that intellect.[1] This (commonly known) function of Ego which belongs to the intellect, being the encompasser of misery, encompasses the knower and the object of knowing also (encompasses) its own semblance.[2] There[3] does not arise the function of Ego in a body without there being any external change.

NOTES

Again, Sureśvara talks in terms of the Sāṁkhya theory of cognition, nevertheless, showing that there is an important difference.

1. Sureśvara does not accept that the Ātman is the natural enjoyer.

2. It is *ahaṁkāra* 'Ego' (inseparable from *buddhi*) that is responsible for experience — it is (by mistake) understood for the Ātman and *vice-versa* and therefore these are statements like 'I know' etc.

3. This sentence points out how the function of Ego and a change in the body (*not in the Ātman* in any way) are simultaneous and also how there is an error of identifying the Ego and the Ātman as one. This is amplified in the following verses.

स्वस्थेन्द्रियमनोबुद्धेर्नैवाहमिति वीक्ष्यते ।
पुत्राभिमानजे त्वस्मिन्न देहांशविशिष्टता ॥३५२॥

352. When (a person's) sense-organs, *manas* (and) the intellect are (in fact) in their own form,[1] there is not seen the Ego (functioning). However, when this (i.e. the Ego) is noticed

(to function) by attachment to a son (etc.), it (i.e. Ego) is then qualified as being the part of some particular body[2].

NOTES

1. That is, they are not affected by any external object of misery or joy — e.g. by a prick of a thorn or some soft touch.

2. This is in contrast with the first line. The Ego can persist even without an external object, since it may retain some attachment to a son etc.

तत्तद्वस्तु समुद्दिश्य दुःखित्वं तत्र मानिनः ।
अज्ञानादभिमानोऽयं बुद्ध्यादौ विषयावधौ ॥३५३॥

353. Referring[1] to different objects a person is stricken by misery when he regards them as his. (And)[2] the notion, (this is) mine (i.e. Ego[3]) is due to ignorance in respect of the intellect and insofar as the (external) objects (exist).

NOTES

1. One who possesses *abhimāna*, viz. the notion 'this is my son etc.' with reference to a wide range of objects, has misery. Further, it is then indirectly superimposed on the witnessing consciousness within.

2. This explains that misery arises from the misconception such as 'this is mine', which really the witnessing consciousness does not entertain.

3. *abhimāna*=*ahaṁkāra*. Cf. SK 24: *abhimāno 'haṁkāraḥ* . . . .

न तु निःसङ्गकूटस्थप्रतीचः स्यादहंमतिः ।
न कार्यप्रलयो दृष्टो यस्मादन्यत्र कारणात् ॥३५४॥

त्वगारम्भकसामान्यं त्वग्गिराऽतोऽत्र गृह्यते ।
कार्यत्वान्नेन्द्रियेष्वेव विषयप्रलयो भवेत् ॥३५५॥

354-355. The thought 'I am (this or that)' could not be on the part of the individual consciousness which is free from all attachment and immutable,[1] since merger of an effect is not seen elsewhere than in the cause.[2] Therefore, the word skin[3] (etc.) is understood here, in the sense of the common origin of the skin (etc.), for[4] the merger of the objects would not be in the sense-organs inasmuch as they (themselves) are of the nature of an effect.

NOTES

1. This is a reply to the doubt that the misconception of Ego and that of 'mine' are on par, then how can you say the misconception of 'mine' really exists ?

2. According to SP, Sureśvara refers to this as the refutation of the view of Bhartṛprapañca (*bhedābhedavādin*)—though SP did not say so on verses 328-330. Sureśvara obviously follows his master Śaṅkara who cites this view of Bhartṛprapañca in BUB 5.1.1 (see the Introduction section 9).

3. Cf. next verse which mentions *tvagādi.*

4. SP states : The sense-organs are the effects of the objects and, therefore, not their origin.

न मृदोऽन्यत्र कुम्भादेः शरावे प्रलयो यतः ।
तस्मात्त्वगादयः शब्दास्त्वगाद्यारम्भकाभिधाः ॥३५६॥

सर्वत्र प्रतिपत्तव्या नान्यत्र प्रलयो यतः ।
गन्धशब्देन कृत्स्नाऽपि पृथिवी परिगृह्यते ॥३५७॥

356-357. Since the merger of a pitcher etc. is not elsewhere than in clay, i.e. in a plate[1], therefore the words *tvac* etc. (here in this discussion) are (properly) to be understood everywhere as expressive of that which originates skin etc. Since their merger is not found anywhere else, therefore, by the word *gandha* is to be understood the whole earth[2].

NOTES

1. A possible objection is : 'Would it be wrong to hold that the objects merge into the sense-organs ?' This is answered here : If the effect gets merged into something else than a cause, then a pitcher etc. would also get merged into a plate. Therefore, the merger of objects into the sense-organs cannot be established.

2. Here concludes the explanation of the Śruti 'of all touches . . .' Now follows the explanation of the word *gandha* in the Śruti, 'Of all smells . . . . The word *gandha* indicates the gross earth in the form of collection of five *guṇas* such as the sound etc.

यदि वा परिभागोऽस्या गन्धस्यानेकभेदतः ।
गन्धो गुरुः क्षितिप्रायो ह्लादो शीतोऽप्प्रधानतः ॥३५८॥

तेजोभूयस्तया तीक्ष्णो लघुर्वायुप्रधानतः ।
शान्तोऽथ विशदो व्यापी स्याद्व्योम्नोऽथ प्रधानतः ॥३५९॥

358-359. Or, perhaps, (by the word *gandha* is understood) the minute part of this (earth), on account of the variety of smell : (Thus) the smell[1] is intense (strongly fragrant) when it is abounding in (the element of) earth. It[2] is pleasant (and) cool when it is abounding in the (element of) water. It is sharp when it is abounding in the (element of) fire (lit. lustre). It is gentle when it is abounding in the (element of) wind. And it is mild, pleasant and (all-) pervading owing to the abundance of the element of ether.

NOTES

1. The meaning of the word *gandha* is the most minute part of the earth, because smell appears (is felt) in manifold forms.
2. This explains the different kinds of smell.

पार्थिवाप्यांशयोस्तेजः परिक्लेदात्तथाऽधमः ।
दुर्गन्धो जायते गन्धः पापकर्मप्रबोधतः ॥३६०॥

360. On account of the overpowering of the element of the earth and the water by (the element of) fire, there arises the worst (lit. lowest) smell. On account of the rise of (some) evil act,[1] the smell becomes bad smell.

NOTES

Sureśvara makes a reply to the doubt :'How can there be the knowledge of difference of good or bad smell, even if there is difference of the smell in accordance with the element?' First, he speaks of the seen cause and then the unseen (*adṛṣṭa*) cause.

1. See Nais 1. 1 on *adharma* as the cause of misery (*duḥkha*).

समांशपरिणामे तु सुरभिर्जायते शुभः ।
पुण्यकर्मप्रयुक्तः सञ्जन्तोरासङ्गकृत्तथा ॥३६१॥

361. But there arises an auspicious (i.e. fragrant[1]) smell when there (exists) combination (lit. effect) in equal proportion (of the elements[2]). So also, being effected by holy activity (the combination of merit and demerit in equal proportion) creates attachment to (various external objects) in (an individual that is) born.[3]

NOTES

1. *śubhatva = sukhakaratva*. (SP)

2. 'When the equal proportion of the earth etc. are heated by fire'. (SP)

3. This explanation is forced by the words *pāpakarma-bodhataḥ* (in the preceding verses) and *śubha* with *double entendre*.

रसरूपरवेष्वेवं यथोक्तं प्रतिपादयेत् ।
प्रधानगुणभावेन गुणानां भूरिरूपता ॥३६२॥

362. In respect of the taste, the form and the sound (of five objects, the touch and the smell) also should one state (or, explain) as (stated) before. Variety (of objects and individual) arises from the relation of the principal and the subordinate among the various properties.

NOTES

The manifoldness of the touch and the smell stated above is extended to the taste etc. in the passage 'Of all tastes . . .' The *guṇas* are manifold due to the increase and the decrease of the elements. The case is the same with individuals—this is implied by two preceding verses.

असाधारणगन्धादिग्राहकत्वानुमानतः ।
ग्राह्यभूतप्रधानत्वं घ्राणादिष्वपि निर्दिशेत् ॥३६३॥

363. On the basis of inference[1] of a capacity to grasp the uncommon (*guṇas* like) smell etc. one should attribute to the sense of smell etc.[2] what are grasped as the principal elements among those entities.

NOTES

This verse answers the possible objection : 'When the said difference in respect of the smell etc. is established in the Śruti, how is it said in the passage 'that common origin of the touch . . .' (verse 355) that the smell etc. are the origin of the smell etc.?'

1. SP refers *anumāna* to *liṅga*.

2. SP understands *api* 'etc.' in the sense of *yathā* or *iva* as implying a simile.

स्वग्राह्यार्थसजातीयमिन्द्रियं स्यात्प्रदीपवत् ।
रूपस्यैवावभासित्वान्न चेत्स्याच्छ्रोत्ररूपवत् ॥३६४॥

364. As the light (is not different from the object which is illuminated by it, so) does a sense-organ belong to the same category as the object which is grasped by it, because (it)[1] illuminates that which is a form. If (this was) not (so)[2], then it would be (related to the form) in the same way as the ear and the form.

NOTES

1. This 'it' means *pradīpa*.

2. If the lamp is not of the same nature of the form which is to be understood, the form is not grasped even by the lamp as it is not grasped by the ear. This evidence proves the point by an instance of contradiction. The eye is very easily understood from the instance of the lamp, for the lamp and the eye share the same *guṇa*, viz. they are both *taijasa* and, therefore, illuminators.

न चेदर्थसजातीयं सर्वार्थग्रहणं भवेत् ।
एकैकस्येन्द्रियस्येह मनोबुद्ध्योर्यथा तथा ॥३६५॥

सर्वभूतात्मकत्वात्तु सर्वार्थग्रहणं तयोः ।
मनोबुद्ध्योरिति ज्ञेयमन्यथा तदसम्भवात् ॥३६६॥

365-366. If a sense-organ would not belong to the same category (as its object), then there would be the grasping of all the objects; as each of the sense-organs would here (in our worldly dealings) grasp all objects so do *manas* and the intellect (grasp all of them). It should be remembered (i.e. known) that as for *manas* and the intellect, they grasp all objects since they are of the nature of all the elements (together), for, otherwise, it would be impossible (for them to grasp them all).

त्वगादिज्ञानशक्तीनां बुद्धिः सामान्यमुच्यते ।
प्राण एव क्रियाशक्तिसामान्यं तद्वदुच्यते ॥३६७॥

367. The intellect is said to be the generality[1] of the powers of knowing, viz. the skin etc., likewise is the vital force said to be the generality of the powers of action.

NOTES

1. The word *sāmānya* means the common quality of them all.

शब्दादिभोगसिद्ध्यर्थं श्रोत्राद्या ज्ञानशक्तयः ।
तद्वत्कर्मोपभोगार्थं वागाद्याः कर्मशक्तयः ॥३६८॥

368. (As) there are the powers of knowing, viz. the ear etc., in order to achieve (lit. to secure) the enjoyment of the sound etc., likewise there are the powers of action, viz. speaking etc.[1] for (the securing of) the enjoyment of action.

NOTES

The reasons why the organs of knowing and those of action are stated in this context are indicated in the first and the the second lines respectively.

1'. SP quotes SK 21 where the functions of powers

of action are described, i.e. *vacana* 'speaking' by *vāc*, *ādāna* 'taking' by *hastau*, *viharaṇa* 'moving' by *pādau*, *utsarga* 'excretion' by *pāyu* and *ānanda* 'joy' by *upastha*.

यथोक्तशक्तिविक्षेपो मनोबुद्धिपुरःसरः ।
संकल्पाध्यवसायाभ्यां तयोर्भेदोऽपि च द्विधा ॥३६९॥

369. The application (i.e. the appearance) of the powers (already) stated proceeds (only) from (the inner-organs, i.e.) *manas* and the intellect.[1] The distinction between them is (also) divided into two categories, viz. imagination and ascertainment.

NOTES

This verse states how the different sense-organs act.

1. According to PKV 33, 34, the inner-organs are four-fold, i.e. *manas*, *buddhi*, *ahaṁkāra* and *citta*. And their functions are *saṁkalpa* 'imagination', *niścaya* or *adhyavasāya* 'ascertainment', *abhimāna* 'misconception' and *anusaṁdhāna* 'investigation' respectively. But here Sureśvara seems to follow the Sāṁkhya view of three-fold inner-organs. This could lead one to hold that PKV is not the work of Sureśvara Cf. SK 23, 24 and 27, where three-fold inner-organs (*manas*, *buddhi* and *ahaṁkāra*) and their functions are described.

योग्येन्द्रियस्य या यस्य ततोऽन्यत्रापि लक्षिता ।
वृत्तिस्तस्यैव सा ज्ञेया न स्वभावविपर्ययः ॥३७०॥

370. Whatever modification (i.e. function) of some sense-organ is noticed on the part of another sense-organ it should be taken to belong, in reality, to that particular sense-organ alone; there (has) not (been) change (as regards the modification).

एवं ज्ञानक्रियाशक्तिविक्षेपाज्जगदात्मनः ।
करणायतनत्वाय देहाविर्भूतिरात्मनः ॥३७१॥

371. In this way, on account of the application (i.e. appearance) of the powers of knowing and action (on the part) of the soul of the world, there is the manifestation in a body of the Ātman (Jīvātman merely) for serving (as) the support of the sense-organs.

NOTES

SP clarifies Sureśvara's idea thus: The old authorities say that the Ātman becomes, i.e. appears as transmigratory due to the two-fold functions of the sense-organs as stated before. The creation of a body is the necessary basis for the functions of sense-organs which are impossible without its support. Moreover, the body also is made up of the five elements, because the five-fold objects, viz. sound etc., are found in the body (of a being).

एवं च सति यद्यस्मात्कार्यमाविरभूत्पुरा ।
तत्तु तत्रैव विलयं कार्यमेति स्वकारणे ॥३७२॥

372. Such being the case, whatever effect has first manifested from whichever cause properly gets merged into its own cause.

NOTES

Sureśvara thus reiterates how the various sense-organs get merged into the five elements which are their 'cause'.

मूलकारण एवैषां सर्वेषां विलयो भवेत् ।
तत्कारणत्वात्कार्याणां न तु कार्यान्तरे लयः ॥३७३॥

373. All these (entities) would get merged into their root-cause, (being) the products of that cause.[1] Indeed, they do not get merged into other effects.[2]

NOTES

1. This is to remove the doubt that the sense-organs would then merge into the five elements, something else than the Brahman. Sureśvara asserts that the idea of a merger (*laya*) is associated with the effects merging into the 'root-cause'.

2. The sense-organs as well as the elements being effects, it is improper to say that the sense-organs which are some of the effects (of the root-cause) get merged into the five elements which are some other effects.

पिण्डादिष्वेव प्रात्यक्ष्याद्घटादीनां लयादियम् ।
भ्रान्तिः पूर्वेषु कार्येषु लयोऽयमिति मोहतः ॥३७४॥

374. It (lit. this) is misapprehension (to say): "On account of directly perceiving the merger of a pot etc. into a lump (of clay)[1] etc., it is possible to hold that every effect merges into every another preceding effect"; (and this is) owing to infatuation (i.e. ignorance).

NOTES

SP points out a possible doubt which is the basis for this verse—; the argument could be: 'All effects do not merge into the Brahman, because (i) we notice that the pitchers etc. merge into clay etc.; and (ii) all the sense-organs, which are effects, merge into the five elements; according to the Vedāntin himself.' The answer is: This argument originates in ignorance. On *sāmānya* and *mahāsāmānya* see note on verse 289.

1. The foot-note on *piṇḍādiṣv eva* reads a variant *mṛdādiṣv eva*: It seems a better reading. The translation follows the text of the edition.

एवं त्वगादिवाच्यासु स्पर्शादीनां यथायथम् ।
स्पर्शादिमात्रासु लयस्तासामपि लयस्तथा ॥३७५॥

मनोविषयसामान्ये तस्यापि प्रलयो धियः ।
स्वगोचरैकसामान्ये सरितां सागरे यथा ॥३७६॥

बुद्धेर्विषयविज्ञानसामान्यमपि चाऽऽत्मनि ।
परस्मिल्लँयविक्षेपरहितेऽपरिणामिनि ॥३७७॥

375-377. Thus, there is (the merger of the effects such as) the touch etc. into the sense-organs expressed by the words *tvac* etc[1].; similarly, there is (the merger) of them also into their generality, viz. the objective *manas*; further, that also has its merger in the one (greater) generality, viz. the intellect—(this is) just the same way as there is the merger of rivers into the ocean. Also, the (great) generality of objective knowledge merges into the Ātman (which is) above (itself and is) without any (further) merger and which does not undergo any modification.

NOTES

Having thus explained the merger of the elements and their products into the root-cause (the Brahman), the author points to the meaning of the statements in BUB on 'thus of all touches...'

1. The word *yathāyatham* informs us that the merger of particular objects such as touch into the particular sense-organ, viz. the sense of touch, is denoted by the word *tvac*, and so on.

वदनादिस्वसामान्यविषयेषु तथा लयः ।
कर्मेन्द्रियाणां सर्वेषां तत्सामान्येषु पञ्चसु ॥३७८॥

378. In the same way, there is the merger of all actions, viz. speaking etc., into their own generality and further that of all the organs of action into their own generality.

NOTES

Now is shown the purport of the passage: *evaṁ sarveṣāṁ karmaṇāṁ hastāv ekāyanam evaṁ sarveṣām ānandānām upastha ekāyanaṁ . . . . sarveṣāṁ vedānāṁ vāg ekāyanam* (BU 2.4.11).

परिस्पन्दः प्रकाशश्च ज्ञानशक्तिषु विद्यते ।
केवलस्तु परिस्पन्दः कर्मशक्तिषु निष्प्रभः ॥३७९॥

379. Movement and lustre are found in the powers of knowing; however, movement alone, i. e. devoid of lustre, is found in the powers of action.

NOTES

This verse states the purport of the passage in BUB: *prāṇaś ca prajñānamātram eva* (p. 334, *line* 8)

सर्वोऽप्येष परिस्पन्दो बुद्धीन्द्रियसमाश्रयः ।
प्राणात्मक इति ज्ञेयो हन्तास्यैवेति च श्रुतेः ॥३८०॥

380. It is to be known that all movement which rests on the organs of knowing, is of the nature of the vital force, for there is the Śruti statement, *hantāsyaiva.*[1]

NOTES

This is the purport of BUB (p. 334, *line* 8). Because the movement is of the nature of the vital force and because manifold sense-organs are of the nature of movement, therefore, organs of action are vital force. This is based on the Śruti *yo vai prāṇaḥ sā prajñā* (KausU 3.3), which is quoted in BUB (p. 334, *line* 8). And because the vital force and the knowledge (*buddhi*, *prajñā*) are considered as identical, organs of knowing are, therefore, the vital force. Thus, the two-fold sense-organs are proved to be the vital force (*kāryakāraṇayor abhedaḥ*, *ādhārādheyayor abhedaḥ*).

1. The source of this quotation is not traceable.

पड्वीशशङ्कुदृष्टान्तात्प्राणस्यैव तु शक्तयः ।
कर्मेन्द्रियाणि सर्वाणि तथा बुद्धीन्द्रियाण्यपि ॥३८१॥

381. The power of all the organs of action as well as those of knowing belong only to the vital force as seen from the illustration[1] of the nails which are driven into the foot (of a horse).

NOTES

In addition to the Śruti, *hantāsyaiva*, the author quotes yet another Śruti to prove that two-fold organs (i.e. sense-organs and the organs of action) are of the nature of the Ātman, i.e. the vital force.

Just as an excellent (i.e. strong) horse uproots simultaneously all the four spikes which are on its hoofs, in the same way the vital force overcomes (i.e. pervades) speech etc. Therefore, the sense-organs stated in the Śruti are dependent on the vital force.

1. Cf. CU 5.1.12 : *yathā suhayaḥ paḍviśa-śaṅkūn saṁ-khidet* /; also BU 6.1.13 : *yathā mahāsuhayaḥ saindhavaḥ paḍviśa-śaṅkūn saṁvṛhet* /

आर्पातकरणग्रामे पुंसि स्वात्मन्यवस्थिते ।
तथा प्राणाग्नयः शुद्धा जाग्रतीति श्रुतेर्वचः ॥३८२॥

382. There is a statement in the Śruti : "(When the Man i.e. the Ātman, has concentrated on himself and all of his

sense-organs have been merged (lit. drunk) within himself, then the fires of *prāṇa* remain (alone) in the waking state."

NOTES

This seems to be a paraphrase of the ideas in PU 4.1.2-3 : *tasmai sa hovāca / yathā gārgya marīcayo'rkasyāstaṁ gacchataḥ sarvā etasmiṁs tejomaṇḍala ekībhavanti / tāḥ punaḥ punar udayataḥ pracaranti / evaṁ ha vai tat sarvaṁ pare deve manasyekībhavati / tena tarhyeṣa puruṣo na śṛṇoti / na paśyati / na jighrati / na rasayate/ na spṛśate / nābhivadate / nādatte / nānandayate / na visṛjate / neyāyate / svapitīty ācakṣate // prāṇāgnaya evaitasmin pure jāgrati / gārhapatyo ha va eṣo' pānaḥ / vyāno'nvāhāryapacanaḥ / yad gārhapatyāt praṇīyate praṇayanād / āhavanīyaḥ prāṇaḥ //* Thus the words *iti śruter vacaḥ* should not be taken to conclude a quotation of the Śruti.

सहैव कर्मशक्त्याऽतो ज्ञानशक्तिर्विलीयते ।
प्राणात्मनि श्रुतिश्चाऽऽह कस्मिन्निति च सादरा ॥३८३॥

383. Therefore, along with the powers of action do the powers of knowing get merged into the Ātman, the vital force, and[1] the respectful Śruti says in this connection, *kasmin* . . .[2]

NOTES

The result of the merger of the two-fold sense-organs in the vital force is mentioned ; and consequently, it points out that the vital force is the highest and the cause.

1. The first *ca* refers to the experience of the vital force, as stated in the Śruti; the other *ca* indicates another Śruti, *sa prāṇam asṛjata* (PU 6.4)

2. PU 6.3 : *kasminnvaham utkrānto bhaviṣyāmi*, 'As a result of whose (departure) shall I rise up ?'

साधारणोऽयं विलयः समानान्तोऽभिधीयते ।
स्वहेतुमात्रसंसर्गान्नायमात्यन्तिको लयः ॥३८४॥

384. It is stated that this merger which has one common end is the common (merger), and (the effect) being united with its own cause alone, there does not follow the absolute merger.[1]

NOTES

The natural (i.e. commonly known / perceived) merger which is common to all beings is spoken of at the end of BU 2.5, i.e. 2.5.18, also—all beings (i.e. their bodies) end in the cause known by one common word.

The second line of this verse gives the reason why this merger at 2.4 and that at 2.5 are similar.

1. Meaning 'destruction'.

ज्ञानशक्तिक्रियाशक्तिविभुत्वात्परमक्षरम् ।
व्युह्याऽऽत्मानं जगत्त्वेन स्वात्मन्येव समूहति ॥३८५॥

385. The highest indestructible having first expanded itself in the form of the world through its powers of knowing and action and pervasive nature, withdraws (lit. collects) it all into itself again.

NOTES

This verse explains why the common merger is mentioned once again at BU 2.5.18. The Brahman is nothing but the Ātman because of its omnipotence; it spreads itself as the world gathers it back in itself but it remains in its own.

निरुह्योति तथा श्रुत्या कारणात्माऽभिधीयते ।
अत्यक्रामदिति त्वस्य निर्बीजावस्थतोच्यते ॥३८६॥

386. The Śruti[1] mentions the Ātman as the cause (of all this) in the words, 'Having completed....,' but the words 'it went beyond....' is the statement of its condition, viz. not being the cause (of all this).

NOTES

Here Sureśvara explains how that Śruti statement includes the word referring to the cause also, for the effects, viz. *prāṇa* etc. are specifically mentioned. The first line refers to the cause, viz. the Ātman, which spreads out the world as well as enters into itself and finally remains (alone). One should not understand that the Ātman together with these its effects (viz. the world) is the ultimate reality—this is understood from the second line.

1. Cf. BU 3.9.26 *sa yas tān puruṣān niruhya pratyuhya atyakrāmat taṁ tvā aupaniṣadaṁ puruṣaṁ pṛcchāmi* / "I ask you of that being who is to be known only from the Upaniṣads, who definitely projects those beings and withdraws them into itself."

यत एवमतोऽशेषज्ञानशक्तिलयात्परम् ।
सर्वकार्योपसंहारी प्राण एकोऽवतिष्ठते ॥३८७॥

387. Since this is so, there remains only the vital force after the merger of the entire (group of) powers of knowing etc., it is the withdrawer (i.e. the collector) of all effects.

NOTES

Since the Śruti, *niruhya...*, mentions the root-cause of this world, therefore the Śruti : *kasmin nu tvaṁ cātmā ca pratiṣṭhitau stha iti prāṇa iti...*/ "On what do the body and the heart (you and yourself) rest ? On vital force." (BU 2.9.26) mentions the merger-sequence. And, as such, one may ask 'why is not there (i.e. in the latter passage) the statement of the absolute merger ?" This verse is an answer to this doubt : 'Vital force alone remains.'

प्राणोऽपाने तथाऽपानो व्यानात्मनि विलीयते ।
व्यानोऽप्युदानमप्येति ह्युदानोऽपि समानगः ॥३८८॥

388. The *prāṇa*[1] merges[2] into the *apāna*, likewise the *apāna* into the *vyāna*, the *vyāna* into the *udāna* and the *udāna* into the *samāna*

NOTES

The word *prāṇa* indicates the specific function, viz. 'breathing', because it is impossible to accept the merger of *prāṇa* in the principal sense 'vital force'; cf. the Śruti,... *prāṇa iti / kasmin nu prāṇāḥ pratiṣṭhita iti apāna iti* / "On *prāṇa* On what does *prāṇa* rest ? On *apāna*" (BU 2.9.26).

1. The five kinds of *prāṇa* are described in BU 1.5.3, 3.9.26; TU 1.7.1; Mai U 2.6 etc. cf. verse 299 above.

2. The word *apy-eti* is used in the sense 'to get merged'; cf. Nais 1.52.

कारणात्मैव जगतः समानोक्त्याऽभिधीयते ।
सर्वसाधारणः सोऽयं प्राकृतः प्रलयो मतः ।।३८९।।

389. The Ātman which is the cause of the world is mentioned in the word *samāna*. This merger which is common to all is accepted as the natural (i.e. common) merger.

NOTES

The word *samāna* is used not in the sense of the specific function, 'downward movement of the wind' but like the word *prāṇa* in the sense of *kāraṇātman* 'the prime-cause Ātman'. This is explained in brief as the natural merger.

प्रज्ञानघनताऽप्यस्य न बुद्धिप्रज्ञयोच्यते ।
प्रत्यक्प्रज्ञोत्थिताभाससंबन्धात्प्राज्ञ उच्यते ।।३९०।।

390. (Take for instance:) This (vital force) is said to be a mass of knowledge not because of the knowledge through the intellect; it is called Prājña because of its connection with the apparent rise of the knowledge on the part of the individual consciousness.

NOTES

Since Upaniṣadic time, the Prājña, which stands for the individual consciousness in sleep, is very clearly declared to be the *ābhāsa* of the Brahman. It means that terms *prājña*, *taijasa* and *vaiśvānara* known from GK are also related to some sort of ignorance about the true nature of the Ātman. The true condition of the Ātman is knowledge par excellence. SP refers to GK 1.7 and 11 on the word *prājña*. For the word *prajñānaghana*, cf. MāU 5 and 7; BU 4.5.13.

यन्निमित्तं प्रमाणानि प्रामाण्यमिह बिभ्रति ।
तदविज्ञातयाथात्म्यमेतत्कारणमुच्यते ।।३९१।।

391. That on account of which these means of knowing have an authoritativeness and whose real nature is not known is the origin of this (world).

NOTES

An objection could be raised thus : 'When the root-cause of the world is knowledge because of its connection with the appearance of the knowledge on the part of the Ātman, the view that the root-cause *prajñānaghana* would not stand to reason. Since there is accepted in that view a difference between what is cause and what the Ātman.' To this is given the reply : The direct perception etc. are authoritative on the plane of the worldly existence by making the then unknown Ātman as its object. And this Ātman is shown in the Smṛti and the Śruti as the cause of the world. There is thus no duality at all.

यस्मिञ्ज्ञाते भवेज्ज्ञातं जगदेतच्चराचरम् ।
अज्ञाते च तथाऽज्ञातमेतदेव तदुच्यते ॥३९२॥

392. Here is a statement about that which being known, this entire world, movable, becomes known, and which not being known, this world is not known.

NOTES

That the Ātman is the cause so long as ignorance persists is supported by the Śruti informing that all worldly knowledge is derived from the knowledge of that alone. Cf. CU 6.1.3 :

... *yena avijñātaṁ vijñātaṁ* (*bhavati*) 'By which being known (all becomes) known.' Further it is declared to be the cause of all this (world). This is to say that the *upādeyā* 'worldly knowledge' does not exist without its *upādāna*, the prime-cause Ātman, i.e. knowledge itself.

नन्विह प्रलयः श्रुत्या विषयस्यैव भण्यते ।
करणस्य तु नैवोक्तस्तत्कस्मादिति भण्यते ॥३९३॥

स्वगोचरसजातीयं करणं मन्यते श्रुतिः ।
विषयस्य लयोक्त्याऽन्तःकरणप्रलयोक्तता ॥३९४॥

393-394. (Objection:) It is pointed out that the Śruti mentions the merger of the objects alone, and not that of the cause;

why then do you say this? (Reply:) The Śruti holds that the cause belongs to the same category as its own object. (Therefore) by the statement of the merger of the object is to be considered the statement of the merger of the inner-organs (also).

NOTES

The objection is based on the acceptance of the Śruti as the authoritative means of knowing these matters : "Even if the merger of the intellect etc. is proved to be the natural merger, it is not declared by the Śruti anywhere—therefore, that argument of the author is unauthoritative." On verse 394, cf. verse 395 which states that the sense-organs belong to the same category as their respective objects. As such the objection that there is no authoritative Śruti does not hold.

[Verses 395-398 constitute the commentary on the introductory part of BUB 2.4.12.]

एवं मन्तव्य आत्माऽयं तर्कतः प्राग्यथोदितः ।
दुन्दुभ्याद्युक्तदृष्टान्तन्यायमार्गेण यत्नतः ॥३९५॥

आत्मसामान्यसंभूतिलयहेतुसमाश्रयात् ।
आत्मैव सर्वमित्येष प्रतिज्ञार्थः समर्थितः ॥३९६॥

395-396. Thus, the Ātman is to be considered (i.e. understood) as already mentioned, through reasoning with effort, in the light (lit. in the way) of the illustrations that are cited, viz. the drum etc. That all this (world) is the Ātman is justified by taking recourse to the reasoning, viz. the rise and the merger coming commonly from the same source which is similar to the Ātman (the source of the world).

NOTES

Here SP remarks : 'The elaborate discussion on *mananavidhi* is now concluded.' But I believe that the word *mantavyaḥ* in verse 395 does not refer to *mananavidhi* as SP would have it, the word *mantavyaḥ* should be paraphrased as *jñeyaḥ*. There is no *mananavidhi* at all.

स्वाभाविकोऽयं प्रलय इति पौराणिका जगुः ।
बुद्धिपूर्वस्तु विलयः सम्यग्ज्ञानैकपूर्वकः ॥३९७॥

397. The Paurāṇikas have declared that this merger is the natural (merger). As against that, the merger preceded by the proper reasoning (about the nature of the worldly existence) is preceded by the right knowledge (of the world etc.)

NOTES

This is a comment on BUB 2.4.12 (p. 335, *line* 6): *svābhāviko 'yam pralaya iti paurāṇikā vadanti*. There is agreement of the Paurāṇikas with the Upaniṣadic thinkers in respect of this said merger which forms the remaining part of the text. Cf. the *Vāyupurāṇa*, 4.100.135ff.; the *Agnipurāṇa*, 368.2 ff; the *Padmapurāṇa*, 13.1.19. Cf. BG 9.7 : *sarvabhūtāni kaunteya prakṛtiṁ yānti māmikām / kalpakṣaye...//*

शक्तिमात्रात्मना स्थानं कार्याणां यत्स्वकारणे ।
इत्यनात्यन्तिकलयो भूयोजन्मकृतक्षणः ॥३९८॥

398. The non-absolute merger consists in that the effects reside in their own cause in the form[1] of efficiency alone and with the fixed condition that they would be produced again.

NOTES

It is stated that the natural merger is different from the merger preceded by knowledge. In the case of the natural merger, the effects get merged into and stay in the cause in the form of its efficiency to produce those effects; but it never steps further, it is non-absolute.

1. Cf. SK 9 : '*śaktasya śakyakaraṇāt...sat kāryam*/

अतीतानागतेहत्यजन्मनाशादिहेतुनुत् ।
यस्तु धीपूर्वको ध्वंसस्तदर्थेयं परा श्रुतिः ॥३९९॥

399. This (subsequent) part of the Śruti intends to speak the destruction (of the transmigratory existence), which removes the causes of the origin, the destruction etc. of the worldly existence in the past and in the future and which is preceded by proper reasoning (about the real nature of the Ātman).

NOTES

This is a comment on *avidyānirodhadvāreṇa yo bhavati tayārtho 'yaṁ viśeṣārambhaḥ* (BUB 2.4.12, p. 335, *line* 8).

The destruction of ignorance, which is the cause of the births in three times, is preceded by knowledge.

The Śruti BU 2.4.12 clarifies that knowledge is the means of the destruction.

यथोक्तवस्तुसिद्ध्यर्थं दृष्टान्तोऽयमिहोच्यते ।
यथा सैन्धवखिल्योऽस्तः स्वयोनावुदधाविह ॥४००॥

कठिनोदकविलयमनु खिल्यो विलीयते ।
विलीनस्याद्भ्य उद्धृत्य ग्रहणाय न कश्चन ॥४०१॥

निपुणोऽपि नरः शक्तः खिल्यरूपेण पूर्ववत् ।
सामुद्ररूपान्नान्येन ग्रहीतुं कश्चन क्षमः ॥४०२॥

400-402. In order to prove the matter (already) mentioned is here (i.e. now) stated an illustration[1]: As when a lump of salt is thrown into its own cause (viz. the ocean), the lump melts after[2] gross (i.e. solidified) water has merged (into liquid water). When it (the lump of salt) has melted (in water), even a skilful person is not capable of picking it out of water in the earlier form of a lump. No one is capable of picking it up in a form other than that of sea (i.e. sea-salt).

NOTES

This is an explanation of *sa yathā saindhava-khilya udake prāsta udakam evānuviliyeta na hāsyodgrahṇāyeva syāt . . .* (BU 2.4.12).

1. It was earlier stated in general terms that the world merges into its cause, the Brahman, when there arises knowledge of reality. Now, in order to prove this, the Śruti adduces an illustration.

2. Cf. SP : *kaṭhinodakavilayānantaraṁ liyata iti yojanā.*

[Now follows a paraphrase of *yato yatas tv ādadito lavaṇam eva* . . ., up to verse 409.]

आददीत समुद्राम्भस्तं जिघृक्षुर्यतो यतः ।
ततस्ततस्तल्लवणं वेत्ति खिल्यं न कुत्रचित् ॥४०३॥

403. He may take water from whatever part of the ocean, as he is desirous of taking that lump. But he notices that it is everywhere the salty water, but not anywhere the lump (of salt).

सामुद्रमम्भः खिल्यत्वं याति भानुविपाकतः ।
सिन्धोरायातः स यतस्तस्मात्सैन्धव उच्यते ॥४०४॥

404. Owing to the heating by the sun, the water of the ocean gets the nature of a lump. (And) since it has come from the ocean (*sindhu*), it is called *saindhava* 'originating from *sindhu*'.

NOTES

The second line follows BUB (p.335, *lines* 9-10) : *sindhor vikāraḥ saindhavaḥ sindhuśabdenodakam abhidhīyate syandanāt sindhuı udakaṁ tadvikāras tatra bhavo vā saindhavaḥ*.

असंभिन्नस्वावयवः खिल्यः सोऽथ निगद्यते ।
सोऽयं सैन्धवखिल्योऽस्तो यथैवेह महोदधौ ॥४०५॥

405. Then it is called a lump, in that no part of it is distinguished (or, separated) from any other; it is this lump of salt that is (said to be) thrown (here) into the big ocean.

NOTES

In the first line is given the meaning of the word *khilya*; cf. BUB (p. 335, *line* 11) mentions *khila eva khilyaḥ svārthe yat-pratyaya* . . ., "*khila* itself is called *khilya* —in this word the suffix *yat* is used (with the intention of restraining) the original sense". The meaning of the word 'that whose part is not separated' is the grossness due to the parts being mutually combined. The word *atha* means 'in the condition before it was thrown into water, its cause'. After the meaning of the words *saindhava* and *khilya* has been stated, there follows in the second line the meaning of the sentence. The lump of salt gives up the heat through which it obtained the nature of the lump contradictory to that of water. See the next verse for this. This explanation of Ānandagiri is based on the contents of the following verse.

तेजो विरोधिनीं प्राप्य प्रकृतिं विजहात्यथ ।
तेजोवियोगात्काठिन्यं ध्वस्ती भवति तद्घनम् ॥४०६॥

406. Having entered into its original form (viz. water) which is of the opposite nature, it (the lump) gives up the heat stored within it[1]. (Then) owing to the loss of the heat, that (earlier acquired) grossness gets destroyed.

NOTES

This verse states that after the loss of the heat, one should not hold that there would have remained the condition of a lump; it gets destroyed.

1. See the note on the preceding verse.

काठिन्यकारणध्वस्तौ खिल्यस्येह महोदधौ ।
कठिनोदकविध्वंसमनु खिल्यो विलीयते ॥४०७॥

यदेवाकृत्रिमं रूपं तदेवास्यावशिष्यते ।
तेजोवयवसंबन्धसमुत्थं विनिवर्तते ॥४०८॥

407-408. When, in respect of a lump, there is the destruction of the cause of its grossness in the big ocean, the lump (also) melts just in the manner the gross water gets destroyed. There (thus) remains the unacquired form (viz. water of the lump); but that form which had arisen due to its contract with the part of (i.e. some heat) disappears (i.e. gets destroyed).

NOTES

These two verses amplify the briefly stated thought of the preceding verse.

तेजआद्यभिसंबन्धः कारणं खिल्यरूपिणः ।
तद्भावभावतस्तस्य तद्ध्वस्तौ ध्वंसतस्तथा ॥४०९॥

409. The connection (of that) with heat etc. is of the cause of (the existence of) the one in the form of a lump. Its existence is owing to the existence of the heat (which is the cause), and likewise its destruction follows the destruction of that (cause).

NOTES

One should not doubt that mere contact with heat is the cause of the existence of the lump of salt, for the earth etc. would also help its formation. This is stated in the first line. But the second line states why the earth etc. are also specifically mentioned as the cause, just like heat. The cause is understood from the method of *anvayavayatireka*.

[Now begins the explanation of *evaṁ vā ara idaṁ mahadbhūtam anantam apāraṁ vijñānaghana eva* (BU 2.4.12); it continues up to verse 416.]

एवं वा अर इत्यस्य कार्यकारणरूपतः ।
प्रतीचो वास्तवं वृत्तं विरुद्धमभिधीयते ॥४१०॥

410. In the statement, *evaṁ vā are* is stated the real nature of that individual consciousness which is contradictory to its being in the form of the cause and the effect.

NOTES

The verse brings out in full the purport of the illustration (which has been earlier stated in brief). The word *idam* in the passage quoted refers to the natural condition of the individual consciousness which contradicts the cause etc.

अव्यावृत्ताननुगतब्रह्मत्वप्रतिपत्तये ।
महदित्यभिधानं स्यात्कौटस्थ्यार्थं च भूतगीः ॥४११॥

411. For the purpose of understanding the nature of the Brahman which is not differentiated from and followed by anything else, there is the expression (viz. the word) *mahat* and the expression *bhūta* (occurs) for indicating its immutability.

NOTES

The significance of the words *mahat* and *bhūta* is thus clarified.

वास्तवं वृत्तमाश्रित्य प्रतीचः प्राक्प्रबोधतः ।
स्वतःसिद्धस्य विज्ञप्त्यै महदित्यादि भण्यते ॥४१२॥

412. Having kept in view (lit. depending on) the actual state of things, has the Śruti stated (the word) *mahat* etc., for the purpose of making known the individual consciousness which is self-established, (but) before it is realized.

NOTES

This is to avert the doubt that the nature of *mahat* etc. is possible only in the state of liberation.

कारणस्य निषेधोक्तिरनन्तमिति यद्वचः ।
अपारमिति कार्यस्य पारः कार्यस्य कारणम् ॥४१३॥

413. (The use of) the word *anantam* is expressive of the denial of the cause, (and the word) *apāram* is (the denial) of the effect, (since)[1] (the word) *pāra* means the cause of the effect.

NOTES

Now are stated the meanings of the words *ananta* and *apāra*.

1. This answers the objection : 'How is it negated by the word *apāra* that the highest is an effect ?' Sureśvara means to say that as by the word *apūrva* one negates that the highest has some cause, so does one negate by the word *apāra* that the highest is the effect. Cf. *anaparam* which is also used along with *apūrvam* in BU 2.5.19 : *apūrvam anaparam anantaram abāhyam . . .*, or GK 1.26 : *apūrvo 'nantaro' bāhyo'naparaḥ*.

कारणस्य तथा कार्यमन्तोऽनादेः प्रसिद्धितः ।
जात्यन्तरनिषेधाय विज्ञानघनगीरपि ॥४१४॥

414. In the same way, (we[1] know that) every effect is the end of some cause, (this) from the well-known information about the beginninglessness of the (ultimate) cause (viz. the Brahman). So also,[2] the word *vijñānaghana* (is used) for warding off any other effect being produced.

NOTES

1. One seeks to know how it is possible to negate that the highest (Brahman) is the cause (of this world) by the use of the word *ananta*. And the reply is : A cause should have no beginning, for otherwise it would involve absence of *anvaya* and infinite regress, and have the nature of an effect. And an effect is the end of a cause, because there is an endness in an effect. Clay etc. having got the nature of a pot cannot give rise to a plate, that is to say : The potness is the end of clay and plateness cannot result from it. Then, the word *anapara* is capable of negating that the highest is a cause because of the denial of any effect proceeding from it.

2. This is the meaning of the word *vijñānaghana*. It is clear that an effect being produced is different from knowing (the nature of reality).

क्षेत्रज्ञाकाशयोरेवं कार्यकारणसंगतिः ।
अब्धिस्थानीयमैकात्म्यं प्राप्योक्तेर्विनिवर्तते ॥४१५॥

415. Thus is the relationship as the cause and the effect between the individual consciousness and the Ākāśa (viz. Brahman). Obtaining (i.e. understanding) the oneness (of the Ātman and the Brahman) which is comparable to the ocean the awareness of the world outside the Jīvātman goes away.

NOTES

The meaning of the word *eva* is stated in this verse.

The oneness of the Jīvātman and Īśvara is known from the sentence, 'Thou art that'. Thereby is removed the world which is made up of cause and its effects. Such being the case, the homogeneousness of the Jīvātman and the Brahman is ascertained.

कार्यकारणविध्वस्तौ ब्राह्मैकात्म्यप्रबोधतः ।
न विशेषात्मलाभोऽस्ति खिल्यस्येव महोदधौ ॥४१६॥

416. When (the notion of the individual consciousness and the Brahman as) the cause and the effect is (completely) lost

owing to the realization of the oneness of the Brahman, it (viz. the Ātman) never comes into existence as any particular individual (i.e. Jīvātman) as the lump (of salt thrown) into the big ocean (does not regain any of its property).

NOTES

One might argue that even if the nature of the Jīvātman is lost through knowledge leading to the destruction of the cause and effect relationship, it, i.e. the Jīvātman, may be born again. That would mean there is no final liberation as such. To this is given the following reply : No. The Jīvātman is not reborn because of the absence of the cause. Like the lump thrown into the big ocean Jīvātman which has been once and for all destroyed does not again arise.
[This is an explanation of *etebhyaḥ bhūtebhyaḥ*; it continues up to verse 422.]

तेजःसंबन्धमासाद्य यथाऽम्भः खिल्यतामगात् ।
तथैवाज्ञानभूतेभ्यः परः क्षेत्रज्ञतां ययौ ॥४१७॥

417. As the water has attained the state of a lump after having come into contact with the heat, so also has the highest one come to the state of an individual consciousness though above (i.e. different from) the elements and ignorance.

NOTES

Sureśvara points out that the destruction of the nature of the Jīvātman has come about on the occasion of the destruction of ignorance because the entire non-Ātman is produced from ignorance—this he does in answer to the possible objection that there is the destruction of ignorance owing to knowledge, but not that of the nature of the Jīvātman and of the relation between the Brahman and the Jīvātman being a cause and an effect.

कार्यात्माऽपचयं गच्छन्यत्र निष्ठां निगच्छति ।
तानि भूतान्यविद्येति प्राहुस्त्रय्यन्तनिष्ठिताः ॥४१८॥

418. The persons who take their stand on the texts of the Vedāntas have declared as ignorance (*avidyā*). The elements

(*bhūtam*) where the origin (lit. nature) of effects, reducing itself (in qualities), goes down to some other things.

NOTES

An objection could be thus stated: 'Since the word *bhūta* is associated with the elements, how is it said that the highest, the individual consciousness arises from the elements which are of the nature of ignorance?' Sureśvara says in reply to this: That which all effects get merged is the root cause. That is expressed by the word *avidyā* and also by *bhūta*. Cf. Vācaspati's remark : *nāmarūpabījaśaktibhūtam avyākṛtaṁ bhūtasūkṣmam*, as stated by SP; it does not stand to reason that the elements can give rise to the individual consciousness.

परः कारणकार्येभ्य आत्मा पूर्णत्वकारणात् ।
एतेभ्योऽविद्याभूतेभ्यः कार्यकारणतामगात् ॥४१९॥

419. The Ātman is beyond causes and effects on account of its fullness. It becomes the cause of all effects on account of these elements which are (products of) ignorance.

NOTES

One may say that those which give rise to the individual consciousness are causes and effects as well are the elements. To this, this verse is an answer. The Ātman, which is different from the limited (*paricchinna*) cause because of its fullness, is taken as the cause producing all effects owing to the element of ignorance. Cf. the preceding verse which explains *avidyā* as *bhūta*. SP points out that the Ātman is said to have produced effects on account of *mūlāvidyā* 'basic, or natural, ignorance' about the Brahman and also that the word *bhūta* in *avidyābhūtebhyaḥ* means *kārya* in *avidyākārya*.

यतोऽविद्यैव तद्धेतुस्तदुच्छित्तावतो न सन् ।
कार्यकारणभेदोऽयं ब्रह्मास्मीतिप्रबोधतः ॥४२०॥

420. Since it is ignorance that is the cause of it,[1] therefore, when this ignorance is eradicated, the distinction such as the

cause and the effects does not remain (any more) — (this proceeds) from the knowledge 'I am Brahman'

NOTES

1. This is all worldly existence.

तस्मिन्ध्वस्तेऽथ संबोधात्केवलैकात्म्यशेषतः ।
विशेषसंज्ञा नास्त्यस्य पूर्णप्रज्ञप्तिमात्रतः ॥४२१॥

421. When that[1] is destroyed by the knowledge[2] (arising) from the remainder, viz. the oneness of the Ātman alone, there is no particular awareness for it,[3] only on account of the knowledge[4] that it (viz. the Ātman) is full.

NOTES

Some might say : 'The result of the cessation of difference is voidness.' This verse seeks to refute this.

1. 'Distinction such as the cause and the effect.'
2. Cf. *brahmāsmītiprabodhataḥ* in the previous verse
3. See the last remark in SP on verse 420. The word *saṁjñā* means 'awareness'; see verses 437, 444, 448 and 449 below.
4. *prajñapti* = *prajñāna* = *jñāna*

[Now begins the explanation of the word *samutthāya* (BU 2.4.13), it continues up to verse 429.]

अविचारितसिद्धीनि यान्यविद्येत्यवादिषम् ।
एतेभ्यो हेतुभूतेभ्यो भूतेभ्योऽकार्यकारणः ॥४२२॥

कार्यकारणवद्रूपं समुत्थायेति शब्द्यते ।
अविद्यासंगतेरस्य जायतेऽनेकरूपवान् ॥४२३॥

422-423. (That Ātman which is) neither a cause nor an effect, (arising) from these very elements which have become the causes (of the transmigratory existence) and which I have (earlier) mentioned as ignorance and the existence of which cannot be subjected to any examination — becomes described (in the words); having arisen from (the *bhūtas*) in the form of causes and effects and, owing to its (so-called) association, with ignorance, it becomes possessed of many forms.

चेतनाचेतनाभास आत्मानात्मित्वलक्षणः ।
कार्यकारणरूपेण मिथोपेक्षाश्रयं तमः ॥४२४॥

424. The appearance of sentiency and insentiency has the nature of the Ātman and the non-Ātman, (standing) in the form of causes and effects, (and) thus mutually dependent — this is darkness (i.e. ignorance).

NOTES

Desiring to explain the appearance of the Ātman in manifold forms, Sureśvara points out to the characteristic appearance of sentiency.

कार्यकारणतां यात आत्माऽप्येवं तमोवशात् ।
स्वाभासैर्बहुतामेति मनोबुद्ध्याद्युपाधिभिः ॥४२५॥

425. Having thus reached the nature of causes and effects, due to darkness (i.e. ignorance), even that Ātman attains manifoldness by its limiting adjuncts, viz. *manas* and the intellect etc., (which are) its own appearances.

NOTES

Here, Sureśvara states what follows from the individual consciousness assuming manifold forms due to ignorance. Not only does the Ātman get the nature of causes and effects due to ignorance, but also it comes to possess the nature of a knower etc.

तमोहेतु समुत्थानं न वेद्मीत्यग्रहात्मकम् ।
मिथ्याज्ञानं तमः कुर्वदीदृगेव करोति तत् ॥४२६॥

426. Any[1] activity (of the Ātman) originates from darkness (i.e. ignorance). Ignorance produces false knowledge of the nature of non-grasping (of reality, which is expressed in the words) 'I do not know' and that (false knowledge) produces such (further ignorance).

NOTES

All activity of the Ātman is born of ignorance which first causes false knowledge of the form of non-grasping (*agrah-ātmaka*) expressed in words 'I am ignorant, I do not know' and at the same time it causes yet further false knowledge which is similar to it, viz. grasping reality otherwise (*anyathāgraha*).

1. Activity of the Ātman = rise of the Jīvātman.

अविद्याकार्यबुद्धिस्थप्रत्यगाभासरूपवत् ।
बोद्धेत्यादिसमुत्थानं भण्यते परमात्मनः ॥४२७॥

427. What is described as the activity of the highest Ātman, viz. the knower etc.,[1] has the appearance of the individual consciousness residing in the intellect which is the effect of ignorance.

NOTES

1. The word *ādi* refers to the condition of the Jīvātman as the *bhoktṛ* 'enjoyer', the *kartṛ* 'agent'. This will be clear from the following verses.

श्रोता स्प्रष्टेतिरूपः स्यात्तथैवेन्द्रियवृत्तिभिः ।
दुःखी गौरो द्विजश्चेति शरीरोत्थानतः परः ॥४२८॥

428. Likewise, he (the highest Ātman) would be having the form of one who listens, one who touches etc., thanks to the (different) organs and their functions. Also, he[1] who is above (i.e. aloof from) the activity of the body, (appears as) miserable, fair and twice-born.

NOTES

1. Cf. BSB 1.1.1 (p. 3):.... *tathā dehadharmān sthūlo'haṁ kṛśo'haṁ gauro'haṁ tiṣṭhāmi gacchāmi laṅghayāmi ceti / tathendriyadharmānmūkaḥ kāṇaḥ klībaḥ badhiraḥ andho'ham iti /*

धनी गोमान्दरिद्रो वा धनाद्यर्थात्मसंगतेः ।
अतद्वानपि संमोहाद्यथोक्तात्मकतामगात् ॥४२९॥

429. (The highest Ātman) is (described as) wealthy, or possessed of cows or poor owing to his[1] association with objects such as wealth etc. Even though he does not have that (character) (he has) become known as such due to infatuation.

NOTES

1. 'His' stands for 'that of his body; cf *ātmaśabdo dehaviṣayaḥ* . (SP)

प्रत्यग्याथात्म्यमोहोत्था विरिञ्चोपक्रमा मृषा ।
क्षेत्रक्षेत्रज्ञभेदेन ह्या स्थाणोरुत्थितिदृंशेः ॥४३०॥

430. The activity of the 'seer' consisting in the distinction as the body and the individual consciousness beginning with the (appearance as a) creator and up to (that of) a pillar is false, as[1] it arises from ignorance about the real nature of the individual consciousness.

NOTES

[This is the explanation of *tāny evānuvinaśyati*; it continues up to verse 436 in 8/9th lines.]

1. The word *hi* emphasises that the cause of falsity is 'ignorance'.

यथावस्तु यदा बोधो वेदान्तोक्तिश्रुतेर्भवेत् ।
तदा नश्यन्ति भूतानि येभ्यः क्षेत्रज्ञतां गतः ॥४३१॥

431. When there results knowledge of the thing (viz. the Brahman) as it is, on hearing the statements of the Vedāntas, then get destroyed the elements[1] (as distinct from the individual consciousness) on account of which the Ātman has got the status of the individual consciousness.

NOTES

1. I.e. the awareness of them as distinct from the Ātman.

स्वरूपलाभमात्रेण सम्यग्बोधोऽखिलं तमः ।
यतो हन्ति ततो नासावभ्यासं प्रति वीक्षते ॥४३२॥

432. Because right knowledge (about the nature of the Ātman) removes total darkness (i.e. ignorance), merely by its rise (lit. acquiring its natural form), it does not look to (i.e. expect) any more repetition (of knowledge-acquiring practice).

NOTES

The verse seeks to set aside the view that the right knowledge depends on repeated practice (of meditation) in order that it destroys ignorance and its effects. Cf. the *Brahmasūtra* 4.1.1 : *āvṛttir asakṛt upadeśāt.*

व्यङ्ग्येष्वर्थेषु नाऽऽवृत्त्या व्यञ्जको हन्ति तत्तमः ।
व्यञ्जकस्य स्वभावोऽयं न प्रयोगमपेक्षते ॥४३३॥

433. The manifestor (viz. the individual consciousness) does not destroy darkness (i.e. ignorance) in respect of things which are to be manifested[1] by repetition (of meditation etc.) Such (indeed) is the nature of the manifestor that it does not have to apply itself to (lit. expect) repeated practice of meditation.

NOTES

There is a suggested illustration of the lamp that illuminates objects once for all, it does not have to repeat the act of illuminating. The Ātman is like the lamp.

1. What are these *vyaṅgyārthas* ? Perhaps, there is Śleṣa and *vyaṅgyārthas* refer to (i) the objects in the world (as false) and (ii) the objects of the world to be brought to light by the lamp.

2. For the word *prayoga* see NKL (p. 902) : *prayogam abhyāsakriyām iti yāvat.*

मोहतत्कार्यनीडो यस्तस्याज्ञानसमन्वयात् ।
प्रत्यगात्माऽपि तद्ब्रह्म परोक्षमभवन्मृषा ॥४३४॥

तद्वदद्वयतत्त्वोऽपि तदसम्बोधहेतुतः ।
आत्मा संसारितां यातो यथा कार्ष्ण्यं वियत्तथा ॥४३५॥

434-435. Even for the individual consciousness, who is the abode of infatuation (i.e. ignorance) and its outcome owing to the inherent relation to ignorance, the Brahman becomes falsely beyond perception. In the same way, that Ātman becomes possessed of the transmigratory existence on account of not knowing its nature, although there is no other Truth beside itself (this happens) as the sky (becomes) dark[1].

NOTES

The verse 434 anticipates the objection : If ignorance is abandoned due to the rise of knowledge of the oneness of the Ātman, then because of the ever non-existence of this oneness : (i) How can one say that the Brahman is beyond perception, since the Brahman is held as identical with the individual consciousness which is directly perceptible. (ii) Also, how can one say that the Ātman is transmigratory, though the Ātman is identical with the Brahman which is non-transmigratory. And this is the reply : (i) is not fault, for it is ignorance that makes one feel the Brahman as not directly perceptible. Cf. the Śruti : *yat sākṣād aparokṣād brahma* (BU 3.4.1, 3.5.1), "The Brahman that is immediate and direct." Verse 435 refutes (ii) as stated in the note on the previous verse. The illustration of the sky becoming dark, i.e. getting to possess the quality of darkness is owing to the onlooker's misconception. Cf. BSB 1.1.1 (p. 2): *apratyakṣe 'py ākāśe bālās talamalinatāyāmadhyasyanti.*

आत्मनो ब्रह्मता यस्माद्ब्रह्मणोऽप्यात्मता स्वतः ।
तमोमात्रान्तरायत्वात्तद्ध्वस्तावेव साऽऽप्यते ॥४३६॥

436. Since the Ātman has the nature of the Brahman and the Brahman, of the Ātman in its own right, therefore, on account of eradication of the obstruction, viz. merely darkness (i.e. ignorance) (of the true nature of the Ātman), is attained that (oneness of the two).

NOTES

The purport of the passage *tāny evānuvinaśyati* is concluded in this verse. When knowledge of the true nature of the

Ātman arises, ignorance is eradicated. And the Brahman shines in its own form.

[This is the meaning of *na pretya saṁjñāstīty are bravīmiti hovāca yājñāvalkyaḥ* (BU 2.4.13); it continues up to verse 444.]

सर्वमात्मेतिसम्यग्धीजन्मनैवाखिलं तमः ।
ध्वंसमेति ततः संज्ञा नाविद्योत्थाऽवशिष्यते ॥४३७॥

437. The total darkness (i.e. ignorance) is destroyed merely by the rise of the right knowledge (in the form), 'all (this) is the Ātman'. And then, there does not remain any awareness (etc.[1] for the Ātman) arising from ignorance.

NOTES

1. This is most probably in the form, 'I am this; I have this name,' etc.

सदोत्पन्नाऽऽत्मनि मितिरुत्पाद्याऽकारणादिधीः ।
कारणादिधियः पूर्वं प्रतीचि ब्रह्मधीस्ततः ॥४३८॥

438. The knowledge[1] is ever-existent in the Ātman. The knowledge that (the Ātman) is not the cause etc. is to be effected (lit. produced). The (various) knowledge of the cause etc. on the part of the individual consciousness (occurs) first (lit. before, i.e. in the beginning) and the knowledge that it is only the Brahman (occurs) later.

NOTES

The objector might ask: 'When the knowledge of the Ātman arises, how is it that there remains no awareness (of name etc.) The reply is: The awareness such as 'I am the agent of this action' etc. on the part of the Ātman is accepted by everyone as a general rule, but the knowledge that 'the Ātman is non-agent' is created by the statement of the Śruti. Moreover, by the knowledge of the oneness of the Ātman, from the statement of the Śruti, the awareness of the agentship is destroyed at first and then the awareness in the individual consciousness, viz. it is the Brahman, is destroyed—just as the fire burns out when it is without any fuel.

l'. *mati* = *jñāna*.

अपास्ताशेषभेदस्य यद्रूपं भेदवद्गतम् ।
तज्ज्ञानेनैव तज्ज्ञातं तदन्यानवशेषतः ॥४३९॥

439. Only by the (proper) knowledge of that which is known as the form consisting in variety of that (consciousness) whose all variety has been set aside (i.e. thrown away as unreal) becomes known that (viz. consciousness, since there does not remain anything else than itself.

NOTES

A question arises: 'How does one grasp that there does not remain anything else than the Ātman that is wholly devoid of variety? For, it is heard that *ākāśa* etc. exist apart from the Ātman.' The reply is: True, that nature of the homogeneous individual consciousness possessing difference like ether (*ākāśa*) etc. is known only by the knowledge of the individual consciousness and that is the effect of ignorance alone. So, when the notions about the Ātman regarding his agentship etc. are removed, all so-called difference such as ether etc. is also destroyed. And there remains consciousness alone.

अहेतुफलरूपेण प्रतीचा तद्विलक्षणम् ।
कार्यकारणवज्जग्ध्वा द्रष्टैवैकोऽवशिष्यते ॥४४०॥

440. Having become one with (lit. eaten) is which consists in causes and effects and which is in characters different from the individual consciousness that has the nature neither of cause nor of effect, the seer (i.e. the Ātman) remains alone.

प्रत्यङ्मात्रेक्षणादात्ममोहतज्जनिराकृतेः ।
असंभवाद्द्वितीयस्य स्यामपूर्वादिमानहम् ॥४४१॥

441. Since, on thinking of (lit. seeing) the individual consciousness alone, there is removal of infatuation (i.e. ignorance) about the Ātman and its (i.e. of the ignorance) products and therefore there is no possibility of a second

existence, (there remains the thought;) may I be one without any beginning etc.

NOTES

One might think that since the individual consciousness is declared to be one thing, it can have the nature of cause as well as effect; this is totally averted.

व्यपेततमसस्तत्त्वमागमापायसाक्षिणः ।
ज्ञानेन गम्यते साक्षात्तावन्मात्रानुरोधिना ॥४४२॥

442. The Truth of the Ātman from whom has (all) darkness (i.e. ignorance) withdrawn and who is the witness of the appearance and the disappearance (of the worldly objects) is known by the knowledge which is in keeping with that (Ātman) alone.

NOTES

This verse conveys that it is not possible to remove ignorance of the Jīvātman by means of knowing of a pot etc. that cannot be the witness (*sākṣin*).

दृष्टिमात्रात्मयाथात्म्यात्कार्यकारणवस्तुनः ।
नाज्ञातं किञ्चिदप्यस्ति नानपास्तं तमोऽप्यतः ॥४४३॥

443. There is nothing unknown (that is other) than the real nature of the Ātman which consists only in seeing itself, and which (in reality) is (the thing at the basis of) causes and effects. And darkness (i.e. ignorance) also does not remain unremoved by this (i.e. the knowledge of the individual consciousness).[1]

NOTES

Here is shown the difference between the knowledge of the individual consciousness and that of a pot etc.

1. Cf. *ataḥśabdena pratyagjñānoktiḥ*. (SP)

क्षेत्रज्ञेश्वरभेदेन संज्ञा नैवेह विद्यते ।
तद्धेतौ तमसि ध्वस्ते कुतः संज्ञाऽनिमित्ततः ॥४४४॥

444. There does not exist here (i.e. in the state of knowledge)[1] any awareness of the distinction as the individual consciousness[2] and Īśvara (the Brahman). (For) when the cause of that, i.e. darkness (i.e. the ignorance), is destroyed where could there be (such) awareness which has no cause (to effect it)?

NOTES

1. Cf. *iheti vidyāvasthoktiḥ.* (SP)
2. *kṣetra = pratyag, Īśvarā = brahman.*

संज्ञा प्रेत्याऽऽत्मनो नास्तीत्येतच्छ्रुत्वा त्वचूचुदत् ।
शङ्कमानाऽऽत्मनो नाशं मैत्रेयी पतिमादरात् ॥४४५॥

445. On listening, "After departure, there is no awareness of one ('I am such and such etc.')," Maitreyī feared the destruction of her own self and through reverence (or, with a little fear) implored (lit. goaded) him (with a question).

विज्ञानैकघनोक्त्या च निःसंज्ञवचसा तथा ।
उक्त्योर्मिथोविरुद्धत्वादात्मा मोमुह्यते मम ॥४४६॥

446. By the statement that the Ātman is a mass only of consciousness and also by the statement that there is no (more) consciousness (after death) which are mutually opposed, my mind (lit. Ātman) is in (great) infatuation (i.e. feels great apprehension).

NOTES

This explains *mā bhagavān amūmuhan na pretya saṁjñāstiti* (BUB 2.4.13).

[Now follows up to verse 452 the explanation of *sa hovāca vā are 'haṁ mohaṁ bravīmi* (BUB 2.4.13).]

अविरुद्धं सुविस्पष्टं मया तुभ्यं प्रभाषितम् ।
स्वापराधात्तु मद्वाक्यं विरुद्धार्थं त्वमीक्षसे ॥४४७॥

447. (Yājñavalkya answered) "I have told you (what is) non-contradictory and clear. But you understand (lit. see) my say as involving contradictions on account of your own fault.

विज्ञानैकघनोक्त्याऽहं कृत्स्नैकात्म्यं तवावदम् ।
संज्ञानाशेन चाविद्याहेतुत्थापह्नुतिं तथा ॥४४८॥

448. "In the statement 'the Ātman is a mass only of consciousness,' I have declared to you the complete oneness (of the Jīvātman) with the Ātman and by (the statement of) the absence of awareness (of name, form etc., I have declared) likewise the overpowering (lit. covering), (of reality) arising from ignorance."

विशेषसंज्ञा याऽस्याभूद्विज्ञानात्मादिलक्षणा ।
सम्यग्धीध्वस्तमोहस्य सा कृत्स्ना विनिवर्तते ॥४४९॥

449. Whatever special awareness there was spoken of the Ātman as characterized by some definite knowledge etc.[1], all that (awareness) disappears (from it) whose infatuation (i.e. ignorance) is destroyed by the right knowledge.

NOTES

This is reiteration of the idea in the latter half of the previous verse.

1. *jñātṛtva* of the Ātman in relation to *jñeya* 'knowable (object) beside it; cf. verses 427 and 435 above—this refers to the Ātman's discrimination between one object and another.

यत्त्वपारमनन्तं च वास्तवं ज्ञानमात्मनः ।
कूटस्थं तत्स्वतःसिद्धेस्तत्कस्माद्विनिवर्तते ॥४५०॥

450. The knowledge on the part of the Ātman which does not produce any (later) existent effect[1] endless and immutable, since it is self-established, how can it (ever) disappear ?[2]

NOTES

1. Cf. verse 413 and note thereon.
2. I.e. get removed by any cause.

इतीममर्थं भार्यायै याज्ञवल्क्योऽभ्यभाषत ॥४५१॥

कार्यकारणनाशेऽपि स्वतःसिद्धमनन्यगम् ।
यद्वस्तु तदलं स्वात्मसंवित्त्यै निरपेक्षतः ॥४५२॥

451-452. Such a thing did Yājñavalkya speak unto his wife. That thing which is self-established and which is without anything else[1] is, even when there occurs the destruction of (the notion regarding) the cause and effect (relation), capable of making itself understood independently (of anything else).

NOTES

This is an explanation of *alaṁ vā ara idaṁ vijñāya* (BU 2.4.13).

1. The text reads *ananyamam*, qualifying *tad vastu*. It is difficult to make out its sense. Possibly the correct word could be *ananyagam* 'which does not follow any other', that is to say 'which is one without a second' . . . cf. the *Bṛhadāraṇyakavārtikasāra* 2.4.163 (p. 1523).

[This is the significance of *yatra hi dvaitam iva bhavati* (BU 2.4.14); it runs up to verse 464.]

यत्राज्ञातात्मतत्त्वात्माऽविद्यासंवीतशेमुषिः ।
तत्र मिथ्याग्रहग्रस्तो द्रष्टृदृश्यादिभेदधीः ॥४५३॥

453. Whoever is one that has not known the Truth of the Ātman and has the intellect overpowered (lit. wrapped) by ignorance; is overwhelmed by wrong knowledge and has the notions of distinction such as the seer, the object of the seeing etc.

यत्राज्ञातात्मयाथात्म्यस्तत्तमोपिहितेक्षणः ।
तत्राविद्योत्थबुद्ध्यादिगुणभूतात्मविन्नरः ॥४५४॥

454. The person, who has not known the real nature of the Ātman, has eyes covered by darkness (i.e. ignorance) about that, understands the Ātman as being possessed of properties such as the intellect etc. which have arisen from ignorance.

अविद्यामात्रशेषत्वं जगतः प्रागवादिषम्
नर्तेऽविद्यां कार्यमिदं हीति हेतावतः पदम् ॥४५५॥

455. I have already declared that the world is the product of ignorance alone; there would not be this effect, (viz. the world) without ignorance. The word *hi* is used for indicating the reason.

NOTES

The purport of the passage from the BU is already stated; now, the meaning of the word *hi* is explained. Cf. BUB (p. 340, *line* 9) : *hi yasmāt.*

सतोऽभिव्यञ्जकं मानं स्वभावोऽयं मितेर्भवेत् ।
अविद्यायाः स्वभावोऽयं यदसत्करणं मृषा ॥४५६॥

456. The means is that which manifests the existent——— such is the nature of the (right) knowledge. But the nature of ignorance is such that it falsely creates that which is non-existent.

NOTES

The world is (i) existent, or (ii) non-existent. If (i), there would be no use of ignorance. If (ii), how is it possible to see the non-existent through ignorance—this doubt is removed by means of illustration.

The nature of knowledge and that of ignorance are clarified in contrast. Knowledge is that which manifests what is existent. Ignorance gives rise to what is non-existent.

उक्तहेत्वर्थदीप्त्येतद्धीति तस्य निपाततः ।
द्वीतं द्विधेतमेकं सत्तद्भावो द्वैतमुच्यते ॥४५७॥

उपमार्थं इवेत्येतद्भवतीति क्रियापदम् ।
तत्रैव विद्यावस्थायां संज्ञेयं युज्यते मृषा ॥४५८॥

457-458. This[1] word *hi* is to clarify the thing which has been already stated on account of its being an adverb. (The[2] word) *dvitam* is explained as *dvidhā itam* 'that which, being one has proceeded in two ways'—the nature of that is *dvaita*. The word *iva* is for conveying the sense of comparison. (The word) *bhavati* is a verbal form. In that, viz. in the condition of ignorance, is this name falsely used.

NOTES

1. The question, 'How can one say that the word *hi* clarifies its reason ?' is answered thus : Since the world is caused by the nature of being the seen etc., it is nothing but the product of ignorance like a serpent in a rope.

2. The second line of verse 457 and verse 458 explain *yatra hi dvaitam iva bhavati* (BU 2.4.14).

ननु द्वैतमिवेत्येतदुपमानं कथं भवेत् ।
द्वैतं वस्तु न चेदस्ति सर्वस्यैकात्म्यमात्रतः ॥४५९॥

459. One might object : How can (the words) *dvaitam iva* serve as the standard of comparison, for all this is but one Ātman and therefore there is no duality (or, lit. nothing else beside one reality) ?

NOTES

The *upamāna-upameya* relation is impossible in case there exists but one thing.

नैष दोषो यतो दृष्ट एकस्मिन्नपि वस्तुनि ।
उपमेयोपमाभावो दिग्धीरिव विहायसि ॥४६०॥

रामरावणयोर्युद्धं रामरावणयोरिव ।
यथा प्रसिद्धो जगति तथैवेहापि गम्यताम् ॥४६१॥

460-461. (The answer is :) This is not a fault, because the relation of the standard of comparison and the object of comparison is noticed even in the case of only one thing—thus, for example, it is there in the case of the sky where there is the notion of different quarters. As there is the example known in the world, viz. the fight between Rāma and Rāvaṇa was like that between Rāma and Rāvaṇa, so also may be understood (the relation of comparison and the object of comparison) in this case as well.

NOTES

Even in the absence of a thing different from the Ātman, the word *iva* can be used for the sake of comparison. The notion of different quarters which is known about just one and unique sky is an example. It should be borne in mind that *sādharmya* can be spoken of only two different things—cf. *sādharmyam upamābhede* (the *Kāvyaprakāśa* 10.1). Likewise, even if there is no duality in respect of the Ātman, it is possible to say that the Ātman appears to be manifold. Cf. *ekaṁ sat viprā bahudhā vadanti* (the *Ṛgveda* 1.164.46).

Another illustration is given to prove the same in verse 461. One should remember that there is the idea of similarity volitionally conceived of—the purport is to point out the incomparableness of the thing (*ananvaya*). Cf the *Kāvyaprakāśa* 10.5 *vṛtti* : *upamānāntarasambandhābhavo'nanvayaḥ*. The basic idea in *ananvaya* is *anyasadṛśavyavaccheda*.

अद्वैतात्परमार्थाद्वा मायाद्वैतमपीष्यते ।
तेनोपमार्थसंसिद्धेर्यथा स्वप्नेन्द्रजालयोः ॥४६२॥

462. Or, from the non-duality which is the highest reality is understood the false duality also, for thereby is established the idea of comparison as in the case of sleep and the show by a magician.

NOTES

Sureśvara points out that the duality spoken of is not really existent, it is imagined to be so. Thereby, he wants to establish the propriety of the comparison used by the Śruti as in BU 4.3.10; MaiU 4.2, 7.10; GK 3.29 ff. etc. The use of similes based on experiences in the dream and in the magic show only help to point out the unreality of the non-Ātman. Read SP : *kalpitadvaitenopamāsiddhiṁ sphuṭayati*.

मिथ्येव भाति सत्योऽपीत्यापि लोकेऽभिधीयते ।
मिथ्याभावो न नास्तीति वक्तुं कश्चिदपि क्षमः ॥४६३॥

463. It[1] is said in the world that even[2] a real thing appears to be false; (and[3]) no one can ever say that there is no unreality.

NOTES

1. This verse is an answer to the doubt : 'How can the

false duality of sleep etc. be the illustration of the real Ātman ?'

2. The word *api* implies that the false thing also appears to be real. According to SP, the second *api* is used for giving the two arguments in the Śruti.

3. This part of the verse seeks to obviate the possible question : 'Because of invariable concomitance in the form that whatever is visible is unreal, how can one say that a false (unreal) thing does not exist ?' The answer is : They often establish the contradiction and sublation of falsity by Truth.

समस्तव्यस्ततारूपं यो वक्तीहाऽऽत्मनः श्रुतेः ।
तत्पक्षस्य निषेधोऽयं यत्र हीत्यादिनोच्यते ॥४६४॥

464. This statement, *yatra hi* . . . (BU 2.4.14), is the refutation of the view of one who propounds, on the basis of the Śruti[1], that the Ātman has a condition (consisting) in whole and its parts.

NOTES

This is the purport of *yatra hi* . . ., that is to say : Seeing duality is possible only in the condition of ignorance, not otherwise. It is only through ignorance that one would talk of creation of the universe from the Brahman (=Ātman). Or, in other words, one would consider the Brahman (=Ātman) as a whole and the various objects its parts.

1. Cf. PU 4.9 : *eṣa hi draṣṭā spraṣṭā śrotā* . . . "And this one is the seer, the feeler, the hearer . . .", also BU 2.4.6 : *idaṁ sarvaṁ yad ayam ātmā* "All this is what is this Ātman."

[This is the meaning of *tad itara itaraṁ jighrati* . . .*tad itara itaraṁ vijānāti*; it continues up to verse 468.]

तस्यामविद्यावस्थायां स्वप्नावस्थां गतो यथा ।
घ्रातेतरः सन्नितरं गन्धं घ्राणेन जिघ्रति ॥४६५॥

465. In that condition of ignorance, a person like the one who is in the dream-state, smells a thing by the sense of smell, being different from that which is smelt.

घ्रातृघ्रेयाभिसंबन्धाद्घ्राणाद्याहृतिरिष्यते ।
जिघ्रतीत्यपि निर्देशः क्रियातत्फलयोर्भवेत् ॥४६६॥

466. It is on account of the connection of one who smells and that which is smelt one that one understands the statement about the act of smell etc.[1] Also, the expression *jighrati* can become the mention of both the action and its result.

NOTES

One might doubt that the expression *ghrāṇena* is not proper, because we hear words which have the meaning of the agent, the object of action and the action. The first line of the verse states the purport of BUB (p. 341, *line* 6): *itara itaram iti kārakapradarśanārthaṁ* . . . , "The words *itara itaram* are used to show the functionaries." Yet, one might ask 'what is the fruit ?', for it is not intended here there is no word denoting that.

1. The word *ādi* conveys to us the idea of all that causes contact with objects in respect of *ghrāṇa*.

उत्तरेष्वपि वाक्येषु योजनेयं यथोदिता ।
प्रत्यगज्ञानमात्रोत्थं ग्राहकाद्यत्र भण्यते ।४६७॥

467. In the subsequent sentence also is applicable what is here, thus stated. (Indeed) the statement about cognizer etc. is made as it does arise merely from ignorance about the individual consciousness.

NOTES

The first line states that the subsequent passages *tad itara itaraṁ paśyati* . . . should also be explained in the same manner as the statement *tad itara itaraṁ jighrati* is explained. In the second line concludes the meaning of the passage *yatra hi dvaitam iva bhavati tad itara itaraṁ jighrati* . . . .

क्रियाकारकसंज्ञाया विषयोऽयं समीरितः ।
अतोऽविद्यासमुच्छित्तावियं संज्ञा निवर्तते ॥४६८॥

468. (All) this matter is discussed in respect of the name,

viz. action and that which helps action. Therefore, this name vanishes when there is the eradication of ignorance.

[Now begins the explanation of *yatra vā asya sarvam ātmaivābhūt tat kena kaṁ jighrati—tat kena kaṁ vijānīyāt* (BU 3.4.14); it continues up to verse 478.]

विज्ञानघन इत्युक्तेर्विषयोऽयमथोच्यते ।
यत्रं वा इति वाक्येन ध्वस्ताविद्ये विपश्चिति ॥४६९॥

469. Then is discussed the matter mentioned in the words *vijñānaghana* . . . . , in the sentence *yatra vā* . . . . , in respect of the wise (knower) whose ignorance has been destroyed.

यत्र त्वस्याऽऽत्मनोऽज्ञस्य शास्त्राचार्यप्रसादतः ॥४७०॥

प्रत्यग्याथात्म्यविज्ञानभास्वद्भास्करदीधिति-
संप्लुष्टनिखिलाविद्ये तत्र कः केन किं वद ।
जिघ्रेदैकात्म्यमात्रेण सर्वस्यास्याऽऽत्ममात्रतः ॥४७१॥

470-471. But where, that is to say, in the case of one who is ignorant about the Ātman and whose entire ignorance is destroyed by the rays of the bright sun in the form of the knowledge of the true nature of the individual consciousness through the favour of the exponent (lit. preceptor) of the Śruti, tell me, who could smell what and with what? (I ask this,) because to him all this is the Ātman alone on account of (i.e. through the fact that there is) oneness (of reality).

NOTES

Sureśvara refers to the other reading *yatra tv asya* in place of *yatra vā asya* (*sarvam ātmaivābhūt*) of BU 2.4.14. This *yatra tv asya* is noted in BUB (p. 342, footnote no. 1).

षष्ठगोचरवत्सर्वं कार्यकारणवज्जगत् ।
ध्वस्तात्मान्ध्यस्य विदुषः सम्यग्ज्ञानोदये भवेत् ॥४७२॥

472. All (this) world (which is) made up of causes and effects, would become like the world which falls within the range of the sixth sense-organ, viz. *manas*,[1] when there arises the right knowledge on the part of one whose blindness as regards the true nature of the individual consciousness is destroyed.

NOTES

Doubting that, when all the agents are the Ātman and nothing else, the nature of the existent is only like that, he concludes the purport of *sarvam ātmaivābhūt*.

1. The word *ṣaṣṭhagocara* is used in Nais 1.30, 2.114 and Cand explains it as the *pramāṇa* called *abhāva* in 1.30, otherwise as *asat* in 2.114, cf. further HIRIYANNA's note on Nais (p. 220), HACKER, *op. cit.*, p. 39 footnote. It is nevertheless uncertain if this could be correct, inasmuch as, in Śaṅkara's time, *abhāva* (*anupalabdhi*) was not considered as a *pramāṇa*—Śaṅkara accepted only three *pramāṇas*, i.e. *śabda*, *anumāna* and *pratyakṣa*. In fact, BSB 2.1.2 (p. 436) reads *ṣaṣṭhasyaivendriyārthasya na smṛtir avakalpate* which shows *ṣaṣṭha* to refer to *manas*. And, as such *ṣaṣṭhagocara* may better be paraphrased as *manogocara*. It is, therefore, doubtful that Sureśvara, a direct disciple of Śaṅkara, accepted *abhāva* as a *pramāṇa*.

अव्यावृत्ताननुगतमतिहेतु सदैकलम् ।
विज्ञानधनमानन्दमैकात्म्यं व्यवतिष्ठते ॥४७३॥

473. There remains only the oneness which is not differentiated and followed by anything else, beyond cause, ever alone, a mass of consciousness, and bliss.

NOTES

One might say that, like duality, non-duality could also be insignificant. Therefore, Sureśvara asserts that there remains just the oneness which has neither particularity nor generality and which is self-luminous. In other words, duality ends into what is not void.

ग्राहकादिविभागोऽत्र नास्ति तद्धेत्वसम्भवात् ।
चिन्मात्रस्य स्वतः सिद्धेर्विज्ञानघनगीरतः ॥४७४॥

474. Distinction (lit. division) (of reality) such as a knower etc. does not exist here[1] owing to the impossibility of there being any cause of that (ignorance). Since consciousness, one (without a second), is self-established, there is the word (of the Śruti) *vijñānaghana* (about it).

NOTES

Sureśvara asserts here that the Ātman is self-luminous and therefore does not fall within the purview of the usual knowing mechanism such as the knower, the means of knowing etc.

1. This refers to the state of pure knowledge on the part of the individual consciousness; *atreti vidyāvasthoktā*. (SP)

आत्माविद्यामनाश्रित्य कारकत्वं न लभ्यते ।
कारकं चानपाश्रित्य न क्रियेह प्रसिध्यति ॥४७५॥

475. Here (i.e. in the worldly dealings) the character of an agent (on the part of the individual consciousness) is not noticed (lit. found) by one who has not resorted to ignorance about the Ātman. And there is no activity established without resorting to (the character of) agent.

NOTES

It is possible to translate the first line of this verse in two alternative ways which depend upon two translations of the word *kārakatva*: (i) the character of an agent and (ii) the character of a means. The translation above is in keeping with the alternative (i); the other translation of the first line in keeping with the alternative (ii) is thus: In the worldly dealings the character of a means of knowing is not noticed by one in what has not depended on ignorance about the Ātman. Cf. SP: *kriyākārakavyavahāraḥ saptamyarthaḥ*, where *saptamī* means *adhikaraṇārthaḥ*.

अन्तरेण क्रियां तद्वत्फलं नैव प्रसिध्यति ।
कारकाद्यात्मना सेयमविद्यैव प्रकाशते ॥४७६॥

476. Similarly, no result is ever secured without some activity. Thus, in the form of the different *kārakas* this ignorance itself manifests (to one).

NOTES

One might argue that a result could be obtained only through activity which involves the thought of *kārakas*, i.e. of duality. But Sureśvara argues that the notion of different *kārakas* proceeds only from ignorance about the true nature of the Ātman.

यत एवमतोऽविद्यासमुच्छित्ताविदं जगत् ।
व्याकृताव्याकृतं कृत्स्नमात्मतामेति बोधतः ॥४७७॥

477. Because this is so, there being complete eradication of ignorance, the entire world, manifest and/or unmanifest, becomes one with the Ātman, through knowledge (of the real nature of it).

NOTES

Once again, Sureśvara asserts the absence of any division of this world into the agent, activity etc.

भूयोऽपि लभते संज्ञां लीनं सत्कारणात्मनि ।
जगदेतद्यथा तद्वन्नाविद्याविलये भवेत् ॥४७८॥

478. As this world which has (earlier) merged into its existential cause once again gets the awareness (that it exists etc.), so does it not get that awareness in case there is the disappearance of ignorance.

NOTES

One might argue that, as at the end of the dream state, a person may become aware of duality. Sureśvara does not tolerate this idea of similarity between dream state and the experience of reality. Once ignorance is destroyed, there is no return of worldly existents.

[This is the clarification of *yenedaṁ sarvaṁ vijānāti taṁ kena vijānīyāt*; it continues up to verse 482.]

ज्ञानोत्पत्तौ न संज्ञाऽस्तीत्यास्तां तावदिहाऽऽत्मनः ।
अपि सत्यामविद्यायां न संज्ञाऽस्त्यात्मनीदृशी ॥४७९॥

479. If one says, there cannot be any awareness on the part of the Ātman (viz. I am this etc.) when there arises the knowledge; our answer is: Let that be so, for even when there is ignorance, on the part of the Ātman, there[1] does not exist any

awareness on its part which is like this (viz. dependent on division such as the agent, the activity etc.).

NOTES

The word *idṛśi* means 'that which cognizes the difference such as a cognizer etc.'

ग्राहकादि जगत्सर्वं येन कूटस्थसाक्षिणा ।
लोकः सर्वो विजानाति जानीयात्केन तं वद ।।४८०।।

480. Tell me by what means one should know that one, the immutable witness through whose help people know this whole world, the perceiver[1] etc.

NOTES

Sureśvara puts a rhetorical question only with the intention of asserting that the witness of all is in every condition but the Ātman. Cf. Ānandagiri on BUB (p. 343) : . . . *taṁ sākṣiṇaṁ kena karaṇena ko* . . . . *jānīyād* . . . . /

1. *grāhaka-* = *indriyeṇa grāhaka-*

अचेतने जगत्यस्मिन्साक्ष्येवैकोऽत्र चेतनः ।
ग्राहकादिर्न तत्रापि साक्षिसिद्धावपेक्ष्यते ।।४८१।।

481. In this insentient world, the sentient one alone is the witness. But even that being so, the division such as the knower etc. is not expected for proving (the existence of) the witness.

NOTES

The first line affirms that even in this world of ignorance, a witness is only a sentient being that is unchanging. And the second line points out that, though there is sentient being alone that grasps the oneness of the Ātman, it is independent of any means etc. unlike the sentient being in the world of ignorance.

संज्ञेयं किमु विध्वस्तसंसारानर्थकारणे ।
उदितैकात्म्ययाथात्म्यसम्यग्ज्ञानदिवाकरे ।।४८२।।

482. How could be there this awareness when the Sun (lit. the maker of day) of the right knowledge of the true nature of the Ātman, viz. of its oneness, has arisen and which is the cause of destruction of evil, viz. the transmigratory existence?

NOTES

This clarifies the sentence *yenedaṁ sarvaṃ*—which was earlier indicated by the word *api* in *tatra api* of the previous verse. Since there does not exist any other witness than the Ātman, there is no notion of difference such as the perceiver etc.

बोद्धारमपि चापेक्ष्य न संज्ञा प्रत्यगात्मनि ।
बोद्धृतज्ज्ञानविषयैर्न बोद्धा गृह्यते यतः ॥४८३॥

483. Referring to the knower also, there is not an awareness (viz. I am this etc.) in respect of the individual consciousness, because the knower is not (i.e. cannot be) understood by the usual relation of the knower, the object of knowing.

[This explains *vijñātāram are kena vijānīyāt* in 11th line.]

अविचारितसंसिद्धिः प्रमात्रादिस्वलक्षणा ।
संज्ञेयं प्रथते मोहान्नत्वसौ वस्तुनिश्चितौ ॥४८४॥

484. This awareness, which has its own characteristics consisting in the knower etc. and (whose proof is) established (even) without any thought, (is) well-known on account of infatuation (i.e. ignorance). But (certainly) it does not get established when there is an ascertainment of reality (i.e. Ātman).

यत एवमतः सिद्धं दर्शनं प्रत्यगात्मनः ।
श्रुत्यादिसाधनं साक्षात्सर्वमात्मेत्युदीरितम् ॥४८५॥

485. Since this is so, therefore, the understanding (lit. seeing) of (the true nature of) the individual consciousness is established. And there (in the Śruti) is there a proof mentioned (in the words), 'All this is the Ātman'.

NOTES

Thus is concluded the purport of the section. It has been ascertained that the dealings proceed from difference which can be found only in the condition of ignorance. Also, it is established that what has been stated to be the direct perception of the individual consciousness dependent on hearing etc. is the means to liberation along with renunciation.

BUBV 4.5

निरधारि पुरा ब्रह्म मधुकाण्डागमेन यत् ।
याज्ञवल्कीयकाण्डेन तद्युक्त्याऽथोपपादितम् ॥१॥

1. Now (in this section of Yājñavalkya[1]) is supported with reason (the thought on) the Brahman which is earlier ascertained by the tradition (noted) in the Madhukāṇḍa.[2]

NOTES

It is useful to note how Ānandagiri points out the relation of 4.5 to the preceding section of BU. He says : In BU 4.4 which precedes this section, were narrated the evil, the cause of evil, the aim of human beings, and the cause of human end (viz. liberation) with the help of the Śruti. Further, it was pointed out that the entire Veda teaches the way to obtaining the final end, which is elaborately described by the Śruti itself and that the Brahman, described as *sopādhika* and / or *nirupādhika*, the knowledge of it and the fruit obtained thereby were also stated. Therefore, one may doubt that this section would be of no use, therefore, Sureśvara states the purport thereof.

It is only proper that the necessary logical support to the Śruti should be pointed out. Apparently, Sureśvara follows Śaṅkara who has stressed the need of logical reasoning in '*tadavirodhitarkopakaraṇā vedāntavākyamīmāṁsā*' (cf. BUB 1.1.1, p.6) and '*āgamavaśatarka*' (cf. BUB 2.1.11, p.194)

1. The Yājñavalkyakāṇḍa (= Munikāṇḍa) corresponds to BU ch. 3-4.

2. The Madhukāṇḍa corresponds to BU ch. 1-2. The word *āgama* means tradition recorded in the Śruti texts. Cf. verses 5-6 below.

जल्पन्यायेन तत्पूर्वं पञ्चमे प्रतिपादितम् ।
वादन्यायेन तद्भूयः षष्ठे सम्यक्प्रपञ्चितम् ॥२॥

2. It has been exposed first in the fifth (chapter, viz. BU ch. 3)[1] in the way of the dialectic mode, and (once) again fully elaborated in the sixth (chapter, viz. BU ch. 4) by way of the assertion.

NOTES

Sureśvara thus refers to the two parts of the logical argument in the Munikāṇḍa (BU ch. 3-4); one section adopts the method of *jalpa* and the other, *vāda*. *jalpa* is defined as *yathoktopapannaś chalajātinigrahasthānasādhanopālambho jalpaḥ* in the *Gautama Sūtra* 1.2.2 or *jalpas tu yathāsambhavaṁ sarvanigrahāṇām adhikaraṇam parapakṣe dūṣite svapakṣasthāpanaprayogāvasānaś ceti bodhyam* in the *Tarkabhāṣā pariccheda* 44 (the *Nyāyakośa*, p. 257) and *vāda*, *pramāṇatarkasādhanopālambhaḥ siddhāntaviruddhaḥ pañcāvyayavopapannaḥ pakṣapratipakṣaparigraho vādaḥ* in the *Gautama Sūtra* 1.2.1 (the *Nyāyakośa*, p. 672). And MĀDHAVĀNANDA (p. xi) says, ".... logical explanation of that great doctrine of Advaita through the employment of the dialectic modes of argumentation known as *jalpa* (arguing constructively as well as destructively for victory) and *vāda* (arguing for truth)."

1. Regarding the concordance, see remarks in the Preface.

अथाधुना निगमनस्थानीयमिदमुच्यते ।
मैत्रेयीब्राह्मणं श्रुत्या तथा च न्यायविद्वचः ।।३।।

हेतूक्तितः प्रतिज्ञायाः सिद्धार्थाया यदुत्तरम् ।
वचो निगमनं तत्स्याद्वाक्यस्यावयवोक्तिभाक् ।।४।।

3-4. Now, the Śruti declares this Maitreyī-section (viz. BU 4.5) as the *nigamana*.[1] For, in that sense there is a statement of logic. That later statement of the enunciation which is (earlier) proved by the statement of the cause is called *nigamana* 'conclusion'. It should form a part of (the whole) statement (of the syllogism).

NOTES

Cf. the *Nyāyasūtra* 1.1.39 : *hetvapadeśāt pratijñāyāḥ punarvacanaṁ nigamanam*, "*nigamana* is the re-statement of the proposition, pointing out the reason."

vākya means *mahāvākya* consisting of five parts, i.e. syllogism; these five parts are: *pratijñā*, *hetu*, *udāharaṇa*, *upanayana* and *nigamana*.

The conclusion is a restatement of the proposition, but now standing proved.

ससंन्यासाऽऽत्मविद्या या मधुकाण्डागमोदिता ।
उपपत्तिप्रधानेऽपि सैव मोक्षेऽवसीयते ॥५॥

5. The lore (about the nature) of the Ātman, together with (its means viz.) renunciation which has been discussed by the tradition (of the Vedāntins recorded) in the Madhukāṇḍa is itself shown to culminate into liberation, even, in (the Munikāṇḍa which has) the predominence of reasoning (in it).

NOTES

Another purpose served by this section is now stated. The Maitreyī-section in the Madhukāṇḍa (viz. BU 2.4) stated the knowledge of the Ātman together with renunciation as the means to liberation, on the strength of tradition (of the Vedāntins); in this Munikāṇḍa also it is understood that the knowledge of the Ātman is the cause of liberation, but on the strength of reasoning.

आत्मज्ञानं ससंन्यासं मोक्षायेत्यागमाद्यथा ।
युक्तितोऽपि तथा ज्ञेयमिति चेहोपसंहृतिः ॥६॥

6. (And such) is the conclusion here (i.e. in this chapter): Just as the knowledge of the Ātman from its description in the Śruti leads to (lit. is for) liberation,[1] so can it be known from reasoning also.

NOTES

One might ask: In respect of the questions of Kahola and others (cf. BU 3.5 ff.) this knowledge was proved by reasoning, what then is the use of this section? The verse is an answer to this objection. Since this section intends to conclude the matter already established by the Śruti and reasoning, it is not useless. The two *dharmas* mentioned in the example (*udāharaṇa*) are proved to have *sādhya-sādhana* relation : (In *parvato vahnimān, dhūmāt, yathā mahānase, vahnimat* is *sādhya* and *dhūma* is *sādhana* (*sādhaka, siddha*). The conclusion is restated for denying the opposite view in respect of the *sādhya* — this brings the significance of the word *upasaṁhṛti* in the verse.

1. SP supplies *jñānam* after *mokṣāyeti* in the first line (cf. *itiśabdād ūrdhvaṁ jñānam ity adhyāhāraḥ*) and, accordingly, one could translate the first line as 'it is to be understood that'.

व्याख्यातत्वात्पदार्थानां चतुर्थेऽध्याय एव तु ।
तद्व्याख्यानाय यत्नोऽत्तो न भूयः क्रियतेऽधुना ॥७॥

7. But, since the meanings of the (various) words (relevant upon the subject) have been (already) explained in the fourth chapter (viz. BU 2.4), no effort is to be undertaken here to explain them.

NOTES

1. The fourth chapter means the *Bṛhadāraṇyaka* ch. 4, i.e. BU ch. 2, (cf. remarks in the Preface); here the Maitreyī-section of BU ch. 2, i.e. BU 2. 4, is meant.

शब्दस्यैवाऽऽत्मनो जन्म चतुर्थे प्रतिपादितम् ।
सर्वोपसंहृतेरत्र यागादेरपि भण्यते ॥८॥

8. In the fourth chapter,[1] it is stated that the word is born of the Ātman. (And) all (activity such as) the sacrifice etc. is also (to be taken as born of the Ātman), since here (i.e. in the Ātman) is all concluded (withdrawn).

NOTES

If the meaning of the word is not to be stated, this section should be taken as completed here because the purport has been already mentioned in verses 1-6. Therefore for the removal of such a doubt is mentioned the purport of the sentence *iṣṭaṁ hutam āśitaṁ*····(BU 4.5.11).

1. See note (1) on the preceding verse.

शब्दोऽयं बहुधा भिन्नो नामैव परमात्मजम् ।
यागदानादिकं कर्म रूपं लोकपुरःसरम् ॥९॥

9. 'Word' (i.e. the Śruti) which is variously divided is but the name that is born of the highest Ātman. (And) the activity

such as sacrifice, giving of gifts etc. which precedes the word *loka* is its form.

NOTES

'Word' is divided into different parts : Śruti, Brāhmaṇa etc. But these are nothing but different names of one and the same Ātman. This is the purport of the sentence *yad ṛgveda ... vyākhyānāni* (BU 4.5.11), also of the sentence *iṣṭaṁ hutam āśitaṁ ... pāyitam* the purport is similar, viz. all that is born of the highest Ātman refers to the form of the Ātman. The sentence *ayaṁ ca lokaḥ .... niḥśvasitāni* (BU 4. 5. 11) concludes the list of all that is said to be born of the highest Ātman. This refers to the section of creation.

सर्वमेतदयत्नेन तत एव विनिःसृतम् ।
अनन्यभूतं तेनातः साक्षात्तत्त्वं प्रगीयते ॥१०॥

10. All this has proceeded only from that without any effort (on the part of that) and is, therefore, not different from that (viz. the Ātman). (Thus) is stated here the reality of all (which is clearly) perceptible.

NOTES

The first line presupposes the question : 'Since there is total absence of effort on the part of the highest Ātman, how does the world which is of the nature of name, form and action arise from the highest Ātman?' and answers the same thus: The Veda also is included in this world created from the Ātman without any effort on its part. Let this be similar to the illusory creation only in that the rule *sarvadharmopapatteś ca* (the *Brahmasūtra* 2.1.37) applies to it. The rule is: Although an actual change is impossible in respect of the Ātman having no attributes, an apparent modification is possible. Because of ignorance, all the attributes are superimposed on the Ātman which is supposed to be the cause for such a creation. The second line points to the significance of this statement about creation : The oneness of the apparent *kārya* with the *apparent kāraṇa*—in reality there is (and there remains) but one Ātman—this is shown by the word *ataḥ*; that is to say, there is no effect apart from the cause.

अन्तर्बहीरसघनः सैन्धवस्य घनो यथा ।
विज्ञानघन एवायं विज्ञानात्मा तथैव च ॥११॥

11. As a lump of salt is both inside and outside the lump of (but one) taste, so is this knowing Ātman (but) a mass of consciousness.

NOTES

This is the meaning of *yathā saindhavaghanaḥ kṛtsnaḥ prajñānaghana eva* (BU 4.5.13).

स्वविकारोपसंश्लेषाद् विज्ञानात्मत्वमेत्यतः ।
तद्धेतुनाशात्प्रकृतिं स्वामेव प्रतिपद्यते ॥१२॥

12. It becomes the knowing Ātman owing to its close contact with the modification(s)[1] of its own[2]. Therefore, after the destruction of the cause of it (viz. the contact which was caused by ignorance) it gets back its own nature, viz. pure consciousness.

NOTES

The first line explains the sentence : *etebhyo bhūtebhyaḥ samutthāya* (BU 4.5.13) and the second, *tāny eva anuvinaśyati* (BU 4.5.13). When sentiency is related to the intellect etc., the nature of the Jīvātman exists. By overcoming ignorance through the knowledge of its own, the Jīvātman begins to shine in its true nature of the Brahman.

1. *svavikāra* means 'the intellect etc.'
2. The word *sva* means the *pratyagātman* 'individual consciousness.' (SP)

परिणामनिषेधः स्यादविनाशिगिराऽऽत्मनः ।
अनुच्छित्तिगिरा नाशो वार्यते यो निरन्वयः ॥१३॥

13. In the word *avināśi*, there is rejection (of the idea of any) transformation of the Ātman and by the word *anucchitti*, is warded off the complete destruction.

NOTES

Commenting on *avināśi vā are'yam ātmānucchittidharmā* (BU

4.5.14), Sureśvara points out that the two words are not tautology (*apunarukti*).

मात्रासंसर्गजस्त्वेष यो विनाशादिधर्मवान् ।
अविद्यामात्रहेतूत्थो रज्जुसर्पादिवन्मतः ॥१४॥

14. But this one that is born due to the contact with the sense-organs, and has the properties, perishing etc.[1] is understood as one arisen from but (one) cause, viz. ignorance, like a serpent arising from a rope etc.

NOTES

Incidentally, Sureśvara explains the reading *mātrāsaṁsargas tv asya bhavati* in the Mādhyandina recension of this Upaniṣad.

1. Here, *mātrāsaṁsargaja* is *viśeṣa* and *jīva, viśeṣya.*

ब्रह्मैवैकः स आत्मोक्तो ह्यध्यायेषु चतुर्ष्वपि ।
उपायमात्रभेदोऽत्र न तूपेयः प्रभिद्यते ॥१५॥

15. In all the four chapters of the Upaniṣad, it is declared that the Ātman (i.e. Jīvātman) is said to be only the Brahman[1]. There is differentiation only as regards the means (to understanding the real nature of the Ātman) but not as regards the goal (viz. the Ātman that is to be known).

NOTES

In various chapters of this Upaniṣad, are mentioned various means to obtaining the Brahman. But this should not lead one to say : The Brahman is not homogeneous, but *anekarasa* 'heterogeneous'. To such a doubt this verse is an answer.

1. That is, nothing else or not different from it.

नेति नेति चतुर्थोऽसौ यथैव प्रतिपादितः ।
नेतीति पञ्चमेऽप्येवं निर्विकल्पोऽवधारितः ॥१६॥

षष्ठेऽपि जनकाख्यानप्रारम्भे तद्वदीरितः ।
निर्विकल्पो यथैकोऽर्थो नेतीत्यत्रोपसंहृतः ॥१७॥

नेतीति शास्त्रावसितौ तथैवात्मोपसंहृतः ।
एकरूपमतस्तत्त्वं सर्वत्रैव विवक्षितम् ॥१८॥

16-18. As it is described in words '(The Brahman is) not this, not this' in the fourth chapter (viz. BU 2.3.6) so is that ascertained in words 'not this' in the fifth chapter (viz. BU 3.9.26) and having no specifications[1]. In the beginning of the narrative of Janaka of the sixth chapter (viz. BU 4.2.4 also), (it is) described in the same way; there (also) it is concluded in words 'not this' and one having no specifications. Just so, in the end of the Śruti (viz. Maitreyī-section, BU 4.5.15) it is concluded that the Ātman (which is to be described as) 'not this'. Therefore (i.e. thus), it is everywhere intended to point out that reality is of but one form.

NOTES

Sureśvara points out that the goal is the same; though there are many ways to it as stated in various parts of the BU, it is mentioned as *eṣa neti nety ātmā* (BU 4.5.15).

1. The word *vikalpa* refers here to some definite attributes etc.

नेति नेत्यात्मकात्तत्त्वात्प्रकाराणां शतैरपि ।
निरूप्यमाणे नान्यादृग्यस्मात्तत्वं समीक्ष्यते ॥१९॥

तर्कतो यदि वा वाक्यादय एवेदमेव तु ।
नेतिनेत्यात्मविज्ञानममृतत्वैकसाधनम् ॥२०॥

ससंन्यासं विनिश्चेयमिति शास्त्रस्य संग्रहः ।
अमृतप्राप्तयेऽलं स्यात्साधनान्तरनिःस्पृहम् ॥२१॥

यथोदितमिदं ज्ञानं सहकार्यन्यसाधन-
निरपेक्षमलं मुक्त्या इत्येतदभिधीयते ॥२२॥

19-22. Since they have not seen the reality as anything other than what is of the nature of (being grasped as) 'not this, not this', even if it is explained in hundreds of ways; therefore, one has to obtain (lit. ascertain) this very knowledge of the Ātman alone as the mean to immortality[1], together with renunciation, whether by means of reasoning or from the Śruti (statement). Such is the gist of the whole Śruti[2]. This knowledge as stated (herein) is capable of securing (i.e. effecting/bringing about) immortality without expecting (help of) any other means. It is so stated (in the Śruti) that (this knowledge) non-expectant of any other ancillary means is capable of achieving (for one) liberation[3].

NOTES

1. It is repeatedly spoken that the knowledge of the non-dual Ātman which has no attribute whatever, together with renunciation, is the cause of liberation.

2. The word *saṁgraha* means 'a brief statement of the whole teaching'; cf. Bharata's *Nāṭyaśāstra* 6.9 : *vistareṇopadiṣṭānām arthānāṁ sūtrabhāṣyayoḥ nibandho yaḥ samāsena saṁgrahaṁ taṁ vidur budhāḥ//*

3. This is based on the Śruti sentence : *etāvad are khalv amṛtatvam.* Immortality consists in only knowing the oneness; after knowing, one does not have to do anything else.

एतावदर एवैतदमृतत्वस्य सिद्धये ।
प्रत्यग्याथात्म्यविज्ञानं नान्यत्किञ्चिदपेक्ष्यते ॥२३॥

23. In this statement *etāvad are khalv...* is mentioned the knowledge of the real nature of the individual consciousness as (sufficient) for attaining immortality. It does not expect anything else[1].

NOTES

1. I follow the variant reading *apekṣate* (recorded in footnote no. 1); that expresses the original idea better and also explains *nirapekṣaṁ* in the previous verse. But following *apekṣyate*, one could translate alternatively : In this statement *etāvad are khalv...* is mentioned the knowledge of the real nature of the individual consciousness as (sufficient) for attaining immortality. (In this context), nothing else is expected.

इत्युक्तार्थपरिज्ञानदार्ढ्यार्थं सर्वसाधनम् ।
कर्माणि चापनुद्याऽऽशु प्रवव्राजाविचारयन् ॥२४॥

24. Then, in order to reaffirm that the knowledge which has been mentioned becomes the means to all (human endeavour

towards liberation) after having set aside all the action, he renounced immediately[1] after this conversation, not (even a little) thinking[2] (i.e. hestitating).

NOTES

This is the explanation of *vijahāra* (BU 4.5.15).

1. It is suggested that on the occasion of renunciation, there is on the part of a knower, no necessity to look to any injunction.

2. The words *āśu* (in verse 24) and *tvarayā* (in verse 26) point out that the seeker of the knowledge of the Ātman does not have to perform any rite for renunciation and that renunciation of all desires in action is a necessity for such knowledge.

न केवलमिदं ज्ञानं कर्मसाधननिस्पृहम् ।
निःशेषकर्मसंन्यासापेक्षाऽपि स्याद्यतो मुनिः ॥२५॥

सम्यग्विज्ञाततत्त्वत्वात्कृतार्थोऽप्यखिलं स्वयम् ।
तत्याज कर्म त्वरया वाङ्मनःकायसाधनम् ॥२६॥

25-26. Since not only is this knowledge non-expectant of (all) action and means, but there is (together with it) the expectation of abandonment of entire action also, therefore, the sage, though he had accomplished the objects (of desire) on account of having well understood the nature of that (reality), hurriedly[1] himself gave up (all) action which has speech, *manas* and body as the means.

NOTES

1. See note (2) on the previous verse.

अतोऽवगम्यते नूनं न कर्म सहतेऽखिलम् ।
आत्मज्ञानं यतोऽत्याक्षीत्सम्यग्ज्ञानोऽपि तन्मुनिः ॥२७॥

27. Since the sage possessed of the right knowledge (of the Ātman) gave up all action, from this, it is understood that the knowledge of the Ātman does not tolerate whole action.

NOTES

The implication is that knowledge and action stand in contradiction.

कर्महेतुविरुद्धत्वात्सम्यग्ज्ञानस्य कर्मणा ।
विरोधोऽस्त्यर्थमेवातस्तत्त्यक्तं ज्ञानशालिना ॥२८॥

28. Since right knowledge is opposed to the cause of (any) action (viz. ignorance), this (said) contradiction (of knowledge to action) is to the extreme. Therefore it is renounced by the sage who excelled with knowledge.

एवं काण्डद्वयेनेयं सफलताऽनवशेषतः ।
सर्वसंन्यासनिष्ठा च ब्रह्मविद्या समीरिता ॥२९॥

29. Thus, in the Madhukāṇḍa and the Munikāṇḍa, are stated in full the lore about the Brahman to be fruitful and (that it is) resting on complete renunciation.

NOTES

Thus is restated the purport of both the *kāṇḍas*.

एतावानुपदेशः स्याद्वेदे श्रेयोर्थिनां नृणाम् ।
कृतकृत्यो भवेत्क्षिप्रमेतज्ज्ञात्वाऽनुशासनम् ॥३०॥

30. (Only) this much is the instruction in the Veda[1] for man who is desirous of the highest good[2]; having understood this instruction, he would immediately become one who has accomplished his end[3].

NOTES

1. This suggests that there is no need of any other instruction in order to attain liberation.

2. The instruction about paying homage to the temple etc. is possible for persons who are not striving for liberation.

3. This suggests that there is expectancy of no other means to bliss.

SELECT GLOSSARY

[Figures in the parentheses indicate the number of verses under translation. Verses of BUBV 2.4 are indicated only by the verse number, e.g. (100) for BUBV 2.4.100, and verses of BUBV 4.5 are indicated by prefixing 4.5 to the verse number, e.g. (4.5.15) for BUBV 4.5.15.]

akṣara	indestructible (246, 385)
akṣādi	direct perception etc. (154, 176, 177, 326)
ajñātajñāpana (*vidhi*)	(an injunction) that informs one of what is not known (198)
atītānāgata	past and future (399)
atīndriya	beyond sense-perception (153, 155, 165, 170)
advaya	one having no other (Truth) beside itself, i.e. the Ātman (435)
advaita	non-duality (462)
adhyavasāya	ascertainment (369); [function of *buddhi*]
anartha	evil (482); cf. note on 10
anubhava	experience (131, 192); awareness (221); *vicāryamāṇo anubhavaḥ* experience which is subjected to reasoning (132)
anubhūti	experience (95, 132); experience as the result of all means of knowing (=*sarvamānaphala*) (123)
anumā	inference (172)
anumāna	inference (172, 363); cf. the Introduction section 7
anumiti	inference (226)
anuvāda	restatement (232)
anṛtantra	not dependent on (the activity or desire of) a person (143, 153)
antaḥkaraṇa	inner-organ (s) (369, 394); cf. note (1) on 369
antarāya	hindrance (108, 150); cf. *nirantarāya* without any hindrance (110)

antarmeyabala	the strength of the object of knowing within oneself (viz. the Ātman) (256); cf. the Introduction section 6
anvayavyatireka	the method of *anvayavyatireka* (11,18,107, 112, 114, 271, 274, 190); cf. Introduction section 7
apariṇāma	(the Ātman) which does not undergo any modification (377)
apavāda	exception to the general rule (311)
apuruṣatantra	not dependent on (the activity or desire of) a person (121); cf *anṛtantra* above
apūrvānapara	having nothing preceding and subsequent to it (229, 343, 299); [a phrase from BU 2.5.19 that 'describes' the Brahman]; cf. *apūrvānaparānanta* (299)
apauruṣeya	(sentence) having no human agency (165)
apyaya	merger (296)
abuddhipūrvaka	not preceded by any deliberate thinking (306, 330); cf. *buddhipūrvaka* below
abhidhā	simple affirmation (147, 148, 153, 154, 156, 158, 159, 160, 161, 162, 165, 168, 169, 181, 182); (the function called expression (315); cf. the Introduction section 5
abhidhā	expression (182, 315, 411)
abhidheya	what is to be expressed (315)
abhimāna	misconception; [function of *ahaṁkāra*]; cf. note (1) on 369; the notion (this is mine) (i.e. Ego) (353); cf. note (3) on 353; attachment (352)
abhyāsa	constant meditation (202, 207, 453); repetition (of knowledge acquiring practice) (432)
amṛta	immortal (25, 49); immortality (54, 65, 70; 4.5.21); cf. note (1) on 54
amṛtatva	immortality (48, 51, 54, 55, 59; 4.5.20, 23); [amṛtatā (73)]
avacchinna	differentiated (186); *anavacchinnayāthātmyabrahmaikātmya* the oneness of the

	Brahman whose nature is not differentiated (from the individual consciousness)
avaccheda	differentiation (185)
avicāritasiddha	established (even without any thought) (422,484)
avidyā	ignorance (6, 54, 185, 186, 187, 195, 196, 199, 200, 201)
avyāvṛtānanugata	not to be differentiated from and followed by anything else (14, 110, 411, 473)
avyutthitamanas	a person whose *manas* has not become operative (106)
avyutthitātman	a person who has not arisen from (64, 106)
asambhava	impossibility (291, 325, 365, 441, 474)
ahaṁkāra	(the notion of) Ego (100, 351, 352)
ahammati	the thought 'I am (this or that)' (354)
ahaṁvṛtti	the function of Ego (350, 351)
ākāśa	ether; [one of five elements]; Ākāśa (viz. the Brahman) (415)
ākhyāta	verbal form (160, 161)
āgama	Śruti (7, 140, 214, 219, 309; 4.5.6); cf. note (1) on 6-7; statement in the scripture (163); tradition (4.5.1); cf. note (2) on 4.5.1; appearance/emergence, as in *āgamāpāya* below
āgamāpāya	appearance and disappearance (442)
āgraja	result of previously performed action (3)
ātman	body (129); [particular usage]; in other cases, the word is translated as 'the Ātman, (individual) consciousness, or the Jīvātman'
ātmadhimātragamyārtha	an object to be understood only from the knowledge of the Ātman (240)
ātmayāthātmya	the real nature of the Ātman (98,254)
ātmalābha	one's or a thing's coming into existence (119, 190, 275, 416)
ābrahmastambaparyanta	from the Brahmā (i.e. Hiraṇyagarbha) up to the blade of grass (71, 93, 134)
ābhāsa	semblance (351); appearance (424, 426);

svābhāsa its own appearance; cf. *pramābhāsa* below & the Introduction section 4

ārambhaka — expressive (355, 356)

āśrama — the stage of life (22, 33, 34); cf. *brahmacarya, gṛhastha, vānaprastha* (27)

itihāsa — MBh and the *Rāmāyaṇa* (314); cf. note (3) on 314; narratives in the sacred texts (317, 318, 319, 321); note (2) on 314

iśvara — lord (303); Īśvara (the Brahman) (321, 444)

(sam) ucchitti — eradication (194, 195, 349, 420, 468, 477)

utpattyādicatuṣṭaya — four-fold (fruits of action, viz.) origin, attainment, change and purification (189); cf. note on 189

utsarga — exception (311)

upapatti — reason (103); reasoning (4.5.5)

ekāyana — one meeting-place (329, 332)

aikātmya — the oneness (of the Brahman and the Ātman/Jīvātman) (19, 25, 68, 109, 135, 146, 151, 164, 175, 176, 177, 181, 186, 194, 199, 235, 297, 301, 415, 416, 421, 448, 459, 471, 473, 482)

aiśvarya — freedom (liberty, capacity, power) (152)

kañcuka — robe (284); [a technical term in Kashmir Śaivism]; cf. note (1) on 284

kaṭhina — gross (344, 401, 407); [=*sthūla*]; cf. the Introduction section 10

kāṭhinya — grossness (341, 406, 407); cf. *kaṭhina* above

kāraka — that which helps action (194, 468); cf. note (1) on 194; *kāraka* (viz. duality) (476); cf. note on 476; agent (475)

kāraṇātman — the material (cause) (viz. the Ātman) (196); the Ātman having the nature of a cause (242); cf. *kāryātman* (242); the Ātman which is the cause of the world (389)

kāryakāraṇavastu — the thing which is both the cause and the effect (192)

kūṭastha	immutable (284, 354, 450, 480)
kṛtrima	a product (307)
kevalādvaita	the absolute non-duality (295)
kaivalya	renunciation (22); liberation (26, 93); reality (252); state of the absolute (Ātman) (205, 206); cf. the Introduction section 10
kauṭasthya	immutability (411); cf. *kūṭastha* above
kriyāvirodha	impossibility of that activity (137)
kriyāśakti	the power of action (367, 371, 385), [=*karmaśakti* (368, 379, 383)]
kṣetrajña	the individual consciousness (as the knower) (186, 415, 430, 444); cf. notes on 186 & 444
kṣetrajñatā	the state of the individual consciousness (as the knower) (417, 431)
gandha	smell (333, 334, 338, 357, 358, 360, 363, 465, 466); cf. notes on 357 & 358-359
guṇa	property (335, 337, 338, 340, 362, 454)
ghrāṇa	nostril(s) (333, 363, 465)
cit	cognizer (129); [=*saṁvid*]; sentiency (282); consciousness (474)
citi	knowledge (204)
cidābhāsa	appearance of sentiency; [=*caitanyābhāsa*] (346); cf. the Introduction section 4
cetana	the sentient (481); cf. *acetana* the insentient (481)
cetanācetanābhāsa	appearance of sentiency and insentiency (424); cf. *ābhāsa* above
caitanyākāra	a form of sentiency (124, 125)
jñāna	knowledge; cf. the Introduction section 6
jñānaśakti	the power of knowing (367, 368, 371, 379, 383, 385, 387)
tattva	Truth (98, 295, 435, 442, 453); essence, nature (237,255,302); truth (252); reality (91; 4.5.10, 18, 19); the nature of reality (4.5.26)
tamas	darkness (i.e. ignorance) (151, 201, 209,

230, 231, 238, 256, 258, 347, 424, 425, 426, 432, 433, 436, 437, 442, 443, 444, 454)

tarka — reasoning (216, 395; 4.5.20); logical reasoning (226); cf. the Introduction section 7

tejas — fire (334, 337, 339, 341, 359, 360); [one of five elements]; heat (408, 409, 417)

tyāga — renunciation (23, 318)

trayyanta — Vedānta (151, 418)

tvac — skin (329, 332, 333, 342, 344, 355, 356, 367, 375)

darśana — seeing (213, 232); vision (261); perception (299); understanding (lit. seeing) (485)

dārṣṭāntika — the illustrated; cf. the Introduction section 8

duḥkha — misery (87, 348, 359, 350)

duḥkhin — miserable (349, 353, 428)

dṛś — seer(=Ātman) (342, 430); cf *sadādṛś* ever-seeing (36); cf. *sākṣin* below

dṛṣṭānta — the illustration; cf. the Introduction section 8

dṛṣṭi — seeing power (284)

deva — god (24)

draṣṭṛdraṣṭavya — the knower and the object of knowing (97)

dhī — intellect (2, 349, 376), knowledge (145, 152, 344, 438); knowing (96); (act of) knowing (97); *dhīpūrvaka* [=*buddhipūrvaka* below]; *samyagdhī* right knowledge (437, 449); *bhedadhī* notion of distinction (453); *śuddhadhī* one of pure intellect (71), *viśuddhadhī* (25)

dhyāna — meditation (233, 234); cf. the Introduction section 3

nāmarūpādi — name, form etc. (264, 301); *nāmarūpakriyā* name, form and function (293); *nāmarūpa*

	(328); cf. *nāmarūpādisambhinnaṁ jagat* (264)
nāśa	destruction (195, 196, 452; 4.5.13)
niḥsaṅga	free from all attachments (354)
nigamana	conclusion (4.5.3,4)
nityakarmādi	the daily action etc (2); cf. the Introduction section 2
nityamukta	eternally liberated (111)
nididhyāsana	the culmination of *śravaṇa* and *manana* (70, 217, 232, 233); cf. the Introduction section 3
niyamavidhi	injunction for restriction (146); cf. note on 146
niyoga	employment (184)
niyogaviṣaya	the one who is enjoined and the object towards which his act is directed (97)
niyojya	one on whom the injunction is enjoined (152)
nivṛtti	liberation (55)
niṣprabha	devoid of lustre (379)
nṛ	person (53, 67, 71, 222, 402, 454); a man (75, 93); one (250; 4.5.30); a human being (254, 308); cf. *anṛtantra* above
nyāya	reason (115, 168); manner (128, 297); rule (109, 214); the way (4.5.2); logic (4.5.3)
pañcabhūta	five elements (335)
padārtha	meaning of word(s) (4.5.7); that which is signified by word(s) (108, 109, 111, 112, 226); cf. the Introduction section 7; *ātmānātmapadārtha* objects denoted by the words *ātman* and *anātman* (91); thing (293)
paraṁ padam	the highest place (23)
pariṇāma	transformation (341; 4.5.13); combination (lit. effect) (361)
parisaṁkhyāvidhi	injunction for exclusion (146); cf. note on 146
parispanda	movement (379, 380)

parokṣa indirect (434)
pāpa sin (253); *pāpakarman* evil (act) (360)
purāṇa Purāṇa (317, 318, 319, 321) [class of texts held authoritative next to Vedic texts and epics]
puruṣārtha end of human life (48, 64, 310)
pṛthivī earth (334, 338, 354, 360); [one of five elements]
prakāśa lustre (379)
prakṛti nature (406; 4.5.12)
prajñapti knowledge (421) ; [= *prajñāna, jñāna*]
prajñā knowledge (390)
prajñāna knowledge (= the Brahman) (327)
prajñānaghana a mass of knowledge (390) ; cf. *vijñānaghana* below
pratijñā enunciation (4.5.4)
pratipatti understanding (220, 226, 357)
pratyakṣa direct perception (163, 164, 172, 285, 324); cf. *akṣādi* above; directly (320)
pratyañc the individual consciousness (15, 23, 36, 79, 87, 88, 89, 92, 94, 95, 104, 125, 154, 170, 201, 203, 221, 228, 229, 330, 238, 255, 262, 265, 272, 274, 283, 284, 291, 294, 296, 299, 410, 412, 438, 440, 441, 467) ; *pratyagbuddhi* the awareness of the individual consciousness; *pratyagdhī* the knowing principle within (i.e. *pratyagātman*) (285); *pratyagābhāsa* appearance of the individual consciousness (427) ; *pratyagātman* the individual consciousness (434, 483, 485); *pratyagīśvara* the lord, the individual consciousness (303) *pratyaṅmoha* infatuation (i.e. ignorance) on the part of the individual consciousness (79, 113, 256) ; *pratyagdhīmātragamya* (object) to be understood only from the (correct)knowledge of the individual consciousness; cf. *ātmadhīmātragamyārtha* above.

pratyag yāthātmya	the true nature of the individual consciousness (4, 38, 102, 187, 193, 242, 331, 430, 471; 4.5.23); *pratyanmātraikayāthātmya* essentially of the nature of the individual consciousness (103), *ātmayāthātyma* the real nature of the individual consciousness (454)
pradhānaguṇabhāva	the relation of the principal and the subordinate (362)
prapañca	elaborate explanation (263); *prapañcita*, elaborated (4.5.2)
pramā	the right knowing (of the object of knowing) (95); right knowledge (1, 51, 167, 224)
pramāṇa	a means of knowing (124, 148, 155, 163, 168, 173, 189, 224, 243, 266, 322, 391); valid or invalid knowledge (132)
pramātṛ	knower (103, 120, 127, 130, 133, 183, 237, 484)
pramābhāsa	appearance of right knowing (124)
prameya	the object of knowing (95, 120, 164, 166, 200, 238); the object to be known (224)
prayatnataḥ	zealously (218); cf. *yatnāt* below; *prayatna*, effort (304), *aprayatna* without any effort (305)
pralaya	merger (327, 328, 330, 331, 354, 355, 356, 357, 376, 389, 393, 394, 397)
pravṛtti	activity (32, 56)
prājña	Prājña (390); [the individual consciousness in the state of deep sleep]
prāṇa	vital force (=the Ātman) (367, 380, 381, 383, 387, 390); cf. notes on 380 & 387; *prāṇa* (295, 299, 303, 346, 347, 382, 388); [one of five winds, 'breath']; cf. note on 345-346, 388 & note on 388
prāmāṇya	authoritativeness (319, 326, 391)
bādhaka	stultifier (258)

bādhya	stultified (258)
buddha	(Gautama) Buddha (320)
buddhi	intellect (329, 330, 345, 346, 350, 352, 353, 365, 366, 367, 369, 377, 380, 381, 390, 425, 427, 454); knowledge (120); thought (129); human intellect (306); *ātmabuddhi* awareness of one's own individual consciousness (96)
buddhipūrvaka	preceded by some deliberate thinking (331); preceded by the proper reasoning (about the nature of the worldly existence) (397)
brahmayāthātmyavijñāna	the knowledge of the real nature of the Brahman (7)
brāhmaṇa	Brāhmaṇa text (313, 314, 316)
bhāktam	metaphorically (83); *bhaktyā* secondarily (82)
bhāvaka	one who repeatedly meditates on the nature of the Ātman (203)
bhāvanā	imperative force (157, 158, 181, 193); constant meditation (205, 206)
bhāsvara	blazing (218)
bhū	earth (337); [=*pṛthivi*, one of five elements]
bhedaka	the cause of differentiation (200)
bhrānti	misapprehension (374)
mati	thought (129)
manana	pondering over, (122, 219); cf. the Introduction section 3
manas	inner-organ called *manas* which organizes sense-perception (329, 344, 352, 365, 366, 369, 376, 425)
marut	wind (339); [=*vāyu*, one of five elements]
mahāsāmānya	great generality (287, 288, 292, 296)
mātṛ	knower (143, 152, 225, 238); [cf. *pramātṛ* above]
mātrādi	sense-organs etc (126); cf. note (1) on 126.

māna	a means of knowing (148, 149, 168, 169, 170, 181, 212, 227, 237, 238, 290, 291); cf. *pramāṇa* above
mānatva	authoritativeness (326); [cf. *prāmāṇya* above]
māyā	false (duality) (462)
mithyā	false (239, 426, 453, 463)
mukti	liberation (24, 55, 64, 68, 234)
mukhyam	primarily (83); *mukhyayā* by its primary operation (188)
mumukṣu	one who is desirous of liberation (28)
mumkṣutva	the desire of liberation (142); *amumukṣutva* (65)
mūrtāmūrta	concrete and/or abstract (thing) (9, 20, 325); cf. note (1) on 9
mṛṣā	(adj.) false (430, 434); (ad.) falsely (456, 458)
meya	the object of knowing (130, 132, 133, 266); cf. *prameya* above
mokṣa	liberation (15, 33, 67, 94; 4.5.5, 6); [cf. *mukti* above]
moha	infatuation (i.e. ignorance) (24, 25, 31, 236, 242, 256, 374, 434, 441, 449, 484)
yatnāt	specifically (213) [a technical term in the Mīmāṁsā]; particularly (241); with effort (75); *yatna* effort (303; 4.5.10); *yatnataḥ* by effort (i.e. activity) (74)
yathāvastvavabodhin	that which enlightens one about a thing as it is (183)
yathāsthitātmavastū-tthajñāna	knowledge that arises out of the existential entity (viz. the Ātman) as it is (151)
yāga	sacrifice (187; 4.5.9)
yukti	reasoning (199; 4.5.6); cf. Introduction section 7
yogipratyakṣa	direct perception of the ascetics (170, 171, 175)
yoṣidagnyādidṛṣṭi	looking on a woman as fire etc. (215)
rajjusarpa	rope-serpent (186, 268; 4.5.14); cf. *rajjusarpādivat* (229, 236)
rava	sound (862); [=*śabda*]

rasa	taste (334, 362)
rūpa	form (362, 364); [=*akṣaviṣaya*]
laya	merger (373, 374, 375, 377, 378, 384, 387, 394, 396); cf. *anātyantikalaya* non-absolute merger (398); cf. *pralaya* above
liṅga	characteristic (222, 227); characteristic mark (170); *liṅga* (214); cf. note (1) on 214
vastuyāthātmyavṛtta	the (very) nature of the thing as it is (197)
vastuvṛtta	the real nature of the thing (viz. the Brahman) (5, 331); (mere) existence of reality (196)
vākya	authoritative sentence (i.e. the Śruti) (225); Śruti (statement) (226, 227; 4.5.20)
vākyārtha	sentence-sense (110, 111, 113, 226)
vāṅmanaḥkāyasādhana	one having speech, *manas* and body as the means (4.5.26)
vāc	speaking (368)
vācyavācakasambandha	the relation between a word and its expressed sense (216)
vāyu	wind (334, 336, 339); [one of five elements]
vāstavavṛtta	the real state of thing (410, 412); *vāstavaṁ vṛttam* (197, 410, 412); cf. *vastuvṛtta* above
vikāra	modification (340)
vikriyā	change (347, 348, 351)
vikṣepa	application (369, 371)
vijñapti	making known (412)
vijñāna	knowledge; cf. Introduction section 7
vijñānaghana	a mass of consciousness (414, 469, 473, 474; 4.5.11)
nijñānātman	the knowing Ātman (4.5.11, 12); *vijñānātmādilakṣaṇa* characterized by some definite knowledge etc. (449); [=*pratyañc saṁjñā*]
vijñānaikaghana	a mass only of consciousness (446, 448)
vidhi	injunction; cf. Introduction section 6
vinirmukta	fully free from (94)
vibhāga	distinction (298, 299)

vibhutva	pervasive nature (385)
vimukta	liberated (5)
viyat	sky (145, 435)
virakta	turned averse to (3, 6, 65)
viriñca	creator (430)
vilaya	merger(287, 372, 373, 384, 397, 401); [cf. *pralaya* & *laya* above]
viśeṣa	particularity (269, 270, 277, 279, 280, 282, 287, 289, 292); distinct property (336)
viśeṣaṇa	distinguishing attribute (278, 283, 287)
vṛtti	function (346, 349, 350, 351, 370, 428)
vairāgya	aversion (6, 72, 73,)
vaiṣṇavaṁ padam	the place of Viṣṇu (22); [=the state of liberation]
vyañjaka	revealing (189, 190); manifestor (433)
vyabhicārin	variable, (125, 126, 155, 255, 256, 266, 276); not different (129); *avyabhicārin* invariable (125, 126, 255, 256, 266, 275)
vyākṛtāvyākṛta	manifest and/or unmanifest (477)
vyāpin	pervading (359)
vyāpti	acquisition, i.e. attaining proper understanding of the object of knowing (130); concomitance (271); association (346)
vyāpyavyāpaka	the pervaded and the pervasive (271)
vyāvṛttānvayarūpin	having forms mutually distinguished and related (287)
vyutthitātman	one whose Ātman has risen above (all the non-Ātman) (106); cf. *avyutthitātman* above
vyoman	sky (305)
śabda	sound (368)
śamadamādi	tranquillity, controlling sense etc. (122)
śābdī	verbal (219)
śāstra	Śāstra (i.e. scriptures and law books) (45); Śruti (6, 7, 219, 222, 470; 4.5.20)
śuddhātman	the pure Ātman (33)
śravaṇa	hearing about (122, 212, 213, 218, 221); cf. Introduction section 3
śrutiliṅgādika	*śruti, liṅga* etc. (214); cf. notes (1) & (2)

on 214 regarding the meaning of the word *śruti*

śrotra — ear (364, 368)

ṣaṣṭhagocara — comprehensible by *manas* (472); cf. note (1) on 472

saṁkalpa — imagination (369); [function of *manas*]

saṁgatyasaṁgati — agreement and disagreement (132); cf. *saṁgati* (136, 137)

saṁjñā — awareness (421, 437, 439, 444, 445, 448, 449, 458, 468, 478, 479, 482, 483, 484)

saṁnyāsa — renunciation 6, 7, 20, 27, 28, 29, 32, 35, 38, 39, 40, 46; 4.5.5, 6, 21, 25, 29) [=*nyāsa* (44)]; cf. Introduction section 2

saṁbhūti — rise (396); [=*utpatti*]

saṁmoha — infatuation (249); cf. *moha* above

saṁvid — cognizing principle (126)

saṁvyāpti — co-existence (135)

saṁsarga — merger (196); union (384)

saṁsāra — transmigratory existence (3, 5, 17, 33, 64 65, 71, 73, 141, 142, 195, 482)

saṁsārin — transmigratory (16); *saṁsāryātman* (138); *saṁsāritā* [=*sāṁsāra*]

saṁskāra — impression (76)

saṁhata — made up of parts (285)

samastavyastatā — condition (consisting) in whole and its part (241, 464)

samāna — *samāna* (388); [one of five winds]; *samāna* (389): [as the sense of prime-cause Ātman]; cf. note on 389

samuccaya — combination (21)

sarittīraphala — fruits on the bank of a river (159, 162); cf. note on 159

sarvānarthanivṛtti — the removal of all undesirable results (89)

sarvāntaryāmin — one who resides within all (248)

sāṁkhyasiddhānta — the Sāṁkhya doctrine (20)

sākṣin — witness (145, 343, 442, 480, 481)

sādhāraṇa — common (330, 384)

sāmānya	generality (267, 269, 270, 277, 282, 288, 292, 367, 376, 377, 378); common (396)
sukha	pleasure; *ātyantikasukha* the pleasure which is absolute (86), *sāṁsārikasukha* worldly pleasure (87)
sūkṣma	subtle (294, 345)
sthitikāla	the time of sustenance (296, 297)
sthitisarga	(the time) of the creation and sustenance (327)
sthūla	gross (293)
sparśa	touch (329, 332, 333, 336, 337, 338, 339, 341, 342, 343, 375)
svaccha	subtle (344); [*sūkṣma*]; cf. *kaṭhina*; cf. Introduction section 10
svataḥsiddha	self-established (117, 154, 156, 157, 158, 412, 450, 452, 474); cf. 117
svapnāvasthā	dream state (465)
svapnendrajāla	sleep and the show by a magician (462)
svārājya	domain of light (61); [=the state of liberation]
hetu	reasoning (396); [=*jñāpakahetu*]; cause (118, 422): [*kārakahetu*]

BIBLIOGRAPHY

TEXTS (CONSULTED)

[The mark * shows the text under reference in this work]

Agnipurāṇa, Poona : ĀnSS 41, 1947.

Arthasaṁgraha, (ed. and tr.), A. B. GAJENDRAGADKAR and R. D. KARMARKAR, Poona : 1934.

Bhagavadgītā with Śaṅkara's Commentary, Poona : ĀnSS 34, 1909.

Brahmasiddhi, (ed.), S. KUPPUSWAMI SASTRI, Madras: University of Madras, 1937.

**Brahmasūtrabhāṣya*, (3rd. ed.) : Bombay : Nirnaya Sagara Press, 1948.

Brahmasūtra Śāṅkara Bhāṣya with the Commentaries Bhāmati, Kalpataru and Parimala, Bombay : Nirnaya Sagara Press, 1917.

Bṛhadāraṇyakopaniṣad with Śaṅkara's Commentary, Poona : ĀnSS 15, 1891.

Bṛhadāraṇyakopaniṣadvārtika with Ānandagiri's Commentary : Śāstraprakāśikā, 3 vols, Poona : ĀnSS 16, 1892-94.

Bṛhadāraṇyakavārtikasāra, 2 vols., Varanasi : Acyutagranthamala, 1941-1943 (Saṁvat 1997-1999).

Chāndogyopaniṣad with Śaṅkara's Commentary, Poona : ĀnSS 14, 1902.

Gauḍapādakārikā, (ed. and tr.), R. D. KARMARKAR, Poona : BORI, 1973.

Jaiminiyanyāyamālāvistaraḥ, Varanasi : KSS 126, 1937.

Kāvyālaṅkārasārasaṁgraha of Udbhaṭa, Poona : BORI, 1925.

Kāvyaprakāśa Ullāsa X, (ed. and tr.), S. S. SUKHATHANKAR, Bombay: Karnatak Publishing House, 1941.

Mahābhārata, (critical ed.), 19 vols., Poona : BORI, 1933-1960.

**Māṇḍūkyopaniṣad with Gauḍapādakārikā and Śaṅkara's Commentary on Gauḍapādakārikā*, Poona : ĀnSS 10, 1936.

Manusmṛti, Bombay : Nirnaya Sagara Preess, 1946.

Mīmāṃsādarśana, 7 vols, Poona : ĀnSS 17, 1970-1974.

**Naiṣkarmyasiddhi with Jñānottama's Candrikā*, (revised ed.), Poona : Bombay Sanskrit and Prakrit Series 38, 1925.

**Naiṣkarmyasiddhi of Śrī Sureśvarācārya with the Kleśāpahāriṇī*, (ed.), S. S. SARASVATI, Holenarsipur : Adhyatma Prakasha Karyalaya, 1968.

Nāṭyaśāstra, Bombay : Nirnaya Sagara Press, 1943.

Nyāyakalpalatikā, (ed.), V. SUBRAMANYA SASTRI, Tirupati : Kendrīya Sanskrit Vidyāpīṭha, Vol. II, 1975.

Padmapurāṇa, 4 vols., Poona : ĀnSS 131, 1893-1894.

Pañcīkaraṇam by Shree Shankaracharya with Six Commentaries, Bombay : Gujarati Printing Press, 1930.

Paribhāṣenduśekhara of Nāgojibhaṭṭa, Poona : BORI, 1962.

**Sambandha-Vārtika of Sureśvara*, (ed. and tr.) T. M. P. MAHADEVAN, Madras : University of Madras, 1972.

**Saṁkṣepaśārīraka* 2 vols., Poona : ĀnSS 83, 1918.

Saṁkṣepaśārīraka of Sarvajñātman, (ed. and tr.), N. VEEZHINATHAN, Madras : University of Madras, 1972.

Śaṅkaradigvijaya, of Vidyāraṇya Poona : ĀnSS 22, 1932.

Śaṅkaravijaya of Anantānandagiri, (ed.) N. VEEZHI NATHAN, Madras : University of Madras, 1971.

Siddhāntabindu, Baroda : GOS 64, 1933.

Ślokavārtika, Varanasi : Tara Publication, 1978.

Śrīśaṅkarācāryaviracitagranthasaṁgraha, (ed.), H. R. BHAGAVAT, Poona : 1924.

Taittirīyasaṁhitā, Bombay : Bharata Mudranalaya Svadhyaya Mandala, 1957.

Taittirīyopaniṣad with Śaṅkara's Commentary, Poona : ĀnSS 12, 1929.

Taittirīyopaniṣadbhāṣyavārtika with Ānandagiri's Commentary, Poona : ĀnSS 13, 1977.

Upadeśasāhasrī, (3rd. ed.), Bombay : Nirnaya Sagara Press, 1930.

Vāyupurāṇa, Calcutta : Gurumandal Series 19, 1159.

Vedāntaparibhāṣā, (ed. and tr.), S. S. SURYANARAYANA, Madras : Adyar Library Series 34, 1971.

Vedāntasāra, (6th ed.), J. B. JACOB, Varanasi : Chowkhamba Amarabharati Prakashan, 1971.

BOOKS and ARTICLES :

ALSTON, A. J., (tr.), *The Realization of the Absolute*, London : Shanti Sadan, 1971.

BALASUBRAMANIAN, R., (tr.), *The Taittiriyopaniṣad Bhāṣya-Vārtika of Sureśvara*, Madras : University of Madras, 1974.

BASHAM, A. L., *The Wonder That was India*, Calcutta: Rūpa and Co., 1967.

BOETZELAER, J. M. van, (tr.), *Sureśvara's Taittiriyopaniṣad Bhāṣya Vārtikam*, Leiden : E. J. Brill, 1971.

CARDONA, G., "Anvaya and Vyatireka in Indian Grammar," *The Adyar Library Bulletin*, vols. 31-32, (1967-1968), pp. 313-52.

DASGUPTA, S., *A History of Indian Philosophy*, vols. 1-2, Delhi : Motilal Banarsidass, 1975.

DATTA, D. M., *The Six Ways of Knowing*, Calcutta : University of Calcutta, 1972.

DEUSSEN, P., *The System of the Vedānta*, (Eng. tr., C. JOHNSON), Delhi : Motilal Banarsidass, 1972.

DEVARAJA, K. K., *An Introduction to Śaṅkara's Theory of Knowledge*, Delhi : Motilal Banarsidass, 1972.

DEVARAJA N. K. and N. S. HIREMATHA, *A Source Book of Śaṅkara*, Varanasi : Banaras Hindu University, 1971.

DEVASTHALI, G. V., *Mimāṁsā*, Bombay : Booksellers' Publishing Co., 1959.

GAMBHIRANANDA, (tr.), *Eight Upaniṣads*, 2 vols., Calcutta : Advaita Ashrama, 1972-1973.

GAURINATH SASTRI, *The Philosophy of Word and Meaning*, Calcutta : Sanskrit College, 1959.

GHATE, V. S., *The Vedānta*, Poona : BORI, 1960.

GHURYE, G. S., *Indian Sadhus*, Bombay : Popular Prakashan, 1964.

GUPTA, SANJUKTA, *Studies in the Philosophy of Madhusūdana Sarasvati*, Calcutta : Sanskrit Pustak Bhandar, 1966.

HACKER, P., *Untersuchungen über Texte des frühen Advaitavāda*, 1. *Die Shüler Śaṅkaras*, Wiesbaden : Akademie Der Wissenshafter und der Literatur, 1950.

HARGOVINDA SASTRI, (ed.) *Amarakośa*, Varanasi : KSS 198, 1970.

HASURKAR, S. S., *Vācaspati Miśra on Advaita Vedānta*, Darbhanga, Mithila Institute, 1958.

HIRIYANNA, M., *Outlines of Indian Philosophy*, London : George Allen and Unwin Ltd., 1932.

HIRIYANNA, M., *Essentials of Indian Philosophy*, Bombay : George Allen and Unwin (India) Private Ltd., 1973,

HIRIYANNA, M., "Śaṅkara and Sureśvara", *Dr. C. K. Raja Presentation Volume—A Volume of Indological Studies—*, Madras : Adyar Library, (1949), pp. 1-4.

HIRIYANNA, M., "Bhartṛprapañca : An Old Vedantin," *Indian Antiquity*, vol. 53, (1924), pp. 77-86.

INGALLS, D. H. H., "The Study of Śaṅkarācārya, "*Annals of Bhandarkar Oriental Research Institute*, vol. 33, pts. 1-4, (1952), pp. 1-14.

JACOB, J. B., *Laukikanyāyāñjaliḥ*, 3 vols., Bombay : Nirnaya Sagara Press, 1907-1910.

JACOB, *A Concordance to the Principal Upaniṣads and Bhagavadgitā*, Delhi : Motilal Banarsidass, 1971.

JHA, G., (tr.), *Śābara-Bhāṣya*, 3 vols., Baroda : GOS 66, 70 and 73, 1973-1974.

JHA, G., (tr.), *The Tattvakaumudī*, Poona : Oriental Book Agency, 1965.

JHA, G., (tr.), *The Chāndogyopaniṣad*, Poona : Oriental Book Agency, 1942.

JHA, G., (tr.), *Ślokavārtika*, Calcutta : Bibliotheca India, 1906.

JHA, G., *Pūrva Mīmāṁsā in Its Source*, Varanasi : Banaras Hindu University, 1964.

JHA, G., *The Prābhākara School of Pūrva Mīmāṁsā*, Delhi: Motilal Banarsidass, 1978.

KANE, P. V., *History of Dharmaśāstra*, vol. 2, pt. 2, Poona : BORI, 1941.

KARMARKAR, R. D., *Śaṅkara's Advaita*, Dharwar : Karnatak University, 1966.

KEITH, A. B., *The Karma-Mīmāṁsā*, London : Oxford University Press, 1921.

KEVALANANDA SARASVATI, (ed.), *Mīmāṁsākośa*, 7 vols., Satara : Prajna Pathashala Mandal, 1952-1966.

KOKILESWAR SASTRI, V., *An Introduction to Advaita Philosophy*, Calcutta : University of Calcutta, 1926.

LIMAYE, V. P. and R. D. VADEKAR, *Eighteen Principal Upaniṣads*, vol. 1, Poona : Vaidika Saṁśodhana Maṇḍala, 1958.

MACDANELL, A. A. and A. B. KEITH, *Vedic Index*, 2 vols., Delhi: Motilal Banarsidass, 1958.

Mādhavānanda, S., (tr.) *The Bṛhadāraṇyaka Upaniṣad*, Calcutta: Advaita Ashrama, 1975.

Mahadevan, T. M. P., (ed.), *Word Index to the Brahmasūtrabhāṣya of Śaṅkara*, 2 vols., Madras University of Madras, 1971-1973.

Mahadevan, T. M. P., *The Philosophy of Advaita*, Madras : University of Madras, 1969.

Mahadevan, T. M. P., *Gauḍapāda*, Madras : University of Madras, 1975.

Mahadeva Sastri, A., (tr.), *Dakshinamurti Stotra*, Madras : Samata Books, 1978.

Mahadeva Sastri, A., (tr.). *The Bhagavad Gitā*, Madras : Samata Books, 1977.

Mainkar, T. G., (tr.), *Sāṁkhya Kārikā of Īśvarakṛṣṇa with Gauḍapāda Bhāṣya*, Poona : Oriental Book Agency, 1972.

Markandeya Sastri, C., *Sureśvara's Contribution to Advaita*, Vemur : Sundari Samskrita Vidyalaya, 1973.

Max Müller, F., *Three Lectures on the Vedānta Philosophy* Varanasi : CSS 62, 1967.

Mayeda, S., "On an Advaita Method of Exegetico : Anvaya and Vyatireka," (Japanese), *Journal of Indian and Buddhist Studies*, vol. 19-2, (Mar. 1971), pp. 74-80.

Mishra, Chhabinath, *Nyāyoktikośaḥ*, Delhi: Ajanta Publications, 1978.

Murti, K. S., *Revelation and Reason in Advaita Vedānta*, Delhi : Motilal Banarsidass, 1974.

Nikhilananda, S., (tr.), *Māṇḍūkyopaniṣad with Gauḍapādakārikā and Śaṅkara's Commentary*, Mysore : Sri Ramakrishna Ashram, 1974.

Pandey, R. B., *Hindu Saṁskāras*, Delhi : Motilal Banarsidass, 1976.

Pashupatinath Sastri, *Introduction to the Pūrva Mimāṁsā*, Calcutta : Ashoka Nath Bhattacharya, 1923.

Prasad Sastri, H., (tr.), *Pañcadaśi*, London : Santi Sadan, 1965.

Radhakrishnan, S., *The Principal Upaniṣads*, London : George Allen and Unwin Ltd., 1953.

Raghavachar, S. S., (tr.) *Naiṣkarmyasiddhi of Śrī Sureśvarācārya*, Mysore : University of Mysore, 1965.

RAJA, C. K., *In Defence of Mīmāṁsā*, Madras : Adyar Library, 1952.

RAJA, K. K., *Indian Theories of Meaning*, Madras, Adyar Library Series 91, 1977.

RAMACHANDRAN, T. P., *The Concept of the Vyāvahārika in Advaita Vedānta*. Madras : University of Madras, 1969.

RANADE, R. D., *Vedānta, The Culmination of Indian Thought*, Bombay : Bharatiya Vidya Bhavan, 1970.

RAO, RAMAKRISHNA, *Advaita as Philosophy and Religion*, Mysore : University of Mysore, 1969.

RICHARAV DE SMET, S. J., "The Logical Structure of 'tat tvam asi' According to Sureśvara's Naiṣkarmayasiddhi,' *Philosophical Quarterly*, vol. 33-34, 1961.

ROER, E., (tr.), *The Twelve Principal Upaniṣads*, vol. II, Madras : Theosophical Publishing House, 1931.

SEN GUPTA, A., *Sāṁkhya and Advaita Vedānta—A Comparative Study*, Lucknow : 1973.

SHARMA, B. N. K., *Lectures on Vedānta*, Dharwar : Karnatak University, 1973.

SHARMA, H. D., (tr.), *Brahmasūtra-Catuḥsūtrī*, Poona : Oriental Book Agency, 1967.

SINGH, R. D., *The Vedānta of Śaṅkara*, vol. 1, Jaipur : Bharat Publishing House, 1949.

SINHA, J., *Problems of Post-Śaṅkara Advaita Vedānta*, Calcutta : Sinha Publishing House Ltd., 1971.

SINHA, J., *A History of Indian Philosophy*, vol. 2, Calcutta : Sinha Publishing House Ltd., 1956.

SRINIVASACHARI, P. N., *A Synthetic View of Vedānta*, Madras Adyar Library Series 81, 1952.

SRINIVASACHARI, P. N., *The Philosophy of Bhedābheda*, Madras : Adyar Library Series 74, 1972.

SUNDARAM, P. K., *Advaita Epistemology*, Madras : University of Madras, 1968.

SURYANARAYANA SASTRI, S. S., (tr.), *The Bhāmati of Vācaspati*, Madras : Theosophical Publishing House, 1933.

THIBAUT, G., (tr.), *The Vedānta-Sūtra*, 2 vols., Delhi : SBE 34 & 38, 1973.

THRASHER, A. W., *The Advaita of Maṇḍanamiśra's Brahmasiddhi*, Unpublished Ph. D. dissertation submitted to Harvard University in 1972.

TIWARI, K. N., *Dimensions of Renunciation in Advaita Vedānta*, Delhi : Motilal Banarsidass, 1977.

UPADHYAYA, V. P., *Lights on Vedānta*, Varanasi : CSS 6, 1959.

WARRIER, A. G. K., *The Concept of Mukti in Advaita Vedānta*, Madras : University of Madras, 1971.

INDEX OF VERSES

Verse No.